web developer's guide to

multicasting

CORIOLIS GROUP BOOKS

an International Thomson Publishing company I(T)P®

Albany, NY ▪ Belmont, CA ▪ Bonn ▪ Boston ▪ Cincinnati ▪ Detroit ▪ Johannesburg ▪ London ▪ Madrid ▪
Melbourne ▪ Mexico City ▪ New York ▪ Paris ▪ Singapore ▪ Tokyo ▪ Toronto ▪ Washington

PUBLISHER	**KEITH WEISKAMP**
PROJECT EDITOR	**DENISE CONSTANTINE**
COVER ARTIST	**GARY SMITH**
COVER DESIGN	**ANTHONY STOCK**
LAYOUT DESIGN	**NICOLE COLÓN**
LAYOUT PRODUCTION	**APRIL NIELSEN**
COPY EDITOR	**MARY MILLHOLLON**
PROOFREADER	**DENISE CONSTANTINE**
INDEXER	**KIRSTEN KING**

Web Developer's Guide To Multicasting
Copyright ©, 1997 by The Coriolis Group, Inc.

Limits of Liability and Disclaimer of Warranty

The author and publisher of this book have used their best efforts in preparing the book and the programs contained in it. These efforts include the development, research, and testing of the theories and programs to determine their effectiveness. The author and publisher make no warranty of any kind, expressed or implied, with regard to these programs or the documentation contained in this book.

The author and publisher shall not be liable in the event of incidental or consequential damages in connection with, or arising out of, the furnishing, performance, or use of the programs, associated instructions, and/ or claims of productivity gains.

Trademarks

Trademarked names appear throughout this book. Rather than list the names and entities that own the trademarks or insert a trademark symbol with each mention of the trademarked name, the publisher states that it is using the names for editorial purposes only and to the benefit of the trademark owner, with no intention of infringing upon that trademark.

The Coriolis Group, Inc.
An International Thomson Publishing Company
14455 N. Hayden Road, Suite 220
Scottsdale, Arizona 85260

602/483-0192
FAX 602/483-0193
http://www.coriolis.com

Printed in the United States of America

10 9 8 7 6 5 4 3 2 1

To Blair

Acknowledgments

The following people made the completion of this book possible: Kim Dimick, Judy Estrin, John Cole, Neena Taskar, Dan Mapes, Anne Flatte, Connie Nicholas, Eric Gilbert, Ada Hunter, Lisa Birch, Randall Isaac, Blake Sorrel, Kieran Kane, Leslie Ellis, Bonnie Levitan, Denise Constantine and April Nielsen.

As usual, special thanks are due to Cathie Nelson, JoAnn Uhelszki, Holger Petersen, Keith Weiskamp, Fred Gault, Galan Bridgman, Heinz Geisler, Tim Byars, Gary Clayton, and Barry Poss.

Contents

Chapter 8 Live Multicasting And Maintaining A Production Studio 199

Chapter 9 LAN-Based Video 223

Chapter 10   Multicasting On Internetworks   253

Chgapter 18   White Papers From The First IP Multicast Summit   449

Chapter 19   Interview With Judy Estrin, CEO Of Precept Software   489

Chapter 20   Interview With Anne Flatté, Video Producer At S.C.P.D.   509

Introduction

Several of the people from companies whose products are featured herein felt that a detailed book on multicasting for Windows machines and Macs would be premature if published in the first half of 1997. As it turned out, by the time the manuscript was completed, stable multicast products for these platforms were already shipping.

Still, there is a lot of confusion surrounding the exact nature of multicasting, which is why books such as this particular one are important right now. If you don't understand how multimedia data travels in a multicast-enabled network environment—whether that environment is a LAN, a WAN, or the MBone itself—you'll risk being part of the problem that multicasting hopes to solve.

You do not need to be a programmer, a video technician, or a network systems integrator to profit from reading this book, although a background in PC-based multimedia (as well as Web-based media) will certainly help. If you're unfamiliar with network routers and high-speed communications lines (such as ISDN), what you'll need most are patience and perseverance in getting such hardware properly connected to your system. But you can do it, and the rewards are worth it.

The primary goal of *Web Developer's Guide to Multicasting* is to give you a meaningful context for creating, serving, and consuming multicast media. To perform these tasks well, you'll need a combination of skills that few people currently possess. This book will point you in the right direction for acquiring such skills, but to master them you'll have to jump and get your hands dirty (while setting up hardware, for example), which certain chapters show you how to do in great detail.

As in most areas of desktop multimedia, today's multicasting environment is heavily tool-centric. This means that, to get any work done, you need to rely on specific applications. Fortunately, the media creation and editing tools are highly mature. The actual multicast server and viewer tools are currently in the Release 1.X phase, but ready for professional use right now.

The chapters of this book are organized and grouped according to their content: An overview of today's streaming video solutions, an introduction to general multicast technology, multicasting on private internet-works, multicasting on the global Internet (the MBone) and interviews with established multicast practitioners.

In the first group, we cover unicast products like VDOLive, Vivo, Vxtreme, and (to some extent) RealAudio so that we can differentiate them from the multicast solutions which form the basis of this book. We'll also cover today's video conferencing products for the same purpose. For the record, Progressive Networks' RealVideo was just released as this book went to press.

The second group of chapters deals with the basics of multicasting technology, such as the new network transport protocols, the new router hardware requirements, high speed communications issues (ISDN, ADSL, cable modems, satellite delivery, etc.), as well as creating and editing content suitable for multicasting. Finally, integrating all of these components is discussed.

Multicasting on private internetworks (as opposed to the Internet at large) is covered in group three. We start with a summary of existing network-based video delivery—on LANs and WANs—then move on to address setting up routers on multicast servers and clients. Test drives of various software products (like Precept's IP/TV and Microsoft's NetShow) are performed, all from a perspective of providing a meaningful context for these applications.

The fourth group is generally devoted to the MBone. Specific attention is given to tunneling, bandwidth considerations and, again, delivering a sense of scope and proportion in relation to the Internet as a whole. Finding an MBone provider is discussed, as well as event scheduling and the tools (Unix, Windows, and Mac) currently available for MBone access.

In the final group, interviews are conducted with pioneers in the field of multicasting. Judy Estrin, CEO of Precept Software (arguably the leader in Windows-based multicast solutions) presents a detailed technical analysis of the current environment. Also, Dan Mapes documents the Summit of Hope, a live event in which his company brought together Jimmy Carter, Nelson Mandela, and Shimon Peres on the MBone. Finally, Anne Flatté, Producer/Director at the Stanford Center for Professional Development, provides some valuable insight into the process of creating and editing content suitable for multicasting.

If you are excited about delivering (or just consuming) multimedia across LANs, WANs, and the Internet itself—without flooding the network with redundant data streams—you will find this book valuable. Multicasting is the next generation of networked multimedia, and the show has already started.

Chapter 1

- **Understanding the Video On Demand Model**

- **Working with the current Video On Demand products**

- **Reviewing the Video On Demand compressors and file formats**

Chapter 1

Video On Demand

In the 1996 Paramount movie *Mission Impossible*, a spymaster, played by Jon Voight, coordinated a covert operation with a laptop sporting multiple video windows. Each window on the computer screen showed a different view of the operation. Voight monitored the activities of his agents and updated them accordingly on the progress of the mission.

For networking and desktop video professionals, several things didn't add up here. First off, the video streams were broadcast directly from tiny (digital?) cameras hidden on agents participating in the operation. For another thing, all the data transfer seemed to be happening over the Internet. Last, and certainly not least, this was apparently being done with cellular phone connections!

Of course, it was pure Hollywood. Even worse, it was a gadget-rich spy caper where only the highest technology can keep an audience happy. The catch was that the equipment looked *familiar* (and possibly even affordable). Though Voight's computer bore no Apple brand or *Intel Inside* sticker, he still used it like a standard laptop. And the live video windows looked suspiciously like QuickTime clips, right down to the movie controller bars.

Figure 1.1   Where do you want to spy today?

So, what's the problem? Simply put, it felt like a commercial for existing technology (if not for existing companies). The video was clear and fluid, the com links simple and apparently reliable, and the novelty factor for the agents pretty darn low. Fortunately, the movie was entertaining enough to keep even Web and video professionals from getting too bogged down in the details.

The Changing Scene

In the real world, such technology is only now trickling down to corporate and consumer desktops. But it *is* finally arriving, and it's just as exciting and ready for commercial exploitation as that *Mission Impossible* scene suggests. Okay, maybe the digital lipstick cameras and complete cellular solutions are a bit further off. But high-quality Internet video, as well as private network video, is starting to happen right now. The hard part is knowing how to put together cost-effective systems using a mixture of off-the-rack components (hardware and software) and a few pieces of special equipment.

Another challenge is understanding the abstractions involved in creating and using wide area digital networks. For example, it's one thing to feel comfortable consuming Web-based multimedia on your workstation, or even installing complex server software. But it's quite a different feeling when you want to invest money in a digital media delivery network but have trouble visualizing how data packets flow through the system at large.

In other words, only at an abstract level can you appreciate what's going on system-wide (both locally and remotely). And only with that appreciation can you make the right decisions when it comes to purchasing and installing networked equipment and software applications. Such an approach is significantly different from traditional Web site development (if there is such a thing) where most of the server-side abstractions have already been worked out and are much less formidable to begin with.

Oddly enough, *Mission Impossible* does dramatize three basic directions that networked desktop video is now taking:

- Video On Demand (the subject of this chapter)

- Video Conferencing (the subject of Chapter 2)

- Multicasting (the subject of the rest of this book and, arguably, more interesting than the first two)

What Is Video On Demand?

This chapter takes stock of the current environment for desktop video on demand (sometimes called *unicasting* or *narrowcasting*) with the goal of using it as a basis for comprehending the braver new world of multicasting. Chapter 2 takes this approach a step further by crystallizing the desktop video *conferencing* market. As you'll see, multicasting has roots both in video on demand and desktop video conferencing (at least as of Fall 1996).

The best way to characterize video on demand in the PC universe is to consider a clip that plays in a Web page window on your desktop. When you click on it, the video starts playing from the beginning (after a few seconds), as shown in Figure 1.2. This may sound oversimplified, but it is how the average Web surfer generally consumes streaming video— assuming the browser is configured properly.

Video Room Service

It's supposed to be like ordering a movie in a high-tech hotel room, but with less quality expected. You choose the programming you want, *when*

Figure 1.2 Getting instant gratification.

you want it. This type of consumption is fundamentally different than cable TV and even satellite-based pay-per-view. With the latter two, you can wind up waiting an hour or two before your movie starts fresh again, and you usually can't jump in part way through. (As you'll see, this is more the way multicasting works—but with many more benefits.)

In a high tech hotel room, any movie the establishment offers is available immediately. This is true video on demand. Customers don't need to know where their broadcast originates, nor do they likely care (as long as they know what it's going to cost). When this service was first available, hotels reportedly had people in the basement running around putting tapes in VCRs to simulate computerization.

In the very near future, products from such companies as Microsoft and Oracle really will completely computerize this sort of movie delivery for hotels (and, eventually, the modern office). The video assets themselves will be stored on hard disks or next-generation optical disks, likely as MPEG-2 files, and probably broadcast over Ethernet cables stretching from the basement to the guest rooms. The presentation will be at least as good (probably better) as from consumer video tape and, ultimately much more manageable for the hotel. Figure 1.3 illustrates a hotel wired to deliver video on demand.

Why are hotels such good proving grounds for emerging digital technology? Because all the pieces come together: standard length media packages (feature length movies), standard rules for requesting such

Figure 1.3 A wired hotel.

media packages (on-screen ordering), numerous, willing, and relatively homogenous users (hotel guests), all on one big local area network (the hotel itself). What better proof of concept—assuming it all works— could a network media designer ask for?

The Early Days Of Streaming Video

Keep this model of video on demand in mind as we now head back to the Web. Despite big quality differences between movies served in wired hotels and Web-based video streaming from, say, Japan to New York, the mode of *consumption* inherent in this model remains the same: You click it, you get it. (Don't forget that we'll be contrasting this with the multicasting model later.)

Early in 1996, when streaming video software was first available, it was third party companies (as opposed to the likes of Apple and Microsoft) who published the first round of products. The big players were, of course, working on their own solutions for the Web-based video on demand market, but they weren't ready to compete with the smaller companies right out of the gate—for a number of reasons.

As it turned out, the big companies were heavily committed during that time to other advanced Web technology, such as video conferencing, *high-end* video on demand (as in the hotel example), 3D rendering, and VRML. Many of the fruits of these diversified development labors— notably in the 3D area—have already been harvested successfully. Extra dividends, like products evolved from R&D investments in Web video conferencing, are just now being introduced. Future multicasting technology may indeed stem directly from the engineering efforts undertaken during this time.

The above state of affairs probably accounts for the original lack of hype surrounding Web-based video on demand. It also underscores the fact that most multimedia software written by third-party companies cannot be true enabling technology. In other words, key elements of small-company solutions (such as server software and tools for creating streaming media) cannot be given away for free. When Apple, Microsoft, and Intel do it (like with QuickTime, Video for Windows, and Indeo) it generally *is* free.

Challenges Met

The early contenders in the Web-based video streaming arena employed software that did a couple of things very well, at least for that early period. This is not a value judgment—all multimedia software just naturally gets better over time. Those particular technical achievements were:

- Scalability

- Data integrity maintenance over the Web

Scalability is the means by which video and audio quality (for the consumer) will increase in proportion to the throughput of the communications link, such as a telephone circuit. *Data integrity maintenance* is just what it sounds like: ensuring that high-quality data is delivered to the user. This is difficult enough when Web connections are reliable and do not fluctuate. On the Web, neither of these conditions is a given (also a problem in multicasting technology).

In terms of supported platforms, the streaming video on demand developers went where the market was first: Windows 95. (Remember, we are talking about mass market PCs here.) Support for the Mac followed eventually, with some exceptions, as noted below. Workstations, like those from Sun and SGI, were effectively absent from the original equation, probably based on marketing decisions.

Implementation was usually accomplished via the user's Web browser of choice—either Netscape Navigator or Microsoft's Internet Explorer. Plug-ins supplied by the streaming video developers allowed movies to be presented in pop-up player applets, as shown in Figure 1.4. In

Figure 1.4 Playing a movie in the Netscape browser.

some cases, a streaming video can be integrated into an overall Web page tableau.

As for media processing tools for creating streaming movies, all that was ultimately needed was a way to convert an existing desktop video clip into a format suitable for streaming. If your existing clip was uncompressed, so much the better. Most streaming media companies provided at least one tool for this purpose, and several found ways to let content creators use applications like Adobe Premiere for the job.

The Original Players

The next section of this chapter surveys what are considered the leading companies and products in the PC-based, Web video on demand field. It is worth downloading each of these solutions (the player components of most of them are free) to get a feel for them and the levels of performance they offer. Armed with this knowledge, you'll be able to better appreciate the way multicasting fits into the bigger picture of packet-switched media delivery.

VDOLive

Arguably the most prominent of the early streaming video developers was VDOnet, maker of the widespread VDOLive player and server solutions. As this book is written, VDOLive is at release level 2.0 and still going strong. It is fair to say that they have set the standard for this class of software. Their server software is supported on a wide variety of platforms and several ancillary products—such as an Internet video phone—are also available at VDO's Web site: **www.vdolive.com**.

VDOnet's user tools for creating streamable movies include both a capture application and a compression program.

tip

CAPTURING VIDEOS WITH PREMIERE

One good strategy when working with VDOLive and other types of streaming media is to capture the video either with Premiere or the software that comes with your capture card, then bring that clip into Premiere's editing environment for final compression into streamable format.

Unlike some of its competitors, VDOLive 2.0 gives you a lot of control over a clip at playback time. The audio level is adjustable, and you can switch to a special slide view of the video stream for greater clarity (but less fluidity). Also, you can separate a clip from your browser and watch it in the standalone VDO player if you need to multitask. Adopters of VDOnet's various products include CBS, Fox, and CNN. Figure 1.5 shows a standard VDOLive clip being played.

VDOnet offers a free *personal* version of their server and tools so that prospective buyers can do a test drive prior to making an investment in the software. The company seems committed to improving their products and will soon offer the ability to record movies while they play—a feature missing from the early versions of the player. It will

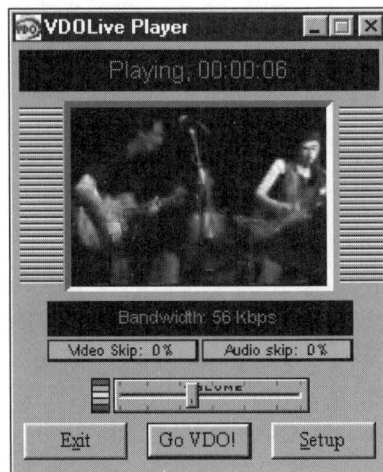

Figure 1.5   Playing a VDOLive clip.

be interesting to see whether VDOnet decides to get into the multicasting business.

Xing

Another early entrant in the video (and audio) streaming sweepstakes was Xing Corporation (**www.xingtech.com**), with their StreamWorks software, now at version 2.0, as shown in Figure 1.6. Xing's original client-side products tended to work as standalone viewer programs—as opposed to player/plug-ins for use with Web browsers. Both the Mac and the PC (as well as Unix machines) were supported initially. The early user interfaces had a certain multicasting feel to them in that you could select from a preset list of stations.

As one of the pioneers in MPEG video for the desktop, Xing leveraged off this technology in both its video and audio streaming products. While performance at 28.8 was often marginal (unlike with VDOLive), Xing maintained that things would improve dramatically at ISDN rates and beyond (which they eventually did).

Like VDOLive, StreamWorks 2.0 doesn't yet allow for saving a clip at stream time, nor does it have a volume control, but it does let you resize the streaming video window. Although Xing has also attracted some major video broadcasters, its mission in the multicast universe is still less than clear (as of this writing). Don't hesitate to call and ask them.

Note! *One of the keys to the success of VDOLive and Xing is that they use the UDP (User Datagram Protocol) network transport layer. Briefly stated, UDP allows data packets to be skipped in the interest of keeping the*

Figure 1.6 Playing a Xing clip.

media presentation streaming as well as possible. In concept, this is similar to how movie playing engines like QuickTime allow drop video frames if necessary. Several other of the video on demand products employ UDP as well. We'll be getting into the details of UDP—especially in a multicasting context—in the next few chapters.

VivoActive

A later arrival to the scene was Vivo Software, with its VivoActive Player and VivoActive Producer. Unlike VDOLive and StreamWorks, Vivo supplies a solution without server-side executable software. In other words, you just make your movies and post them on the server for user access, like GIF and JPEG files. To make Vivo movies, you need the $500 VivoActive Producer program, which converts AVI files to the proprietary Vivo format.

Consuming Vivo-ized media is accomplished via the Vivo Player plug-in or Microsoft's ActiveX player, both of which are free. Figure 1.7 displays the Vivo player interface. Currently, the Player supports both Mac and Windows, while the Producer only supports Windows 95 and NT. Support for MacOS is promised.

Reports from the field indicate that overall performance is not as robust as with VDOLive and StreamWorks, but that seems to be the quid pro quo for not having to deal with server programs. As you might imagine, the Vivo compressor works best with clips in which there is not a

Figure 1.7 The Vivo Player interface.

lot of action—like talking heads. While this is usually fine for messages from the company president, it's not what most video consumers really want to see. To be fair, Vivo's competitors also suffer from these conditions.

The bottom line on Vivo, so far, is that it's a good compromise if you are posting certain types of video assets on your site. People getting into multicasting are probably already comfortable with server-side programming, so Vivo's lack thereof won't seem like such a big advantage. For further information, visit Vivo's Web site at **www.vivo.com**.

Vxtreme

Another relative newcomer to the medium-quality video on demand arena, Vxtreme (**www.vxtreme.com**), competes almost head-on with VDOLive. The current version of their player has some interesting VCR-like controls but overall performance is generally no better than VDO. Plus the product may always be playing catch-up if VDO continues to push its current lead. Figure 1.8 shows Vxtreme playing a video clip.

This brings up an interesting problem. Trying to compare products from competing companies like VDOnet and Vxtreme is often an exercise in futility (assuming one isn't *obviously* better than the other). To make a valid quantitative judgment, you would have to start with the same content in each case, then compress it with exactly the same settings for each product's encoder.

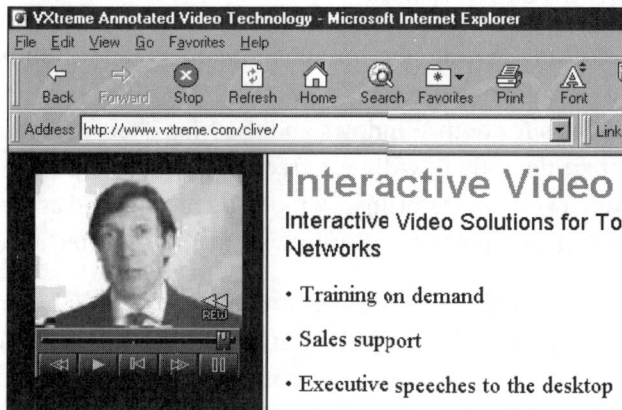

Figure 1.8 Playing a Vxtreme clip.

Furthermore, you would have to stream the resulting movies under identical conditions—not an easy job on the Internet. Of course, you could always hire a Ph.D. in mathematics to prove that one product's compression and scaling algorithms were better than the other's (if you really wanted to make your point).

Vosaic

Now, here's a product that may have an interesting future. In fact, it may already be slightly ahead of its time. What differentiates Vosaic from its competitors is how it manages its media streams (not to mention increased difficulty factors for both setup and maintenance). The URL for Vosaic's site is **www.vosaic.com**.

In essence, the Vosaic server component monitors and calibrates the stream size during the data transfer (other products do it once at the beginning of the transfer). Like VDO and Streamworks, Vosaic exploits UDP technology, polling the Vosaic Player to see if it's being starved or stressed. If so, the server application adjusts the data flow accordingly.

Down in the engine room, the Vosaic server is actually managing three separate files: a GSM audio file, an MPEG file, and a third file consisting of data regarding the MPEG file. If you're the hands-on Webmaster, you may have extra work to do keeping track of these extra files (and the other files that reference them), but you're probably used to it by now.

As of this writing, the Vosaic software suite (still in beta) includes the server component, a set of media tools for MPEG conversion, and player/plug-ins for both Windows and the Mac. According to their marketing department, there will be a free version of the player and a nominally priced version featuring rewind and fast-forward controls, among other amenities. Figure 1.9 displays Vosaic's user interface.

Unfortunately, Vosaic (like StreamWorks) only begins to shine when it has enough bandwidth. But its design is sophisticated enough to make it a product to consider once you upgrade to dual-channel ISDN or higher. Also, once MPEG decoding hardware becomes standard on PC motherboards, Vosaic will get an additional performance boost. It will be interesting to see where they position themselves in the multicasting realm.

Figure 1.9 The Vosaic UI.

Note! *There are some other small-company products out there as well, but you should be the judge as to whether they qualify as bona fide video on demand solutions. If you're interested, check out Digigami's CineWeb (**www.digigami.com**) and Iterated Systems' Clearfusion (**www.iterated.com**). Also worth noting here is that Progressive Networks' streaming video product will probably be shipping by the time this book is published. The company's RealAudio software set an important standard for streaming audio.*

Apple

Now for the heavy hitters. As noted above, Apple and its peers were late getting up to speed in dial-up video streaming (video on *demand* streaming, that is). Unfortunately for the smaller players (like VDO and Xing), this is no longer the case. What's interesting to note is that not all of the big guns have been equally aggressive.

As you'll see in Chapter 2, Apple has got some powerful offerings in the video conferencing market. Unfortunately, the best they've been able to do for Web-based QuickTime on demand in the 28.8 leagues is something called QuickStart. This feature, manifested as a QuickTime plug-in for Netscape 3.0, lets you play the part of the movie you've already downloaded as you download the remainder of the movie. This is great for small audio-only QuickTime clips, but not much more than a novelty for longer movies with video tracks. Figure 1.10 shows QuickStart in action.

Marketing tactics aside, this is not true streaming video—but who cares anymore? Back when VDOLive first came out, it seemed significant that Apple wasn't picking up the gauntlet (despite its other troubles, at the time). Since that time, two factors have become clearer.

First, it is not in Apple's best interest to make QuickTime movies look blurry. This would have been inevitable if QuickTime clips were made to stream freely at 28.8 like VDO clips. Desktop video producers have worked hard perfecting the art of making pristine QuickTime assets. Why change the rules on them if you don't have to?

Second, Apple can now afford *not* to compete directly in the 28.8 video on demand rodeo. As the higher end technologies (like multicasting) gather momentum, Apple can leverage off its R&D investments in these technologies to hit the ground running where it will probably matter.

In the meantime, of course, there has been the often confusing QuickTime Live Web entity, complete with the Web site shown in Figure 1.11. Back when it mattered, Apple characterized QuickTime Live as a "production mechanism" that employed Plain Old QuickTime (POQT), QuickTime VR, QuickTime Conferencing, and even some non-Apple products to bring multimedia to the Web in realtime.

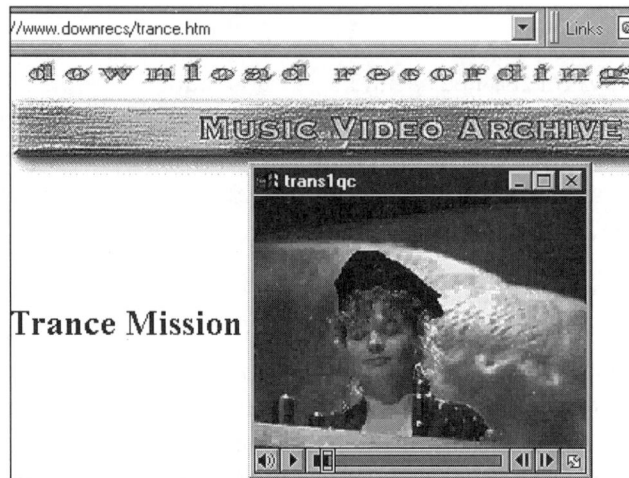

Figure 1.10 A QuickStart clip.

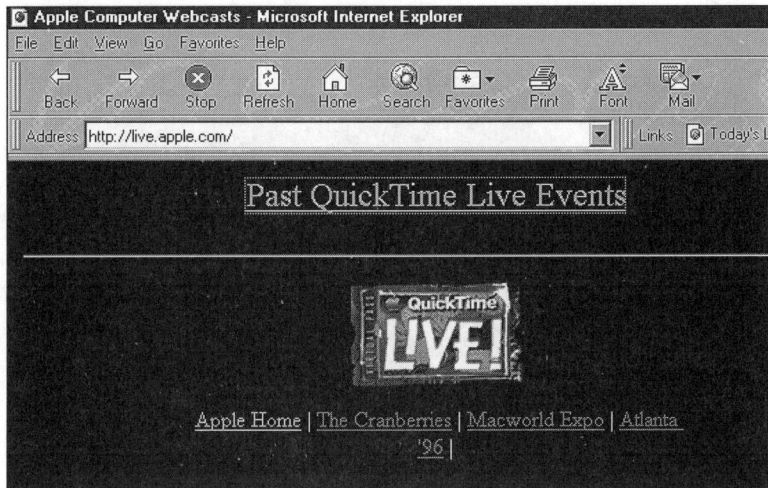

Figure 1.11 The QuickTime Live site.

Right! Based on what was then available at **http://quicktime. apple.com**, QuickTime Live seemed to boil down to coverage of gala affairs in Hollywood, multimedia land, and the music industry. Lots of POQT files were available for downloading, the design was compelling, and there were often URLs available for receiving "live" coverage of newsworthy events. Ah, the good old days.

Does Apple have a complete video on demand strategy? It's hard to say at this point. Does it matter? Maybe not. Not all the smoke has cleared yet in this area. Again, as QuickTime Live reminded us, Apple has POQT, QuickTime VR, and QuickTime Conferencing. All three of these technologies continue to advance, as does the Mac-specific hardware that runs them.

Microsoft

It is staggering to consider the progress Microsoft made in colonizing the Web from the Spring to the Fall of 1996. Not only did they give Internet Explorer 3.0 the power to entice users away from the venerable Netscape Navigator, they also slipped in ActiveX and, more importantly for desktop video producers, ActiveMovie (the software previously known as *Quartz*).

If you have installed Explorer 3.0 and ActiveMovie on your Windows 95 or NT 4.0 desktop, you'll notice that all your video clips (QuickTime, AVI, and MPEG) now get played with the ActiveX player—as opposed

Figure 1.12 The ActiveX player in action.

to QuickTime's standard movie player or Microsoft's old Media Player. See Figure 1.12 for a view of the ActiveX player.

If you go to Microsoft's Web site (at the time this chapter was written), you'll even see multicasting mentioned frequently, as well as ActiveX conferencing. Third-party multicast developers have found ActiveX/ActiveMovie to be highly stable in supporting their proprietary solutions.

ActiveX comprises such a large set of individual technologies that we cannot do it justice in a few paragraphs. What's most important to note is that it is built upon Microsoft's mature OLE code base, which allows for data documents (including media files) to be edited, presented, and otherwise exploited with their native player/editor software (if appropriate and available) with no muss and as little fuss for the user as possible.

ActiveX brings all of that OLE-type functionality to a desktop connected to the Internet. In other words, if a document such as a video clip is played by a user, it shouldn't matter whether that clip is streaming from a remote Web location or a local CD-ROM drive. Of course, it will matter if the bandwidth isn't available, but that's not Microsoft's fault in the short run.

The best way to keep up-to-date on ActiveX is to visit the Microsoft site daily (**www.microsoft.com**). As noted above, there is already plenty of discussion concerning ActiveX's role in multicasting and video conferencing.

Video On Demand Compressors

No discussion of video on demand would be complete without at least a cursory review of the video compressors and file formats employed by this technology. As it turns out, several of these codecs and file types are being used in the multicasting world as well.

In fact, let's set down a complete set of the current desktop video data types. It's a relatively short list and will provide a quick reference area for when we drop these names later in the book. Not too much has changed in the last five years, at least in the mainstream. Several smaller players took a run at mass market acceptance, but failed because they weren't free or didn't fully understand the politics involved.

QuickTime

QuickTime is Apple's venerable and highly mature engine for playing multimedia files on the PC desktop. Most of those QuickTime multimedia files turn out to be video clips. Unlike Microsoft's frame-based Video for Windows engine, QuickTime is time-based. This is just one of the reasons it is used by professional videographers, as well as multimedia producers.

QuickTime movies can range from individual still images to audio-only clips to MIDI sequences. Each discreet media element can occupy a separate *track* in a QuickTime movie (unlike with Video for Windows). The great thing is, you can assemble a QuickTime movie with all sorts of tracks, each of which can be controlled independently at playback time.

When this chapter was written, Apple's most recent editions of QuickTime were 2.5 for the Mac and 2.1 for Windows. The latter is still a playback-only solution, even though you can save QuickTime movies from products like Premiere for Windows. Apple generally maintains the latest revisions of each product on its Web site: **www.quicktime.apple.com**. Figure 1.13 shows the QuickTime MoviePlayer playing a video clip.

Figure 1.13   Playing a clip with the QuickTime MoviePlayer.

It's hard to know whether the original QuickTime development team had video on demand in mind (much less multicasting) when rev 1.0 was being assembled. The fact that QuickTime Conferencing leverages off this technology says something, but the rest may have been plain old retrofitting. We'll get into this more in the next chapter.

The best way to get the most out of QuickTime is knowing when to use the right codec. The first QuickTime compressors were Animation, Graphics, JPEG, Apple Video, Raw (a.k.a Apple None), and, later, Cinepak. These core codecs remain supported by the Mac QuickTime init and also by QuickTime for Windows (for playback).

In a video on demand context, all of these codecs seem to be supported by the QuickStart functionality mentioned earlier. As far as multicasting goes, we should expect some newcomers (as we'll see in Chapter 2). For now, here is a rundown of the workhorse QuickTime codecs to date.

RAW

Also known as *None*, this is less a standard compressor than an uncompressed encoding scheme. In other words, no serious compression is applied when you save (or capture) a QuickTime movie in this format. In fact, you may be effectively *un*compressing a movie if you do this, with no gain in data richness. One good use for None is transporting raw Mac movies to the Windows environment, where they can be loaded and then compressed with another codec by Premiere 4.2.

ANIMATION (RLE)

The Animation codec was developed to compress and play QuickTime animated movies. Because Run Length Encoding (RLE) is the compression algorithm, this is not a good choice for compressing real video clips, although it does do well for sequences with lots of single color planes (like cartoons). Given the resurgence of animation on the Web, perhaps this codec will get renewed attention. Still, Animation is not by nature a streaming compressor.

GRAPHICS (SMC)

Akin to the Animation codec is the Graphics compressor, although the latter usually wins in both rendering speed and compressed file size. The Graphics codec, displayed in Figure 1.14, is commonly used for traditional computer-graphics sequences where the images have been created by rendering software as opposed to by hand. Not likely to see much direct action in the multicasting or video on demand worlds.

JPEG

Based on the ANSI standard (document 10918-1), the JPEG codec is mainly used for archiving QuickTime movies. You can play a JPEG movie with MoviePlayer, but performance will likely be unacceptable—unless you have special hardware in your system, in which case the movie will probably look great. Many of the high-end video capture cards use some type of so-called *motion* JPEG (MJPEG) compressor to encode and playback raw capture files. Because these cards are often used in systems that output to videotape, high image quality is crucial. Also not a strong contender for multicasting action (or video on demand, for that matter).

Figure 1.14   A movie compressed with the Graphics codec.

VIDEO (ROAD PIZZA)

This was the original QuickTime compressor, and the codec of choice for all the 160 × 120 movies that circulated in the early days of multimedia. Unlike Cinepak, Video-encoded movies take as long to compress as they do to decompress, although their file sizes are usually larger than otherwise similar Cinepak movies. There are still times when the Video codec is a viable or even preferable alternative, but Cinepak has pretty much stolen the show at this point. Is the Video compressor suitable for video on demand and multicasting? It doesn't seem likely at this point.

CINEPAK

This codec was created for the specific purpose of compressing movies for speedy decompression and playback from CD-ROM. The trade-off is that Cinepak movies take a relatively long time to compress (as opposed to, say, Video). This is less of an issue now that PCs are much more powerful than they were two or three years ago.

As far as software-only decompressors go, Cinepak may rule for the foreseeable future in the kingdom of non-streaming codecs. It's free, it's fast, it's cross-platform (covered in later chapters), and everybody uses it. What more can you want from a codec (apart from streaming and multicast support)?

INDEO

Indeo on the Mac hasn't caught on like it has on the PC, despite Intel's marketing efforts, but it is a worthy adversary of Cinepak on both platforms. The general wisdom is to use Cinepak if you want your movies a little smoother, and Indeo if you want slightly better resolution—especially on slower computers. See Figure 1.15 for a ranking of the relative attributes of all common codecs.

The best place to go for the latest version of Indeo is Intel's Web site (**www.intel.com**). It's worth the trip because new releases of Indeo don't necessarily track new versions of QuickTime itself. Intel also has quite a body of literature concerning cross-platform development with Indeo on their site. By the time you read this, the Mac version of Indeo Video Interactive may be available (see the description of IVI in the Video for Windows codec section later in this chapter). Intel is just beginning to unleash its Web-centric MMX technology, in which IVI will likely have an important role.

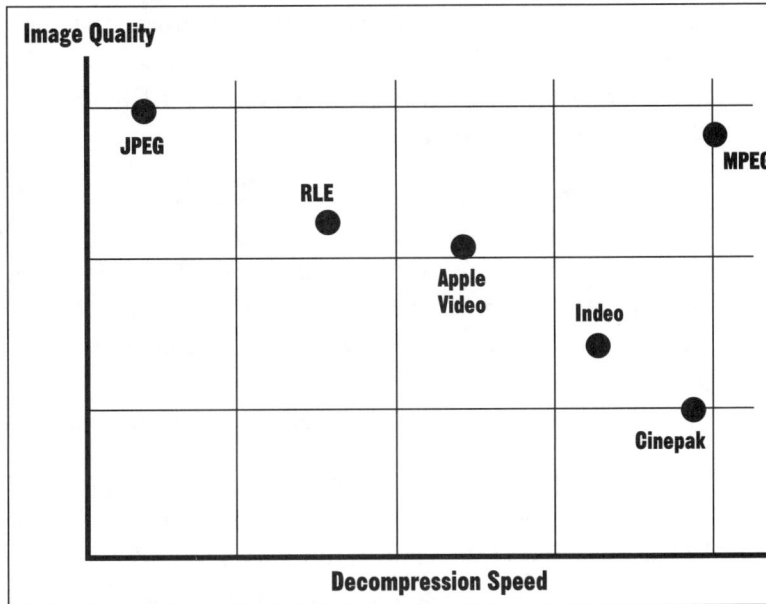

Figure 1.15 Relative attributes of common codecs.

Getting back to QuickTime in general, the bottom line is usually that QuickTime is a complex enough technology to be different things to different people. Software developers usually exploit it as a powerful toolkit for playing time-based media from within their applications.

For users, especially graphics professionals, QuickTime is perceived as a standard way of dealing with almost all multimedia data—such as audio, video, and still images. This means even more on the Mac, where QuickTime ships standard with the operating system (which is optimized for working with QuickTime).

Video For Windows (AVI)

When it debuted late in 1992, Microsoft's Video for Windows was a direct response to the 1.0 release of Apple's QuickTime for Windows (developed by the San Francisco Canyon Company, under contract to Apple). Back then, VfW was a relatively poor performer compared to QuickTime, although now both are mature enough to perform equally well (despite knee-jerk protests from Mac purists).

From a technical perspective, an AVI movie is a Microsoft RIFF (Resource Interchange File Format) file. Other kinds of RIFF files are WAV audio files and Windows bitmaps. You can learn much more about RIFF files (among other things) in the Microsoft Press books *Windows Multimedia Programmer's Guide* and the *Video for Windows Development Kit Programmer's Guide*.

As of this writing, the most recent versions of Video for Windows is 1.1e, although that version is specifically targeted to work with Windows 3.1. Windows 95 and NT 4.0 effectively have their own version of VfW built in (generally manifested in the ActiveX/ActiveMovie player). In other words, in the Win95 and NT environments, AVI movies just play as shown in Figure 1.16—assuming you have installed the operating systems and the multimedia components correctly.

Granted, AVI files follow a much less elegant design scheme than QuickTime movies, but their goals are more modest. All the original Video for Windows wanted to do was play video frames and audio chunks, which it ultimately did quite well. As noted above, there was no sophisticated track ordering and no means of setting frame duration (like there is in QuickTime).

As with QuickTime, satisfaction in working with Video for Windows lies in knowing when to use the right codec. The first round of VfW compressors included RLE, Video 1, and Indeo (Cinepak came later). A Raw codec (similar to Apple None) named YUV9 was also on board. All VfW codecs are utilized as standalone DLLs, as are the QuickTime for Windows codecs.

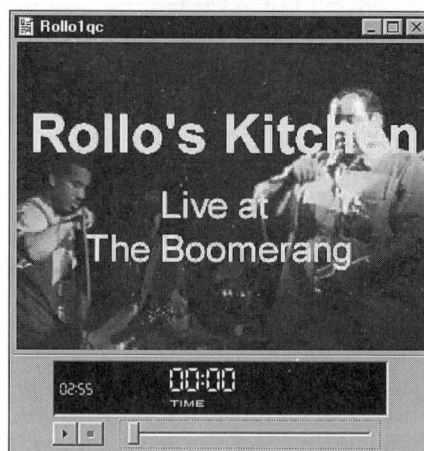

Figure 1.16   An AVI movie in the ActiveMovie player.

INDEO

Intel's Indeo Video codec has been through numerous changes since its inception. The latest version (4.1, also known as Indeo Video Interactive or IVI) has been rewritten from scratch. It is based on an advanced hybrid wavelet algorithm and is a formidable piece of software engineering.

As is the trend in newer multimedia software, IVI's full potential is realized only on high-end PCs, such as Pentiums and Power Macs. On 486s and below, you should probably stick with Indeo Video version 3.2. If you are already working with Indeo but have not looked at IVI yet, you'll be impressed with the new features it offers.

We should expect Indeo to have a role on the multicasting stage. Several third party developers have added support for this codec to their multicast solutions, based on its general merits. In fact, Intel used Indeo to stream LAN-based video in its original WorldView product.

CINEPAK

Cinepak under Windows works just like its Mac counterpart. In other words, if you convert a Mac Cinepak movie to a VfW Cinepak movie with one of the tools described in Chapter 15 (cross platform issues), the encoded data stream will remain the same.

Is Cinepak better than Indeo? Certainly the former has a bigger market share, but it depends on what you want from it. Again, one rule of thumb many people use is to go with Cinepak for greater playback smoothness and Indeo for better image resolution (on fast machines).

Is Cinepak going to play a part in video on demand and multicasting? Like on the Mac, it doesn't seem likely. Apparently, Radius still controls the development of the Cinepak codec (much to Microsoft's now fading chagrin), and they have not announced a new strategy as of this writing.

VIDEO 1

Originally developed by Media Vision, Video 1 was acquired by Microsoft as the original video compressor for VfW. It has pretty much seen its day, although occasionally it finds some special uses, especially when 8-bit encoding is required. Cinepak is usually better.

RLE

This codec can be very useful for making movies from screen captures, as shown in Figure 1.17. Similar to the Animation compressor on the QuickTime side, RLE is lossless by design, although it only supports 4-bit and 8-bit pixel depths (unlike the QuickTime version).

JPEG

Although Microsoft announced a standard Device Independent Bitmap (DIB) extension format for storing JPEG-format still images and motion sequences, there is no JPEG codec per se for Video for Windows as of this writing. As desktop video experts are aware, most high-end video capture cards come with their own MJPEG codecs, which tend to be proprietary and incompatible with each other.

MPEG

There has been a lot of hype about MPEG for the desktop over the last few years, and, until recently, a lot of it did not translate into viewer satisfaction. The big problem was that you needed a separate add-in board (such as Sigma's ReelMagic card) to play MPEG clips back with acceptable performance.

This situation has effectively changed with the event of Pentium computing. A Pentium 90 is now fast enough to play a standard SIF

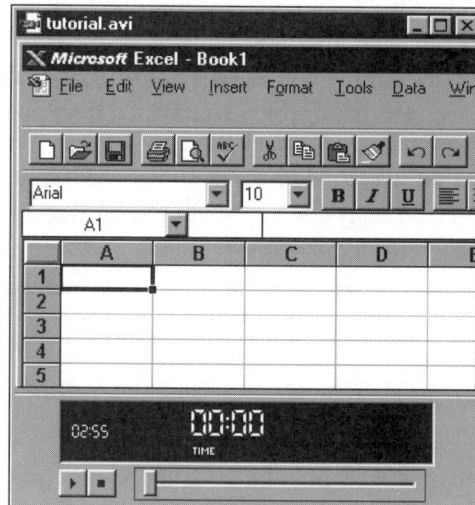

Figure 1.17 A typical RLE movie.

(352 × 240 pixels) MPEG clip without any extra hardware. If you do it with the ActiveX/ActiveMovie player, you don't even need special software because ActiveX/ActiveMovie is built into Microsoft Internet Explorer 3.0.

Does this spell trouble for Cinepak and Indeo? Maybe. Even though you can now play an MPEG clip in software only (as opposed to with a ReelMagic card), you still can't bring it into a desktop movie editor like Premiere 4.2 (the latest version). Also, the encoding hardware for high-quality MPEG clips is still expensive, although it is coming down fast. Game software developers got burned by MPEG once. The resultant wariness may slow down the second date to some degree.

For the record, MPEG is an acronym for the Motion Picture Experts Group, which has defined several MPEG standards for storing sound and video. The first such standard, MPEG 1 (or just MPEG), assumes the video storage is CD-ROM.

MPEG 2 video is generally targeted for the broadcast and movie theater markets and is just now being put into practice. The next incarnation, MPEG 3, was originally aimed at the HDTV world but was dropped when MPEG 2 was found to fill this role as well. MPEG 4, still in development, is planned to take advantage of fiber optics networks.

SHOCKWAVE

Currently implemented as a Netscape plug-in (also supported by ActiveX/ActiveMovie), Macromedia's Shockwave, shown in Figure 1.18, provides a way to play Director movies in your Web browser—including audio (you can get the plug-in at **www.macromedia.com**).

Shockwave provides enough of a video on demand experience to warrant mention here. It is free for the downloading, and no server-side software or special handling is required, save for some minimal configuration details. If you want animated banners and logos, Shockwave will do the job nicely. If you are looking for something more on the video side, it is worth going to some shocked sites to see how other people are doing it.

Figure 1.18 A standard Shockwave movie.

Summary

Understanding video on demand isn't hard once you start using the software that fleshes out the model (like VDOLive). What is more difficult is keeping the model in perspective as you introduce other abstractions, such as so-called *video servers* and, ultimately, the multicasting model.

If you are new to these concepts, you should download as much of the free video on demand software as you have time for and put it through its paces. By the time you get a sense of the inherent limits, you will probably be ready to start considering the multicasting model.

Chapter 2

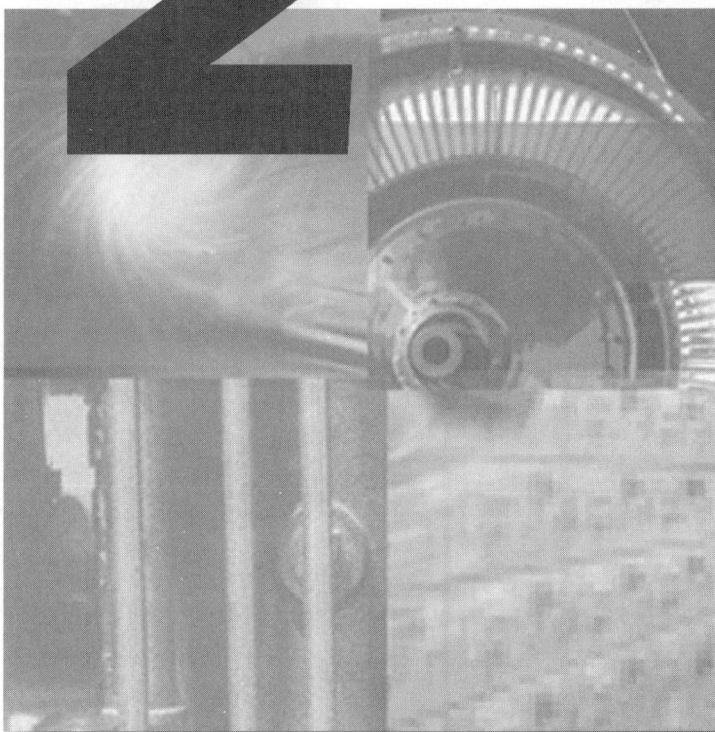

- **Understanding Internet video conferencing**

- **Working with the current video conferencing products**

- **Pushing the video conferencing limits**

Chapter 2

Video Conferencing

Generic video conferencing is nothing new. Big corporations like AT&T and Sprint have been doing it for years, presumably making a profit. According to the marketing literature, they save their customers significant airfare and hotel expenses (if not headaches and disorientation). What we'll be talking about in this chapter, however, is *digital desktop* video conferencing, which is relatively new and operates under quite different principles.

Like in Chapter 1, we'll look at the existing models for video conferencing (especially desktop video conferencing) as a basis for better comprehending the multicasting model described in the chapters that follow. As you might suspect, we'll also reprise the importance of understanding the abstractions inherent in any digital communications network. Finally, we'll continue to stress the wisdom of procuring and experimenting with the available free software.

Currently, a major commonality shared by PC-based video on demand, PC-based video conferencing, and PC-based multicasting is the way the video and audio presentation on the desktop feels to the user. What it feels like is multimedia. To people unaware of the remote data communications issues (or those who took the technology in *Mission Impossible* at face value), it sometimes feels like multimedia from 1992.

The point is that, bandwidth being equal, the image in a VDOLive window (video on demand) generally behaves like an image in a CU-SeeMe window (video conferencing). Figure 2.1 puts this idea in context. Moreover, the video streams in each of these windows may feel much the same as a stream you'll receive in a multicast window (again, subject to bandwidth being the same). Also, remember that multimedia improved *a lot* between 1992 and 1996.

If you go to the trouble of downloading and running as much free software as possible in each of these three categories (assuming you want this direct experience), you can really appreciate the field conditions faced by most users. This is really the only way to get a gut feeling for desktop video technology operating in the real world.

Traditional Video Conferencing

There are actually several models for video conferencing per se. This is partly due to a broad definition of the word *conferencing*, but also to the availability of various types of technology used to implement the models. As always, the bigger the budget, the better the performance. Let's take a look at each of these models.

Figure 2.1 VDOLive and CU-SeeMe on the same desktop.

The Corporate Way

Picture a fortieth-floor corporate media center in San Francisco, a sales office in Houston, and a booth at a trade show in Singapore. Each location is equipped with cameras and big-screen video monitors. The gear is all connected via high-capacity phone lines or maybe even satellite links. People at each location act distracted and straighten their ties. All of the equipment was set up for them.

The conference begins. Everybody can see and hear everybody else, even if the video is a little blurry and the audio sometimes suffers a slight delay. Executives at each site proceed to exchange empirical business information—as well as important corporate culture signals—depending on their level of video conference training and on-camera comfort level.

Perhaps there is a separate *document camera*. Such a device is helpful when someone wants to show, say, an outline or a schematic to the other participants. Of course, this means that the document camera has to be switched to, which implies some behind the scenes event management. In any case, when the allotted time is consumed, the conference is over.

Other technical amenities can include acoustically-designed stages, intelligent microphones with noise reduction filters, and remote-control cameras guided with infrared control pads, as shown in Figure 2.2. A leading player in this area is PictureTel, whose products have set new standards for broadcast video and audio data compression.

This is what most people think of as corporate, or *room,* video conferencing. Generally speaking, it works—as long as the participants observe the training rules and the technicians know what they're doing. If it didn't work, big telecommunications companies probably would have stopped providing the service by now. For the record, this scenario involves a fair amount of analog video equipment, in addition to digital.

You could argue, naturally, that this technology is still in the self-promotional stage and that most corporate video conferencing is done to sell more corporate video conferencing—as opposed to simply providing a viable service for disparate customers. In other words, it's all part of the positioning game played by big telecommunications companies.

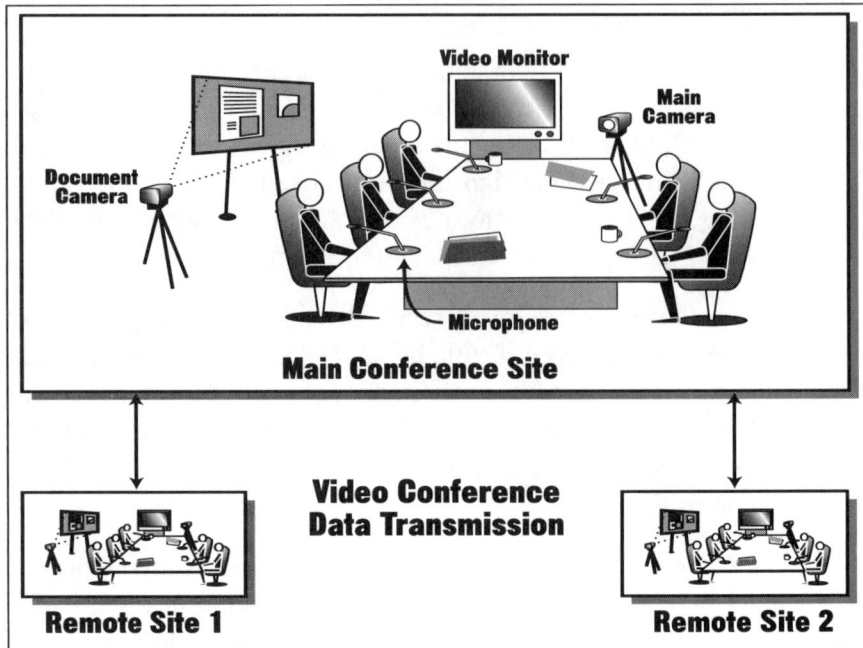

Figure 2.2 Video conferencing with all the trimmings.

But, so what? Maybe we'll learn that we don't need this type of video conferencing in the long run.

The goal of this model, and others detailed in this chapter, is to make it convenient and economical to do the kind of business that requires personal interaction, all without taking a business trip. If it can be just like talking to someone in the same room, so much the better (as if that's going to happen any time soon).

Unlike video on demand, there is no real instant gratification factor or commercial consumption of a video conference data stream. The paradigm is an open communications port, with data flowing in both directions but no *theater* involved. Still, the common medium is a video monitor or a smaller window in a video monitor (as in multimedia). Plus, you can always turn it off.

The Small Business Approach

Now, imagine another scenario where a person (Ms. VC) sits in a rural, home office. Perched on top of her computer monitor is a small camera plugged into the serial or parallel port of the CPU. An ISDN cable runs from the house to the trunk line down the hill (installed at no small cost). At least in this situation, business dress is optional.

Ms. VC places a regular phone call to an executive in a corporation whose office is outfitted with the same dedicated video conferencing gear as she has. She tells the executive that she wants to initiate a video conference. Both parties ring off. Ms. VC fires up her conferencing application, which dials the remote corporate office. The executive's computer answers and the conference begins. Note that this is not being done via the Internet and usually follows a fairly standard sequence of events (as shown in Figure 2.3).

Because an ISDN line is employed and this is a direct dial-up, the A/V aesthetics are not too bad (given the quarter-screen video window). Depending on the type of software, the participants can switch between video and other types of displayable data. Occasionally, one reminds the other that they have drifted away from the microphone (also attached to the computer) or that they need to speak up. Audio can be flaky in this environment.

Ms. VC, a communications consultant, has persuaded her client that this is the way they need to communicate to keep their personal conferencing skills from atrophying, and things have been going

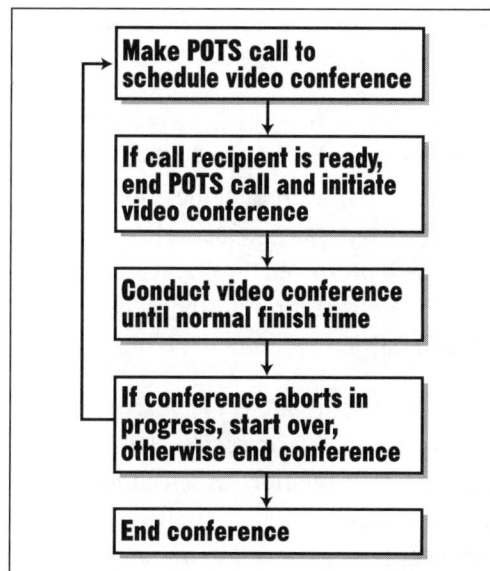

Figure 2.3 Executing a small business video conference.

smoothly so far (it also helps that the business relationship is a good one). The two parties discuss the status of various projects and then sign off.

This is a slightly less prevalent form of video conferencing, though equally as valid (at least conceptually) as the previous all-corporate example. As to whether it just plain works, it depends on who you're talking to. Ms. VC happens to like it and makes money off it. As in the corporate example, certain matters of video conferencing etiquette must be observed, but regular conferees usually adapt to each other's personal style.

Again, you could argue that even this down-sized version of business video conferencing is still justifying its existence via its heavy novelty factor (instead of working in the background as a stable productivity tool). But, again, so what? Business is happening. And, when the novelty wears off, we are essentially talking about a video-enabled telephone (aside from the visual *data presentation* capability), which is a desirable business tool.

It is important to note here that Ms. VC's insistence on using this medium for communication with her client is not all that unusual. At one prominent Northern California corporation, the product group in charge of producing a well-known desktop conferencing solution mandated that all official remote communications within their group employ their product.

Your humble author was, in fact, present in the office of at least one outside vendor when such an official communiqué took place. The occasion was a demo of a product the outside vendor was preparing, which was itself mostly desktop video clips. The product was a CD-ROM adventure which promoted the client's products. The idea was to present the demo to the client through the video conference link by switching to data presentation mode once the normal conference was underway.

Did it work? The short answer is yes. What was most memorable (outside of the idea itself) was seeing the people at the client company—the audience—in a quarter screen video window, all crowded into a gray cubicle to watch what amounted to a video stream within a video stream (conceptually speaking, of course).

The goal of this particular video conferencing model is, like the previous corporate scenario, to make it cheap and easy for people to conduct their business and personal affairs remotely, without the loss of the personal touch. Again, in contrast to the video on demand world, you can reduce it conceptually to a simple communication channel with a minimum of overtly theatrical content (as illustrated in Figure 2.4). Because of this lack of theatrics, there is little instant gratification (unless the participants are desperate to communicate). And the common medium is, once again, the video screen.

The Education Angle

So much for business. Let's now focus on some other communication settings in which video conferencing plays a role. We've all seen those politically correct Apple commercials where a classroom in America is connected to a school in, for instance, Europe or Africa. While entrepreneurs like to call this experience *distance learning*, it is (technically speaking) just another form of desktop video conferencing.

If children are involved, a lot of nonstructured data may flow through the communication link, but who's to judge? Other types of distance learning products are now in development where the delivery of the educational material is highly structured but still fits the video conferencing profile. It's hard to tell in the Apple commercials whether the communications line is supposed to be the Internet or a dedicated dial-up. But since Apple was heavily involved in promoting *Mission Impossible....*

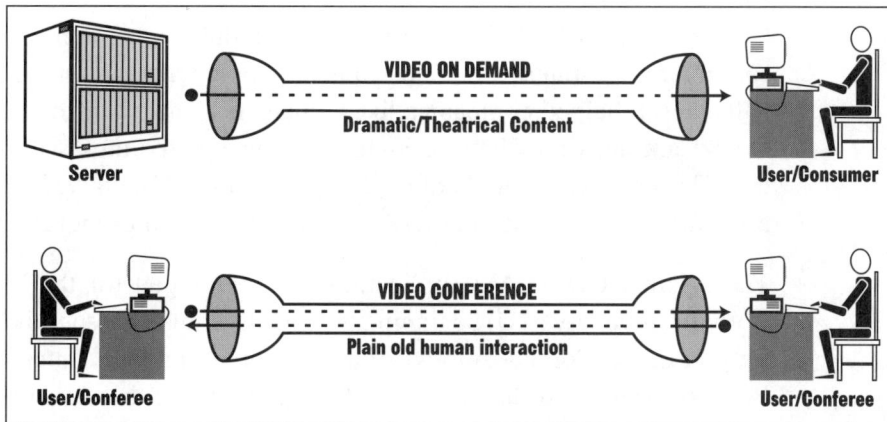

Figure 2.4 Video on demand versus video conferencing.

When you think about it, the video on demand model also works for distance learning. You could make a stored, prerecorded desktop video clip available to students with Web access, just like you might assign them to watch an episode on the Discovery Channel on TV. As you'll soon see, we are almost verging on the multicast model at this point.

The Noncommercial Model

What video conferencing models haven't we discussed? Just one—the one that lives on the Internet at large. Because there are some new levels of abstraction at work here, we'll open up a whole new section of this chapter for the Noncommercial Model on the Internet.

TCP/IP Video Conferencing

This section explores the realm of so-called *TCP/IP-based* remote video conferencing. It also concentrates on one particular player (White Pine Software, developer of CU-SeeMe) to give this exploration a real context. We'll cover the other players and their products in the next section of this chapter.

As noted earlier, many of the key engineering principles in TCP/IP-based conferencing are also important in multicasting (itself basically a TCP/IP-based technology). Taking the time to acquire and experiment with CU-SeeMe as a prelude to investing in multicasting software and equipment is highly recommended.

About CU-SeeMe

CU-SeeMe is considered the first software-only video conferencing solution for the Internet at large. Lots of people went nuts for it originally, and it helped companies like Connectix—maker of the famous QuickCam shown in Figure 2.5—to have some pretty impressive quarters. (This product should not be confused with SayYouSayMe, a program that lets you video conference exclusively with Lionel Ritchie.)

The original CU-SeeMe application was developed for the Mac at Cornell University (CU) beginning in 1992. Eventually, issues like user support drove Cornell to look for a commercial partner. Enter White Pine Software, who shrink-wrapped the program for the mass markets and ported it to Windows. All things considered, a pretty smooth migration. Lots of people still go nuts for it, and it is now used in ways its creators may not have intended, such as members-only Web peep shows.

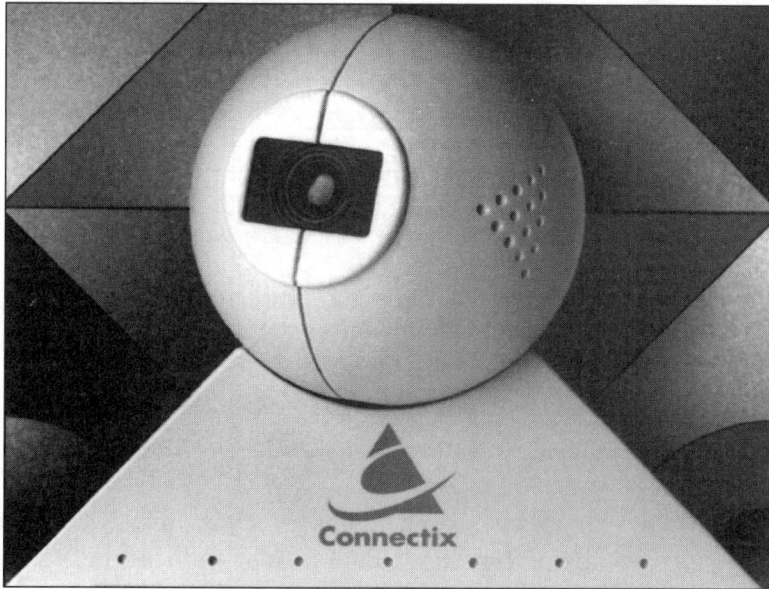

Figure 2.5 The ubiquitous QuickCam.

Although CU-SeeMe is software-only, it still needs some standard hardware components to function at full capacity. Foremost among these is a video camera/video capture board combination or a both-in-one Connectix QuickCam. You'll need a camera if you want other users to see you, although you can still receive images of other users without a camera.

A complete CU-SeeMe solution comprises both client and server software. You can get the client component free from the Cornell University FTP site, as shown in Figure 2.6, or buy the full-featured White Pine version off the rack. Actually, if you want a free version, the best advice is to do a Yahoo or Alta Vista Web search on CU-SeeMe and see what comes up. Server components, implemented as so-called *reflectors*, are discussed in detail below. Note that you don't need a reflector if you just want to connect to one other user.

How Reflectors Work

A CU-SeeMe reflector is essentially a video stream broadcast site. The reflection idea comes into play when a reflector re-transmits a video stream received from a single user to many other users (as opposed to making each user have a separate connection with every other user).

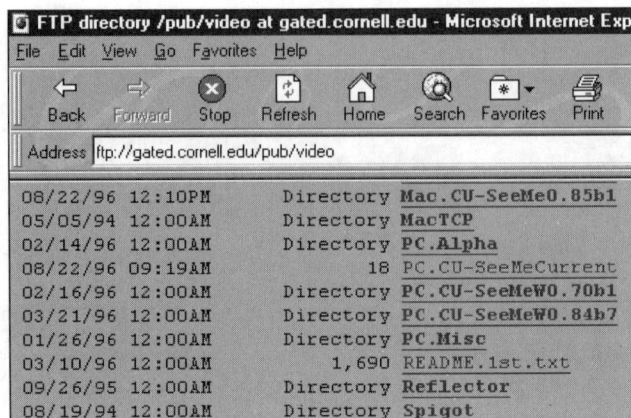

Figure 2.6 Getting the free Cornell version of CU-SeeMe.

Multicasting is also based on this principle. In fact, CU-SeeMe reflectors actually perform a standard type of multicasting.

Reflectors rely on TCP/IP's UDP protocol (briefly described in Chapter 1) as opposed to the basic packet-based protocol also built into TCP/IP. Because the data flow in video conferencing systems is constantly changing in size and composition, UDP protocol—with its packet skipping capability—is better able to handle the job.

To understand the role played by reflectors, let's first consider a video conferencing environment without reflecotrs. As it turns out, some video conferencing solutions still adhere to a unicast model wherein one stream is transmitted but each recipient tunes in with a dedicated connection. Other products perform multicasting well enough on LANs but fall back to unicasting for WAN clients. Neither approach does much for overall bandwidth conservation, obviously.

CU-SeeMe reflectors work their magic by:

- Providing basic multicast services to all users in a particular conference (including MBone clients and other reflectors)

- Adding intelligent broadcasting features (such as transmitting only when users are present)

In other words, each user sends his or her video stream to a given CU-SeeMe reflector. That stream is reflected (retransmitted) to each individual user participating in the conference. Using its built-in intelligence, the given CU-SeeMe reflector can tell whether the stream comes from a unicaster, a multicaster, an MBone client, or even another CU-SeeMe reflector.

When multiple CU-SeeMe reflectors work together on a distributed WAN, the underlying design strengths really start to shine, particularly when CU-SeeMe scales up to add lots of new users to an ongoing conference or deals with changing network conditions. For example, CU-SeeMe reflectors can dynamically readjust video transmission rates of connected users when overall network traffic gets too heavy.

As noted earlier, each of these CU-SeeMe design principles also has meaning in the general world of multicasting. Because they are so important to understand, let's now take a look at how a reflector site is set up. Again, keep in mind that reflectors are required only for video conferences involving more than two users.

Setting Up A CU-SeeMe Reflector

CU-SeeMe's current design spec can handle up to 100 users per reflector. Additional users (which can number in the thousands) are handled via reflector networks. Cornell University's free reflector application is only supported by Unix. If you want an NT or Windows 95 version, you'll have to buy a commercial version from White Pine. Check out their Web site at **www.wpine.com** for details.

Actually, there are some free Windows reflectors out there (which is why a Yahoo search on CU-SeeMe was suggested earlier) but not all of them are defect-free and none have excellent customer support. Also, not all of them have multicast capability. Since this is not a book about CU-SeeMe, we won't document any step-by-step, platform-specific installation procedures. Instead, we'll focus on some abstract reflector design issues, detailed as follows.

For the record, because of the one-to-one relationship between reflectors and IP addresses, you can only set up one reflector per computer (because a physical computer can only have one IP address). The Enhanced Reflector from White Pine supports up to 65,534 conferences with one reflector, while the free Cornell version only supports a single conference per reflector. Figure 2.7 shows the White Pine home page.

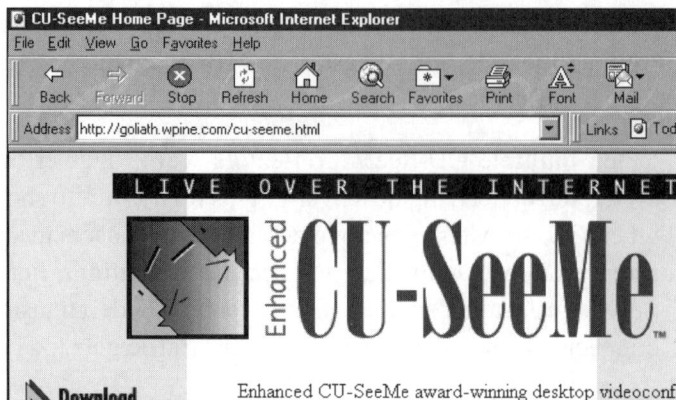

Figure 2.7 Visit the White Pine site.

Choosing Your Broadcast Model

To begin setting up your own reflector, you'll need to determine your broadcasting method. Three such methods are available:

- One-to-many

- Many-to-many

- Hybrid broadcasting

In the one-to-many approach, video streams only flow in one direction. If you plan on broadcasting prerecorded video clips or live A/V feeds (as opposed to interactive conferencing), this may be the best choice. Because traffic is only going in one direction, more bandwidth is available and more users can join the session.

The many-to-many method is the most common for so-called *public* reflectors. Under this model, video conferees can join a conference in progress, exchange information with other participants, then log off. Note that, although the physical connection limit is 100, system performance may fall off seriously with as few as 10 active chatters.

Hybrid broadcasting with CU-SeeMe is still an evolving model. What it promises is the delivery of a small-scale many-to-many broadcast to a much larger viewer community. It's easy to imagine the potential for this type of cybercasting, but the technical challenges are still being surmounted.

Using A Reflector Network

If you get seriously involved with CU-SeeMe, you may ultimately decide to implement a reflector network. If you need to provide service to more than 100 simultaneous users, this decision will likely be made for you, as shown in Figure 2.8. Implementing reflector networks is where CU-SeeMe multicasting can really come into play and where an understanding of multicasting abstractions is essential.

Before setting up a reflector network, you need to carefully evaluate the communications network that will link your host computers. As you'll see in later chapters, not all the pieces in the Internet at large are capable of multicast transmission, nor will they be in the near future. The best place to start for such an evaluation is your Internet Service Provider.

The Future Of CU-SeeMe

Despite competition from some of the new desktop video conferencing players (profiled later in this chapter), CU-SeeMe appears to have a great future. CU-SeeMe's future seems especially bright on the Mac side, where it has a huge installed base and performance often feels more solid (of course, the Windows side will catch up eventually).

Because of how CU-SeeMe utilizes multicast principles, it will probably continue to set standards for practicing bandwidth environmentalism. If you want an immediate hands-on experience with an application that puts multicasting to work in ways that show off its strengths, you should download the free version of CU-SeeMe and tune into some public reflectors. Or, call a friend, ask them to get the program also,

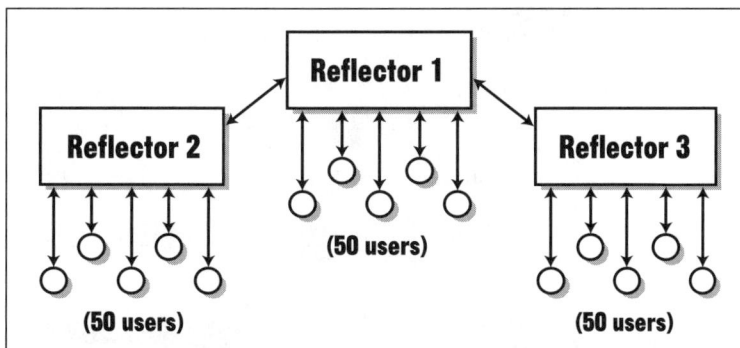

Figure 2.8   A reflector network.

and then immediately dial your respective ISPs and strike up a personal conference (for a quick unicast experience).

A couple of years ago, the types of CU-SeeMe reflectors that a new user could log on to were few and boring (depending on your taste). These days, you can find all kinds of conferences and broadcasts in progress, from online auctions to vacation promotions to sophisticated virtual classrooms. It works, it's free (with the Cornell client), and it's a good way to experience multicasting technology.

The Other Video Conferencing Players

While CU-SeeMe is an excellent role model among video conferencing solution providers, there are other strong contenders—several of whom may steal the point position from White Pine in the near future. We'll look at the big ones first, then cover the third party products.

QuickTime Conferencing (QTC)

This is obviously Apple's product, and it is formidable indeed. As most desktop video professionals are aware, QuickTime Conferencing has been a hot development area at Apple for a while. As with other video conferencing products, the initial target of QTC, however, was the LAN—as opposed to the Web. True, both environments support TCP/IP, but time-based media such as QuickTime can behave quite differently on the Web as opposed to on a LAN. Figure 2.9 shows Apple's QTC home page.

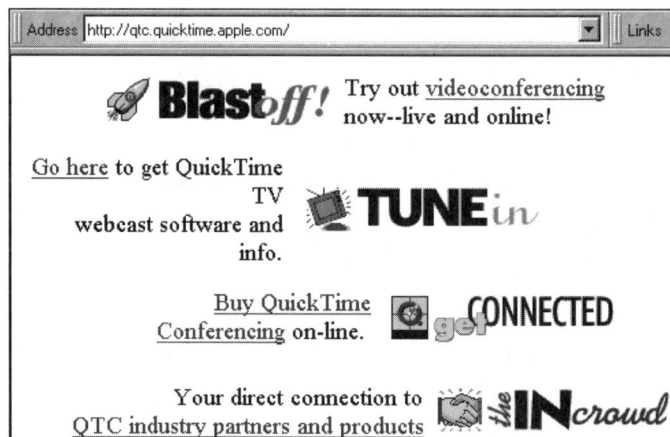

Figure 2.9 The QTC home page.

According to Apple's documentation (which may be revised by the time you read this), "QTC is a foundation and framework for media-rich desktop conferencing and collaborative computing, supporting an array of networked multimedia connections and applications. QTC's long-term viability and strength is based on a number of core software and hardware technologies," including:

- QuickTime itself

- Sound Manager for managing digital audio

- PowerTalk for network browsing and personal address books

- OpenTransport for transport independent networking

- Multiprotocol network services (AppleTalk, MacTCP, ISDN, etc.)

- A/V input for digitizing audio and video

- PowerPC for high performance processing

- Built-in Ethernet for media stream transmission/reception

Apple further documents that, "Functionally, QTC is an extension of the Macintosh operating system, designed to add realtime media communications features to new and existing user applications. QTC is a flexible solution because it is an open architecture and it enables cross-platform communications. QTC consists of an expandable set of software components, each dedicated to a different functional area of the multimedia networking landscape."

QTC has been proven to work well on LANs, but good performance of QTC on the Web is not generally available at modem speeds of 28.8 and below. However, as noted in Chapter 1, this may not be a problem for either QuickTime on demand or QTC—depending on the markets they expect to reach. If you need technical documentation for QTC, Apple has no shortage of it. There is also ample background data on QTC at the URL **quicktime.apple.com**.

As for multicasting with QTC, the company is on the cutting edge software-wise. Apple multicast protocols are available for both AppleTalk and TCP/IP. QTC also supports SMRP (Simple Multicast Routing Protocol) and IP multicast for network routers.

In the early days of QTC, only SMRP was supported. As TCP/IP support was integrated, router manufacturers were forced to upgrade to this standard as well, which not all of them did on the same schedule. By the time you read this, all the multicast components of QTC should be working together harmoniously.

QTC Free

What can you get for free right now to experiment with over the Web? You can start with QTC Free, at **http://qtc.quicktime.apple.com/qtc/qtc.demo.html** (shown in Figure 2.10). QTC Free is a software bundle, based on QuickTime Conferencing that lets you video conference and watch Webcasts.

As of this writing, QTC Free is still labeled beta and requires the latest Mac system software and some specific additional hardware. Specifically, the items are: System 7.5 or higher (7.5.3 recommended), a Power Mac (or 68040 machine) with 16 MB of RAM, an Internet connection of at least 112 Kbps, and MacTCP (if you don't have system 7.5.3).

The current QTC Free package includes three applications:

- QuickTime Web Conference

- QuickTime TV

- Conferencing Helper Application

According to Apple, QuickTime Web Conference is "a feature-limited version of QuickTime Conferencing video conferencing and collaboration software. It lets you establish a two-way video conference, post

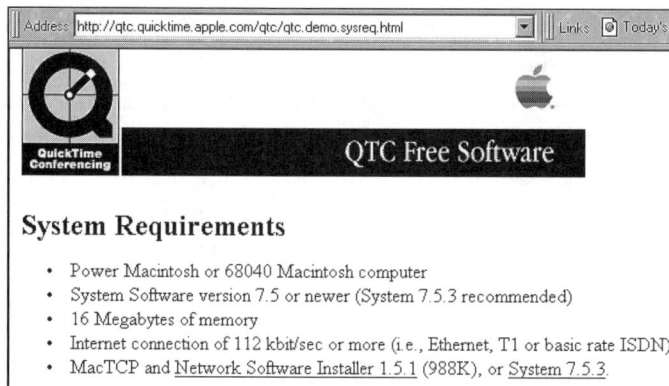

Figure 2.10   The QTC Free page.

graphics and text files to a Shared Whiteboard, and mark-up those files in realtime with the person on the other end. You can record the video conference as a QuickTime movie, and drag-and-drop the contents of the Shared Whiteboard to your desktop as a PICT file."

QuickTime TV allows you to view Internet Webcasts. According to Apple, you'll need network bandwidth of at least 128 Kbps to view a Webcast. QuickTime TV actually works quite well on a LAN but not quite as robustly as CU-SeeMe on the Web at large. Apple has sponsored several high-profile Webcasts to date, but there are not as many 24-hour QuickTime TV stations as there are CU-SeeMe reflectors—at least not yet.

The Conferencing Helper Application is used for "autolaunching video conferences from within a Web page and for creating files which can launch live connections from within a Web page."

Apple provides detailed instructions installing all of this software once you have downloaded it. The standard way to get most of the conferences and Webcasts rolling is to embed them in Web pages using Netscape plug-ins, directions for which are also included. As with CU-SeeMe, it is highly recommended that you get hold of this software and put it through its paces to set your expectation level for multicasting in general.

ActiveX Conferencing

This is a brand new solution (at least for the masses), but it is a completely logical extension of Microsoft's otherwise stable ActiveX code base. According to Microsoft, "ActiveX Conferencing is the technological underpinning of a new class of programs, like Microsoft NetMeeting, that turn your multimedia PC into a communications center." Unfortunately, the initial release of ActiveX Conferencing does not include video (although it does include audio). Figure 2.11 shows the NetMeeting home page.

The ActiveX Conferencing platform rests on a number of industry standards. For example, the data conferencing elements were developed in accordance with T.120, the International Telecommunication Union (ITU) protocol for realtime multipoint data transmission across the Internet.

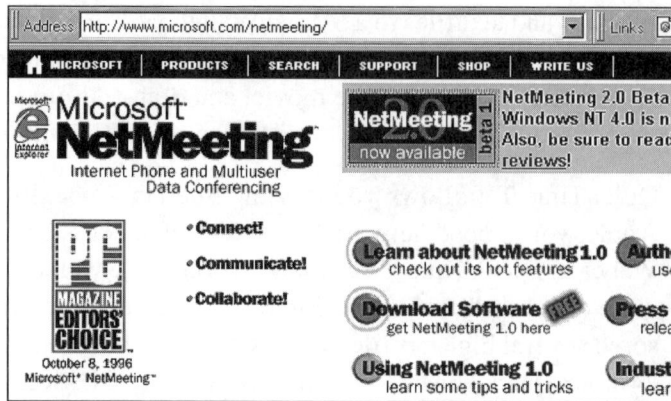

Figure 2.11 Microsoft's NetMeeting home page.

The audio conferencing features are based on RTP/RTCP, which are formal standards from the Internet Engineer Task Force (IETF) for streaming realtime multimedia data on the Web. The planned video conferencing capabilities are expected to support the H.320 and H.324 protocols.

One of the most interesting facets of the emerging ActiveX Conferencing suite is the software layer referred to as MCS, or Multipoint Communications Services. According to Microsoft, "MCS defines the relationship between nodes participating in a conference in a hierarchy called an MCS domain. Conferences always take place within the context of a single MCS domain, but there is no restriction on the number of conferences occurring within the domain."

Sounds a little bit like the CU-SeeMe reflector strategy described earlier in this chapter. It also sounds a little too abstract at this point, but it shows that a good deal of planning has gone into ActiveX Conferencing so far. The rest of ActiveX works well, so it's a good bet that the conferencing part will do the same.

Currently, the major components of ActiveX Conferencing are as follows:

• Data collaboration

• Application sharing

• File transfer

• Video conferencing (not included in v1.0)

This chapter is about video conferencing, so we won't cover ActiveX Conferencing in any more detail here, but it is definitely worth keeping tabs on because video support has been promised and Web product development is now Microsoft's middle name. Check out the NetMeeting area of the Microsoft Web site for frequent updates, as well as **www.microsoft.com/intdev/msconf**.

The rest of this chapter is devoted to third-party Internet video conferencing solutions. There will be even more players soon. As you'll see, just because they come from smaller companies doesn't mean they aren't good performers.

Once again, our mantra: Download these programs and see for yourself how good (or bad) they are. More importantly, let them prepare you for the look and feel of venturing into the more expensive and complex world of full-on professional multicasting.

The Connectix VideoPhone

This application was initially created to support the Connectix QuickCam. As it turns out, the VideoPhone is now a decent contender all by itself—especially in high-bandwidth territory. In 14.4/28.8 land, image fluidity tends to drop off significantly (even though image clarity remains relatively high).

A user initiates a call by either choosing an entry in his or her personal phonebook or calling into the user database maintained by Connectix. If you're the call recipient, you can configure the VideoPhone to launch itself when a call is detected or simply accept calls as they come in. Figure 2.12 shows the VideoPhone's principle user interface.

While VideoPhone works fine with point-to-point communications, it doesn't handle conferences in which multiple participants appear on the user's screen simultaneously (as in CU-SeeMe). You can, however, use the product not only on the Web and LANs but also in modem-to-modem dial-ups.

One of the major problems you should expect with the VideoPhone is poor audio performance at 28.8 (and below). At ISDN (and higher) speeds, the audio is fairly stable. For some reason, Connectix chose not to include a volume indicator, and the volume controls themselves are not accessible from the main screen.

Figure 2.12   The VideoPhone UI.

Another problem area is the unduly complicated installation/configuration scheme. In other words, tweaking the product for optimum performance can take a fair amount of testing (and patience). If you plan on using the VideoPhone a lot, it is probably worth your time to optimize it using the available controls for doing so.

Current list price: $99. For more information, contact Connectix at (800) 950-5880 or **www.connectix.com**.

CineCom's CineVideo/Direct

This Windows-only product offers good point-to-point performance for two participants but, as with the Connectix VideoPhone, it does not provide true video conferencing capability (in which more than one other conferee appears on any user's screen). As you would expect, it works with LANs, the Internet, and with modem-to-modem connections.

Calling another CineVideo user is relatively easy because the UI is relatively clean (unlike with the Connectix solution). You can dial from a list or enter the IP address of the recipient and click to connect. When operating normally, the program shows you call status, incoming and outgoing frame rates, and the IP addresses of both connected parties (see Figure 2.13).

Figure 2.13 The CineVideo/Direct UI.

Unfortunately, CineVideo will not answer a call if it is not running. You can, however, specify that a caller supply a password before a connection is established. Under this condition, you can see the caller's video but he can't see yours until he enters the correct password.

Much to its credit, the program can adapt to changing bandwidth conditions on the fly. This frees it from burdening the user with lots of static configuration controls. Installation is also fairly trouble free, including detection of the user's video capture card. The program apparently checks the SYSTEM.INI file to see if a capture board is present and then works directly with its drivers.

Audio is a potential problem, especially in low-bandwidth environments (no surprises here), but it is not as bad as with some of the competition (the VideoPhone, for example). One nice alternative to audio failure is CineVideo's chat window (also a good way to send a password to a new caller). It kind of makes you wonder, though, if the majority of CineVideo's users settle for text communication instead of wasting their time using the marginal audio feature.

Overall, ease of use and clean design are relatively strong in CineCom's offering. The proprietary video compressor serves the product well, especially in its ability to keep the image of the participant offset from the background. If you wish, you can view the remote conferee in black and white as opposed to color (assuming your camera supports color).

Current list price: $39.95. For more information, contact Cinecom at (703) 680-4733 or **www.cinecom.com**.

VDOnet's VDOPhone

Based on the positive evaluation of VDOLive (video on demand) in Chapter 1, it should come as no surprise that VDOnet's video conferencing product is a powerful application, as well. In fact, two formidable technologies are employed here: VDOnet's video compressor (VDOWave) and Voxware's audio codec (ToolVox). Overall, the results are quite impressive.

As noted in Chapter 1, VDOWave utilizes a wavelet compression scheme to achieve a high level of scalability while maintaining high data integrity. This means that streams transmitted in wide bandwidth situations will appear dramatically better than the same streams transmitted through narrow bandwidth environments.

Like the Connectix VideoPhone and CineVideo/Direct, the VDOPhone is actually a two-party, point-to-point application rather than an extensible video conferencing tool (like CU-SeeMe, with its multiple conferee windows). Another drawback is the fact that, because VDOnet's underlying video compression software is so computationally intensive, the frame rate of the video stream often suffers. This is also true for the video on demand product.

VDOPhone's UI is nice and clean, just like the one in CineVideo/Direct. All the controls are immediately apparent and collectively provide solid ways to tweak playback performance of both audio and video (see Figure 2.14). At ISDN and greater modem speeds, the whole package comes together nicely.

Additional features include the VDOPhone NetAnalyzer and, for $100 more, Dual Mode, which allows VDOPhone to operate over regular phone lines—as opposed to directly over the Internet. VDOnet's Web site also has some other interesting products available for downloading that are worth checking out.

Current list price: $99. For more information, contact VDOnet at (415) 846-7700 or **www.vdolive.com**.

Summary

We noted at the end of Chapter 1 that getting a handle on video on demand wasn't difficult once you played around with the available software. Not surprisingly, the same idea holds true for video conferencing.

Figure 2.14 The VDOPhone UI.

Once again, however, the hard part is keeping all of the conferencing models in mind, as you develop your overall understanding.

So, we'll say it one last time: Get the free software and install it. Find someone with similar interests and make a point of holding at least one short video conference per day until you can't stand it any more—or find out that you like it enough to expand your network of conferees. If you don't like the look and feel of PC-based video conferencing (or video on demand, for that matter) you may want to rethink your plans for getting into full-on multicasting.

Chapter 3

- **Getting familiar with the specialized multicasting hardware vendors**

- **Understanding the role of multicasting software developers**

- **Putting all the pieces together**

Who The Players Are

You can tell a lot about an emerging technology by the company it keeps. While still relatively young, multicasting has attracted enough attention from software developers, hardware manufacturers, and systems integrators to allow a far-sighted promoter to bring these companies together under a common banner (at least for the time being).

That banner bears the title *The IP Multicast Initiative*. The organization that flies it was assembled by Judy Estrin, CEO of Precept Software, Inc., based in Palo Alto, California (**www.precept.com**). The initiative is managed by Stardust Technolgies, Inc., of Campbell, CA. The home page for the IP Multicast Initiative is **www.startdust.com**. Regular meetings are scheduled, as well as frequent updates to the information provided at the Web site (see Figure 3.1).

The First Wave

The official ante for the IP Multicast Initiative, as you'll see when you visit their page, is not cheap: $25,000 for charter membership and $5,000 to $25,000 for general membership (based on company revenue).

Figure 3.1 The IP Multicast Initiative home page.

The clubhouse roll call is an impressive who's who:

- Microsoft

- Intel

- Hewlett-Packard

- Sun Microsystems

- Netscape

- Cisco Systems

- 3COM

- Silicon Graphics

- Xerox PARC

- White Pine Software

- Bay Networks

- Cabletron

- FTP Software

- StarBurst Communications

- Vivo Software

- Precept Software

Curiously absent from this list so far are Apple Computer and Oracle, along with some of the other players noted in the previous chapters concerning video on demand and video conferencing (such as VDOnet). Perhaps these companies are just late joiners, but Apple is certainly well-positioned to enjoy the benefits of membership in this initiative. As for Oracle, they generally like to blaze their own trails.

This chapter will cover the contributions made to date by the major players (and selected smaller companies) to the multicasting environment. If appropriate, we'll recap their announcements regarding future products—with as many grains of salt as necessary. By visiting the Web sites for these companies, you can ultimately make your own decisions about the viability of their solutions based on more timely information. Don't be surprised to see some familiar names in this chapter (from the prior video on demand and video conferencing chapters).

As you cruise around the Web looking for pieces to add to your overall multicast strategy, remember that (for a while, at least) special equipment, such as routers and high-speed modems, is going to be as important for performance as the basic software components.

KEEPING AN EYE ON THE NET

Every few days, try a basic Yahoo or Alta Vista search, as shown in Figure 3.2, just to see if anything new has arrived on the scene.

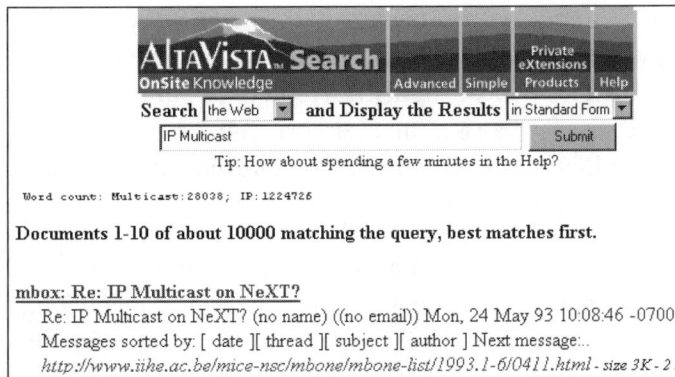

Figure 3.2 Reeling in the Net.

Get It In Writing

One thing you'll find at the sites of many of the companies who provide multicast solutions are white papers and other official documentation on multicasting. In general, it is worth reading all such documents. After you have acquired a basic understanding of multicasting issues (plus hands-on experience with related technologies such as video conferencing and video on demand), it is interesting to see how Company A's views line up with Company B's.

Don't be frustrated if it's confusing in the beginning. This is a new development area for both hardware and software companies, complete with gaps here and there. Make sure to look for technical literature with lots of diagrams and schematics. Multicast technology lends itself very well to visual representations, as you'll see in the chapters that follow.

The Special Hardware Players

Let's start off with the exotic equipment manufacturers. There are not as many of them as there are multicast software developers but, as noted earlier, their role is pivotal. When you start to spend money on system upgrades for multicast capability, this will be one of your first cost centers. The list that follows is not meant to be definitive.

Cisco Systems

This firm's stock price was in the news frequently in 1996. The company itself experienced rapid growth, and for good reason. It made some of the most sophisticated network plumbing products available and almost had the market cornered for a while. Many of the Web sites in the Internet's First Golden Age consisted of a server, a Cisco router, and a T1 line.

The company is still thriving and now offers many products important to prospective multicasters (as well as to the networking professional in general). Figure 3.3 shows a snapshot from their home page, **www.cisco.com**. When you go to their site, remember to do a search on the word *multicast*. Contact them by phone at (408) 527-2033.

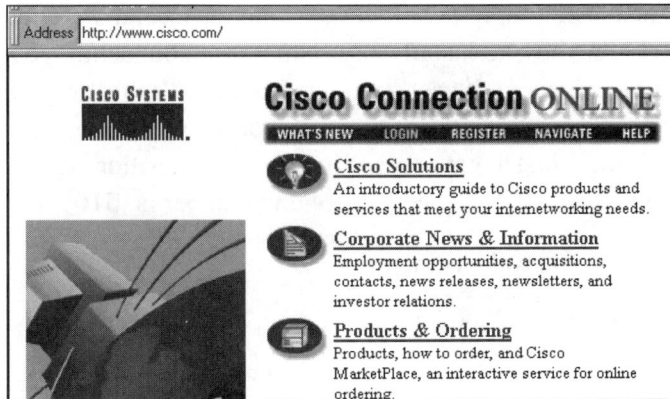

Figure 3.3 Cisco's home page.

Cisco's products include (among many other offerings):

- High-performance LAN solutions

- Routers for *remote* connection to a LAN via ISDN

- Routers for connection to the Internet via ISDN

Ascend

Ascend specializes in advanced remote networking hardware and software. Less well-known than Cisco, Ascend is nevertheless in an excellent position to exploit the coming market for private network and WAN multicasting—or, in their words, "global bandwidth on demand." As shown in Figure 3.4, their Web site is at **www.ascend.com**.

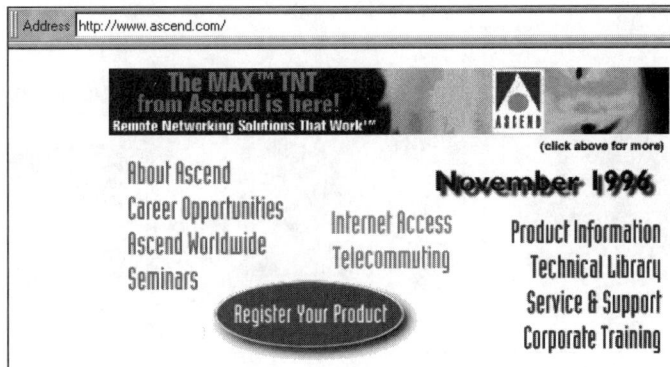

Figure 3.4 The Ascend Web site.

In a later chapter, we'll cover some of Ascend's products in detail, including how to install and use them for connecting your PC to a WAN to receive a multicast transmission. If you're reading this book chapter by chapter from the beginning, you may want to drop by the Ascend site now just to get a feel of how they are positioning themselves among the other players. Their telephone number is (510) 769-6001.

Ascend's products include:

- Routers and modems for high-speed WAN access

- Solutions for digital video conferencing

- Hardware and software for high-end LAN connectivity

Acclaim Communications

This firm's marketing literature uses phrases like "...fusing switching with routing" which is exactly what we're after in the private network multicasting world. Based on information available as of this writing, the hardware appears to be more expensive than average for individual users, but probably offers higher performance or is targeted for the corporate side.

The Acclaim Web presence is at **www.acclaiminc.com**, as illustrated in Figure 3.5. According to documentation for their EtherWAN product, "The integrated architecture of EtherWAN gives customers a single, Windows-based, SNMP platform for managing both the LAN and the WAN. EtherWAN management features configuration data, in-depth

Figure 3.5 The Acclaim Web site.

device management, and a graphic network view. The products offer load balancing, load sharing, and link redundancy. The new EtherWAN products will be available from Acclaim dealers in early Q4, 1996."

Again, this is marketing literature. But it makes this company a player that you should keep youself updated on in the multicasting arena. In general, the buzzwords used above are what you should be looking for as you evaluate multicasting hardware for your system. For more information, contact the company at (408) 327-0100.

Proteon

Proteon seems more focused on routers than on traditional LAN solutions, but it has product lines that make it a contender in both fields. Based on data published at their Web site (**www.proteon.com**—see Figure 3.6), the company has made ISDN one of their strong suits. Contact them by phone at (508) 898-9800.

As noted previously, this is not meant to be a definitive list of router and WAN hardware manufacturers, but it will give you both a place to start and the flavor of the emerging environment. At some point, you will have to jump in and buy some of this gear if you want to consume or deliver remote multicasts, so plan on talking to their technical marketing people by phone, if possible.

Figure 3.6   The Proteon home page.

VARs And Other Resellers

And don't forget the VARs. Some of the hardware manufacturers, in fact, only distribute their products through resellers. A couple of places that handle routers, bridges, and other pertinent hardware are:

- Technical Concepts (**www.techconcepts.com**)

- RTS Limited (**www.dtsdist.com**)

Emerging Hardware

Let's pull back for a moment. So far, in this chapter, we've been profiling the key players (specifically the special hardware companies) in the technology areas upon which multicasting depends. What's important to keep in mind—as you take stock of this landscape—is that the underlying communications systems are also evolving. If you're reading this book, you've doubtlessly heard of xDSL, cable modems, and DirecPC (as well as other satellite-based products).

Most, if not all, of these data delivery systems promise to deliver generic Internet service to Joe Subscriber. This promise raises some important questions:

- Is it truly *plain vanilla* Internet service (just like over the phone line)?

- Will multicast protocols be supported by the special modems/routers that receive the xDSL, cable, and satellite data streams?

Both of these questions will clearly be answered as soon as a particular product line hits the streets and end users start putting the gear through its paces. For a solid technological grounding, we'll look at each generic solution below. When you call a company that makes, say, a router, remember to ask lots of questions about how their product connects to and deals with these new data delivery systems.

ISDN

In practical terms, the next bandwidth plateau up from 28.8 Kbps is Integrated Services Digital Network (ISDN). At peak performance, traditional ISDN service pumps data close to 128 Kbps (depending on the details of your subscription and the type of ISDN modem you have).

Despite announcements to the contrary, the big telecoms do not yet have their ISDN Internet access strategies perfected. When they do, like with AT&T's WorldNet for 28.8 service, life will be better for all ISDN consumers. When this chapter was written, you could get two-channel ISDN service in a major metro area from an independent ISP for under $30 per month. The ISDN line itself is extra and needs to be installed by your phone company (see Figure 3.7).

Running a commercial Web site, especially one that offers multicast events on top of everything else, with just ISDN access to the Internet is a pretty bad idea. If your LAN server offers WAN connectivity via an ISDN port, that's another story (in terms of getting good multicast performance). We'll cover this and related scenarios in later chapters.

Lately, the word is that ISDN is old news, despite the ISDN-specific solutions that some of the hardware vendors listed above are now bringing to market. This is slightly purist and does not take into account real business models. The best advice? Use ISDN as long as it's useful, then upgrade when the time is right.

T1 (And Higher) Lines

Like ISDN service, T1 service is already fairly common for companies that really need it. T3 lines are used by the major ISPs and the phone company itself. The funny thing is, employees of companies with T1 lines often have to share the service with other employees (so-called *fractional* T1 service). Such sharing often leads to sub-28.8 performance across the network.

Generally speaking, a common T1 line provides bandwidth in the neighborhood of 12 common ISDN lines. You could take this a step further

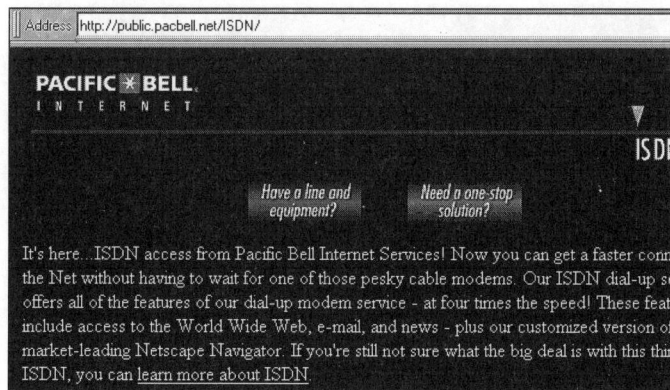

Figure 3.7 One of Pac Bell's ISDN-related Web pages.

by equating a T1 line with around 50 28.8 lines, but the math starts to get pretty conditional at this point. Another way to quantify T1 bandwidth is to think of it as delivering approximately 1.5 MB per second.

Most T1 lines hit routers as they enter company facilities. If companies want to deliver multicasts coming from such T1 lines to their employees, such routers need to be multicast-enabled. Because T1 lines are common, this is already a cut and dried procedure for companies that need it. Figure 3.8 shows the results of a Web search on T1 lines.

xDSL

The last three letters of this acronym stand for *Digital Subscriber Line.* Some people replace the *x* with an *A*, which stands for *asymmetric.* A popular way to think of xDSL is as enhanced ISDN, which it pretty much is (which is why ISDN is said to be outdated). Most of the these enhancements are due to breakthroughs in both hardware and software since ISDN was introduced.

For instance, data compression techniques have improved greatly over the last decade. Also responsible are advancements in chip fabrication and the increasingly dense silicon compounds now being used in miniature electronic components. For more details on xDSL, you can drop by the ADSL Forum Web site at **www.adsl.com/adsl/home_page.html** (see Figure 3.9).

It should come as no surprise that the telcos are jazzed about xDSL. Cable modems will likely be more under control of the cable compa-

Figure 3.8 Yahoo delivers the goods.

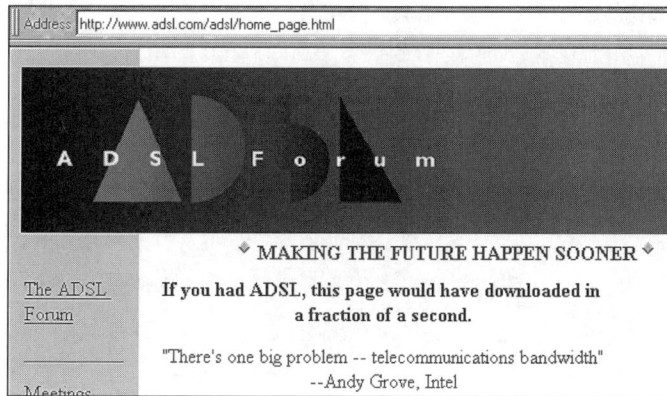

Figure 3.9   The ADSL Forum home page.

nies—who are the natural adversaries of the phone companies. In the current scheme, xDSL service will be delivered over standard twisted pair phone lines. Does this mean that installing and configuring an xDSL modem/router will be just like dealing with today's ISDN modem/routers? The answer may be up to a year away, depending on when you read this.

More bad news: Blazing xDSL speeds only happen in one direction (same as for cable modems). While data coming to the user may arrive at speeds up to 8 MB per second, the back channel performance might be only 15 percent as fast. Keep these numbers in mind, but be prepared to see them change prior to xDSL showtime.

Cable Modems

Cable modems will introduce a fair amount of brand new technology to the PC arena. Field testing (with actual users) has begun in selected parts of the United States. Most analysts predict they won't be generally available (at CompUSA) until Q2 or Q3 of 1997.

The price/performance numbers now being waved around indicate 10 to 40 MB per second for somewhere between $20 and $30 dollars per month per household. The innovation in cabling that makes all of this feasible is named Hybrid Fiber Coax (HFC). Where does the multicast-enabled router fit into the wiring diagram? Details are hard to come by at this point. Frequent Yahoo/Alta Vista searches (as shown in Figure 3.10) are a good way to go until *Consumer Reports* covers the story.

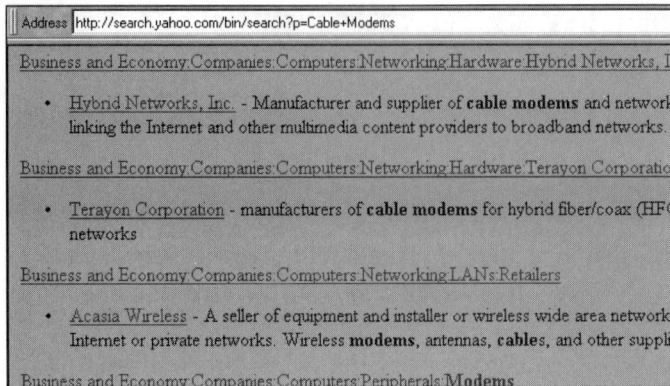

Figure 3.10 The results of a Web search on *Cable Modems*.

Like xDSL, data flow in the current cable modem universe is heavily weighted in one direction. While the user will receive plentiful volumes of data, the outflow will be a small fraction of that inflow (probably near ISDN rates). While this is excellent news for users, Web broadcasters (and multicasters) may not reap such great benefits.

Also, the 40 MB maximum throughput mentioned earlier may need qualification. As in the T1 world described, this bandwidth will likely be shared by other people on your block with cable modems. Some quick math shows that if a cable modem represents roughly 26 T1 lines, and if a T1 line works out to around 50 28.8 lines, then a cable company serving approximately 1300 Web surfers at the same time may only be able to give each one service at 28.8. Granted, this is very rough, but it helps sort out the big picture.

Fortunately, some very heavy hitters are warming up in the cable modem dugout: AT&T, Hewlett-Packard, IBM, Intel, Motorola, and Scientific-Atlanta, among others. Maybe by the time real cable modems are shipping, the formula presented previously will need rethinking.

Satellite Delivery

As anyone who reads consumer electronics ads can tell, 18-inch satellite dishes for movies and sporting events are taking the market by storm. Dishes in the first wave cost $700 at Radio Shack. Lately, the model is becoming the same as for cellular phones: give the hardware away and just sell the damn service. This is the kind of marketing that advances technology like it wants to be advanced.

So, are we now ready for the likes of Hughes Corporation's DirecPC (as opposed to the earlier DirecTV)? You bet. *Wall Street Journal* ads are already running for the hardware and the associated Internet access services. Forget wiring problems. Surf the Web via satellite. Right. As you'd guess, the issues raised above for all the other new types of data transmission hardware are just as sticky. When you go shopping for a multicasting router, be sure to raise them again.

Network Computers

Here's where it may get really interesting. Clearly, if the NC is the success that Oracle and the other companies on the NC freight train want it to be, the overall effect is going to be enormous, even if network computer hardware doesn't proliferate overnight. And, when you think about it, the NC might be just the catalyst that multicasting needs to give it orbital velocity. Figure 3.11 shows the home page for the Oracle NC.

It all depends on how configurable the NC is. While the first models will have built-in network adapters for LAN/WAN access, and their primary purpose will be browser-centric computing—even if just on the LAN—perhaps upgrades will include multicast-enabled routers (not that big a deal if the technology keeps heading in the current direction). When this happens, the NC is going to become a lot more like a TV, both in form and function.

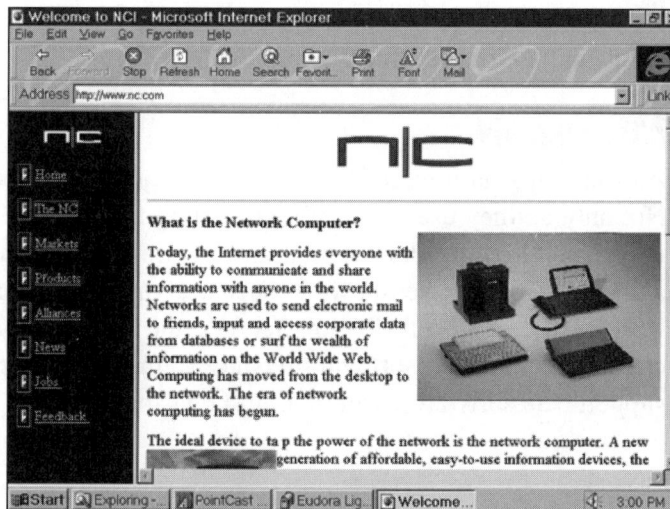

Figure 3.11 The Oracle NC.

Internet Service Providers

Later in this book, we'll devote a chapter to finding and dealing with ISPs that provide multicasting and MBone service. Because these companies are bona fide multicast players just like the hardware and software vendors we've covered so far, we'll give them a bit of coverage here as well.

If you go to the Web page **www.duth.gr/InfoBase/mbone/contacts. html**, you'll find a list of names and numbers for MBone ISPs who can begin to answer your questions and direct you to other multicast service providers, based on your overall requirements and geographical location.

The Software Players

Now for the multicast software companies. As indicated by the member list of the IP Multicast Initiative—presented at the start of this chapter—most (if not all) of the major software companies are staking out at least some part of the multicast landscape. We'll look at where they are now and what they have announced as future directions. As with the hardware manufacturers, this should not be considered a definitive roundup.

Unlike with the hardware vendors, we'll begin in the least exotic territory. Remember that the goal here is to confirm that these big players are involved and getting in deeper. Later chapters will cover the installation and use of their specific products.

Microsoft

As usual, it's hard to catch Microsoft napping anywhere these days. Not only do they use the term multicasting freely in their Web pages, they also have a full-blown multicasting product: NetShow (currently at the beta 2 level). NetShow has been designed to cooperate fully with IIS (the Microsoft Information Server), and it's downloadable free of charge at **www.microsoft.com/netshow** (remember, Microsoft does not support beta software). Figure 3.12 shows the NetShow home page.

Figure 3.12   The glory of NetShow (so far).

Microsoft's marketing literature has this to say about the product: "NetShow enables business users to provide audio and video in online training and communications materials, using minimal network bandwidth. Many leading hardware, software, and service firms are offering network components, compression technologies, authoring tools, administration utilities, applications, and services that build on the NetShow platform to deliver end-to-end networked multimedia solutions."

Furthermore: "NetShow facilitates efficient utilization and management of network bandwidth in a number of ways. For live transmissions, it uses IP multicasting to distribute audio and data files over multicast-enabled corporate networks, allowing one-to-many simultaneous transmission of data using the amount of network bandwidth normally used to send to only one client."

Finally: "For on-demand delivery, NetShow provides the ability to author content at different bit rates. It also includes simple server administration tools that allow management control over network bandwidth usage."

If you look over the NetShow Web pages, you'll see that NetShow comprises server software for Windows NT Server and client components for Windows 95 (and NT). Preliminary authoring tools and administrative programs are also provided. Heavy use is made of ActiveX technology, as you would expect. We'll be covering NetShow extensively in the chapters to come.

The companies Microsoft claims it is working with on NetShow include the usual suspects, as well as some provocative new faces:

- 3Com

- Ascend Communications

- Cisco Systems

- Digital Equipment

- Eastman Kodak

- Precept Software

- Progressive Networks

- Starlight Networks

- VDOnet

- Xing Technology

Apple

Nor has Apple been slacking. As we saw in Chapter 2, Apple embraces multicasting largely through its powerful QuickTime Conferencing software. However, while the company promotes so-called *WebCasts*, it does so by leveraging off the technologies endorsed in its QuickTime Live forum—many of which belong to non-Apple companies. Figure 3.13 shows the Apple WebCast home page.

One of Apple's own solutions, which also depends on QuickTime Conferencing (and therefore, to a large extent, multicasting), is the Apple Media Conference product. According to the marketing literature, "Apple Media Conference and QuickTime Conferencing software leverage the built-in capabilities of Macintosh systems to make videoconferencing and collaboration surprisingly easy and affordable. Just add a camera and you're ready to work with colleagues over an Ethernet local area network or the worldwide Internet."

Furthermore: "The QuickTime Conferencing system extension is based on Apple's QuickTime technology. Because the QuickTime architecture is so extensible, Macintosh developers can easily enhance QuickTime Conferencing for specialized purposes such as video mail, medical imaging, or distance learning. Apple Media Conference's broad-

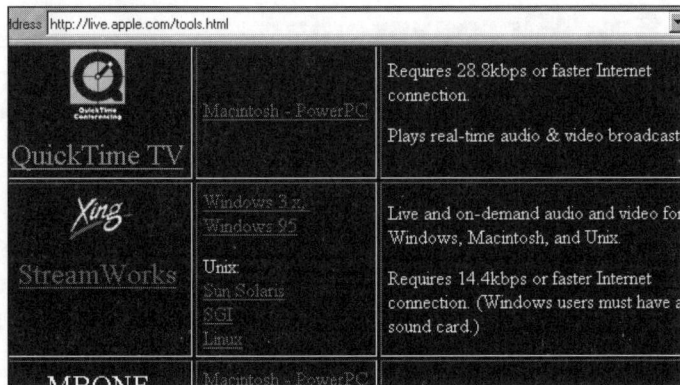

Figure 3.13 Apple WebCast components.

cast capabilities allow one user to broadcast a live video source (cable or broadcast TV, or a videocassette) over a local area network to an unlimited number of viewers. Viewers don't need a camera to tune into a broadcast."

According to Apple, the Media Conference software suite:

- Lets you exchange video, text, graphics, sounds, and movies with other Apple Media Conference users.

- Works over the Internet, local area networks, and ISDN networks (QuickTime Conferencing ISDN Kit required for ISDN networking).

- Offers user-selectable video and audio compression rates, and user-controllable video and audio quality settings.

- Supports multiparty videoconferences and one-to-many broadcasts as well as one-to-one sessions.

More information about Apple Media Conferencing can be obtained by going to the Apple Web site and searching on those three keywords. As noted in Chapter 2, Apple has several core software technologies (QuickTime, QuickTimeVR, and QuickTime Conferencing) which it needs to exploit to the max to keep up with its competitors, regardless of platform. It would be great if they could get something like Microsoft's NetShow cooking, if only for local networks. Perhaps by the time this book is published, they will.

Sun Microsystems

Because of its Unix-based operating systems and high-end workstation focus, Sun has been into advanced networking longer than either Apple or Microsoft. In fact, the first wave of Web servers was composed principally of Sun SparcStations.

With this in mind, let's now consider Sun's role as a player in the multicast arena. One of the company's current multicast solutions for the intranet is named Lyceum (as shown in Figure 3.14). It will be interesting to see if Lyceum (and other Sun multicast products) are implemented on networks that serve Mac and Windows clients.

Some details on Lyceum, in Sun's own words, are as follows:

• Lyceum uses about 500 Kbps of network bandwidth. For a normal Ethernet, this proportion is small, but would swamp low-bandwidth links such as ISDN. Make sure your intranet can handle this bandwidth before using Lyceum.

• Lyceum has been tested only on a low latency network, where little delay occurs between sending and receiving a packet. If you use Lyceum over a link with substantial latency (over one-half of a second), you may have problems.

• You can send an IP packet to a group of hosts with multicast, an extension to IP. Multicast is essential for Lyceum. Without it, every audio and video packet would have to be sent individually to each audience member.

Figure 3.14 Sun's Lyceum page.

- Multicast requires operating system and routing support. Multicast support is built into Solaris. Check to see if your network has multicast routers. Your network must be multicast enabled. The routers that connect the various parts of your network must support multicast.

- Lyceum is an application that can be distributed over a TCP/IP intranet, *not* the Internet.

- Do *not* use Lyceum over the MBone. Lyceum does not use the standard MBONE protocols. To do conferencing on the MBone, you must use standard MBone tools.

Precept Software

As already noted, Precept is the originator of the IP Multicast Initiative. As it turns out, the company is also a star player in the multicast software development world. So far, their product line is confined to Microsoft Windows. Visit their Web site at the address **www.precept.com** (as illustrated in Figure 3.15) for much more detailed information.

Precept's marketing literature describes their flagship products, FlashWare and IP/TV, as follows:

"FlashWare provides the foundation for efficiently broadcasting realtime, synchronized audio/video streams to PC users over local and wide area networks. Using the latest IETF standards such as the Realtime Transport Protocol (RTP) and IP Multicast, FlashWare offers a rich and robust platform for building scaleable, networked audio/video ap-

Figure 3.15   The Precept home page.

plications. It can also be used as a Netscape Plug-in or with Microsoft's Media Player to view worldwide Internet MBone sessions or create your own multimedia broadcasts.

"FlashWare may be installed as a Windows MCI driver allowing network multimedia streams to be manipulated as if they were local. Alternatively, for larger application control, FlashWare offers a comprehensive C++ interface with access to its Realtime Transport Services.

"FlashWare is optionally available with FlashStack, Precept's high performance, WinSock 1.1 compliant, VxD TCP/IP protocol stack. FlashStack has been optimized for multimedia traffic and supports IP Multicast and IGMP capabilities.

"Built upon FlashWare, IP/TV is a client/server application for delivering continuous or scheduled audio/video information over an organization's IP networks to individual users' desktops. Through a friendly user interface, IP/TV lets users view program schedules and channel surf between available sessions.

"IP/TV includes a Web-based Program Guide for easy setup and management of broadcasts, as well as facilities for controlling session access and network bandwidth utilization. Applications for IP/TV include TV to the desktop (e.g. CNN), employee communications, desktop video training, and remote monitoring and surveillance systems."

As you can see, Precept has positioned themselves as a force to be reckoned with. In later chapters, we'll be setting up Precept's software for delivery on both the LAN and the WAN.

Starlight Networks

Starlight has been a player in LAN-based video since before QuickTime and video for Windows. You might have seen demos of their pioneering StarWorks software at past trade shows: a single 486 server with rows of PC and Mac clients stacked like cord wood, each playing movies broadcast by the server over a common LAN.

StarWorks has come a long way since then, as you'll see when you visit the Starlight Web page (**www.starlight.com**), shown in Figure 3.16. It is worth spending a fair amount of time at this site because Starlight is such a (relatively) mature player in networked video.

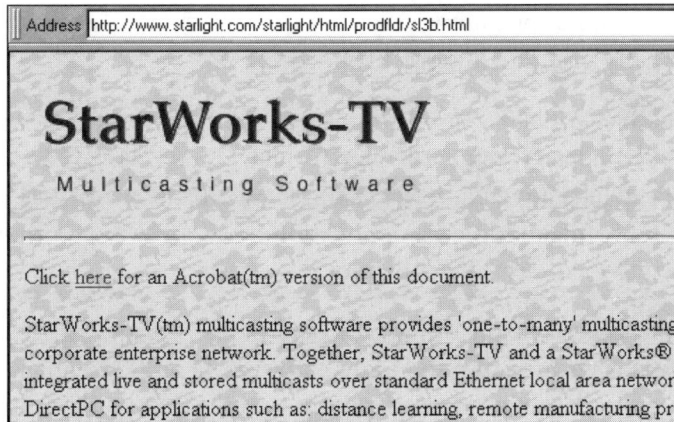

Figure 3.16   The view from **www.starlight.com**.

When it comes to multicasting, Starlight is right on the money with its StarWorks-TV solution. To quote from their Web site:

"StarWorks-TV multicasting software provides one-to-many multicasting services over your corporate enterprise network. Together, StarWorks-TV and a StarWorks video server provide integrated live and stored multicasts over standard Ethernet local area networks or Hughes DirecPC for applications such as: distance learning, remote manufacturing process management, Wall Street live TV news for financial analysts/traders, security/surveillance systems, video conference multicasts, corporate communications, and emergency broadcasts.

"StarWorks-TV consists of a Broadcaster application and a Viewer application that turn your LAN-based PC into a virtual TV. Both applications interact with a StarWorks video server. The StarWorks-TV Broadcaster station receives signals from an analog source (e.g., video tape recorder, cable tuner, and camera), digitizes the signals, and multicasts them over the network 'airwaves.' (Stored digitized files from the StarWorks video server can also be multicast.)

"Hundreds of corporate Viewer stations-using any Video for Windows-compliant player can simultaneously tune in to the 'on-the-air' channel to view the live multicast, as well as stored video from a StarWorks video server. The StarWorks video server acts as a StarWorks-TV Delivery Manager and handles the network resources, such as bandwidth reservation, network connections, and so on. With the StarWorks-TV

Viewer application, you can even schedule to record the multicast locally or to the StarWorks video server.

"StarWorks-TV applications support the Video for Windows interface, use industry-standard video formats (Indeo, MPEG and motion JPEG), and take advantage of existing networks. StarWorks-TV also includes tools for multimedia application developers to incorporate live video into their custom applications."

Another reason to look closely at the material at Starlight's site is their relationship to Hughes and the DirecPC product line. As noted earlier in this chapter, satellite delivery may be a big factor in the success of multicasting.

Progressive Networks

All of the multicast software developers in this section so far have been system-oriented. In other words, they make the software that application software companies take advantage of when those companies write products for use by consumers.

As you'll see in the following text, Progressive Networks (maker of the ubiquitous RealAudio streaming audio product) is an applications developer who is implementing multicast techniques directly. For a complete site dump, please proceed to **www.realaudio.com**. The company's home page is shown in Figure 3.17.

Figure 3.17 Beyond here lies Progressive Networks.

The information you are about to read concerns an architecture Progressive Networks calls RealMedia. Highlights from the RealMedia white paper are as follows:

"Although new and innovative media types and tools appear everyday, the burden of combining them together to create rich applications increases. It is not realistic to expect programmers to combine multiple vendors software platforms, each with different requirements and interfaces.

"Content Providers need to be able to make use of infrastructural improvements, such as the availability of multicast, in a meaningful way and need to be able to manage and measure the delivery of their applications in support of their business.

"The RealMedia Architecture addresses these issues by supporting the following elements:

"...A uniform client integration model which is specifically focused on streaming multimedia and therefore offers the most robust solution in this application environment.

"...Open and extensible protocols, file formats, and an integration model for new data types which guarantees efficient delivery and easy authoring of applications combining media types from diverse vendors into one application.

"...Centralized System Management and infrastructural components, such as support for IP Multicast and Splitters for delivery of applications on a large scale."

The writing is, as they say, on the Web page. Progressive Networks is clearly a multicast software player of the realm. It will be interesting to see how they choose to implement the IP Multicast standard in the RealAudio and RealMedia product lines. The company is reportedly working on a streaming video solution, which apparently will be part of the larger RealMedia package.

Summary

This chapter's objective was to document the extent to which PC hardware and software companies are becoming players on the multicasting field. Clearly, things are well underway. As the field gets more crowded, the necessity for standards will become paramount. Many of the companies profiled in this chapter swear by such standards, but we all know what happens when a successful player thinks it can set its own standards.

One of the good things that will likely come from the IP Multicast Initiative is a set of standards that all of the members agree to abide by. Of course, there will be exceptions, but most of the players will probably do it out of sheer enlightened self-interest.

Chapter 4

- **Reviewing existing multicast protocols**

- **Understanding TCP/IP protocol**

- **Assessing IP Multicast protocol**

Chapter 4

Multicast Protocols

Muticasting is based on some new and enhanced protocols for network data transmission. The existing protocols (such as TCP/IP) for network data traffic cannot accommodate multicasting's one-to-many data transmission requirements. We are speaking very broadly here, of course, but these ideas are big and need to be laid out as clearly as possible, ignoring the special cases and exceptions, at least for now.

The reason multicasting hasn't taken the Internet by storm yet (as of Fall 1996) is simple: not all the industry players have tooled up to exploit the new generation of network protocols. These players include hardware vendors, software developers, and network access providers. As in most industry segments, any time a specific company from one of these player groups incorporates a new protocol into a product, they are taking a serious business risk.

Look at it this way: In the existing unicast world, Joe Web surfer can dial up his ISP and start browsing almost like placing a standard telephone call. This is because his browser, his operating system, his modem, his phone line, and his ISP are all using compatible data transmission protocols (see Figure 4.1). Moreover, these protocols are standard enough so that

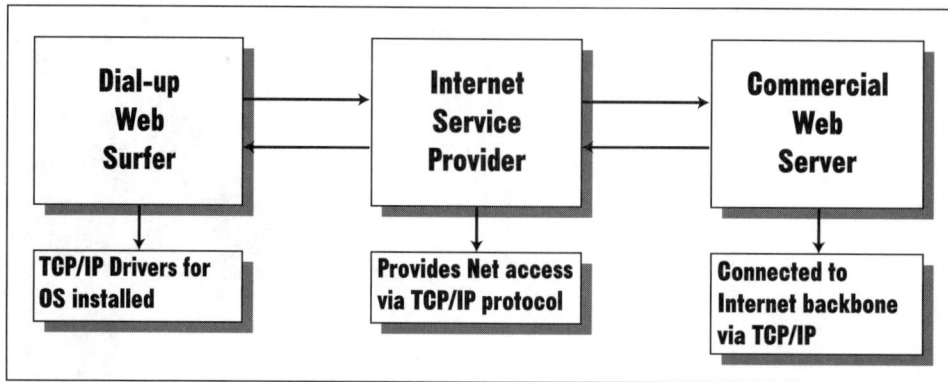

Figure 4.1 Networking with established protocols.

even the installation and configuration process is relatively painless. Multicasting is headed for this blessed plateau, but it's not there yet.

Islands In The Net

From a global perspective, the Internet is now populated with islands of multicasting networks (along with everything else on the Internet). Unfortunately, these multicast islands—such as MBone sites—are generally separated from each other by *unicast-only* routers. Until multicast protocols are standardized and enforced for routing equipment, either by market pressures or official regulation, this separation will continue, at least for the Internet at large.

Interestingly enough, a good deal of multicast protocol standardization is happening in the military (where standards *can* be officially enforced). For instance, the Navy has decreed that all of its shipboard IP router equipment must use consistent multicast protocols. When you visit the multicast-centric Web sites suggested at the end of this chapter, you'll see just how deep the military's fingers are in the evolving multicast pie.

On the commercial side, it makes sense to remember that multicasting per se is essentially a broadcasting/publishing activity, where the burden is on the broadcaster/publisher to deliver content enclosed in standardized packaging. Contrast this with the idea of simply *consuming* a multicast transmission (or any type of networked multimedia programming). When all the hype and headiness burns off, such consumption is usually a matter of traditional viewing and listening.

As noted in prior chapters, enjoying a multimedia presentation often comes down to a desktop video stream (i.e. multimedia) playing in a less-than-full-screen window on your PC desktop. In many cases, you may not even remember that it *is* a multicast (until you think about it), depending on how you interact with that desktop video stream.

The Top-down Approach

When discussing multicast-related protocols, it is easy to get into deep water fast. It is also easy to roll out a lot of data that may have no immediate meaning for the reader. Much of the technical information you can dig up on multicasting is presented in a way that makes it hard to place things in context and come away with a clear overview. Such perspectives are absolutely essential for the user who needs to purchase equipment and set up systems.

The goal of this chapter, therefore, is to present multicasting's new and enhanced protocols from the top down—in context and in relation to each other—only going into technical detail when necessary. As noted in Chapter 1, a fair amount of abstraction will be necessary, which is the best way to truly understand the bigger picture.

Most multicast protocols are implemented in software, usually as installable drivers for the special hardware required (like the equipment discussed in Chapter 3). If you have configured an NT server, you will likely recall installing, say, TCP/IP drivers to add TCP/IP stacks to that server's list of available protocols (see Figure 4.2). Setting up multicasting software is a similar process.

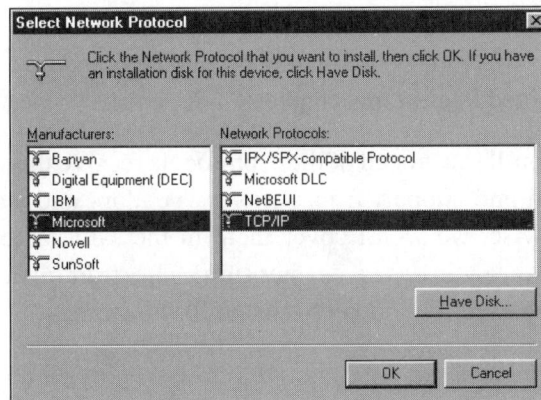

Figure 4.2 Installing TCP/IP protocol on an NT server.

For many users, this frame of reference will also help keep the big picture in focus, which is important because installing drivers is something that PC operators do all the time. And, it will be important for upgrading multicast equipment—which you can expect to do frequently as the multicast environment matures.

The framework for the rest of this chapter will be:

- Enumeration and summary of the top-level multicasting protocols currently recognized by the regulatory and developer communities

- An analysis of the venerable TCP/IP protocol—as a point of departure for discussing IP Multicast (the multicast protocol most likely to succeed in the PC world)

- A detailed discussion of IP Multicast

- A closer look at IP Multicast's competitors

- A discussion of low-level network and router protocols that work with IP Multicast

Note! *Unless otherwise noted, the multicast protocols discussed in this chapter are designed in conjunction with TCP/IP—not to replace it.*

Multicast Protocol Overview

There are at least four significant multicast protocols in use by people working in the multicast developer trenches. This could easily change by the time this book is published (some brand new *emerging* protocols are noted later in this chapter).

As you'll see, not all of these protocols receive the same level of recognition and support from software vendors and standards regulators. Likewise, we won't cover them in the same amount of detail, even though each deserves mention. The four protocols prospective multicasters should keep tabs on for now are:

- IP Multicast

- XTP

- MTP

- ST-II

IP Multicast

IP Multicast is the protocol that receives the most attention in the Windows and Macintosh worlds (see Figure 4.3). It is mentioned frequently in Chapter 3, where major software vendors are quoted concerning their multicasting products. As you'll see later in this chapter (in the section specifically devoted to IP Multicast), this protocol is an enhancement/ extension to the industry standard TCP/IP protocol.

Most experts agree that, market forces being what they are, IP Multicast protocol is the one to bet on in the near future. We'll cover it in detail shortly. For now, let's take a quick look at the other contenders to get a feeling for the density of the landscape.

There is some unavoidable geek-speak in the following capsules (and in the later, more complete descriptions) because they are distilled from official documents, but listing these capsules here is helpful in establishing an overall context. If you want to proceed directly to the IP Multicast section, by all means, do so.

XTP

XTP is a composite network and transfer-level protocol that provides a high level of support for multicast transmission. Unfortunately, XTP cannot ensure data integrity with 100 percent reliability (because it does

Address http://www.microsoft.com/netshow/about.htm

| MICROSOFT | PRODUCTS | SEARCH | SUPPORT | SHOP | WRITE US | Mic |

Microsoft NetShow

about NetShow
software download
samples & providers
support

About Microsoft NetShow

Microsoft NetShow is the software platform for one-to-many multimedia communications and information distribution. NetShow includes two features, NetShow On-Demand and NetShow Live. NetShow On-Demand allows users to stream audio, illustrated au and video over networks. NetShow Live allows users to multicast audio over their corporate networks.

Microsoft NetShow includes two key technologies to enhance use networked multimedia experience, while reducing impact on netw bandwidth:

- NetShow On-Demand - Streaming. Normally, when acces

Figure 4.3   IP multicast on the move.

not keep track of whether sent data actually gets received), but this is an issue faced by all multicast protocols. We'll discuss this problem separately later in this chapter.

MTP

When you come right down to it, MTP is actually a transport-level protocol. It is positioned to enable high-quality multicasting by leveraging off of existing multicast protocols, such as IP Multicast itself. The details are not worth exploring in this brief capsule. To be fair, MTP still gets significant play in academic circles.

ST-II

Invented by the Internet Engineering Task Force (IETF), ST-II was designed to supplant TCP/IP itself for streaming network data. In effect, it provides a consolidated, single-layer solution which includes multicasting, transport, and (theoretically) high-quality service. Like for XTP and MTP (and a couple of other emerging protocols not mentioned earlier), you can get more details in the longer descriptions presented later in this chapter.

TCP/IP

Following our working roadmap, let's now switch gears to consider a network protocol already in widespread operation: TCP/IP (Transmission Control Protocol/Internet Protocol). When we're done talking about TCP/IP, we'll use it as a jumping-off point for understanding new and enhanced technologies—specifically IP Multicast.

TCP/IP is the protocol that effectively fuels the Internet. Generally speaking, it began as a product of the U.S. military establishment. In due course, it migrated to universities and the military-industrial complex at large. As most people now know, this is essentially the story of the Internet (originally the military ARPAnet).

As you'll see when you browse the sites recommended later, the online libraries of many U.S. government agencies are overflowing with technical drafts, Ph.D. Theses, and other types of documentation concerning multicasting, the Internet, and networking in general (see Figure 4.4). Most of it is pretty dry and not aimed at someone with an NT server and an ISDN line who just wants to know which router to buy to tune in to a multicast.

Address http://ntrg.cs.tcd.ie/4ba2/multicast/

A better way to transmit data from one source to many destinations is to provide a **multic** transport service. With a **multicast** transport service, a single node can send data to *many* destinations by making just a single call on the transport service:

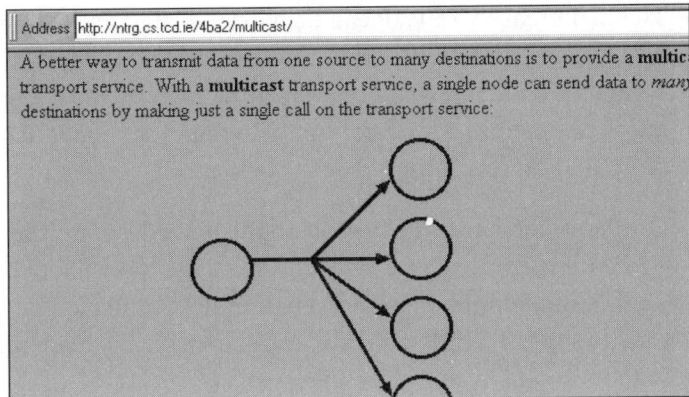

Figure 4.4 Seek and ye shall find.

Key TCP/IP Features

But we digress. What distinguishes TCP/IP from other PC-based network protocols is that it is highly routable (unlike NetNEUI, for example). In other words, data under TCP/IP's control can be transmitted to selected segments of a network, rather than the whole network. As we'll see shortly, this is a very useful feature when it comes to multicasting.

Other key features of TCP/IP include network traffic reduction (due to its routability) and 100 percent reliability when it comes to data integrity. As we'll see, such reliability is an issue in multicasting. On the minus side, installing and configuring TCP/IP often involves a significant amount of work to get it tweaked properly. Most network administrators have drawers full of war stories on this subject.

In general, it is safe to say that TCP/IP has won the greatest acceptance of all the network protocols. If the Internet continues its rapid expansion, this acceptance will only grow stronger faster. IP Multicast has deep roots in TCP/IP, so its future seems assured as well.

As the acronym implies, TCP/IP is effectively a combination of two protocols: Transmission Control Protocol and Internet Protocol. A good way to conceptualize these two pieces is to picture TCP dealing with the content of a given data stream while IP handles the addressing and routing. Again, we are trying to keep things simple as long as possible. This will change in a moment.

The main reason TCP/IP can be hard to install and configure is that its design is so ambitious. On one hand, it is simple enough so that any computer on a TCP/IP network can be identified by a unique IP number (expressed as a series of up to 16 digits separated into 4 subgroups of up to 4 digits each).

On the other hand, TCP/IP is sophisticated enough to link multiple TCP/IP networks which didn't necessarily know about each other previously (and might, therefore, contain IP redundancies). If you take the time to study TCP/IP in detail, you'll come away even more impressed with its sophistication (see Figure 4.5).

TCP/IP In The Abstract

Now we can start testing your powers of abstraction. Imagine the issues involved when dealing with millions of PCs (and other network communications devices) connected through local networks (sometimes call subnets) to one immense *logical* network. Who's keeping it all sorted out? Is there an underlying authority underneath it all (like a bank reconciling all the prior day's transactions during the wee hours)?

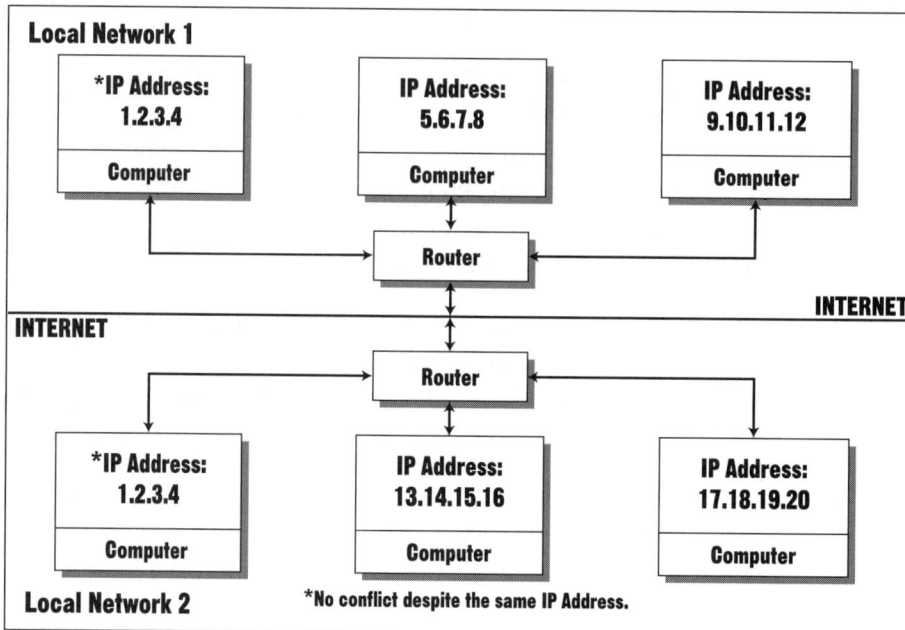

Figure 4.5 The beauty of TCP/IP.

The short answers are 1) Nobody, and 2) it's nowhere near that simple. Fortunately, you will probably never have to worry about TCP/IP's apparent contradictions, as long as you're consistent in your abstractions (and when you configure your network equipment).

Because the underlying design of TCP/IP is both *hierarchical* and *distributed,* you can, in effect, act locally while TCP/IP itself thinks—and acts—globally. In other words, don't be concerned that TCP/IP addresses can seem both permanent or transient, depending on the circumstances.

For example, you can generally use whatever IP addresses you wish when connecting the machines on your standalone LAN. With the same reckless abandon, you can let the Internet powers worry about delivering your email to the IP number. It will later be associated with the recipient's official email address.

Above all, don't worry about how all of TCP/IP's apparent mysteries get resolved (unless you want to be a network programmer). Also, don't feel obligated to explain them to interested parties—unless you *are* a network programmer! Again, just be consistent at equipment configuration time, as shown in Figure 4.6.

If you want a more technical explanation, there is no shortage of dedicated TCP/IP books out there (including one specifically for Dummies). As you'll discover, it's a huge, complex subject and deserves far more attention than what is provided here. For our purposes, we only need to

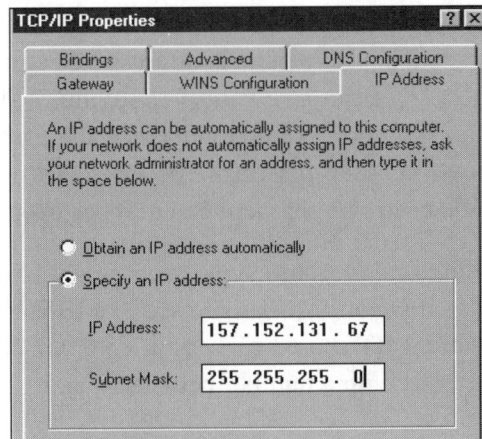

Figure 4.6   Assigning a TCP/IP number to a LAN client.

concentrate on the structure and classes of IP addresses as a basis for understanding the foundation of the general multicasting environment. Let's move on to that now.

TCP/IP Address Classes

If you have set up a computer for Web browsing at home (as opposed to your office, where a network administrator may handle such configuration), you may have seen a reference to the *class* of the IP address your ISP has provided for configuring your browser. Probably this was a *Class C* address, depending on your ISP. Once again, there are lots of real-world variables here, but this point is better made in context.

While such a class designation may seem unremarkable to the average home user, it goes to the heart of how IP addresses are organized by the agency that doles them out: the InterNIC. In the beginning, IP addresses were assigned by the InterNIC based on the anticipated needs of the applicant and the size of the applicant's network.

Originally, there were three classes of IP addresses: A, B, and C. Class D, used for multicasting, was defined later. Class E, even less defined, is currently considered experimental and is generally unused at this point (or so they say). These days, whole blocks of IP addresses get allocated by ISPs at various levels in the Internet food chain—depending on who's getting service from whom—but their address classes don't change.

CLASS DISTINCTIONS

Simply stated, the class of an IP address reflects the number of network (or subnet) IP addresses vs. host (individual) IP addresses that comprise that class. For example, Class A addresses (generally used for large networks) take the form abc.xxx.xxx.xxx. The abc segment is fixed while each xxx segment can number from 0 to 255.

Many addresses in Class A were assigned in the early days of the Internet, so it is not surprising to see that IBM has a class A address of 9.0.0.0 while MIT scored early with 18.0.0.0. For the record, Class A addresses start with a number between 0 and 127.

Class B addresses, normally used for medium-sized networks, use the IP address structure abc.def.xxx.xxx, where the first two segments are fixed. Strange as it seems now, Microsoft (131.107.0.0) has a Class B address, along with 65,535 other subscribers (both actual and potential). An address in Class B starts with a number ranging from 128 to 191.

Class C addresses, of the form abc.def.ghi.xxx are now handed out to small and medium-sized companies (assuming they have small to medium-sized networks). An address in Class C starts with a number ranging from 192 to 223. Check the one assigned to you by your ISP. If you register a domain, you may receive a most excellent Class B address.

Because we'll be discussing them in a moment, note that Class D addresses (for groups of recipients) start with a number ranging from 224 to 239. Class E (the experimental segment) has been allocated addresses starting with 240 and ending with 255. See Figure 4.7 for a visual representation of this allocation scheme.

So what's to stop Joe Website from attempting to stake his claim on the Web using his server's IP number when he's dialed in to his ISP? Remember that the agency that assigns IP numbers for official use on the global Internet is the InterNIC. Also bear in mind that:

- Unless he himself is an ISP, he doesn't have direct access to the Internet *backbone*, which he needs to effectively make his server's IP address visible to the world.

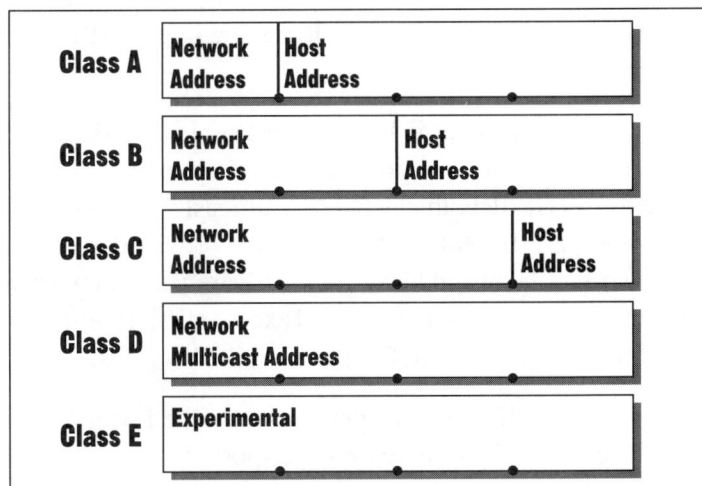

Figure 4.7 The IP Address Classes.

- He doesn't have a way to register his domain name very far up the Name Server tree, if at all. This is what he gains by going through the InterNIC. If his ISP doesn't administer his domain name and its associated IP address, Joe Website's IP address might never be visible on the Web, which is the whole point.

Again, if these concepts seem hard to grasp, don't be alarmed. With enough low-pressure contemplation and exposure, it all makes sense soon enough. In the meantime, let's now get ready to compare the traditional TCP/IP universe with the enhanced world of multicasting.

IP Multicast

IP Multicast (RFC 1112) was endorsed in 1992 by the IETF as the official protocol for developing multicast applications for the Internet. (Speaking of protocols, RFC stands for *Request for Comment*, an institutional designation for U.S. Government technical documents and proposals, among other things.) You'll discover lots of RFCs if you visit the military-industrial Web and FTP sites.

An early proving ground for IP Multicast was the MBone. Soon after IP Multicast was officially embraced, the IETF conducted some now-legendary MBone multimedia audiocasts using its cool new protocol, the results of which were positive enough to ignite the explosive growth of the MBone (and multicasting in general) that has occurred since 1992.

IP Multicast protocol is based on plain old TCP/IP, which is why we covered TCP/IP in some detail. There is, however, a significant departure from TCP/IP both in what IP Multicast does and how it does it. For the most part, IP Multicast capability is provided by hardware vendors at the driver level and by system software vendors (such as Microsoft) at the system extension level. Take another look at Microsoft's IP Multicast positioning in Chapter 3 to confirm this.

As you'll see, IP Multicast depends on some lower-level protocols for specific tasks like routing and transport. These subprotocols are usually implemented as drivers by the switcher/router manufacturers. Unfortunately, this can make the overall implementation process for IP Multicasting a somewhat involved production.

What IP Multicast protocol achieves is the delivery of packetized data from a single source to a particular group of recipients, either on a LAN or via a remote network connection. This is indirect contrast to a unicast (one-to-one data transmission). It is also different from wholesale network broadcasting, which normally involves one transmitter with everyone else on the network receiving the same transmission.

Open Channel D

IP Multicasting does its magic by using IP Class D addresses. Unlike with Classes A through C, Class D addresses are specifically reserved for *groups* of recipients. Such groups can be small or large—from a handful of individual targets to several thousand nodes (or greater).

Because IP Multicast does not do its own address allocation, addresses are usually assigned by multicasting applications. For the global Internet, this will ultimately pose a problem because address contention is always possible when uncoordinated transmitters operate in the same address space, as shown in Figure 4.8. For private networks, it is usually not a serious issue.

From an operational perspective, there is negligible set up time when using IP Multicast. When a Class D address is established, the multicaster starts pumping packets to that address. Routers do the rest (such as resolving the path—or paths—taken by the transmitted packets).

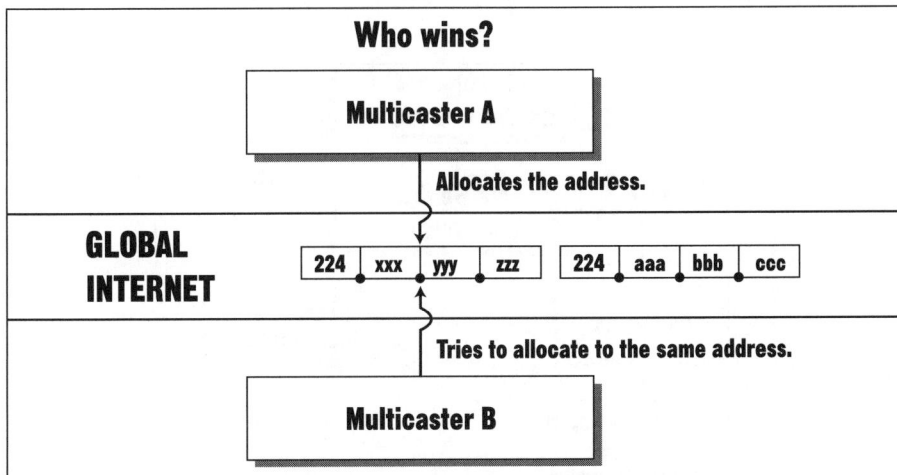

Figure 4.8 When worlds collide.

On the recipient side, a multicast receiver application first fires off an *add membership* request message so that IP Multicast can start scanning for packets from the sender headed toward the established Class D address. We assume here that the recipient is on the same physical network as the sender, such as the global Internet or perhaps even a private LAN.

If this receiver application is the first member of a recipient group to attempt a logon, IP Mulitcast automatically sends (multicasts) its add membership request message to all the routers on the local network. This is done using IGMP (Internet Group Multicast Protocol, discussed below). Otherwise, the application joins the group and starts receiving the appropriate packets (see Figure 4.9).

Of course, we are over-simplifying (again). But we need to do this so that readers unfamiliar with IP Multicast can keep the big ideas sorted out and in perspective to one another. IP Multicast is a sophisticated protocol. Consequently, many other processes are at work in the previous scenarios also. Once again, if you need more information about these lower-level activities, be sure to check out the URLs listed at the end of this chapter.

Limitations Of IP Multicast

IP Multicast protocol is not without its problems. In fact, some people think it is seriously flawed. Market pressures, however, have a way of causing money to be thrown at problems in the PC industry until they

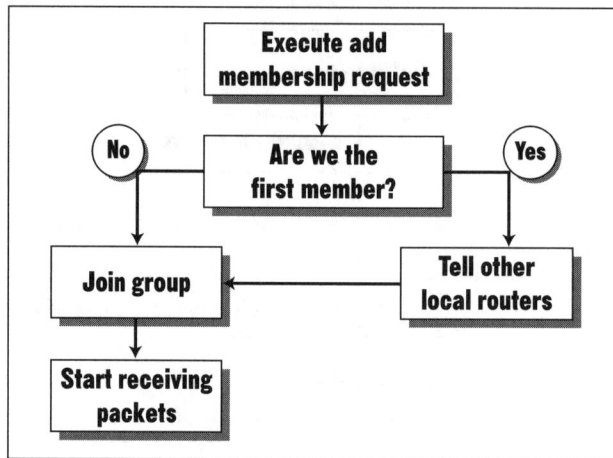

Figure 4.9 Joining an IP Multicast group.

are either fixed or a replacement for the vessel manifesting those problems is developed. It may help to keep this in mind as you consider the IP Multicast shortcomings discussed in the next few paragraphs.

The first problem worth noting happens at set up time. It involves advising hosts about group addresses. Because Class D addresses are allocated dynamically, procedures need to be developed to communicate to multicast recipients which addresses have been associated with groups on a given physical network. In a busy multicast environment on a big network (like the global Internet), any quick solution may well give rise to other issues.

Another problem concerns surplus network traffic being generated after a recipient has logged off, especially when that recipient is the last one in a group. Because of the polling scheme used by IP Multicast to determine who's actively receiving packets in an ongoing session (so that network router tables can be updated), there is always the chance that zombie packets will be in circulation until the polling process catches up to the true state of the multicast.

Finally, there is currently no transport protocol for IP Multicast that has flow control capability and is considered reliable. We'll look at some transport protocols shortly. Presumably, the IETF is working on this and other IP Multicast problems.

The Other Multicast Protocols

Now for the rest of the pack. As you'll recall from the capsule descriptions presented earlier in this chapter, IP Multicast has some competition. A few experts think this competition is formidable, based on the flaws they perceive in IP Multicast. In any case, the following protocols deserve more coverage than they received initially.

XTP

As previously noted, XTP (Express Transfer Protocol) combines network and transfer level protocols to deliver solid support for generic multicast transmissions. Experienced network developers understand that (like IP Multicast) XTP manifests no internal address management scheme. Consequently, external authority (like a multicasting executable) is necessary.

XTP is also akin to IP Multicast in that there is no overt set up processing between the multicaster and the recipient candidate before the commencement of group transmissions. There is, however, a requirement for formal handshaking between the two parties (unlike with IP Multicast).

The XTP design documents do not cover how routers are supposed to deploy a given multicast stream across different linked networks. They do, however, describe the algorithms (cloning, slotting, and damping, for example) that XTP uses to cut down on redundant multicast traffic on a network.

The design specs for XTP further permit the user to tell whether a multicast is unreliable or *semi-reliable*. So called semi-reliable sessions are judged to offer at best a relatively high success rate when it comes to transmitting data. By nature, few—if any—multicast protocols offer 100 percent reliability because they do not keep track of whether sent data has been received (as shown in Figure 4.10).

Error recovery in XTP is handled with a traditional *go-back-n* scheme—provided the bucket algorithm is active—in which dropped packets are re-sent to members of the appropriate multicast group. Unfortunately, this can douse the network even when only one recipient drops a packet (more fodder for professional network developers).

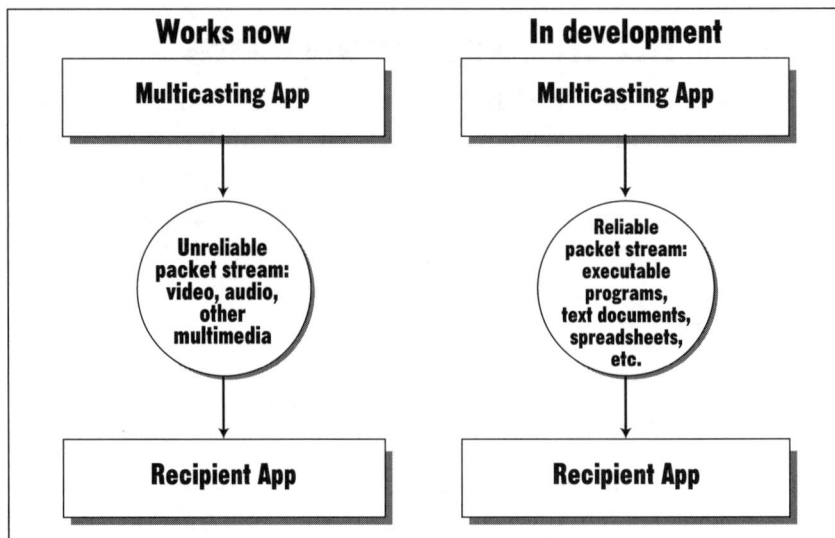

Figure 4.10 The benefits of reliability.

MTP

When you come right down to it, MTP (Multicast Transport Protocol) is actually just that: a transport-level protocol. It is positioned to enable high-quality multicasting by leveraging off of existing multicast protocols, such as IP Multicast itself. A related network protocol, Versatile Message Transaction Protocol (VMT), also supports multicasting but has been judged inappropriate for delivering multimedia.

According to its documentation, MTP is grounded on the concept of a multicast *master*—an abstract entity that "controls all aspects of group communications." As with some of its peers, group address assignment is specifically not handled by MTP itself (this is left to a multicasting application). Likewise for issuing the message asking to join a multicast group once the Class D address has been assigned. Logging off from a group is handled by the multicast master noted in the previous paragraph.

A particularly interesting feature of MTP is how it orchestrates received multicast data. The master delivers *transmit* tokens to the senders in the multicast group. Such tokens specify the rate at which data should be transmitted to the recipients in the group. This helps define the flow control parameters. If the requested flow can't be maintained by a given member of the group, that member is asked to log off.

One problem with MTP is that it incurs a relatively high amount of overheard in terms of required CPU cycles. This is because of all the traffic regulation performed by the master. The resultant delays and increased congestion could take MTP out of the running for multimedia multicasting.

ST-II

One of the interesting things about ST-II (a half-baked acronym for Experimental Internet Stream Protocol, Version 2) is that it ensures end-to-end bandwidth and delay, even though it is a true network level protocol. Consequently, it doesn't need all of the full-blooded functionality of a lower-level transport protocol. Bandwidth reservations are stipulated for all participants in a multicast session employing ST-II protocol, which are established prior to formalizing a given connection.

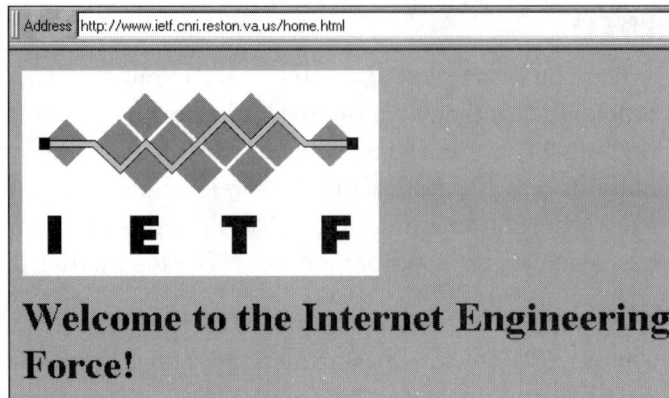

Figure 4.11   The IETF home page.

ST-II was invented by the IETF (see Figure 4.11) and designed to supplant TCP/IP itself for streaming network data. In effect, it provides a consolidated, single-layer solution which includes multicasting, transport, and (theoretically) high-quality service. Unfortunately, because it uses static binding for the addresses of the end nodes, it does not handle scaling very well. Also, it does not provide great service to dynamic groups.

RTP

The IETF's second foray into streaming multicasting protocols, RTP (Realtime Transport Protocol) is split into three pieces:

• Direct multicast support in standard IP

• A bandwidth reservation protocol named RSVP (see the following)

• A new transport protocol, robust enough to handle multicast streaming, named RTCP (not to be confused with RTP itself)

As noted earlier, TCP is the part of TCP/IP that provides the data transport facility. One of its primary design goals was to ensure that packetized data was delivered and processed in the correct order. While this is fine for conventional network trafficking and most unicast scenarios, things get flakey when TCP enters the multicast world.

Specifically, TCP's flow control and error recovery procedures can produce unpredictable delays and spikey data delivery in an environment that depends on minimal delays and a relatively consistent level of data flow. In general, it is fair to say that TCP was not designed to handle streaming multicast data.

Currently an evolving standard, RTP cooperates with TCP to transmit streaming multimedia data. Its packet headers contain the following types of information:

- Synchronization data for coordinating audio and video streams

- Media descriptors to identify, for example, the data compression scheme (such as MPEG)

- Various types of sequencing information

The RTCP component of RTP is designed to report on changing network environment factors. This permits multicasting applications to adjust to such changes in realtime, perhaps by scaling back the richness of their production values to decrease bandwidth requirements.

RTCP is robust enough to provide its reports to all the recipients of a given multicast, including the original multicaster. Also, it can identify the current recipients of the multicast and deliver this information back to the multicasting application.

RSVP

Concerning the RSVP (ReSource ReserVation Protocol) component of RTP, its job is essentially to keep audio and video quality high, as the streams that carry those media compete for bandwidth with all the other data being transmitted on the network. Designed to work with router hardware, RSVP permits applications to reserve network resources dynamically.

RSVP is basically receiver-centric, which means that multicast recipients initiate reservation requests in the same way as they ask to join a multicast in the first place. As of this writing, RSVP protocol is being reviewed by the IETF but is expected to become a standard.

PIM

PIM is an acronym for Protocol Independent Multicast and is also new enough to be still under review by the IETF. As its name implies, PIM attempts to provide scaleable, wide-area multicast service even in environments "where broadcast of data and membership packets is not supported" (according to the spec). When joining a multicast group, PIM employs the network's unicast protocol to send PIM control information. Cisco was a leading early developer of the PIM protocol.

Router Protocols

As noted at the beginning of this chapter, IP Multicast won't work for recipients on a given network until it is supported throughout that network—from the sender through the switcher/router to the end user (see Figure 4.12). Because the switcher/router is the most exotic factor in this equation, let's cover some specific routing protocols. When shopping for a router, it's a good idea to ask which of these mutlicast router protocols supports it.

IGMP

IGMP (Internet Group Management Protocol) is employed by routers to ascertain the presence of group members on their local subnets. It is also used to inform neighboring routers of the members on a given network proper (as opposed to just a particular subnet).

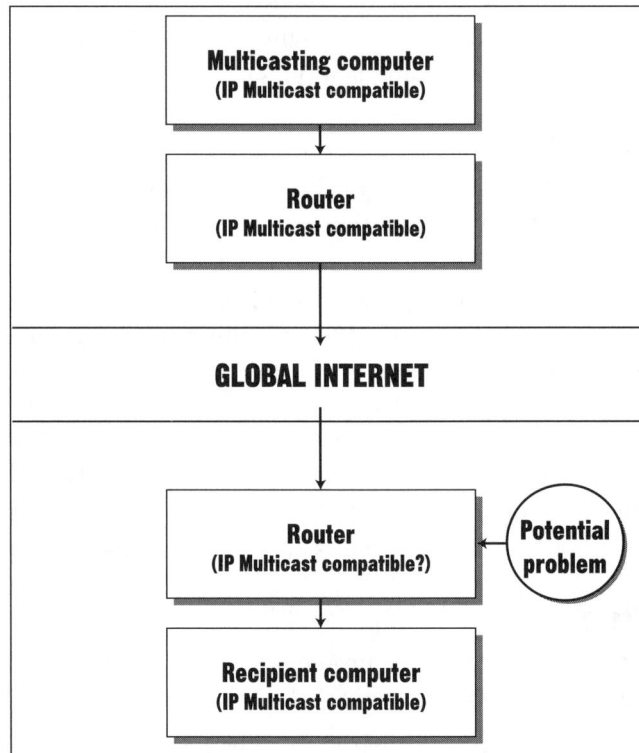

Figure 4.12   The importance of protocol continuity.

IGMP messages essentially fall into three categories:

- Group membership queries

- Group membership reports

- DVMRP (discussed next) routing updates

DVMRP

DVMRP stands for Distance Vector Multicast Routing Protocol. It is the most mature router protocol and is used extensively in MBone multicasting. Several router manufacturers, including Cisco and Ascend, support DVMRP, mainly due to its simplicity and general reliability. The protocol works by transmitting a relatively small amount of information from any multicasts in progress to all of the end nodes, then letting the routers determine which of those nodes don't need further packet transmission (a process referred to as *pruning*).

MOSPF

This router protocol is less robust than DVMRP, and consequently, less widespread, even though it goes back almost as far (over three years). The short story here is that MOSPF is mainly employed as a *unicast* routing protocol in certain MBone scenarios. It functions by distributing group membership data to each network node so that they all know where to send arriving multicast packets. Most multicasters feel that MOSPF works better on LANs than on WANs.

Clearly, this list of router protocol descriptions is generalized (it is also incomplete). It does, however, provide an indication of how sophisticated and differentiated multicast protocols are becoming overall. If you've ever installed traditional LAN software, you'll recall multiple layers of protocols (IPX, NDIS, ODI, etc.) need to work together, depending on the LAN type. Layering of multicasting protocols can be quite similar.

TTL

Not exactly a router protocol, TTL (Time To Live) is basically a mechanism for managing multicast traffic. Once allocated, a given multicast address has a TTL value associated with it. This allows multicast applications to stipulate how far multicast packets should travel on a given network (such as the global Internet) to reach the ultimate destination. In other words, how many router transfers are allowed.

You can think of TTL as part of a method for limiting the scope of IP Multicast datagrams. Each time a datagram goes through a new router, its TTL field is decremented. When the value in the TTL field gets down to zero, the datagram is discarded. TTL is largely an MBone issue, but it can be of interest to IP Multicast users in general.

Reliability Issues

From a technical standpoint, almost all present-day implementations of multicast protocols—and specifically IP Multicast—are inherently unreliable. This doesn't mean they're faulty, just that packets may be dropped. For 100 percent reliability on a TCP/IP network, the TCP part is exploited at the transport level. As we now know, TCP does not support multicasting.

To get on with the show, multicast applications use User Datagram Protocol (UDP) at the transport level, thereby accepting the inherent unreliability. As it turns out, this is not a serious problem when delivering multimedia streams (which can suffer data loss in ways users may not perceive). MBone testing has proven this premise since 1992.

To satisfy networks that require both reliability and muticast capability, work has begun (by the IETF and other interested parties) on some even newer protocols than the ones presented earlier. A lot of the development effort is going into resolving scalability issues. Soon, we'll begin to see the fruits of some of these labors.

Web Sites With Multicast Protocol Information

As noted numerous times in this chapter, the Internet is overflowing with information on multicast protocols. You just have to know where to look. Make sure to check out the following sites as frequently as possible if you're thinking of getting into multicasting on a serious basis. Also, remember to do regular Yahoo and Alta Vista searches (or use another favorite search engine) on terms like *TCP/IP, Multicast,* and *MBone*.

- *Department of Defense Network Information Center*: **http:// nic.ddn.mil** (see Figure 4.13)

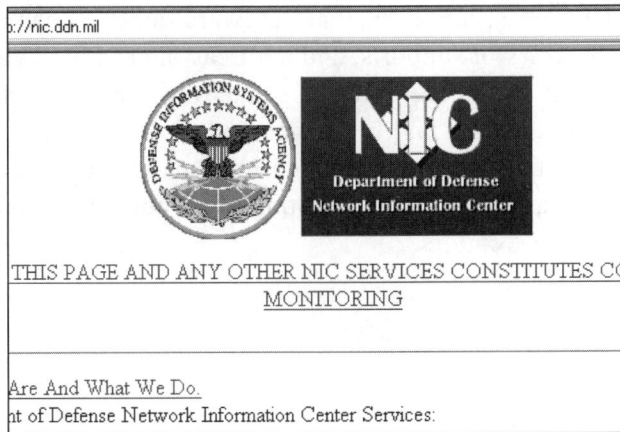

Figure 4.13 The Department of Defense Network Information Center home page.

- *Requirements for Multicast Protocols*: **http://www.cis.ohio-state.edu/htbin/rfc/rfc1458.html**

- *An Introduction to IP Multicast*: **http://ganges.cs.tcd.ie/4ba2/multicast**

- *IP Infrastructure and Multicasting*: **http://skynet.gsfc.nasa.gov/transition/ip-infra/Multicast-refs.html**

- *IP Multicast (Dept. of Navy document)*: **http://www.stl.nps.navy.mil/~jenierle/ch5secD.html**

- *Interoperation with Multicast IP*: **http://www.cs.ucla.edu/~simonw/sigcom/node18.html**

- *RFC Search Index*: **http://nic.ddn.mil/cgi-bin/rfcserach**

Summary

Simply stated, multicast protocols were developed to support network-based group communications—as opposed to one-to-one data transmission and wholesale network broadcasting. Because private-sector multicasting is so new (unlike the MBone research that has been brewing in more academic circles), it often seems like these protocols are mutating too fast to plan a commercial multicast site around.

The fact is, however, that hardware doesn't change as fast as the protocol(s) it supports, and multicasting is a hardware intensive endeavor. If you are going to standardize on one particular protocol, IP Multicast is highly recommended—at least for now. When you set up the systems described in later chapters, you'll find that IP Multicast is winning the approval of most of the major commercial software vendors.

Chapter 5

- **Understanding
  network routers**

- **Modeling
  multicast
  systems**

- **Selecting
  multimedia
  capture
  equipment**

Chapter 5

The New Hardware Requirements

As noted in Chapter 3, multicasting generally requires some special hardware for your PC, depending on whether you are a content publisher or a consumer of such content. Let's put this special hardware in context. We'll begin with some generalizations to provide a feel for how things will be broken down in this chapter, then we'll go into detail for each of the user and equipment categories.

Generalization 1: If you only want to *consume* multicast media streams, and you only plan to do this on an intranet (LAN), you might not need any extra hardware beyond what you need to consume other types of desktop video clips. You will probably need to install some extra software, or have someone do it for you if you're in an office situation.

Or maybe you just like to watch but wish to do so over the global Internet (as opposed to an intranet). If so, you will need special hardware (like an Ascend Pipeline 25 router), as well as extra software. Additional requirements for Internet viewing can include finding the right ISP, plus a few other

	Consumer	Publisher
LAN-Based	**May or May Not Need Personal Router**	**May or May Not Need Router/Telco Switch**
Global Internet-Based	**Need Personal Router**	**Need High-End Router**

Figure 5.1   Types of users and their equipment.

important issues discussed later in this chapter. Same goes for dialing in to a private LAN or intranet. Figure 5.1 sorts this out at an abstract level.

Generalization 2: If you now run a commercial Web site but wish to publish *multicast* content, you may have a powerful router in service already connected to your high-bandwidth communications line. It should be noted that many a pioneering Web site was launched with a Sparc10 server, a T1 line, and a Cisco router. For the record, most routers in this class are bigger and more expensive than the Pipeline 25, but that's because they're for servers and not individual consumers.

In other words, if you are already delivering Web-based media on a professional level, you probably have the gear for publishing multicast content, unless your router is incompatible with multicast routing protocols. If this is the case, you may just need a software upgrade (as opposed to a new router).

Creating A Meta System

As the title indicates, the goal of this chapter is to understand the function and purpose of the new hardware required by the multicasting process. Without such an understanding, it can be very difficult to construct an efficient and reliable multicasting system. Again, our use of the word *new* does not imply brand new or newly invented. Instead, it means unfamiliar for users of *traditional* PC hardware.

One good way to appreciate the function of any piece of equipment, new or otherwise, is to consider it in relation to the other hardware components in a given system. To do this, you need to think abstractly (as noted in earlier chapters). Each piece of equipment in a given system has a role, which contributes to the success (or failure) of the system as a whole. Such an abstract model can be called a *meta system.*

A Video Capture Meta System

Let's consider a desktop video capture station. Abstractly speaking, such a system is composed of four components:

- *CPU*—The computer's central processing unit.

- *Capture card*—Hardware that converts an analog video signal to a digital video stream.

- *Mass storage device*—A big hard drive to hold the freshly captured digital video sequence.

- *Video source deck*—Probably a VCR, VTR, video camera, or laser-disc player.

These abstract components comprise a *video capture* meta system, as illustrated in Figure 5.2. When you understand the role played by each of the components, you can start incorporating real components with known performance limitations. For instance, you might decide to use a fast wide SCSI hard drive in the role of the mass storage device because you know that it can store captured video data at a rate of up to 40 MB per second.

If you do this for all the abstract components in a meta system, you should be able to pinpoint causes of poor performance in the total *physical* system. You should also come away with a much better understanding of how the physical system actually functions as a whole.

In a way, you could say that the video capture card was once the most exotic piece of gear in a desktop video capture station—much like a router is now in a multicasting system. As multimedia producers will tell you, video capture cards have finally become *standard* equipment, with well-defined roles in desktop video capture stations. Soon enough, the same should be true for routers, bridges, and other networking gear that is now relatively exotic (as of this writing).

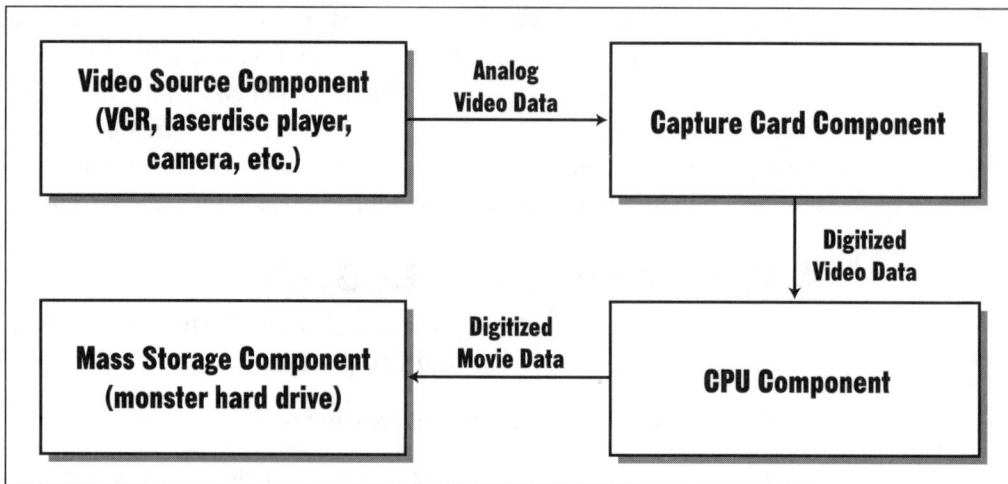

Figure 5.2 A video capture meta system.

Note! *Routers can be used for simple Internet access, as well as for multicasting, assuming your ISP supports routing (discussed later in this chapter). The general advantages of using a router instead of a modem are discussed later.*

Multicasting Meta Systems

Let's now create a meta system for multicasting. Because multicasting can involve more components and types of users than the video capture example, we'll actually create two parallel models. First, we'll list the components of each of these meta systems, then examine the role of each component in detail.

MODEL 1: FOR THE MULTICAST *CONSUMER*

We'll start with the simplest model, which is the meta system a dial-up user (multicast consumer) would use. The core components are:

- *CPU*—The system's central processing unit. This can easily be a mid-range (133/166 MHz) Pentium or an equivalent PowerMac. A Windows machine is assumed to be multimedia ready (with at least a sound card and speakers).

- *Network Card*—The add-in hardware that lets a Wintel CPU's operating system talk to the router—as well as other computers on the local network (a network card's normal job). On newer PowerMacs, Ethernet connectivity is built-in.

- *Router*—The hardware, most likely a standalone box, that connects to a high-bandwidth communications link (the ISP component). In this model, we assume at least an ISDN line. The router component is also connected to the network card component.

- *ISP*—While this is obviously not a piece of hardware, it is an important *abstract* component of our meta system. In a strange way, it is a bit like the analog video source component in the video capture model. In other words, it functions as a tap from which the rest of the meta system gets incoming data streams for processing.

This first multicast meta system is shown in Figure 5.3.

Note! *The simplest model of all—consuming multicast media on a client attached to a self-contained LAN—doesn't necessarily require a router, so we haven't created a meta system for it.*

Obviously, the organization of the boxes in Figure 5.3 does not reflect the way real equipment is connected. (For instance, in a physical sys-

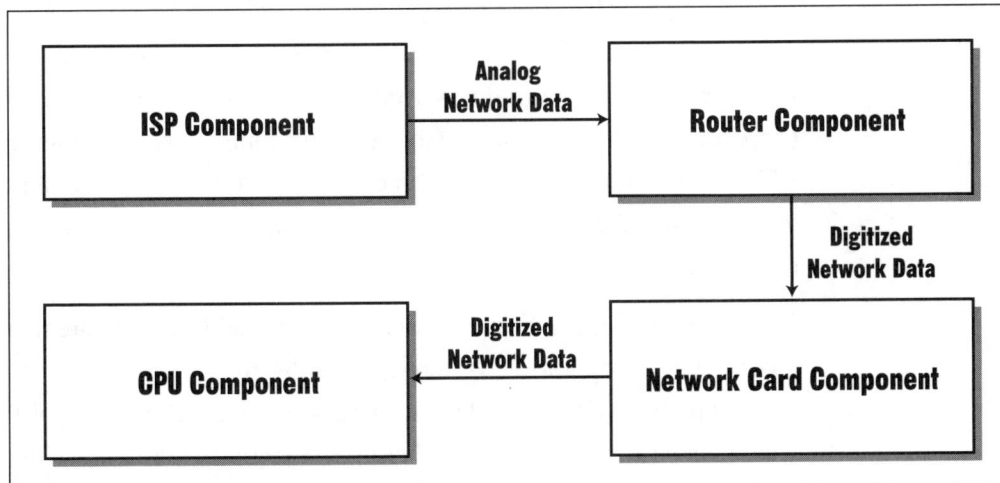

Figure 5.3 The dial-up consumer meta system.

tem, the network card would normally be inside the CPU.) The point is that these abstract components are all you need to receive, process, view, and hear a multicast multimedia presentation—and you must have *all* of them.

We're assuming, of course, that you can find a remote multicast to tune in to. This is the dawn of the multicasting age, so you might have to do some research here, especially if you want to connect to MBone and other multicasting events on the global Internet. These ideas are explained in upcoming chapters.

Fortunately, things are much brighter on the *private* network side. If you know of a private intranet to dial in to (one that has scheduled or ongoing multicasts), you can test the ideas behind Model 1 fairly easily. Expect to see lots of development activity in the private LAN sector in 1997 and beyond.

MODEL 2: FOR THE MULTICAST *PUBLISHER*

Before we examine the components of Model 1 in greater detail, let's take a quick look at the overview of the multicast *publishing* meta system—if only to point out the essential differences. With powerful enough physical components plugged in to Model 2, a publisher can deliver multicast content to properly outfitted multicast consumers at least on a dialin basis and, eventually, over the global Internet.

The core components of the publishing meta system are:

- *CPU*—The system's central processing unit. On a self-contained LAN, which accommodates dial-up consumers via ISDN or (hopefully) better, this can easily be a mid-range Pentium running NT 4.0, or an equivalent PowerMac. CPU components that attempt to multicast to the global Internet need Unix as their operating system (as of this writing).

- *Network Card*—On a Wintel-based system, the add-in hardware that lets the CPU's operating system talk to the router—as well as to other computers on the local network (a network card's normal job). Again, on newer PowerMacs, Ethernet connectivity is built-in. Unix workstations also have their own types of network adapter hardware.

- *Router*—On a Wintel-based system, the hardware that connects to a high-bandwidth communications link (the incoming T1 cable from the phone company, for instance). The router is also connected to the network card component. On Unix-based systems, which may serve MBone events and other multicast programming to the global Internet, the router component is usually a serious piece of hardware.

- *Switch*—The phone line multiplexor (for handling multiple incoming connections). This component effectively replaces the ISP component in Model 1. A better discussion of switches and their role in multicasting systems will be provided shortly.

Our second multicast meta system is shown in Figure 5.4.

TESTING THE META SYSTEM

As a quick test of our meta system approach, let's plug in some real equipment to Model 1. We'll keep our objective modest: dial in to a private LAN as a remote client, consume a bit of multicast content, then bail. The actual hardware necessary for this exercise is as follows:

- *CPU*—A Pentium 133 with 32 MB of memory running NT 4.0 Server.

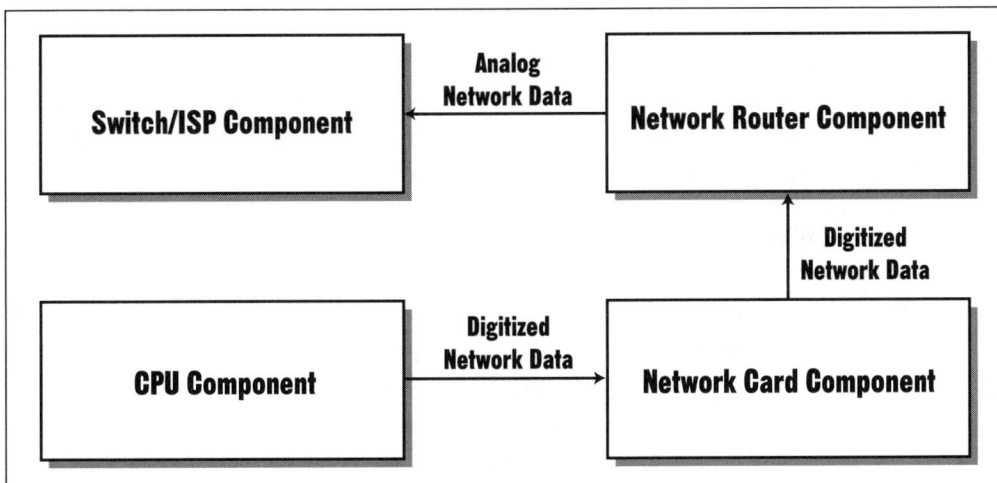

Figure 5.4 The multicast publisher meta system.

- *Network Card*—A 3Com Etherlink III Bus-Master Adapter. The CPU serves several other machines on the local network via this network card, which is rated high enough (bandwidth wise) not to be a bottleneck when plugged into this meta system. Plus, it is a PCI bus card, which guarantees abundant throughput between the card and the CPU, at least for this application.

- *Router*—An Ascend Pipeline 25, 1U-RTR-FX, ISDN. The router is connected to the network card by Thin Ethernet cable, although both the router and the network card support 10Base-T connectivity. Because the Pipeline 25 is specifically designed to handle ISDN lines, we don't expect a bottleneck at that connection point. As for the connection between the router and the network card, the Pipeline 25 is rated to be at least in the same bandwidth ballpark as the 3Com product described earlier.

- *ISP*—A private LAN with an NT-based server, also sporting an Ascend Pipeline 25 router connected to a dual-channel ISDN line (for 128 Kbps bandwidth). Clearly, this so-called ISP is not providing Internet service, it's just the name of the abstract component in our meta system.

Figure 5.5 shows what this model looks like with all the real gear plugged in. As you continue to acquire and set up equipment, make connections, and consume (and publish!) multicast content, you will develop a feeling for which components—and *types* of components—will cause you the most trouble.

Whenever you take on an ambitious installation, you may find that mapping out your strategy in advance with a meta system template can save you time in the long run. Also, it should be stated here that no aesthetic standards (for content quality) are addressed by our meta system(s). In other words, the meta system is meant to be a *quantitative* modeling tool only. Making content look as good as possible prior to multicasting is covered in later chapters.

Multicast System Components

As promised earlier, we'll now talk about multicast system components in detail, based on how we organized them in the meta system

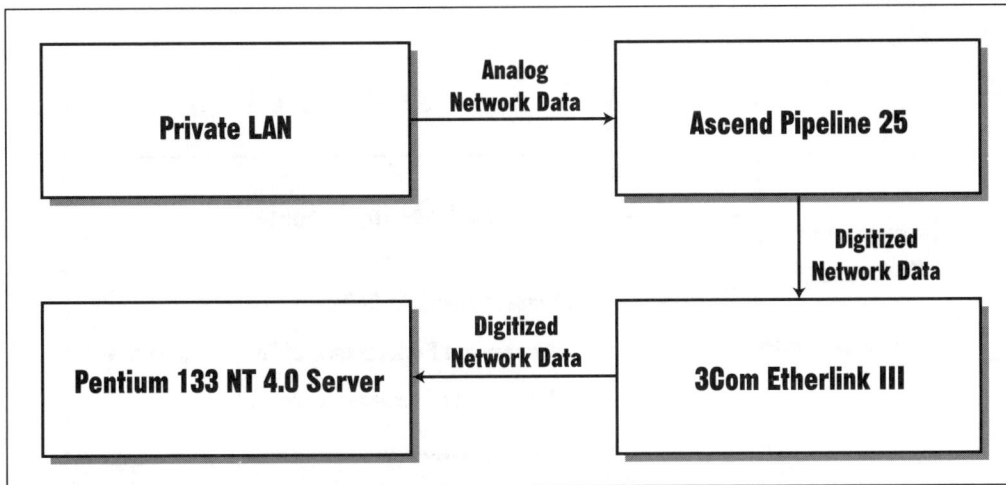

Figure 5.5 A meta system template with real gear specified.

models. We'll discuss the traditional pieces first, then move on to the relatively exotic equipment (like network routers).

The CPU Component

Simply stated, the CPU's role in a multicast meta system is to run the multicasting software and coordinate the activities of the other local components, such as the network card and (as much as possible) the router. In this new era of 166 MHz+ Pentium and PowerPC chips, 32-MB+ RAM pools, PCI buses, and 32-bit operating systems, it is easy to forget that the average PC was a 486-66 less than 2 years ago.

HARDWARE ISSUES

With so much power, it's unlikely that even a P133 with 16 MB of RAM and a PCI network card will be a bottleneck in a multicast meta system, especially on the consumer side. This also applies for similarly classed Macs, Power Computing machines, and other PowerMac clones.

Still, because networking and multimedia playback are such processor intensive activities, you may notice better performance overall if you continue to upgrade your CPU chip speed and add more memory. Figure 5.6 illustrates the role of the abstract CPU component in our multicast meta system.

If your CPU component is multimedia ready, and you can play desktop video clips off a CD-ROM with no problem, you should be able to play

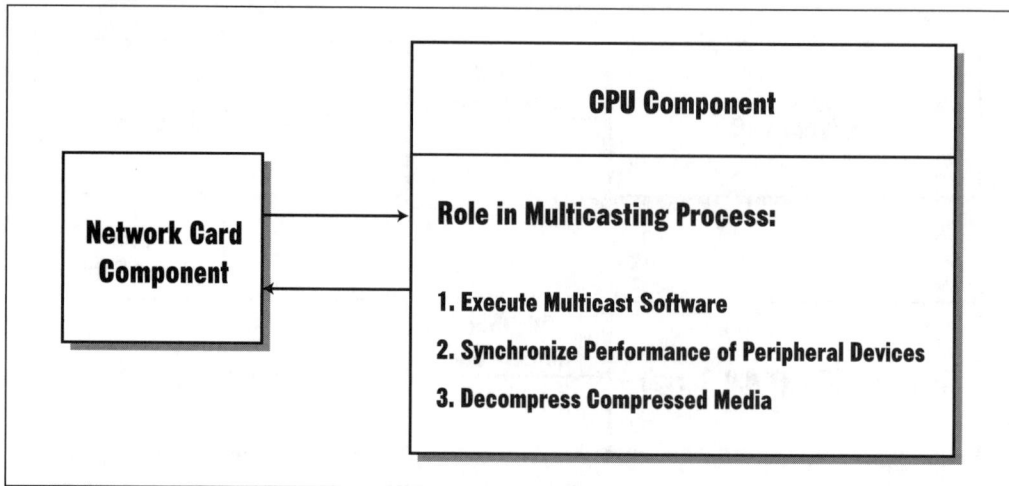

Figure 5.6 The role of the CPU component.

musticast video streams with similar performance characteristics (based on your remote network bandwidth allocation). On a Wintel machine, you'll want a 16-bit sound card (with speakers attached) and at least a 16-bit color video capability. New PowerMacs usually have these features built-in.

For completeness, here are the pertinent specs from the MPC Level 3 standard, currently respected in the desktop multimedia industry:

- *RAM*—8 MB.

- *Microprocessor*—In effect, a Pentium 75.

- *Video*—The official spec is often expressed as performance criteria for a video subsystem, but it boils down to at least 16-bit color (*thousands of colors* on the Mac).

- *Audio*—16-bit, 44.1 kHz, stereo (so-called CD Audio quality).

- *CD-ROM drive*—600 Kbps sustained transfer rate.

To get a more complete picture of the MPC Level 3 spec (and the prior, more succinct Level 1 and 2 specs), try an Alta Vista search on *MPC Level 3* or surf to **www.spa.org/mpc/mpctable.htm**. While these specs officially apply only in the Wintel world, they provide a good frame of reference for the Mac world, as well.

OPERATING SYSTEM ISSUES

As noted earlier (in the meta system overviews), Windows 95, Windows NT, and System 7.5.3+ are perfectly fine OS platforms for consuming and publishing multicast media on *local* networks. This includes LANs that allow clients to connect via remote dial-up.

If you want to consume or publish multicast content on the global Internet, however, things are less straightforward. For instance, a Windows 95 or NT 4.0 machine is certainly *able* to join, say, an MBone multicast—the problem lies in finding an ISP who can provide this kind of service.

Remember, as explained in Chapter 4, the Internet is currently populated with a relatively small number of multicast islands floating on a unicast ocean (see Figure 5.7). The way the multicast islands communicate is by a process known as *tunneling* (this process is described in more detail in upcoming chapters). Generally speaking, if your ISP supports tunneling (and routing), you can join a multicast event on the Internet at large.

ISPs who offer the ability to join a multicast are out there, and their numbers are growing, but they are currently somewhat scarce.

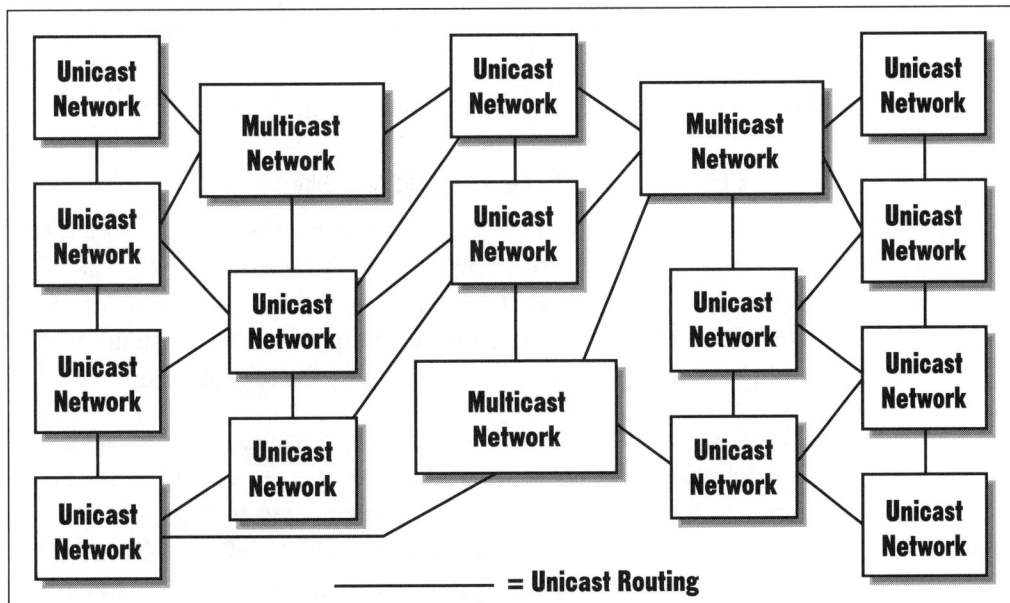

Figure 5.7 Multicast islands.

Chapter 16 covers finding and dealing with a multicast service provider (MSP) in much greater detail. Hopefully by the time this book is published, the MSP community will be much more established.

Which brings us to publishing multicast content on the global Internet (from a meta system CPU perspective). In this arena, OS type is just as important as machine processing power. In fact, as of this writing, only computers running the Unix operating system can serve full-on multicasts to the global Internet with any kind of general reliability. As you might guess, this has everything to do with how multicast protocols (especially router protocols) are integrated with the OS.

By the time this book is published, however, fast Pentium boxes running NT 4.0 with emerging multicast protocols and applications (from Microsoft and a host of third-party developers) are scheduled to be up for the task of global Internet multicasting, including tunneling. You can always surf to the home page of the IP Multicast Initiative—noted at the beginning of Chapter 3—for more timely information on this and related subjects.

APPLICATION ISSUES

There are not many application issues surrounding the CPU component of our multicast meta system, mostly because there are not yet that many applications that do multicasting on Macs and PCs (outside of CU-SeeMe). We'll cover the ones that currently exist, like Precept's *IP/TV* and Microsoft's *NetShow*, a bit later in this book.

The Network Card Component

Like with the CPU, the network card component's job in a multicasting meta system can be stated simply: It provides the link between the CPU and the router component. Of course, this ignores the network card's main job in any real system, which is to function as Ellis Island for data arriving from other computers on the same LAN (see Figure 5.8).

As it turns out, in a *physical* multicast system, the network card performs both jobs simultaneously, depending on how the router is configured and how many machines are connected to the LAN. As you might suspect, this has implications for how you allocate IP addresses on your local network (and it comes up again when you look at things from the router component's perspective).

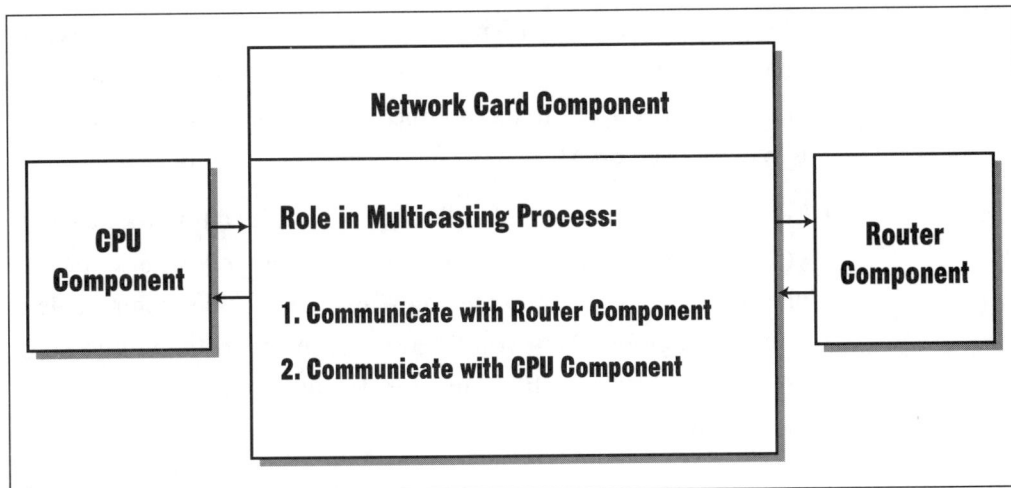

Figure 5.8 The role of the network card component.

Clearly, as multicasting becomes more prevalent in corporate computing, both on the LAN/WAN and the global Internet, network administrators are going to be faced with some new and interesting challenges. To get a flavor of the changing role of the traditional network card, let's consider the following example from the Windows world, step by step.

- You've got an NT Server connected with Thin Ethernet cable to, say, five clients, all on a self-contained LAN. You assigned an IP address to the network card on the server when you installed the card, and did the same for the clients as each was added to the network. As a convenience, you may have made these IP add-resses sequential. For example: 158.150.132.60, 158.150.132.61,…158.150.132.64.

- Because you also installed the Netbeui drivers, your machines communicate with each other just fine at the Network Neighborhood level. If you configured the WINS/DNS services in your Control Panel's Network applet (or made the appropriate entries in each machine's HOSTS file), you can also browse your intranet using TCP/IP protocol as if you were logged on to the global Internet.

- Now, you want to bring a router into this happy home—for connecting to an ISP who supports network routing and, hopefully, IP multicasting (probably via tunneling). The first thing the ISP is going to do is give you a fixed IP address for your router and each of the machines on your LAN that needs to browse the global Web (assuming you want to pay for each one).

- While this is great for global Web browsing, it can wreak havoc on your local intranet, at least temporarily. If you only want to pay for one static IP address, and thus only have one local machine able to browse the global Web, you'll have even more sorting out to do on the local TCP/IP front. It's eminently do-able, but it can be frustrating the first time.

Such are the issues surrounding any physical implementation of the network card component of a multicasting meta system. As indicated in Models 1 and 2 presented earlier in this chapter, network adapters vary in form and function from Windows machines to Macs to Unix workstations, but their underlying roles are essentially the same.

The Network Router Component

Now for the exotic equipment. Abstractly speaking, the role of the network router component is to interface with the incoming communications line from the telecom company (generally ISDN, or better), then determine where on the local network to send the digitized data. Usually, the recipient of that data is the CPU component, via the network card component, as shown in Figure 5.9.

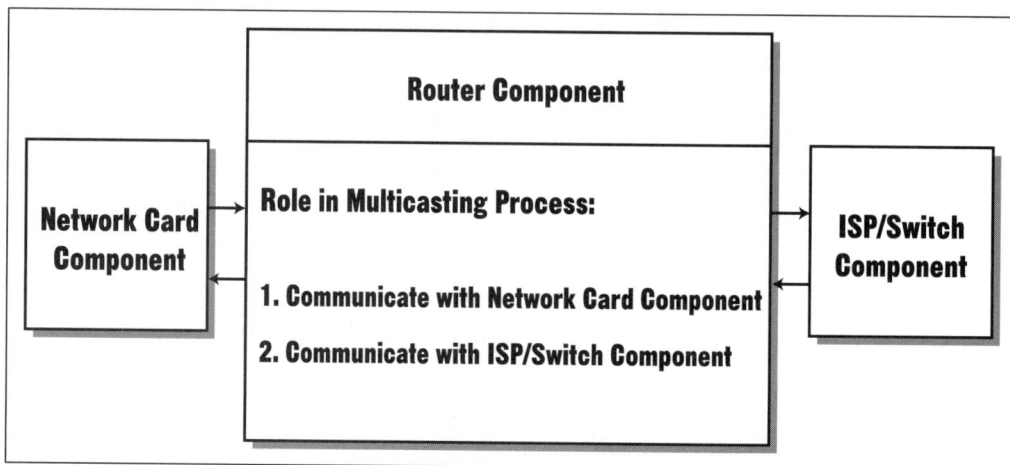

Figure 5.9 The role of the network router component.

In general, if a user on a LAN is running a browser and tries to navigate to a Web page or naked IP address not on the local network, the router takes that situation as its cue to dial out to find the destination on the global Internet. In effect, this is just like firing up your dialer prior to running, say, Explorer or Navigator, except that the whole process is more elegant and can serve multiple users when there is only one incoming telco line.

Don't take the term *router* too literally. Sure it's *routing* digitized data, but it's also doing a modem's job (as opposed to a yeoman's job) digitizing that data for processing by the CPU component. In a *very* abstract way, the router's most important job (aside from giving you the means for enjoying remote multicast content) is to provide connectivity between separate IP or IPX networks. Other types of equipment—such as bridges—provide connectivity among networks based on other protocols.

In Model 1 (the multicast *consumer* meta system), it is useful to imagine the router sorting out incoming data streams for delivery to appropriate local recipients, based on the recipients' assigned (static) IP addresses. If you only pay your ISP for a single static IP address, you should only receive one network data stream, which is passed through your network card to your CPU (and presumably processed into a multimedia presentation).

The role of the router component in Model 2 (the publishing model) is a bit more complex, especially when configuring the meta system for publishing to the global Internet (as opposed to publishing for dialin clients on a LAN). As noted earlier, only Unix computers are capable of delivering respectable multicasts to the Internet at large (generally using tunneling techniques).

Abstractly speaking, the router component in a commercial publishing model is required to connect and interface with either a:

- T1 or better phone line (for global Internet delivery).

- Telecom switch (see the switch component described later in this chapter) for handling multiple dialin clients.

In some high-end routers, switching and routing will be combined in one piece of equipment. Visit some of the Web sites noted in Chapter 3 for more information on this type of gear.

BRIDGING

As you'll soon appreciate, it's hard to talk about routing without at least mentioning bridging—and how it differs from routing. We're already dealing in abstractions (our meta system models), so let's cover bridging in the same manner.

Simply stated, a bridge is a piece of equipment that provides connectivity between networks based on protocols other than IP and IPX. Bridges transmit network data streams at the so-called *hardware address level* or *link layer* (as opposed to a more dynamic address level, like with TCP/IP). Consequently, bridges usually do not involve much protocol-related network configuration.

Speaking more technically, bridges generally require more CPU cycles and memory overhead than routers. This is due to the fact that they look at all the data packets streaming through the LAN (as opposed to just the TCP/IP and IPX packets). On busy networks, this often results in poorer performance, as shown in Figure 5.10.

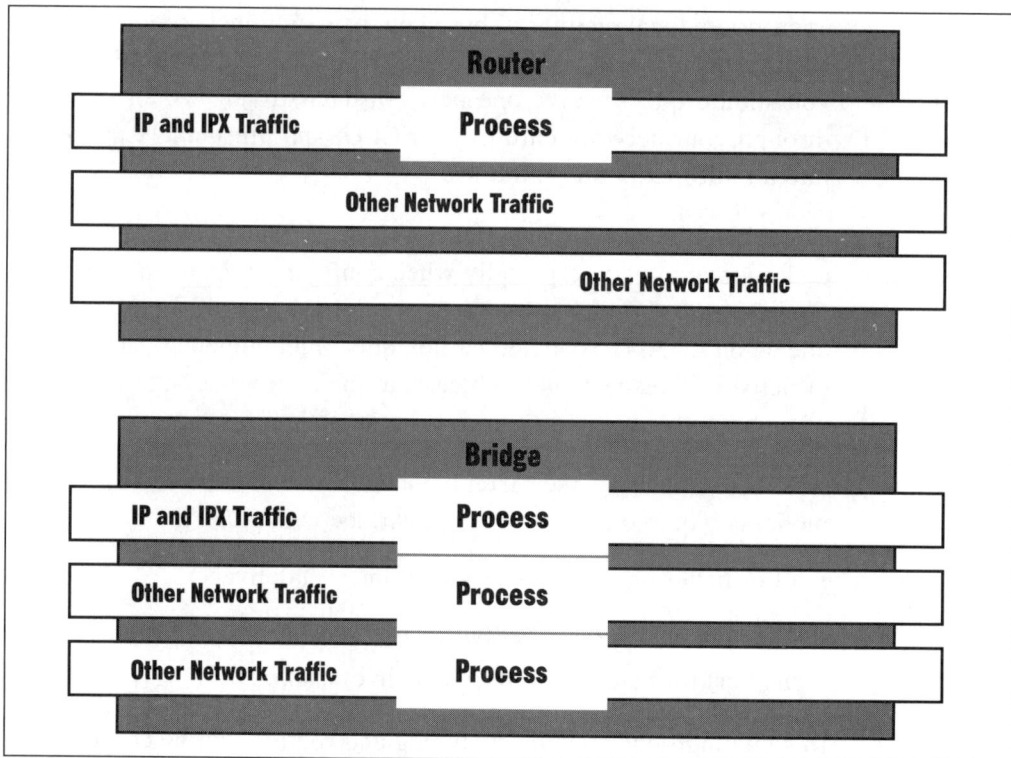

Figure 5.10 Routers versus bridges.

Most router hardware can be configured to operate as bridge hardware—even low-end equipment, such as the Ascend Pipeline 25. In other works, the box can be pressed into service as *either* a bridge or a router, depending on one's network requirements and overall connectivity strategies. When you hear LAN planners talking about bridging, they are often figuring out how to give AppleTalk-enabled machines access to remote networks.

What does this mean for the aspiring multicaster? Not a heck of a lot because multicasting—not to mention the whole Internet/intranet scenario—is based on TCP/IP protocol. Basically, it means that you likely won't be using bridges much as you set up multicasting networks.

The ISP Component

Meanwhile, back at the meta system, we have the ISP component. You'll recall that this component has meaning in the multicast *consumer* model (Model 1). The switch component, to be discussed in a moment, comes into play in the multicast *publishing* model (Model 2).

In the consumer model, where users simply *tuned in* to multicast programming, the ISP (for lack of a better term) was essentially just the source of the multicast. While not a physical piece of equipment (like a router or a network card), the ISP component is nevertheless a meaningful *abstract* component of our meta system. See Figure 5.11 for a crystallization of the ISP component's role.

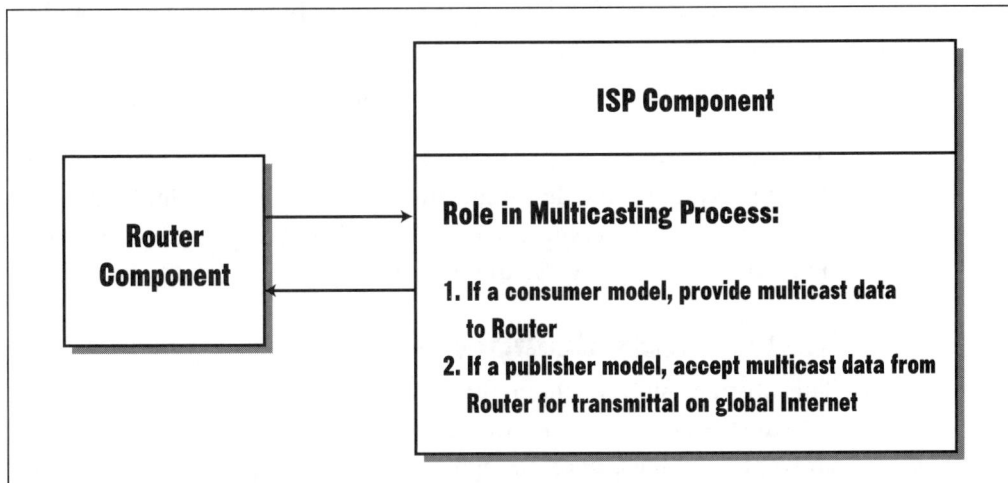

ISP Component

Role in Multicasting Process:

1. If a consumer model, provide multicast data to Router
2. If a publisher model, accept multicast data from Router for transmittal on global Internet

Router Component

Figure 5.11   The role of the ISP component.

In actual practice, the ISP component in a multicast consumer model can take one of the three following forms:

- *A multicasting server on a totally local LAN*—As noted earlier, we don't need to address this scenario because it probably won't involve a router component.

- *A remote server on a LAN that allows dialin clients*—As of this writing, such a setup would most likely be found in a corporate environment. For example, an authorized employee at a remote division of a company might log on as a client of an enterprise-wide LAN/WAN to receive multicast content while conducting company business. Expect this model to expand greatly as network entrepreneurs seek to bypass the congestion and unicast barriers of the global Internet by making commercial multicast content available from private dialin LANs. For a multicast consumer in this expanded scenario, the role of the ISP component remains the same for the meta system, even though the expanded range of content may tend to cloud the abstract function of the underlying model.

- *A genuine ISP per se that can provide multicast services*—Clearly, this is the most straightforward of these three sub-models, even though it is currently the most rare. If you the consumer subscribed to a true multicasting ISP, your online experience would be quite similar to consuming plain old unicast content, depending on how the multicaster's Web site presented the multicast content.

What are the noteworthy bottlenecks inherent in the ISP component of the meta system? By definition, few (if any) that the multicast consumer has any real control over—short of only logging in at off-peak hours or finding a new ISP altogether.

The Switch Component

This abstract piece of the multicasting meta system can be contrasted with the ISP component just discussed. Again, *ISP* and *switch* are merely convenient names, even though their names imply their general abstract function. Also, these names make more sense when put in context with the rest of the meta system, as shown in Figure 5.12. In a

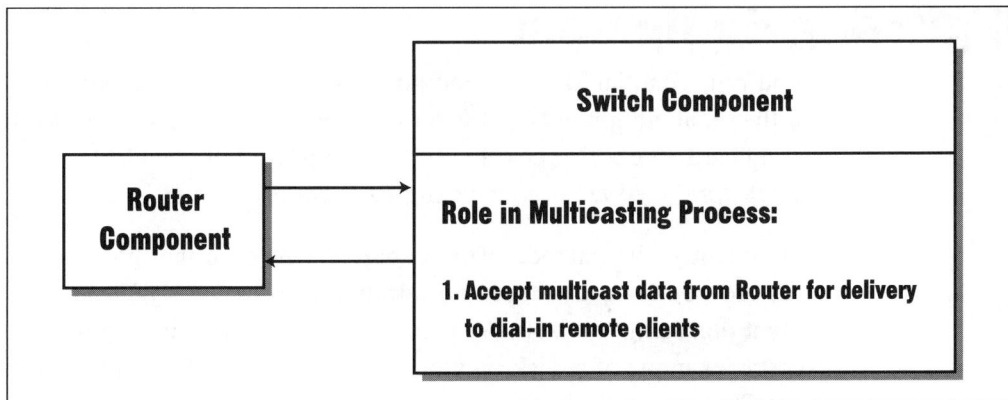

Figure 5.12 The role of the switch component.

telecommunications environment, of course, a switch has a very precise definition: a piece of equipment connected to a trunk line that routes phone calls, usually to user extensions.

As previously noted, the switch component has meaning in the multicast *publishing* model, in which a Web-based media publishing organization wishes to make its content available to consumers via TV-like multicasts. The switch component may take one of two basic forms here:

- If a publisher's multicasts will be transmitted over the global Internet, the switch component may actually be manifested as a physical ISP that can provide commercial multicasting services.

- If that publisher's multicast programming will be available to the public via dialin to a private network, the switch component may be manifested as just that—a phone company switch (or some kind of network router/switch combination). As noted earlier, this may turn out to be a real solution for getting around the congestion and unicast barriers of the global Internet.

All of this might sound needlessly abstract, but it needs to be that way in order to keep the big ideas sorted out. Remember that the goal of these meta system models is to place the hardware involved in multicasting in *context*. Upcoming chapters will describe how to make this equipment work.

Digitizing Equipment

If you're unfamiliar with the equipment used to digitize desktop media, then that equipment qualifies as *new* just like the exotic network routing hardware we've covered so far. Simply put, if you want to start multicasting, you've got to have digitized *content* to multicast.

Consequently, the balance of this chapter will describe the types of hardware you'll have to become familiar with if you wish to do the content digitizing yourself. As you'll see, it's no coincidence that we used the example of a desktop video capture meta system a few pages back. Chapter 7 will deal with the specifics of acquiring and working with multicast content.

Which Platform Is Better For Digitizing?

Not surprisingly, a couple of questions surface right away in any discussion of digitizing media for the PC desktop:

- Is the Mac (or PowerPC Mac clone) still the best platform for this process?

- Is *pretty good* an acceptable quality standard?

The short answer to the first question is that media files (especially video) are best digitized on the platform on which they will be played back. Of course, things are never that simple, because multicast and video on demand servers will ultimately stream the same media files to both Macs and PCs. A better concern is whether Windows machines can digitize media that plays well on both PCs and Macs.

The second question is even more provocative and deserving of a detailed discussion—which this chapter provides. Because new multimedia capture and storage equipment hits the market monthly, we'll concentrate on categories of hardware tools (with appropriate suggestions for proven brand name gear) as opposed to specific products.

Abstract Components

As seen back in Figure 5.2, a multimedia digitizing station can be broken down into four generic hardware components: CPU, capture card, mass storage volume, and media source. If your Mac or PC system incorporates all of these components, you should be able to produce good-quality desktop digital media. As we did for abstract multicasting systems, here is a breakdown of the roles of each of these abstract components.

THE CPU COMPONENT

The role of the CPU is to synchronize the activities of the capture card and the mass storage device, as shown in Figure 5.13. In the early days of QuickTime and Video for Windows, many PCs and Macs (such as 386s and sub-Quadras) were unsuitable for production-quality digitizing, but this has changed now that Pentiums and PowerPCs are common and affordable.

THE CAPTURE CARD COMPONENT

The capture card component is the component category where most of the controversy (Mac versus Windows) originates. In fact, there seems to be a perpetual arms race in this product area, regardless of platform. At the high end are solutions like Data Translation's venerable Media 100 (Mac), which starts at over $10,000, and the DPS Perception and Targa 2000 (Windows) which currently go for about $3,000 to $4,000.

These Cadillac boards are mainly designed for outputting digital video files back to video tape (although CD-ROM producers also like them for the excellent quarter-screen QuickTime and AVI files they capture). For digitizing streaming video files, however, such high-end solutions may be overkill (unless you have already made the investment).

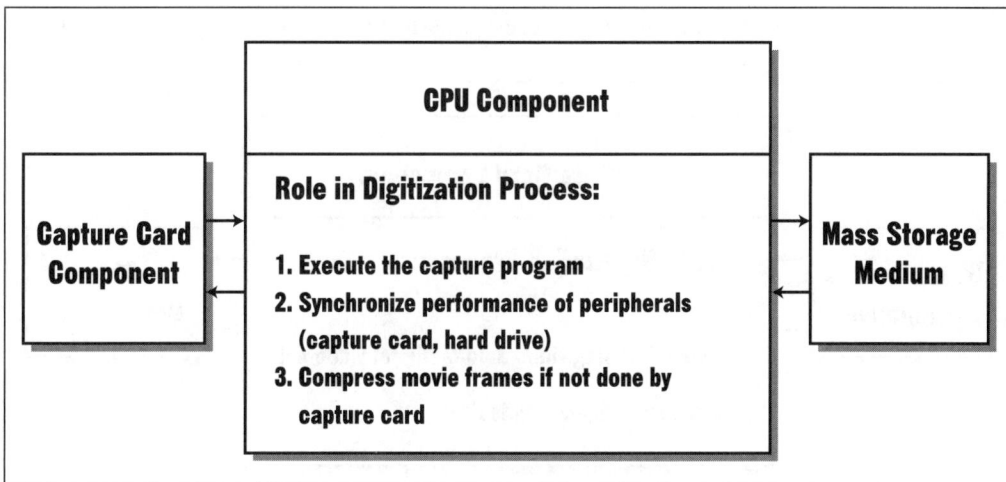

Figure 5.13   The role of the CPU component in digitizing.

If you don't have a capture board yet, consider a Windows card, such as the New PCI-based Intel Smart Video Recorder Pro (somewhere in the sub-$500 range). On the Mac side, the Video Spigot and SpigotPower boards from SuperMac, among others, have good reputations at comparable prices.

In the middle of the Mac spectrum are the workhorse cards used by most producers of CD-ROM video clips: the Radius Video Vision Studio and the RasterOps/TrueVision Targa 2000, among others. Some books spend time detailing the features of these fine products, but that is really the job of the magazine industry.

The things to look for in a capture card are directly related to its role in our abstract component scheme (see Figure 5.14). The bottom line is, if a board can capture up to quarter-screen images at 15 frames per second with good-to-excellent 24-bit quality, it is a fine candidate for inclusion in a multicast digitization station.

MASS STORAGE DEVICES

The role of the mass storage component in our abstract system is to store data captured and encoded by the capture card component. Of course, mass storage capacity is also needed for media files *after* they have been compressed, but not nearly as much on a file by file basis.

For the most part, we are talking about monster hard disks here—external SCSI drives that start at roughly 1 GB and go up from there. Such devices have suffered drastic price cuts in the last few years,

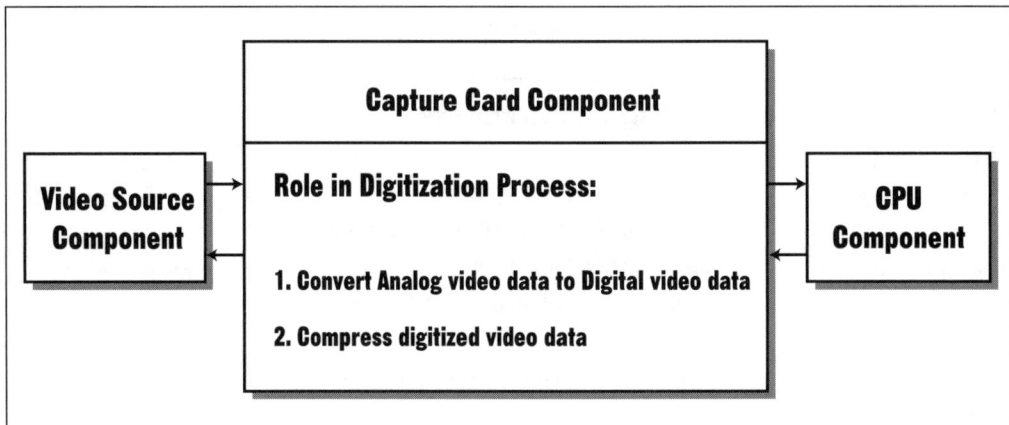

Figure 5.14 The role of the capture card component.

and will get even cheaper as Zip and Jaz drives (fast, high capacity removable storage) proliferate. The basic rule is: either your drives are big enough to hold your raw captures or they're not. For multicast media, it will be safe to think in one-gig units (at least for a year or two) at around $300 or so.

As noted earlier, the data communications protocol that ties almost all mass storage devices together and to their CPUs is SCSI (Small Computer Systems Interface). Don't be intimidated by terms like Fast-Wide SCSI, SCSI-3, or even FireWire (SCSI's hot new competitor). Today's SCSI-2 systems and drives are fine for Web media production.

As a rule, most external SCSI hard drives can be reformatted back and forth between Mac and DOS without much trouble. In cross-platform development, this feature can be a real benefit to digital media handlers—provided they know what they are doing. One good strategy is to keep all your gig drives formatted DOS and let your Mac see them with a program like Formatter Five.

THE ANALOG MEDIA SOURCE

This component comes in many flavors: VCR, VTR, camera, DAT player, laserdisc player, etc. Just as various are the quality standards inherent in these devices: VHS, SHVS, Hi8, and Betacam. Also, don't forget the digital standards: D1, D2, D3, and the newest ingenue, Sony's *consumer* digital format. Figure 5.15 shows the role of this component.

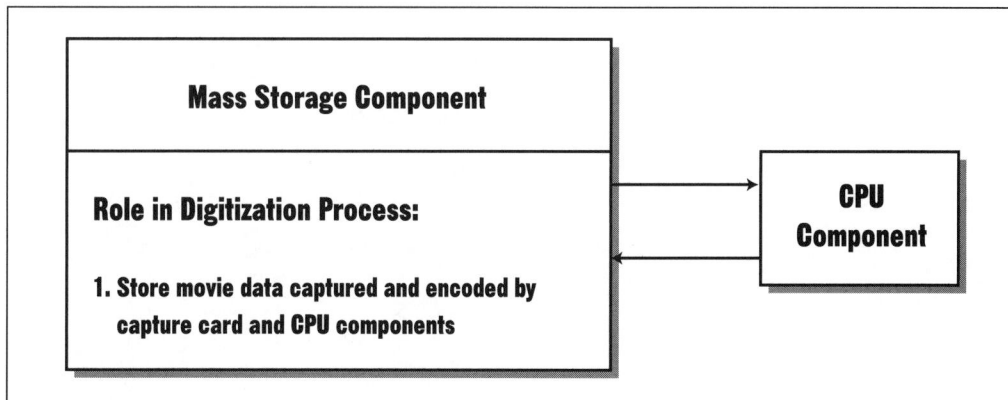

Figure 5.15 The analog media source component.

These days, media files included in consumer CD-ROM titles are generally captured from Betacam SP (video) and DAT (audio) decks. Web site designers are following suit with the downloadable media they offer, but it remains to be seen whether the lower video and audio quality of streaming multimedia assets (both multicast and video on demand) will tempt Internet publishers to relax their standards.

Summary

As the meta system models presented in this chapter illustrate, multicasting in the PC world can take several forms, mostly depending on whether you are a publisher of multicast content or merely a consumer of it. The other major factor is whether you intend to conduct your multicasting business strictly on a LAN with remote dialin capability or whether you will try to make things happen on the global Internet.

These two sets of choices imply at least four clear modes of operation. Whichever mode you choose, you are going to have some new hardware issues to understand, both in how the new equipment works on its own and how it functions in relation to the rest of the hardware in your multicast system. Taking the time to appreciate the meta systems presented in this chapter should help put these issues in context.

Chapter 6

- **Installing and test driving Precept's IP/TV**

- **Setting up and trying out Microsoft's NetShow**

- **Working with NetShow's media editor and conversion tools**

Chapter 6

Installing And Test Driving Multicast Software

If you've been reading the chapters in this book in order, you're probably ready for some actual multicasting by now. This chapter will take you through the installation and initial use of two commercial multicasting products: Microsoft's NetShow and Precept's IP/TV. NetShow is absolutely free and may be downloaded from the Microsoft Web site at **www.microsoft.com/ netshow**, as shown in Figure 6.1. IP/TV is downloadable from the Precept Web site (**www.precept.com**) after you fill out an online registration form (see Figure 6.2).

Both of these products are composed of client-side and server-side software, which means you'll need at least two networked machines to perform the test drives illustrated in this chapter. Both products perform well on the average intranet, despite their relative newness to the PC networking scene. They also perform well in dialin client scenarios and, to the extent you can test them, on the global Internet.

Figure 6.1 The NetShow home page.

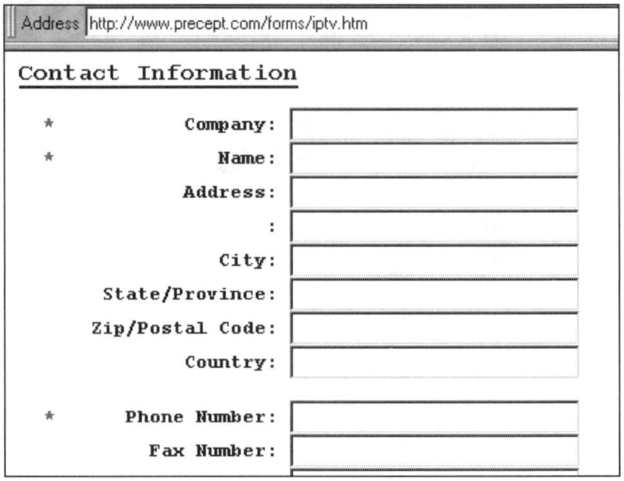

Figure 6.2 The current IP/TV questionnaire.

We'll cover installation and first-time execution from both the client and server perspective, but we'll defer troubleshooting and real-life operational issues until later chapters. If you recall the multicast meta system we developed in Chapter 5, you'll appreciate the following requirements for these test drives:

- Sufficiently powerful CPUs

- Late model network cards in the participating CPUs

- Capable network routers (depending on how clients and servers are connected on your LAN)

Precept Software's IP/TV

Assuming you have procured both the client and server installation programs from the Precept Web site, let's get right to the installation. We'll do the server setup first, then install the client. If you have not yet downloaded the installers, you may want to review Precept's system requirements, quoted in the next section. Precept technology is referenced frequently in this book, and there is a plentiful amount of information on the company and its products on their Web site.

Precept's System Requirements For IP/TV

"Please note the IP/TV Server and the IP/TV Viewer run on Windows for Workgroups 3.11, Windows 95, and Windows NT. The IP/TV Program Guide runs on a Unix-based Web server and requires PERL for CGI support. A beta version of the Program Guide is available for Microsoft's Internet Information Server (IIS) on either NT 4.0 (Workstation or Server) or NT 3.51 Server.

"Here's what you will need to effectively test IP/TV:

- Two or more Pentium PCs running Windows for Workgroups 3.11, Windows 95, or Windows NT.

- For Windows for Workgroups 3.11 or Windows 95, you should have at least 8 MB RAM (16 MB recommended). Windows NT requires at least 16 MB (32 MB recommended).

- Winsock 1.1 compatible TCP/IP stack with IP Multicast and IGMP support. (Precept's FlashStack TCP/IP stack provides IP multicast support for Windows for Workgroups 3.11 only. Please contact support@precept.com if you would like to test IP/TV with FlashStack.)

- Local Ethernet or other IP multicast capable LAN or WAN.

- IP/TV will install Video for Windows and Win32s if they are not already present. (Win32s is only installed on Windows 3.11 systems.)

- For live broadcasts, a video capture card compatible with Microsoft's Video for Windows. For a list of tested capture card vendors, please refer to **www.precept.com/technical/capture.htm**.

- A Unix-based Web server (e.g., CERN, NSCA, Netscape) with PERL installed for CGI support. For access to PERL download sites, please refer to **www.precept.com/technical/sites.htm#perl**.

"An NT Internet Information Server (IIS) version of the Program Guide is about ready for release. If you would like to be a beta test site, please send email to support@precept.com and request download instructions."

Note! *After Precept processes your online application, they will email you their download site location and provide the appropriate passwords for performing the downloads of the IP/TV client and server installation programs.*

Setting Up The IP/TV Server

In this example, we'll install the IP/TV Server on a Pentium 133 with 32 MB of RAM running NT 4.0 Server. Here are the steps you should follow:

1. Put the IP/TV Server installation program in a directory called *TEMP* (if you don't already have one) right off your main hard drive. This is not required, but it makes things easier to keep track of.

2. Double click on the installation program name in the TEMP folder to launch it. Figure 6.3 shows the initial Installer screen.

3. Click on the UNZIP button after specifying the target directory for the temporary installation directory (again, C:\TEMP is an excellent choice).

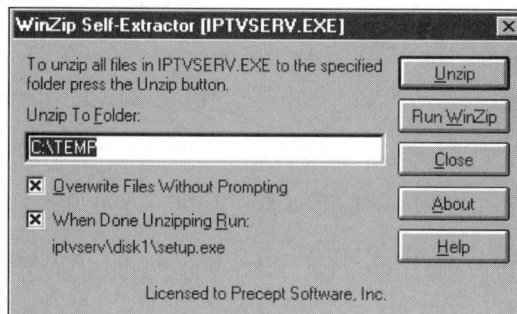

Figure 6.3 Welcome to the IP/TV Server Installer.

4. Click on the OK button in the message box stating that all of the files have been unzipped successfully. The graphic shown in Figure 6.4 will appear briefly, followed by the beginning of a standard Install Shield setup run.

5. When you get to the screen shown in Figure 6.5, fill in your appropriate name and company data, along with the Server serial number assigned by Precept in their return email response to your registration.

6. The setup program lets you specify a target directory for the Precept Server. The default is a directory right off your C: drive. This example deposits the software in c:\program files\iptv\server, as shown in Figure 6.6. A *Typical* installation is fine in this case.

7. In the dialog shown next (see Figure 6.7), check the Microsoft Stack radio button if you are running Windows 95 or NT. If you are running Windows 3.11, check the Other Stack button, and consult the Precept system requirements listed earlier.

8. Select the appropriate program folder from the list shown in Figure 6.8.

9. In the Current Settings dialog box, click on the Next button if the settings are correct.

10. Wait for a moment while the Installer copies files to the specified targets.

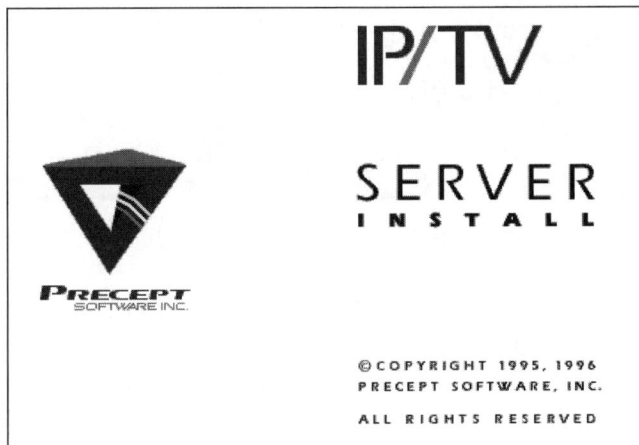

Figure 6.4   The Precept Server Installer splash screen.

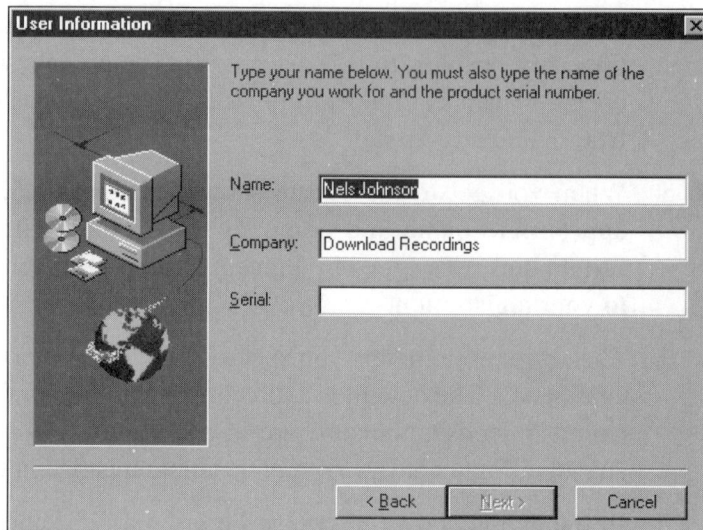

Figure 6.5   Filling in the Precept Server serial number.

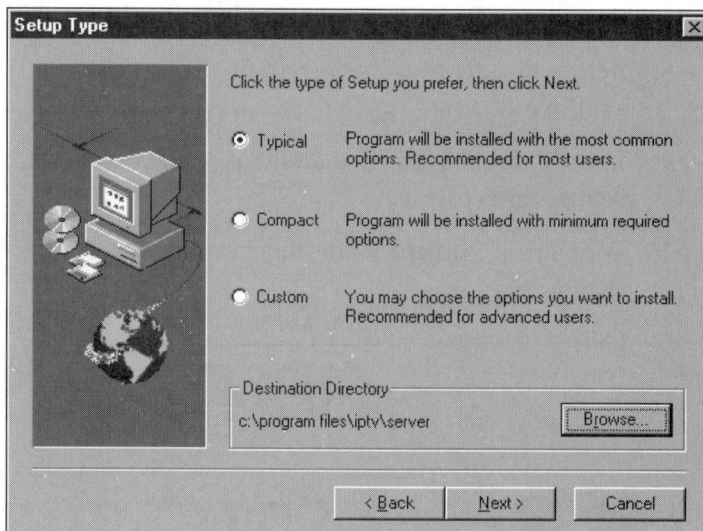

Figure 6.6   Specifying the target directory and installation type.

Note!   *In the version of the Server Installer tested here, there was a minor problem with the creation of a shortcut to the IP/TV Server application (the user is notified in an alert box, which can be dismissed by clicking on the No button). You can fix this by finding the installed executable with the Desktop Explorer and manually creating a shortcut to it. This will likely be corrected by the time this book is published.*

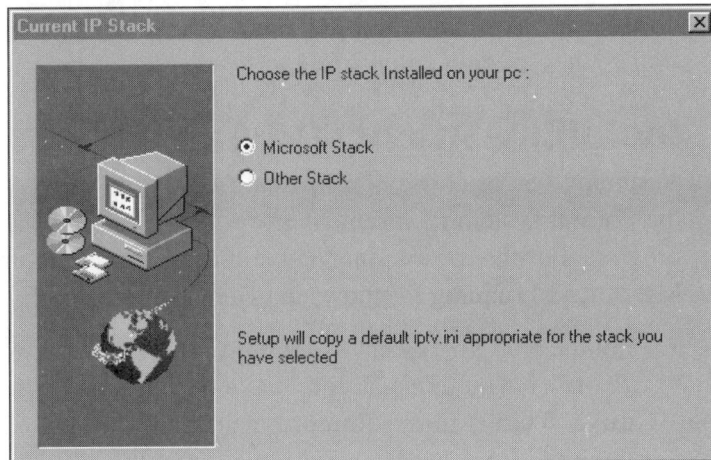

Figure 6.7 Selecting the Microsoft Stack.

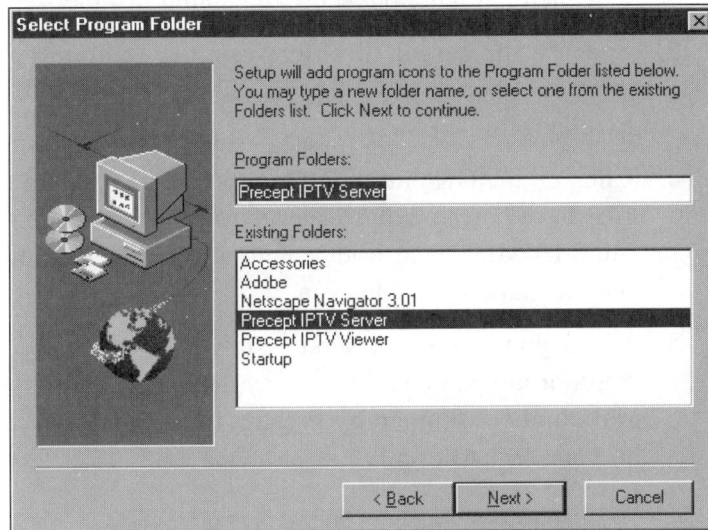

Figure 6.8 Selecting the Precept IPTV Server folder.

11. In the Setup Complete dialog box, click on Next to finish the installation. Check the box to view the Read Me file, and do so at your discretion.

12. In the next part of the Setup Complete dialog box, select the option to restart your computer (highly recommended). The Installer will do this for you now.

When your server is rebooted, you might want to verify that everything is still functioning normally (no reason it shouldn't be) but don't fire up the Precept IP/TV Server application just yet. Let's install the IP/TV Viewer application first.

Installing The IP/TV Viewer

Assuming you're now at a fully qualified IP/TV Viewer machine (see the Precept system requirements), we'll now run the Viewer Installer program. For the record, our Viewer machine is a Pentium 90 with 24 MB of RAM running Windows 95. Here is the recipe:

1. Put the IP/TV Viewer installation program in a directory called *TEMP* (if you don't already have one) right off your main hard drive. This is not required, but it makes things easier to keep track of.

2. Double click on the installation program name in the TEMP folder to launch it. Figure 6.9 shows the initial Installer screen.

3. Specify the target directory for the temporary installation directory, then click on the UNZIP button (again, C:\TEMP is an excellent choice).

4. Click on the OK button in the message box stating that all of the files have been unzipped successfully. The graphic shown in Figure 6.10 will appear briefly, followed by the beginning of a standard Install Shield setup run.

5. When you get to the screen shown in Figure 6.11, fill in the appropriate name and company data, along with the Viewer serial number assigned by Precept in their return email response to your registration.

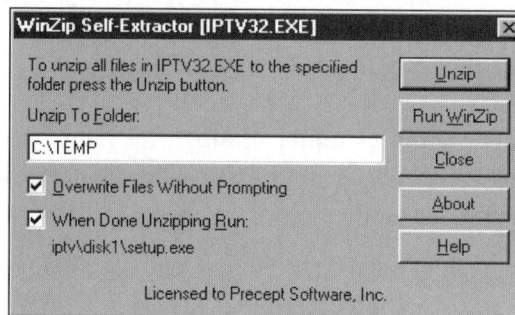

Figure 6.9   Welcome to the IP/TV Viewer Installer.

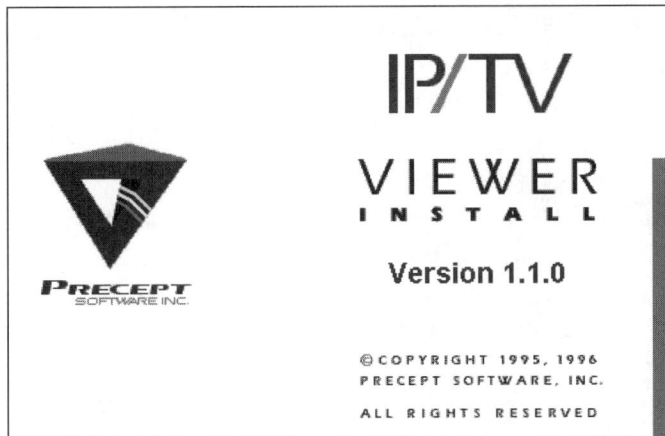

Figure 6.10 The IP/TV Viewer Installer splash screen.

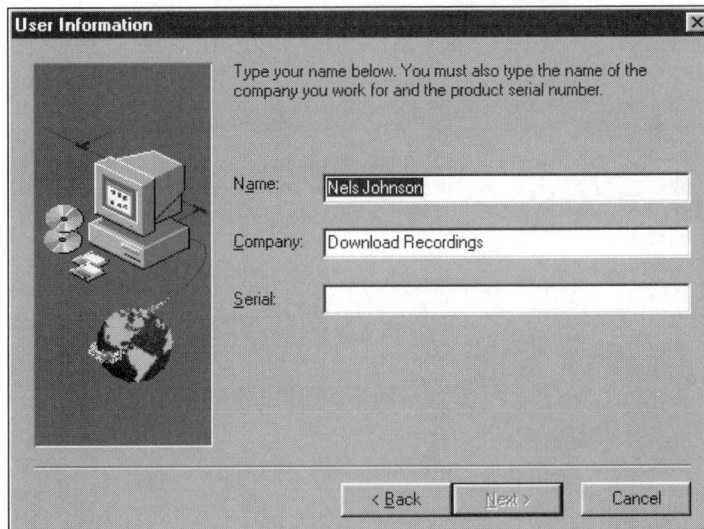

Figure 6.11 Filling in the IP/TV Viewer serial number.

6. The setup program lets you specify a target directory for the Precept Viewer. The default is a directory right off your C: drive. This example deposits the software in c:\Program Files\iptvclnt, as shown in Figure 6.12. A *Typical* installation is fine in this case.

7. Select the appropriate program folder from the list shown in Figure 6.13.

8. In the Start Copying Files dialog box, click on the Next button if the settings are correct.

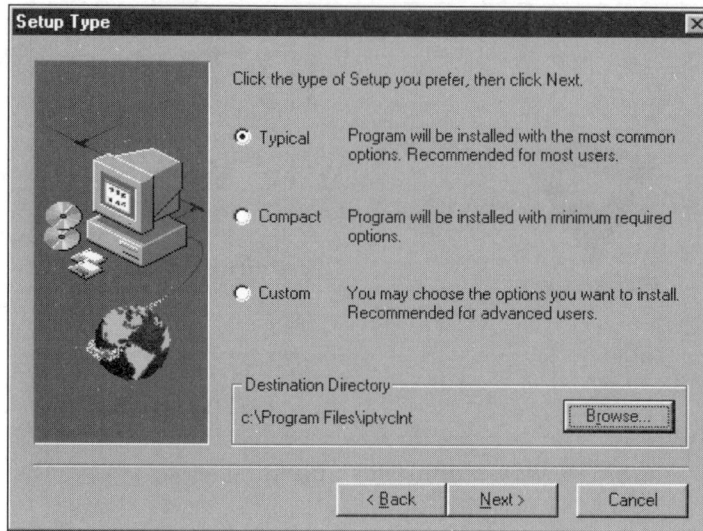

Figure 6.12 Specifying the target directory and installation type.

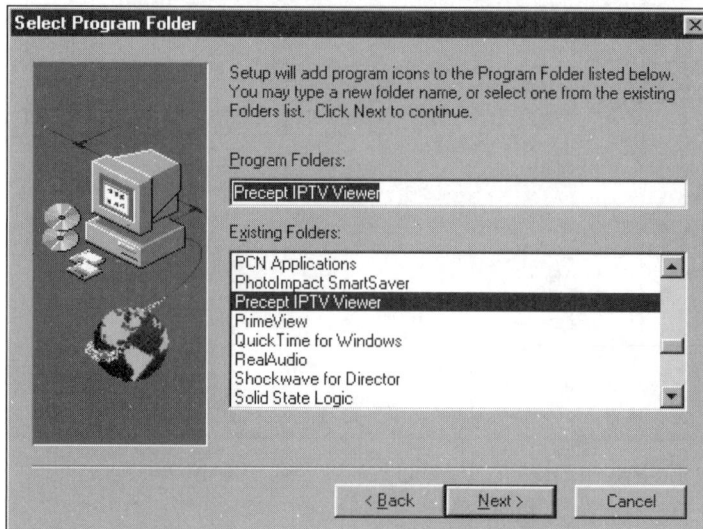

Figure 6.13 Selecting the Precept IPTV Viewer folder.

9. If you see a message box asking if you would like to install the Netscape plug-ins, go ahead and click on the Yes button. Even if you mainly use the Microsoft Explorer, you may find these Netscape plug-ins useful in the future.

10. Wait for a moment while the Installer copies files to the specified targets.

11. In the Setup Complete dialog box, click on Next to finish the installation. Check the box to view the Read Me file, and do so at your discretion.

12. In the next part of the Setup Complete dialog box, select the option to restart your computer (highly recommended). The Installer will do this for you now.

When your client machine is rebooted, you might want to check that everything is still functioning normally (no reason it shouldn't be) but don't fire up the Precept IP/TV Viewer application just yet. Let's now go back and start the Server first.

Running The IP/TV Server

One thing to note here is that the Precept IP/TV Server application does not run as an NT Service per se. In other words, you launch it and shut it down like any other standard executable. As you'll see, Microsoft's NetShow *is* an official NT Service and is controlled from the Services applet in the Control Panel.

So, let's get to it. Assuming your Server was rebooted following the IP/TV installation, and a shortcut is now on your desktop, go ahead and double click on the shortcut icon. As the Server application gets rolling, you will glimpse the panel shown in Figure 6.14, which will segue into the Program Listings user interface, as shown in Figure 6.15

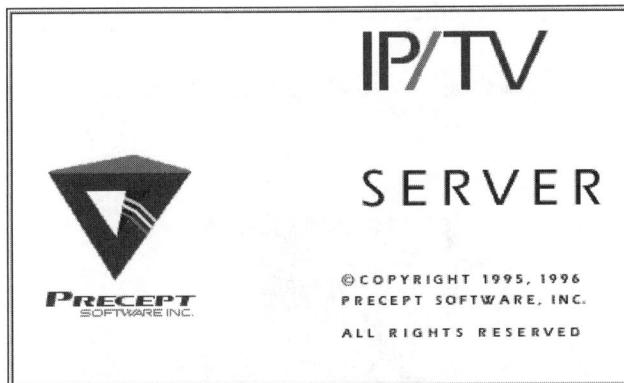

Figure 6.14 The IP/TV server application splash screen.

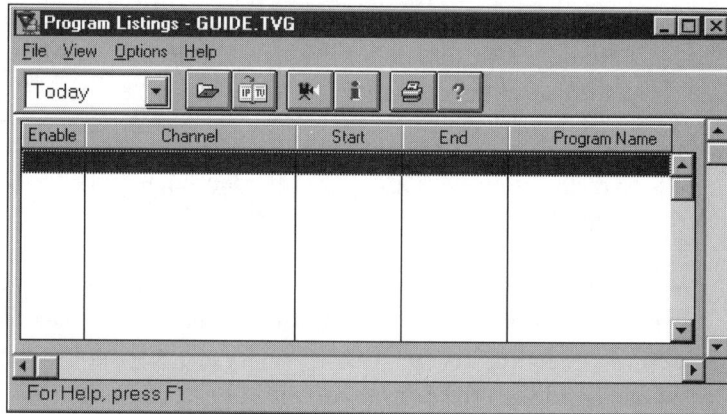

Figure 6.15 The Program Listings window.

To put the IP/TV Server to work, go ahead and execute the following steps:

1. From the File Menu, select the Launch Session item, as shown in Figure 6.16.

2. A File Open dialog box will appear, asking you to select a file with an .SVR extension (see Figure 6.17). This is a text file containing, among other things, a path to a movie file. As you'll see in due course, any movie played by the IP/TV Server application needs an SVR file to point to it and to provide the IP/TV Server with additional information about the movie. You can open the SVR file with a text editor to get a better sense of this.

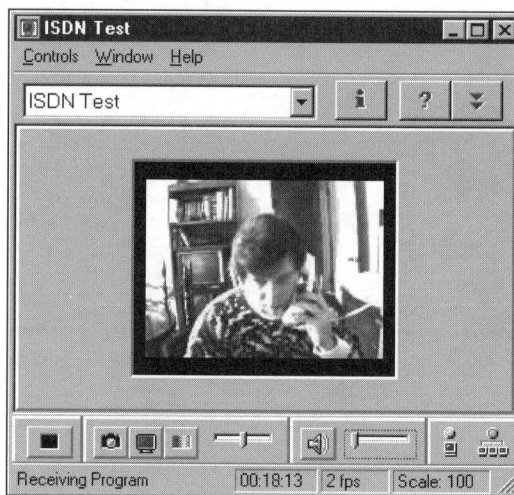

Figure 6.16 Launching a multicast session.

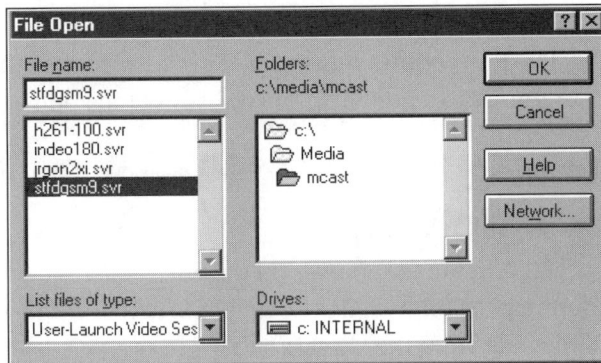

Figure 6.17   Selecting an SVR file.

> **Note!**   *The default SVR file that comes with the IP/TV Viewer Installer points to the ubiquitous Video for Windows snowboarding movie (also included with the Installer). The SVR and movie file used in our test drive were custom made for this purpose.*

3.   When you select an SVR file, the control panel shown in Figure 6.18 will appear (although it may be minimized at first).

4.   Click on the green forward arrow under the left edge of the movie window to start the multicast movie rolling. Your server is now

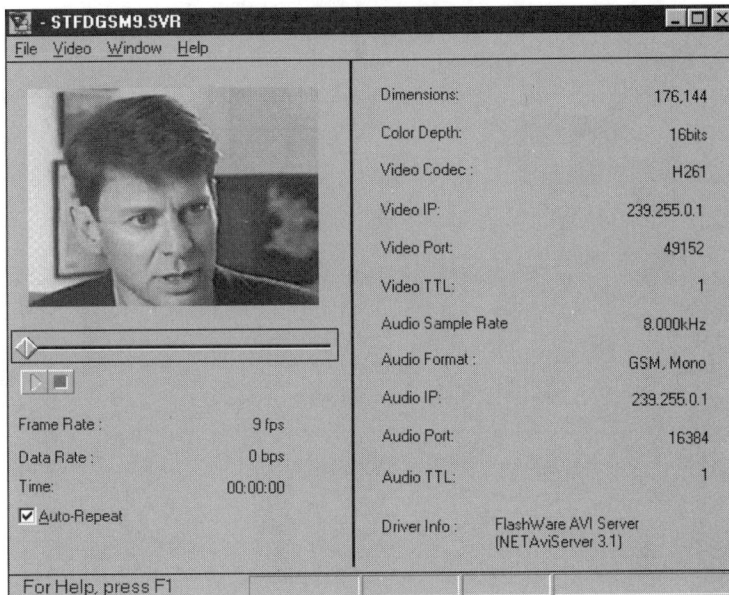

Figure 6.18   The IP/TV Server Control panel.

multicasting! To stop the multicast, click on the red square. Naturally, the yellow control is the pause button. Again, to kill the IP/TV Server altogether, just dismiss the application normally.

Running The IP/TV Viewer On A Local Network

Now, let's fire up the Viewer on the other machine (on the local LAN). Performing the following actions should tune in the movie we just started multicasting from the server:

1. Assuming your client machine was rebooted following the IP/TV Viewer installation, and a shortcut now appears on the desktop, go ahead and double click on the shortcut icon. As the Viewer application gets rolling, you will glimpse the panel shown in Figure 6.19, which will segue into the Program Listings user interface, shown in Figure 6.20.

Note! *If we were connected to a server that had a Program Guide available, we could retrieve it and populate the Viewer UI with scheduled programs. For now, all we want to do is see what the Server is currently broadcasting—make that multicasting.*

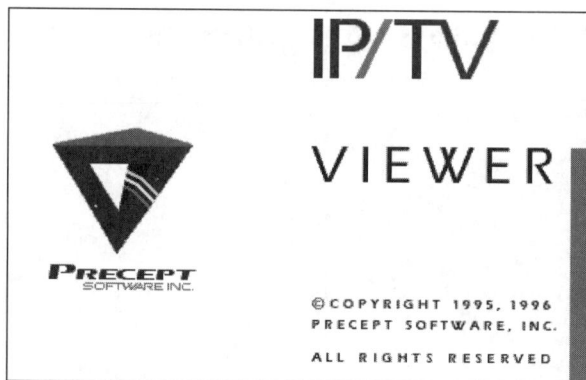

Figure 6.19   The IP/TV Viewer splash screen.

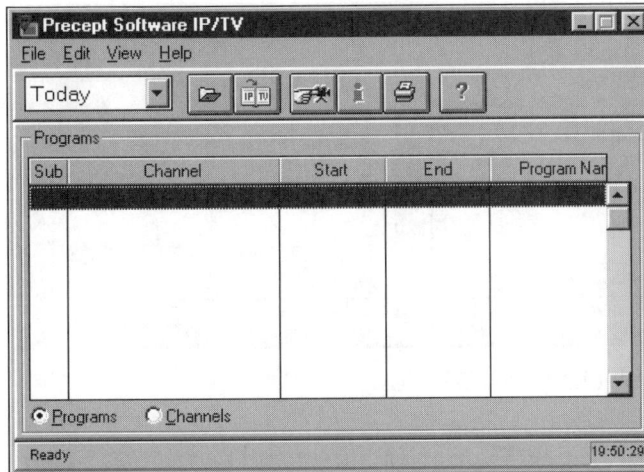

Figure 6.20 The IP/TV Viewer Program Guide.

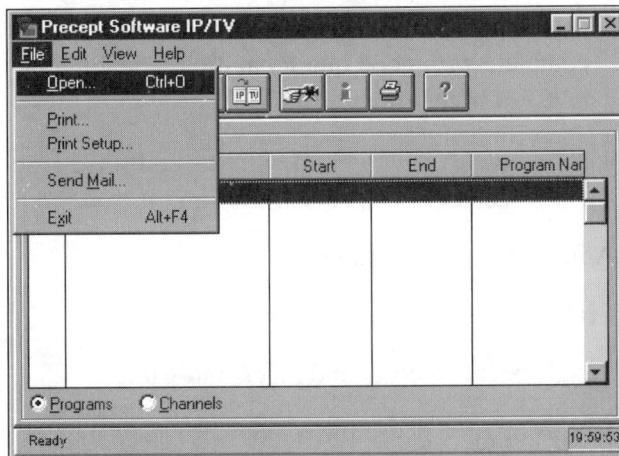

Figure 6.21 Opening a FlashWare file.

2. From the File Menu, select the Open item, as shown in Figure 6.21. A File Open dialog box will appear asking you to select a file with an .SDP extension (see Figure 6.22). This is a text file containing information concerning the movie about to be viewed. In a way, it is a counterpart to an SVR file (used on the Server side). You can open an SDP file with a text editor to get a better sense of this.

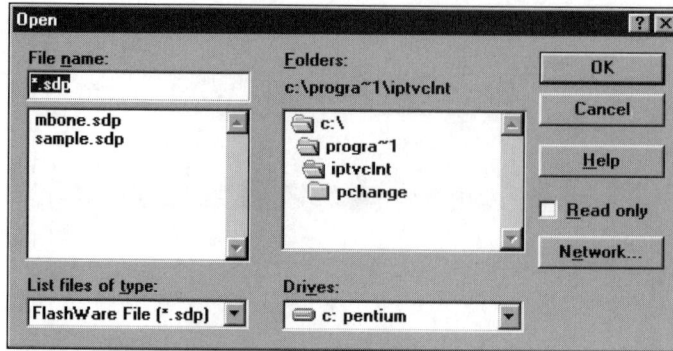

Figure 6.22 Selecting an SDP file.

3. The IP/TV Viewer comes with two sample SDP files, as shown in Figure 6.22. For test drive purposes, choose SAMPLE.SDP.

4. After a moment, the Viewer window shown in Figure 6.23 will come up, hopefully with the movie being multicast from the server, complete with good quality audio (depending on the audio quality inherent in the movie itself).

Take a minute to play around with the controls in the Viewer window. As you'll see, these controls allow you to:

• Adjust the movie volume

• Scale the movie window size

• Toggle between color and black and white

• Start, stop, and pause the movie

More advanced advance features are also available, as shown in Figure 6.24.

If you wish, you can also display statistics on the incoming multicast, as shown in Figure 6.25.

If you have other clients on your LAN, you can install the IP/TV Viewer application and tune in the multicast on those machines also, with the same level of performance for all (such is the beauty of multicasting). In general, if a client has TCP/IP protocol installed and is physically connected to the LAN, they are a candidate for receiving a multicast from an IP/TV server.

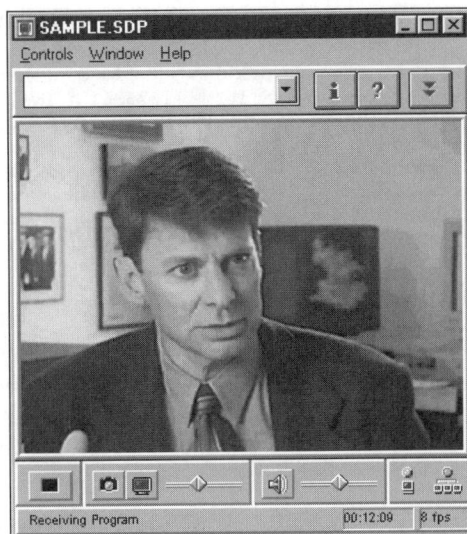

Figure 6.23 Receiving the multicast movie.

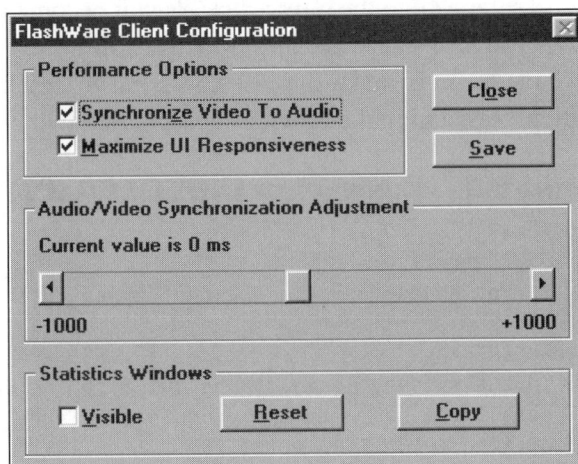

Figure 6.24 Some Advanced IP/TV Viewer features.

Assuming your systems are functioning smoothly, this is the basic multicasting experience, at least on a LAN. Depending on whether you've seen networked video before, the overall effect may not be overwhelming—until you appreciate what is going on here technically. The more you work with multicasting hardware and software, however, the more you should come to understand the potential of this new technology.

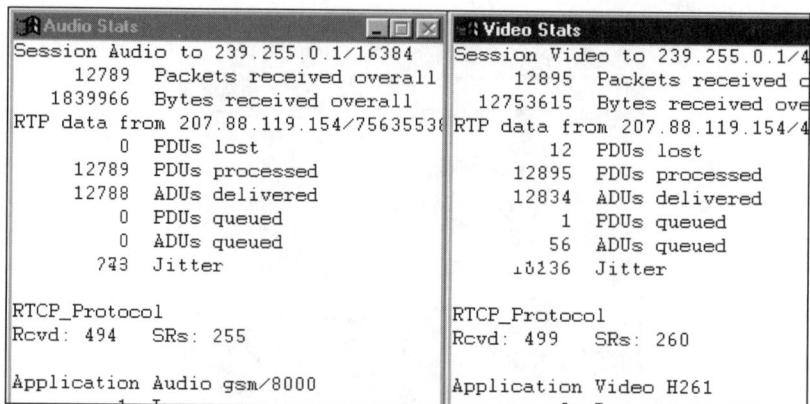

Figure 6.25 Viewing multicast statistics.

If you want to serve some of your own movies right away, you can do so by making SVR files for them. Listing 6.1 shows the contents of the SVR file used in the previous test drive. Notice the last line, which specifies the path to the movie file. As you become more familiar with IP/TV, you will likely get into SVR files in more detail. For now, all you have to do is make the last line point to any movie you want to multicast (assuming the movie is compressed with a supported codec).

LISTING 6.1 CONTENTS OF INDEO180.SVR.

```
[programs]
SampleSVREntry=1
;    Do not change any field except those indicated.

[SampleSVREntry]
;    In the mvideo= line, change 49152 to the UDP
;    port to be used for the video packet stream.
mvideo=video 49152 RTP/AVP 31 96
;    In the maudio= line, change 16384 to the UDP
;    port to be used for the audio packet stream.
maudio=audio 16384 RTP/AVP 0 3 5 96 97 98 99 100 101 102 103
;    In the cvideo= line, change 239.255.0.1 to the IP
;    address to be used for the video packet stream.
;    Change the final 1 to the IP Multicast Range for the
     session.
cvideo=IN IP4 239.255.0.1/1
;    In the caudio= line, change 239.255.0.1 to the IP
;    address to be used for the audio packet stream.
```

```
;     Change the final 1 to the IP Multicast Range for the
      session.
caudio=IN IP4 239.255.0.1/1
a1=video rtpmap:96 WBIH/90000
a2=audio rtpmap:96 L8/11025
a3=audio rtpmap:97 L8/11025/2
a4=audio rtpmap:98 L8/22050
a5=audio rtpmap:99 L8/22050/2
a6=audio rtpmap:100 L16/11025
a7=audio rtpmap:101 L16/11025/2
a8=audio rtpmap:102 L16/22050
a9=audio rtpmap:103 L16/22050/2
;     In the a10= line, change "c:\avi\sample.avi"
;     to the full pathname of the file.
a10=file:c:\media\mcast\indeo180.avi
```

As of this writing, the IP/TV Server supports several types of movie files, not the least of which is Indeo 3.2. Also supported is Precept's H.261 streaming codec, which is installed automatically when you install the Server and Viewer software. If you use Adobe Premiere to make movies under Windows, you'll notice that Precept H.261 is a compression option the next time you run it on a machine which has the Viewer or Server installed.

Running The IP/TV Viewer On A Dialin Client

Which brings us to the dialin client world. Generally speaking, IP/TV works very well in this environment, but you may have to tweak a few extra parameters if you are connecting through routers via ISDN lines and expect the kind of performance possible on a LAN.

Once you get the domain names, passwords, and IP addresses sorted out, however, you won't be disappointed. Router technology is advancing rapidly as the market expands for multicasting, especially on the individual user side. Two Ascend or Cisco ISDN routers connected by a 128 Kbps ISDN line provide a great way to link a Precept Server and Viewer for a good quality off-MBone multicasting experience. We'll get into these issues (and return to Precept's solutions) in later chapters. Figure 6.26 shows the administrator of a LAN talking to a dialin client with a QuickCam. Both parties have Ascend ISDN routers.

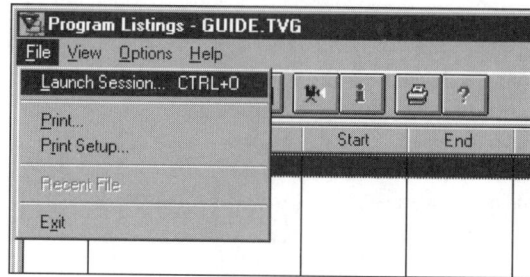

Figure 6.26
Connected to a dialin LAN.

Microsoft's NetShow

As we did for Precept's IP/TV, let's now take a test drive with NetShow, the leading multicast contender (as of this writing) from Microsoft. NetShow differs from IP/TV in several ways, some obvious and some subtle. For one thing, the Server components runs as official NT Services as opposed to running as applications. In effect, this means they:

- Work more closely with the operating system (like all official NT Services).

- Run in the background until specifically stopped (using the NT Control Panel).

Microsoft seems to be positioning NetShow primarily as a corporate intranet solution, with an emphasis on such applications as audio/video conferencing and training. As in the early days of Video for Windows (as opposed to QuickTime), there appears to be less focus on entertainment and entrepreneurial multicasting, at least for now.

NetShow System Requirements

Like IP/TV, NetShow has some minimum platform issues (quoted from its Web page, as of this writing).

CLIENT HARDWARE

- 486/50 MHz processor (minimum); Pentium suggested.

- PCI or EISA bus (PCI recommended).

- 8 MB RAM for Windows 95 (minimum); 16 MB suggested.

- 16 MB RAM for Windows NT (minimum); 32 MB suggested.

- Any Ethernet client adapter for intranet use; modem for Internet use.

- Sound card and speakers.

CLIENT SOFTWARE

- To date, the NetShow Live Client has only been tested with Internet Explorer 3.0.

SERVER HARDWARE

- 486/66 MHz processor (minimum).

- PCI or EISA bus (PCI is recommended).

- 24 MB RAM (minimum); 48 MB suggested.

- Ethernet network interface card (NIC).

SERVER SOFTWARE

- Microsoft NetShow On Demand also requires Microsoft Internet Information Server 2.0 or greater.

Setting Up The NetShow Server

To parallel our IP/TV installation, we'll set up the NetShow Server components on a Pentium 133 with 32 MB of RAM running NT 4.0 Server. As of this writing, there are two principal pieces available on the Microsoft Web site:

- NetShow Live Server

- NetShow On Demand Server

Each of these components does pretty much what its name suggests. The NetShow Live Server is designed to handle live multicasts, while the NetShow On Demand Server handles stored media using some multicast-related protocols. The current design of the On Demand Server allows it to function as a discreet service within the Microsoft Information Server (like Gopher, FTP, and World Wide Web services). A third NetShow component, Content Creation Tools, is also available for downloading. We'll cover that piece in a moment.

Note! *In previous chapters, we have made a distinction between video on demand and multicast video. That distinction is important here as well, because NetShow On Demand does not behave like a true multicast solution.*

We'll install the NetShow On Demand Server first. Here is the flight plan:

1. Assuming you've downloaded the NetShow On Demand Installer program, place it in C:\TEMP (or wherever you put temporary files).

2. Double click on the Installer program in the TEMP folder to launch it. Figure 6.27 shows the initial Installer screen.

3. In the dialog box shown in Figure 6.28, select both options (the Server and the Administration Tools).

4. In the Select Directory dialog box, choose the default directory (unless you prefer not to) \Program Files\Microsoft NetShow\On-Demand.

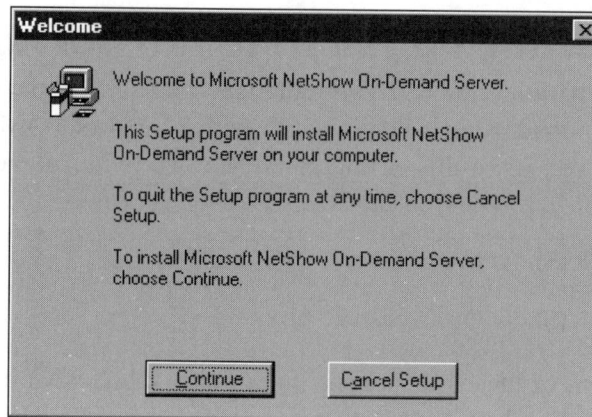

Figure 6.27 Launching the NetShow On Demand Installer.

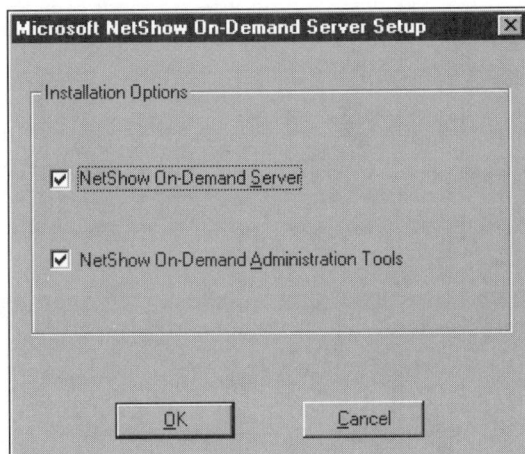

Figure 6.28   Selecting the Server and Administration Tools.

5. In the Server Configuration dialog box, shown in Figure 6.29, accept the defaults for now. You can change these later if necessary.

6. The next dialog box (shown in Figure 6.30) prompts you for the root directory in which to store your On Demand media for multicasting. In this example, we choose a location within our Web server's media bank, although the default is safe for test drive purposes. For now, you can turn off the security feature by checking the No Radio button.

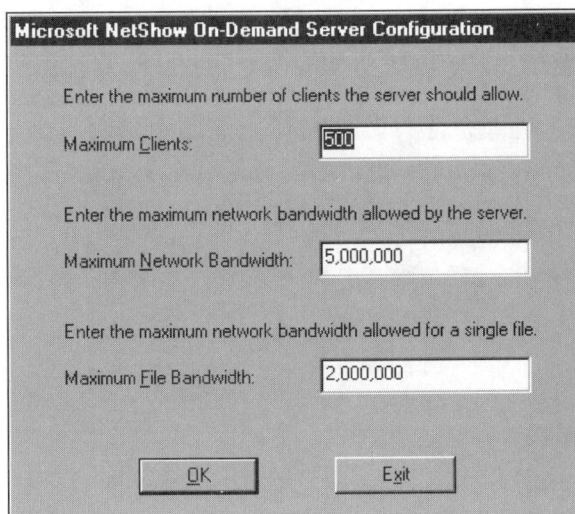

Figure 6.29   Initial configuration of the NetShow On Demand Server.

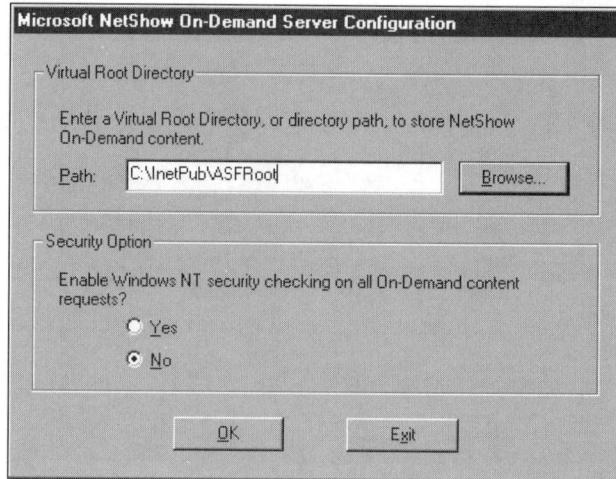

Figure 6.30 Specifying a root directory for your multicast media.

7. The final installation dialog box, shown in Figure 6.31, asks whether you want to restart Windows NT. Go ahead and do this now.

When your Server comes back on line, you can go ahead and install the NetShow Live Server and the Content Creation Tools Package. Because the installation of these components is no more involved than the setup of the NetShow On Demand Server, we'll dispense with a blow-by-blow account of the processes. Figure 6.32 shows the initial screen of the Tools Installer, which gives you some idea of its capabilities. Running the NetShow Live software is covered shortly. First, let's take care of the On Demand Client setup.

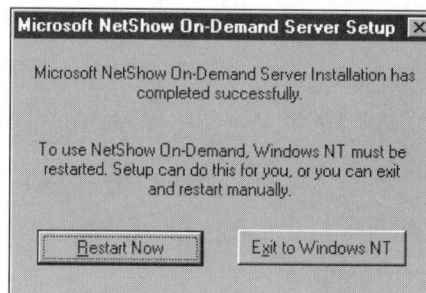

Figure 6.31 Installation is complete.

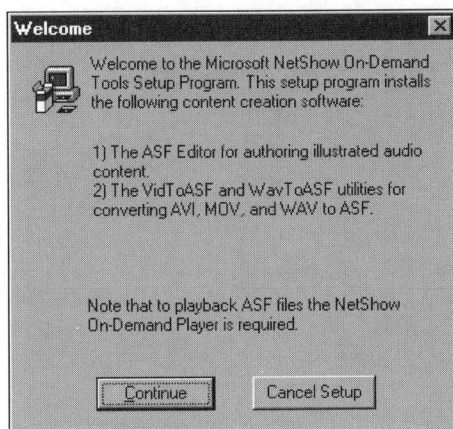

Figure 6.32 Beginning the Content Creation Tools setup.

Installing The NetShow Client

If you're now at your designated client machine for NetShow viewing, we can proceed with running the On Demand Player setup program. The machine used for this test drive, like with the IP/TV test, is a Pentium 90 with 24 MB of RAM running Windows 95. Here's the drill for this installation:

1. Copy the Player Installer program to C:\TEMP (or wherever you wish to run it from).

2. Double click on the installation program to launch it. Figure 6.33 shows the initial dialog box.

3. In the dialog box shown in Figure 6.34, it is safe to accept the defaults for now.

4. In the Select Start Menu Program Group dialog box, select the appropriate group.

5. Wait a moment while the Installer copies files and handles registration formalities. When this process is complete, you'll see the dialog box shown in Figure 6.35.

While you are not prompted to reboot at this point, it never hurts.

Figure 6.33   Firing up the NetShow On Demand Player Installer.

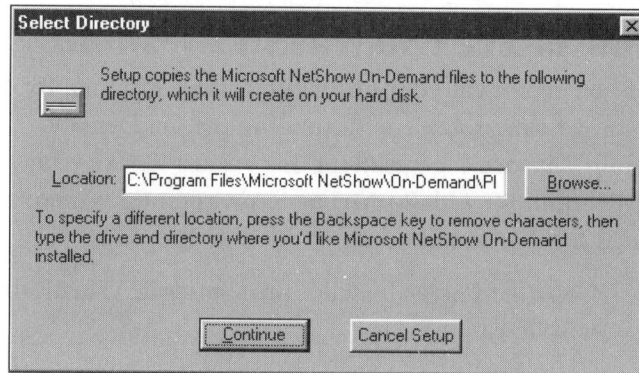

Figure 6.34   Setting the target directory for the Player.

Figure 6.35   NetShow Player installation is complete.

Running The NetShow On Demand Server

And once again, it's show time—or almost. First, we need some suitable content. As you'll see when you start working with the NetShow Tools, the main media editing tool is the NetShow ASF Editor. This program basically allows you to assemble still images and audio files into voice-over slide shows. As of this writing, the ASF Editor does not support importing video files (even uncompressed ones). We'll look more closely at this program in a moment.

Because we're interested in streaming video, it would be nice if there was a way to convert existing video assets into ASF files (the type playable by the NetShow Server). Fortunately, there is—although it is somewhat inelegant.

Actually, two conversion utilities ship with the NetShow Tools:

- *VIDTOASF*—Converts AVI and QuickTime movies to ASF movies.

- *WAVTOASF*—Converts WAV audio files to ASF audio files.

Unfortunately, both of these conversion programs must be run from the DOS command line. In the interest of completing our test drive, however, we'll just deal with this for now. If you plan on using these utilities after the test drive, typing the name of the program (VIDTOASF or WAVTOASF) at the DOS command prompt produces a listing of the flags necessary for setting the conversion parameters, including the input and output file names.

For example, the name of the file we want to multicast is MUS-VID1.AVI. At the DOS command prompt, we'll key in:

```
VIDTOASF -IN MUSVID1.AVI
```

The VIDTOASF program will produce an ASF streaming file named MUSVID1.ASF, based on our command syntax. As of this writing, VIDTOASF prepends a NetShow stinger sequence to the output file, ostensibly for buffering and synchronization as the movie starts streaming (Right!). You can test the output movie immediately with the NetShow On Demand Player program by simply loading and playing it locally, as shown in Figure 6.36.

MUSVID1.AVI was a Cinepak movie with 8-bit, 22.05 kHz, mono audio. Its duration was only about 30 seconds, so it was converted to the ASF format in just a few seconds. It was converted successfully, so we can now serve it up to interested viewers.

Here are the steps for playing our MUSVID1.ASF movie:

1. Put the movie you want to play in the server's ASFRoot directory specified when the NetShow On Demand Server was installed. We'll continue to use MUSVID1.ASF for this test drive.

Figure 6.36 Testing a converted ASF movie with the NetShow On Demand Player.

2. Make sure the NetShow On Demand Service of the Microsoft Internet Information Server is running, assuming you have IIS (version 2.0 or greater) already installed. Do this by clicking on Start|Programs|Microsoft Internet Server (Common)|Internet Service Manager, as shown in Figure 6.37.

Because of how the NetShow On Demand Server is currently implemented, this is all you have to do on the server side. (We'll play the movie with the NetShow Player on our client machine in a moment.) Clearly, the design and functionality of this solution is similar to that of a traditional Web server, even though the underlying technology is substantially different. This will be covered in more detail in later chapters.

Figure 6.37 Ensuring the NetShow On Demand Service is running.

Running The NetShow On Demand Player

With our NetShow On Demand Server operational and ready to deliver ASF movies, let's now try to play one over the LAN.

1. Invoke the Player on your client machine by clicking on Start|Programs|Microsoft NetShow|On-Demand Player. The player interface shown in Figure 6.36 will appear.

2. Click on the File item in the main menu, then the Open Location item. The dialog box shown in Figure 6.38 will pop up.

3. Fill in the name of the location plus the name of the file you want to play, using the sample protocol on the face of the dialog box. In this case, we'll use the server's machine name as opposed to its domain name (see Figure 6.39).

4. Clicking on OK will cause the player to connect to the NetShow On Demand Server and start streaming the movie (see Figure 6.40). While this may feel a lot like regular old video on demand (as defined in Chapter 1), it is actually using multicast protocols, at least according to Microsoft. The hitch is that, if you fire up the same movie on a different client, the movie starts from the begin-

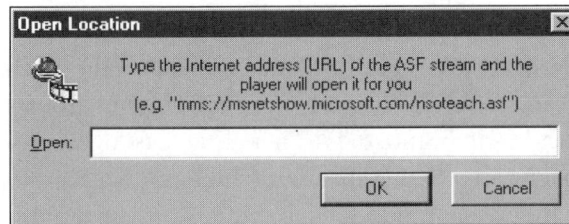

Figure 6.38 Opening a location for a networked NetShow stream.

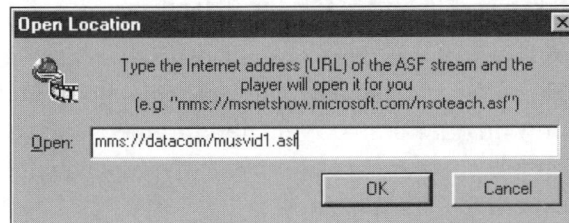

Figure 6.39 Specifying a location and a file name.

Installing And Test Driving Multicast Software

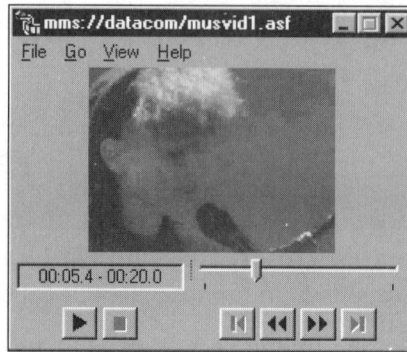

Figure 6.40 Playing an ASF movie on a LAN.

ning for that other client. Invoking the movie on a third client follows the same pattern. In other words, this is video on demand behavior, not a true multicast model. Where Microsoft intends to take this segment of the NetShow product remains to be seen.

This is the basic NetShow On Demand experience, at least for now. Obviously, a whole fabric of applications is expected to grow up around this core technology, just like it did with Video for Windows. A good plan for now is to make and play a wide variety of ASF media, with as much variation in those media as possible.

Using The ASF Editor

If you don't want to be limited to using the VIDTOASF and WAVTOASF conversion programs, you can start playing around with the ASF Editor, shown in Figure 6.41. There is at least one sample ASF project, and also a tutorial that comes with the basic NetShow Tools package. You will find some limitations, but it is worth spending some time with the editor to get a sense of how Microsoft is positioning these tools.

Running NetShow Live

As of this writing, there is a bit of irony regarding the Live side of NetShow. On one hand, it appears to be a true multicasting product. On the other, it does not yet support video—just audio. To its credit, the sample software is very easy to use and equally easy to customize for experimentation purposes.

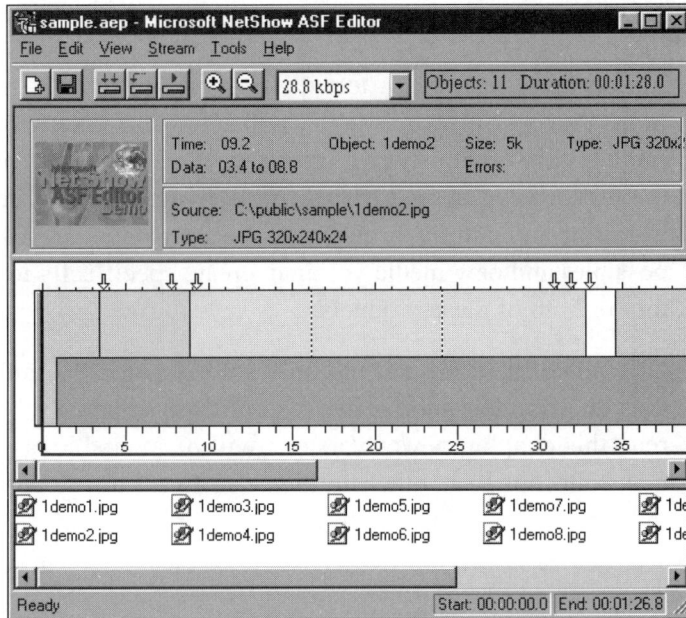

Figure 6.41   The main UI of the ASF Editor.

For now, the basic drill (following a successful installation) is to bring up the NetShow Live administration program, and then:

- Open and play a Microsoft .WAV file (which is then multicast by the NetShow Live Server).

- Start an actual live session using a microphone attached to your audio card. This live session is also multicast by the NetShow Live Server.

On the client side, the recommended way to consume such an audio multicast is via a Web page tuned to the appropriate multicast IP address. Some HTML documents for this are provided by Microsoft in the downloadable NetShow Live installation package. If you tune in the same Web page on two different clients, you'll find two identical audio performances playing from the same point in time. Now that's multicasting!

Summary

This chapter provides a test drive of two prominent multicast solutions: Precept Software's IP/TV and Microsoft's NetShow. While both products are obviously still maturing, they are stable enough to make the test drives rich and thought provoking. They are certainly worth installing and putting through their paces using your existing media (if possible) and new media you may create specifically to work with either or both of these products.

Of course, these are not the only solutions for PC multicasting, but they do provide a good series of contrasts. Hopefully, by the time you read this chapter, newer versions will be available, as well as brand new solutions from other multicast software developers.

Chapter 7

- **Choosing the best production platform (Wintel versus Mac)**

- **Capturing and editing an H.261 AVI movie**

- **Producing MPEG content**

Chapter 7

Producing Multicast Content

Once again, let's lead off with some generalizations:

1. If you are a multimedia producer experienced with tools such as Adobe Premiere, Ulead's Media Studio, and Sonic Foundry's Sound Forge, you can produce multicast content in pretty much the same way you do now for CD-ROM and download-only Internet distribution.

2. Now that the MPEG renaissance is in full swing, you may face a learning curve if you're not already skilled at creating MPEG content—because streaming MPEG files may well become common in the world of multicasting.

3. If you want to produce multicast content but have no prior experience, you may be wondering which platform (Wintel or Mac) is better for this process. The short answer (at least for making multimedia assets, as opposed to full-screen video tape productions) is that both platforms are good, depending on your goals. We'll get into particulars on this issue shortly.

Production Overview

As experienced desktop media producers will tell you, vision is everything. Knowing how to save time when working with limited resources is perhaps the key ingredient to successful desktop production because resources are almost always limited in this environment.

In other words, understanding how to balance the media capture process against the editing and compression processes (when on a deadline) is more important than endlessly tweaking frame rates and key frame intervals just to squeeze out a perceived 2 to 3 percent improvement in image clarity. Remember, this is multimedia—not broadcast television.

One of the facts of desktop production life is that it remains highly tool-centric. To produce good-quality media assets, most people rely on a somewhat disparate collection of software tools as opposed to a unified suite of applications. In fact, the most successful combinations of media production tools often span platforms as well as product lines.

For example, one proven approach for making high quality AVI clips is shown in Figure 7.1 and goes as follows:

1. Capture a raw QuickTime file on a Media100 (Data Translation) capture system.

2. Save the movie on an external hard drive in the flattened Apple None format (some people prefer the Animation format with the highest quality setting).

3. Hook the external hard drive (or FTP the file over your network) to a Wintel box that has Adobe Premiere for Windows installed.

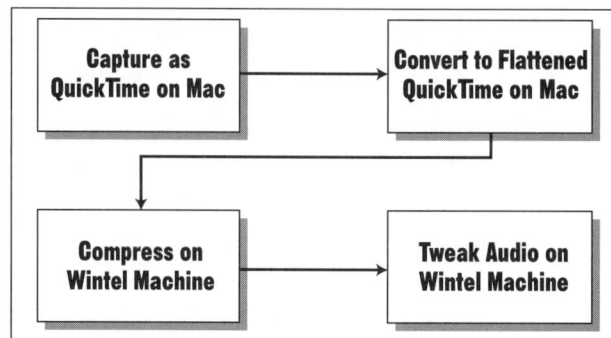

Figure 7.1 Putting the tools to work.

4. Open the flattened Apple None movie in Premiere for Windows 4.2 (or higher). Perform any necessary editing, titling, etc., and compress the file into a Cinepak or Indeo (or even H.261) AVI movie.

5. Open the compressed AVI movie in Sonic Foundry's Sound Forge 4.0 (or higher). Edit the sound track to get the best EQ, volume, and normalization, then save it.

6. If you want a QuickTime movie of the same content, open the finished AVI movie with the San Francisco Canyon Company's TRMOOV program (available at the Web site **www.down recs.com**) and perform the conversion—a one-button process, no re-compression. Of course, you can always compress it into QuickTime from Premiere.

As you can see, it takes both vision and a well-stocked tool chest to boil this sort of production nightmare down to a palatable plan. And the previous example is just one approach, depending on the requirements of the finished production. The recipes that follow illustrate how keeping current with available tools (regardless of your preferred platform) is the only way to make sure you are not wasting time once you go to work on a project.

Getting Down To Cases

Back in Chapter 1, we discussed the standard and emerging file formats for desktop media (AVI, MPEG, QuickTime, etc.), along with the complement of codecs supported by each file format. Consequently, there is no need to reprise that information here. You may, however, want to review the Video Capture Meta System presented near the end of Chapter 5.

In this chapter, we'll present models for capturing and compressing media clips using commercial hardware and software solutions. The goal is to create assets suitable for multicasting, which brings up an interesting question.

Simply put, which file formats and codecs are suitable for this new multicasting environment? Networks are involved (as opposed to just the local desktop), so shouldn't we expect to compress video and audio assets with codecs similar to the VDOLive encoder (and with comparable results)?

Pragmatism Rules

The answer tends to be mostly pragmatic: Use the file formats and codecs supported by the multicast solution manufacturers. Of course, that's what we do already for CD-ROM and download-only media, but there we have many more choices (at least for now). A few existing codecs (such as Indeo and certain types of MPEG) are supported by multicast software publishers, but the movement seems to be toward emerging compressors, such as H.261 and H.301.

Because these new codecs tend to be based on open standards (unlike Intel's Indeo and Radius' Cinepak), third-party companies can exploit them without worrying about cumbersome royalty arrangements (unlike what Apple did originally with QuickTime). Ultimately, third-party companies must decide which file formats they'll implement for their compressors of choice, which will be a function of which platforms their applications run on.

The point is, there is not yet a highly systematic way to look at which types of existing codecs are best suited for multicasting. Companies like Precept, Apple, and Microsoft have chosen to support certain standards based on what works best right now. If you want to judge this short-term thinking, so be it. The situation will certainly mature over the next year or so.

Producing An H.261 AVI Movie

Our first example concerns a movie we want to multicast using Precept's IP/TV solution. The analog version of the movie arrived on an S-VHS video tape. We'll document the whole process beginning with capturing the movie on a Wintel PC, editing and compressing the movie using Premiere for Windows, and,tweaking the audio track using Sound Forge. Because our target codec is Precept's H.261, the IP/TV Viewer needs to be installed on the same machine as Premiere for Windows (the IP/TV setup program also installs the H.261 code libraries).

Capturing The Movie

For the capture process, we'll employ the venerable ISVR Pro (a.k.a., the Intel Smart Video Recorder Pro). Fortunately, Intel has a brand new PCI version of the ISVRP, which allows you to capture raw video clips as 320 × 240 RGB sequences at 15 frames per second—on fast enough machines. Prior versions of the ISVRP weren't quite up to this.

The capture application we'll use is the one that comes with Asymetix's Digital Video Producer product. It's included with the editing suite solution that currently ships with the ISVRP. Intel reportedly has a way to let you use the capture facility in Premiere with this capture card, which will probably be documented on their Web site by the time you read this.

Note! *Full instructions on how to install the ISVRP in your PC are included with the retail product.*

So, let's start the music.

1. Assuming all your gear is connected properly (with the tape in the deck and properly queued), fire up the DVP capture program using the Windows 95 Start button, as shown in Figure 7.2.

2. The UI shown in Figure 7.3 will appear on your desktop. Because the tape is not yet rolling, the Preview window is blank. On the Wintel side (as opposed to the Mac), most mid-level capture environments have a look and feel similar to the one in this example.

3. Time to calibrate the capture settings. First, let's specify the raw file. Because we're working with a professional desktop digitizing machine, we have a couple of one-gigabyte external SCSI hard drives attached for storing uncompressed movie clips as they're captured. Clicking on the Set Capture File option in the File menu (or the file icon with the question mark in the toolbar) brings up the dialog box shown in Figure 7.4. Navigate to the drive you want to use (one of the external SCSI drives), and name the file—in this case, RAW1.AVI.

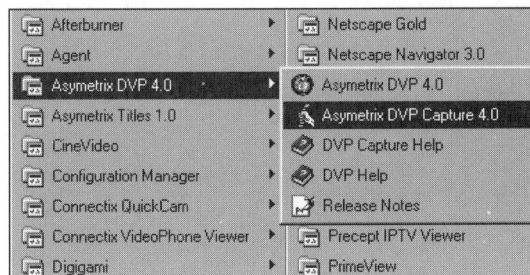

Figure 7.2 Launching the DVP capture application.

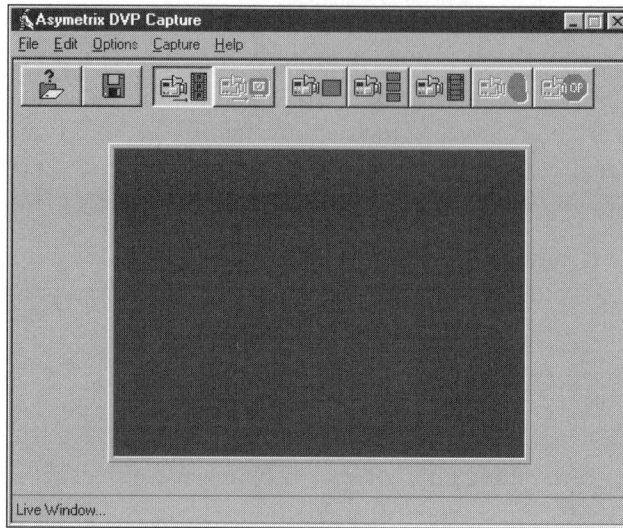

Figure 7.3   The DVP capture program's main UI.

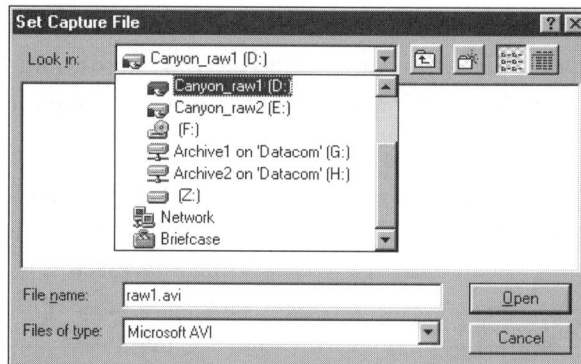

Figure 7.4   Setting the raw capture file.

This menu item actually sets the name of the temporary file used to hold a captured video clip. Use the Save Captured Video As item in the File menu after the capture is complete if you want a more permanent name for your raw file.

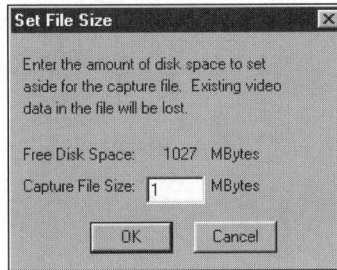

Figure 7.5 Allocating space for your raw file.

4. Next, click on the Allocate File Space item in the File menu. The dialog box shown in Figure 7.5 is invoked. The old wisdom here was that you should allocate just one megabyte and let the program and your system work together to allocate additional space on the fly (all without incurring any performance hits). This is probably still good advice. Do a few trial captures using this technique to see if any frames are dropped. If not, stick with the one-megabyte plan.

5. In the Options menu, shown in Figure 7.6, click on the Audio Format item. The dialog box shown in Figure 7.7 will appear.

6. In the Audio Format dialog box, we'll choose the lowest quality settings because we are going to push them even lower later in this chapter using Sound Forge (something you can't do in most Windows MPC-compatible software). Figure 7.7 shows them already set to 11 kHz, 8-bit, mono.

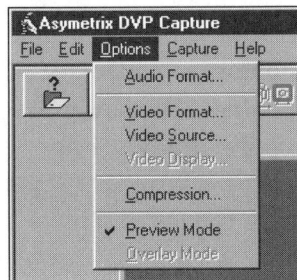

Figure 7.6 The Options menu.

Figure 7.7   The Audio Format dialog box.

Setting the audio attributes in any desktop video capture session deserves your full attention. In this case, we're capturing lower than 44 kHz/16-bit because of the nature of our target (although some desktop audio pros might take exception here). In general, you should always capture with your audio settings as rich as possible, assuming your system won't compromise video quality in the process. Remember, if you don't capture audio with high quality, there is no way you can improve it later. Input volume should be adjusted with the built-in Windows volume control (the speaker icon normally at the bottom right of your Windows 95 desktop).

7. Next, click on the Video Format item in the Options menu to bring up the Video Format panel (see Figure 7.8). As noted earlier, the new ISVRP Mark III can digitize in RGB at 320 × 240, 15 fps, without dropping frames. Prior versions of the card had trouble achieving this performance level. To keep those earlier cards from dropping frames at capture time, Intel supplied a semi-raw codec named YVU9C, which is also included in the new package—except that now it's just called YUV9 (selectable in the Image Format control).

8. Click on the Video Source item in the Options menu to see the Video Source dialog box (presented in Figure 7.9). Like audio, brightness, contrast, and saturation can't generally be made completely right again if they aren't captured correctly in the first place.

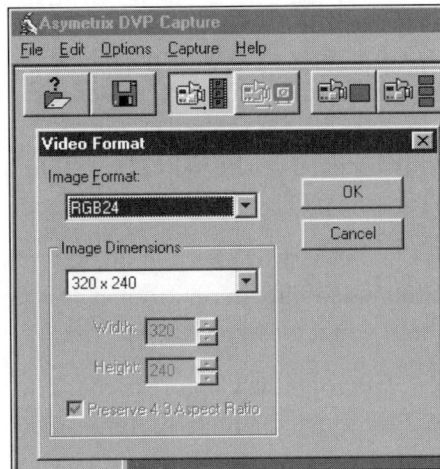

Figure 7.8 The Video Format panel.

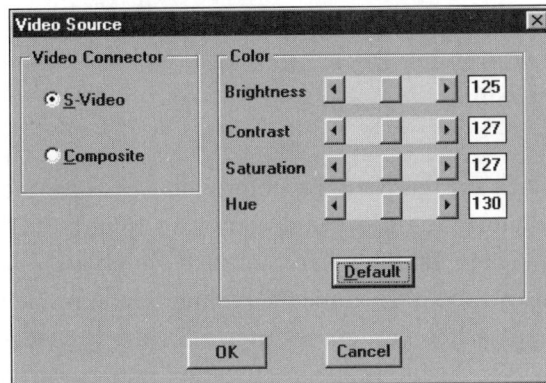

Figure 7.9 The Video Source dialog box.

With this idea in mind, it is good form to experiment carefully with the Brightness, Contrast, and Saturation settings to bring out the best quality in your analog video source. Sometimes, you can make high quality VHS source look as good as, say, fair quality Betacam SP content by carefully calibrating these controls at capture time. For the record, this example uses a VCR with an S-video out port connected to an ISVRP's S-video in jack with an S-video cable. Audio, of course, goes into the PC's sound card via the Line In jack.

9. Unless you are controlling the actions of your VCR (or laserdisc player) from your PC via a special MCI driver, don't worry about the Compression item in the Options menu. While gaining in popularity on high-end Wintel systems, this mode of operation is still relatively unusual on the Wintel side. On Macs, controlling a video deck from the CPU via SMPTE time code is much more common.

10. Check the Preview Mode item in the Options menu if you want to watch the video play in realtime as it is digitized or if you want to see where you are as you cue the video tape on your deck.

11. Figure 7.10 shows the Capture menu. The first three items—Single Frame, Frames, and Video—refer to the capture mode, which you select when the tape is rolling and you're ready to start the capture process. For this example, we're only interested in the Video item.

Note! *As usual, the program's toolbar duplicates the function of many of the menu items. We'll use the Capture Video toolbar button in a moment.*

12. Click on the Settings item in the Capture menu to bring up the Capture Settings panel shown in Figure 7.11. There are several things to calibrate here, most of which are self-explanatory. First, it's always a good idea to capture at the frame rate (and key frame rate) which you expect to use for the finished AVI or QuickTime movie. Again, if you are creating rich raw archives from which to make final movies of yet undetermined quality in the future, you should capture with video and audio attributes set as high as possible. This example requires us to set the frame rate to 15 fps.

13. As for the Capture Storage setting, this can seem confusing, but it really isn't. Checking Capture To Disk makes the program do just that. Capture To Memory means capture to memory until memory

Figure 7.10   The DVP capture program's Capture menu.

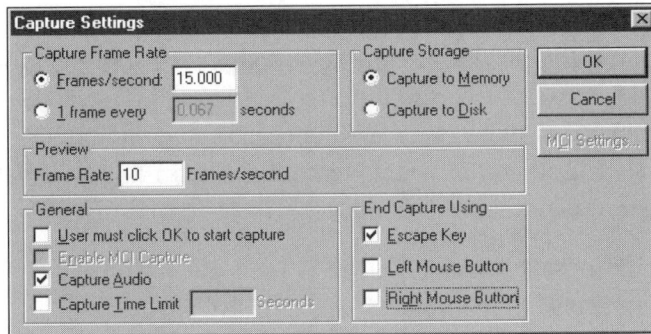

Figure 7.11 The Capture Settings panel.

runs out, then capture to disk. For general efficiency, go ahead and check Capture To Memory.

14. Time to do the capture. Cue the tape to a point several seconds prior to where you want to start capturing, and press the Play button on your video deck. Once the tape is rolling smoothly, click on the Capture Video button in the toolbar. If Preview Mode is enabled, you'll see the video in the Preview window. All the buttons in the toolbar should now be gray except for Stop (see Figure 7.12). The activity light on your external SCSI hard drive should be flashing continuously.

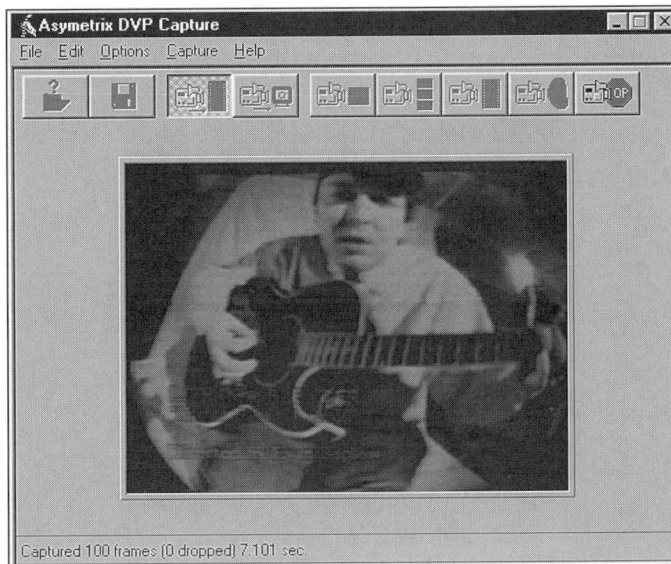

Figure 7.12 A movie grab in progress.

Let the process proceed until the content you want captured has played out, then press the Escape key or click on the Stop button in the toolbar (don't forget to press the Stop button on your video deck). If everything went the way it was supposed to, you should have a fully-formed raw file stored on your external SCSI hard drive. Some good habits to get into at this point include:

• Browsing the external SCSI hard drive with the Desktop Explorer, and checking its file size as a reality check.

• Trying to play the raw movie by simply clicking on it. If you have the ActiveX player installed, you should see something resembling Figure 7.13.

Editing The Movie

With our raw movie successfully captured and stored, it's now time to edit and compress it. Remember, our goal is to produce an H.261 clip suitable for multicasting on a LAN and also in internetworking environments. It's worth noting here that the single biggest time saver when it comes to working with any desktop video editing program is a fast computer.

Even if you are just a talented amateur, you can seem as experienced as a seasoned pro if your movies take 20 minutes to render and compress rather than 4 hours (based on rough differences between, say, a 486-

Figure 7.13 Playing the fresh raw clip.

DX66 and a Pentium 166+). In other words, if you're going to do serious desktop editing, get a serious workstation that won't slow you down (same goes for the Mac).

Our video editing workbench program for this example will be Adobe Premiere for Windows 4.2, although there are other excellent products available for doing this kind of work, such as Ulead Systems' Media Studio Pro. Adobe has worked hard at making the UI for the Windows version feel as close to the UI for the Mac version as possible, with clear success.

If you're not familiar with Premiere, this section will acquaint you with the look and feel of its main features and general way of doing things. If you are an experienced Premiere user, the recipe that follows may give you some new ideas. Aside from its current inability to handle MPEG, Premiere is an almost seamless environment for producing desktop movie clips.

Let's get right to it.

1. When you fire up Premiere for Windows, you are greeted with a splash screen and a configuration panel or two, but you ultimately wind up in the main work area. There are two basic top-level windows: the *Project* window and the *Construction* window. Other windows can be opened to get at other important features, but this is where we'll start (see Figure 7.14).

2. The first thing we need to do is get our raw movie into the active Premiere project. To do this, click on the Import item in the File menu, then select the File item to bring up the Import dialog box shown in Figure 7.15. Navigate to the external SCSI drive, and

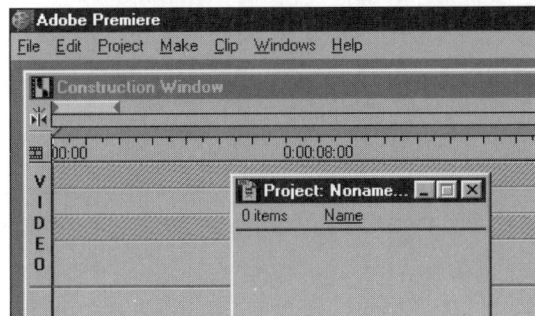

Figure 7.14 Firing up Premiere for Windows 4.2.

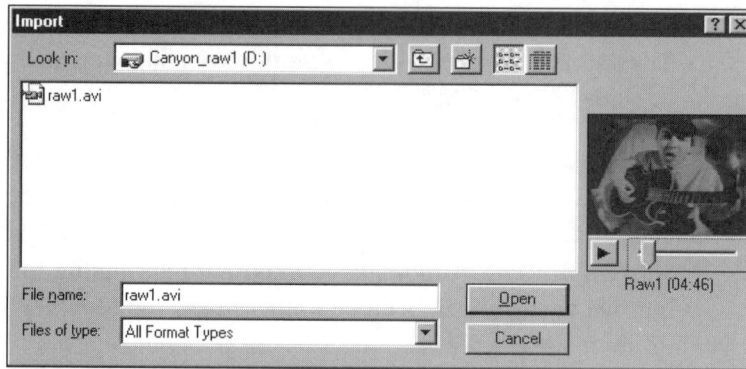

Figure 7.15 The File Import dialog box.

select the video clip to import—in this case, RAW1.AVI. An icon for the imported clip will appear in the Project window. You can double click on this icon to bring up a new window in which you can set the in and out points for the clip (among other things).

3. Next, we need to put this project member into the Construction window. This is done by dragging the file icon from the Project window to the desired timeline in the Construction window. Figure 7.16 shows the result of this action. Now is a good time to save the project (with the File|Save menu item). Saving the project to the same location as the rest of the media in the project (in this case, the external SCSI drive) is usually a good idea.

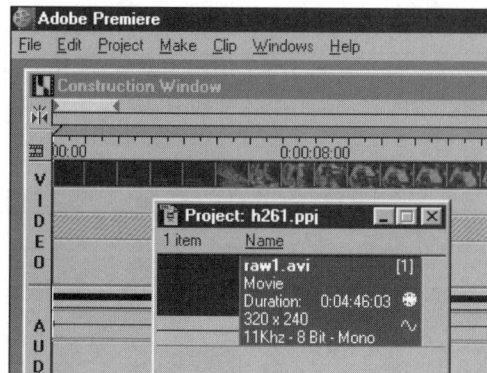

Figure 7.16 Putting a clip in a Construction window timeline.

4. As noted earlier, a good way to set the in and out points of a clip in a Premiere project is to double click on the movie either in the Project window or the Construction window. You can determine where you want to set these points by playing the raw clip frame-by-frame, then clicking on the in and out buttons (depending on whether you're at the beginning or end of the clip). Figure 7.17 shows this particular window. You can accomplish the same goal in the Construction window by zooming in to the frame view and dragging on the appropriate edge of the movie, but the in/out button method is generally more convenient. The more you work with Premiere, the more this kind of discussion will make sense.

5. Let's add a quick title using Premiere's excellent titling facility. To run the title editor, click on File|New|Title. The UI for this utility is shown in Figure 7.18. In the interest of time, we'll dispense with the creation details (they are readily available in the Premiere documentation). We'll store our finished title, H261.PTL, in the same place on the external SCSI drive as the raw movie and the project file. We can save even more time by skipping the details of integrating the title into the project (also covered in detail in the manual); integrating a title is non-essential to the production of our finished movie.

6. Finally, we're ready to render and compress the movie. First, save the project (which now includes the title). Next, click on the Make Movie item in the Make menu. This invokes the Make Movie dialog box, shown in Figure 7.19.

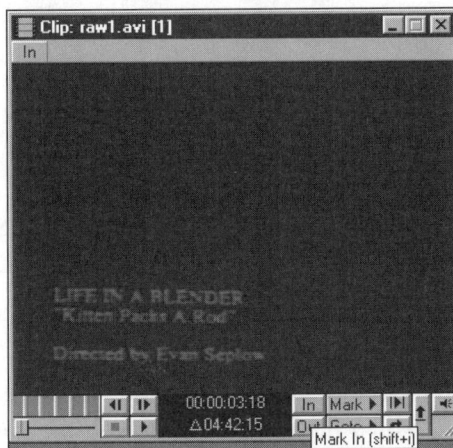

Figure 7.17 Setting the clip's in and out points.

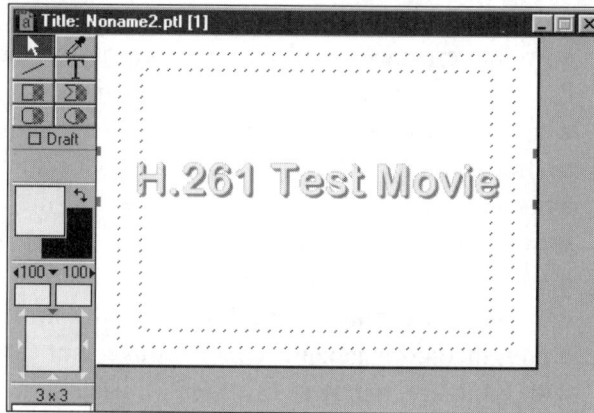

Figure 7.18 Premiere's title editor in action.

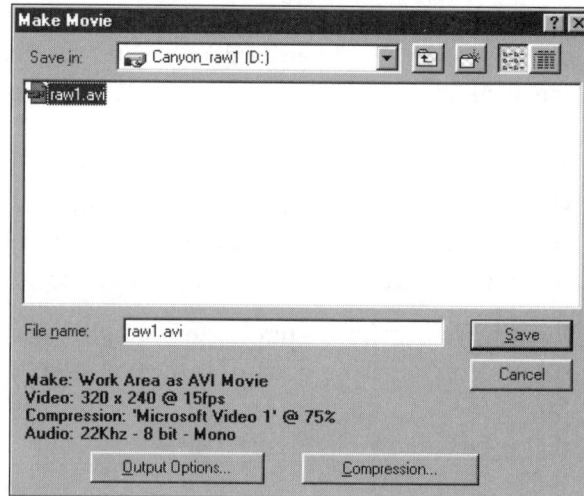

Figure 7.19 The Make Movie dialog box.

7. Navigate to the location of the raw capture file (RAW1.AVI). Key in a name for the finished movie, in this case, H261TEST.AVI. Don't worry about the attributes listed at the bottom of this dialog box because we're about to change them. There are two important subdialogs to deal with here. Let's go to the first one by clicking on the Output Options button. This invokes the panel shown in Figure 7.20.

8. For convenience, Figure 7.20 shows the panel with all the appropriate values filled in, even though the panel normally comes up

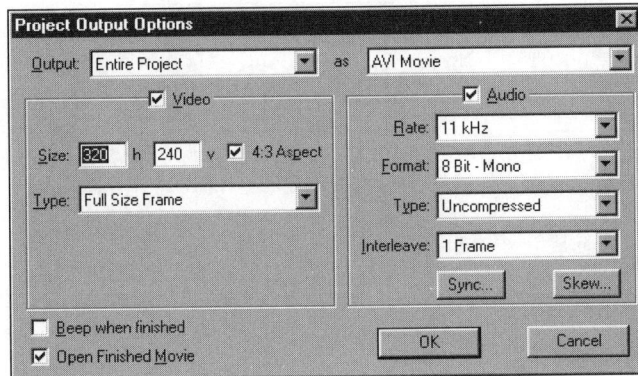

Figure 7.20 Project Output Options.

with default values. Note that we are building the entire AVI Movie (as opposed to the Work Area) at 320 × 240 with 11 kHz/ 8-bit/mono uncompressed audio, interleaved with video at the single-frame level. (Again, remember that we'll change the audio attributes shortly.) Clicking on OK returns us to the Make Movie dialog box.

9. From the Make Movie dialog box, click on the Compression button to summon the Compression Settings panel. As with the Output Options panel, Figure 7.21 shows the Compression Settings panel with the suitable values already selected.

For desktop producers accustomed to making movies with Premiere, this is where things get a bit different. Let's examine the details.

- For the record, we have selected the Precept H.261 Compressor (installed automatically when the setup program is executed for the Precept Viewer or Server).

- Notice, however, that only *Thousands* of colors is specified, as opposed to *Millions* (normal for, say, Cinepak). This helps reduce the data rate.

- Also, notice that we have set the quality slider to 50 percent. This is because Precept's H.261 is more sensitive to different data rate plateaus than Cinepak and Indeo. In other words, you can set this control to less than 100 percent and not see much difference in the quality of the finished movie at show time. In fact, going with a quality setting of 100 percent can produce unwanted side effects in an H.261

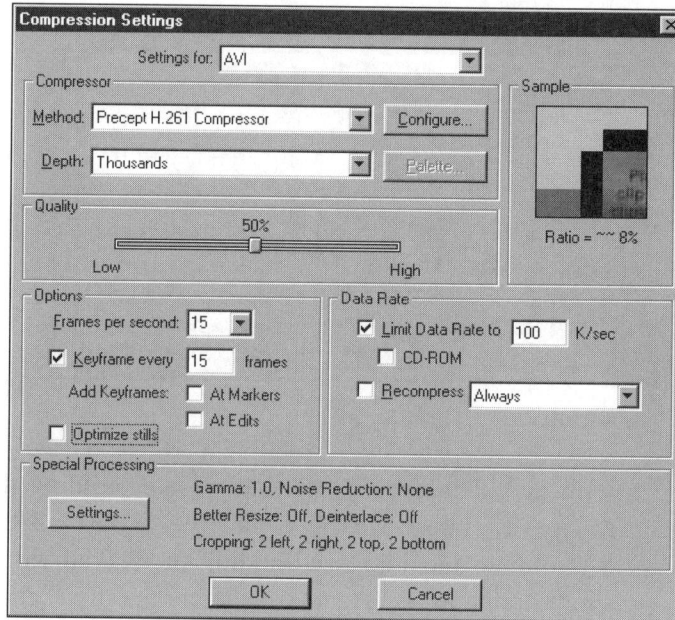

Figure 7.21 Compression settings for H261TEST.AVI.

movie if your data rate is too low. It's worth experimenting with these two interrelated settings (Quality and Data Rate) for a while to get the hang of it.

• Finally, note that we have limited the data rate to 100 Kbps, which is quite low for a 320 × 240 movie. But don't forget that this clip will be played in a networked environment, possibly for a client on the global Internet. Even though we are saving bandwidth by multicasting in general, low data rates for multicast media are going to be the name of the game for a while. As you can see, it's kind of like the early CD-ROM days in terms of AVI and QuickTime production. Sometimes, data rates for 160 × 120 H.261 movies can be even lower than 25 Kbps, depending on the nature of the content.

Note! *Setting the Quality to less than 50 percent is not normally a good idea, although in some cases, it might reduce the side effects (like big pixel blocks) if you are working in highly restrained data rate conditions.*

10. If you wish, click on the Settings button to enter the Special Processing dialog box. Here, you can trim pixel fringe off the sides of your video frames (where lots of video noise lives), as shown in Figure 7.22. Don't forget to scale the video window back to 320 × 240.

11. Click on the OK button to return to the Make Movie dialog box. The attributes at the bottom of the panel should now reflect our new settings. Assuming everything is in order, go ahead and click on the Save button.

12. Premiere's Making Movie dialog box now comes up with a progress bar and a readout of the encoding time remaining. On a midrange Pentium, this may be somewhere around an hour, depending on factors not worth detailing here. You can press the Escape key at any time to stop the compression process and play that portion of the movie that has been compressed so far.

13. When the encoding is complete, play the movie immediately by clicking on it via the Desktop Explorer. This makes for more reliable performance than playing the movie back from within Premiere. If you have the ActiveX components installed, things should look like Figure 7.23.

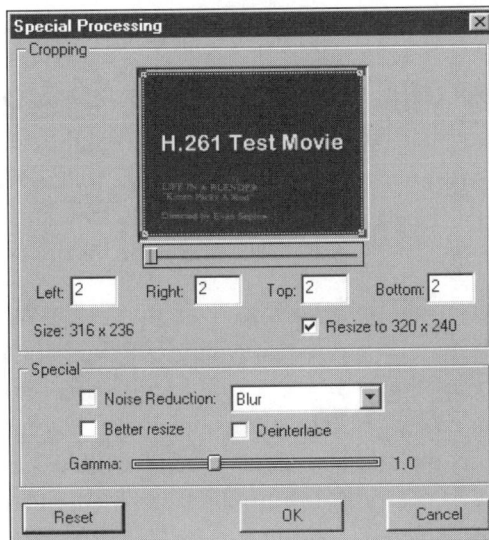

Figure 7.22 Special processing.

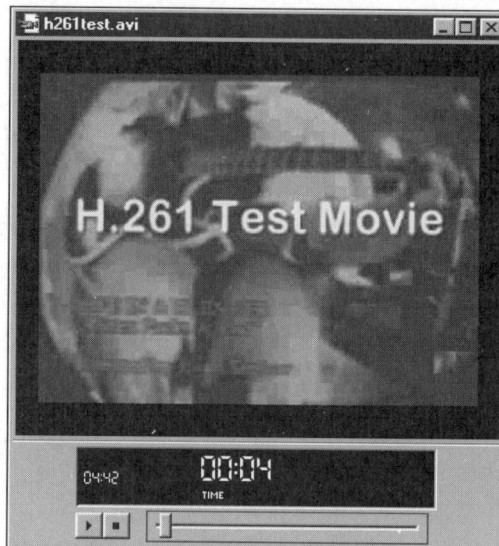

Figure 7.23 Testing the new movie.

15. If the clip performs well on your local machine (good lip-synch, unbroken audio, etc.), it is ready for the next step. Remember that we are still making a Precept H.261 movie for multicasting with Precept's Server and Viewer software. The next step is audio track processing—in this case, with Sound Forge 4.0. At this point, the video track encoding is complete.

Tweaking The Movie's Audio Track

Here's another curve ball for conventional desktop media producers: 8 kHz audio—as opposed to the 11.025, 22.050, and 44.1 kHz MPC standards. If you've been making VDOLive movies, you'll already be used to this new standard and the issues it raises.

The main problem with 8 kHz audio is that Wintel multimedia tools generally handle audio with only MPC attributes. In other words, if you have a WAV file (or a movie with a sound track) with an audio sampling rate of 8 kHz, you'll be lucky if your Windows audio tool even loads the file (let alone saves it with a sampling rate other than 11.025, 22.050, or 44.1). Sophisticated applications like Premiere for Windows can often load such non-MPC audio but are unable to save it in a non-MPC format.

Enter Sound Forge 4.0. If you already have this program, you know how great it is. If you don't, it is an indispensable solution for working with Windows-based desktop audio at all quality levels. We'll use it in the recipe that follows to perform several operations in the same session.

1. One of the cooler things about Sound Forge is that it can open an AVI movie and allow you to edit the movie's audio track in place (without separating it from the video track). You can then save the whole movie without re-compressing the video track, just as if you had detached the audio track, edited it in a separate program, then reattached it to the compressed video track. Figure 7.24 shows Sound Forge's main UI with H261TEST.AVI opened.

Note! *Some desktop audio pros may disapprove of the over-all fatness of this waveform and the apparent clipping in spots, but the clip is noisy to begin with. More importantly, streaming audio (with less rich attributes than CD-ROM-based audio) needs to run somewhat hotter to be as dramatic as possible.*

2. We'll do two things to this audio track: Normalization and re-sampling to 8 kHz (8,000 samples per second). Normalization ensures

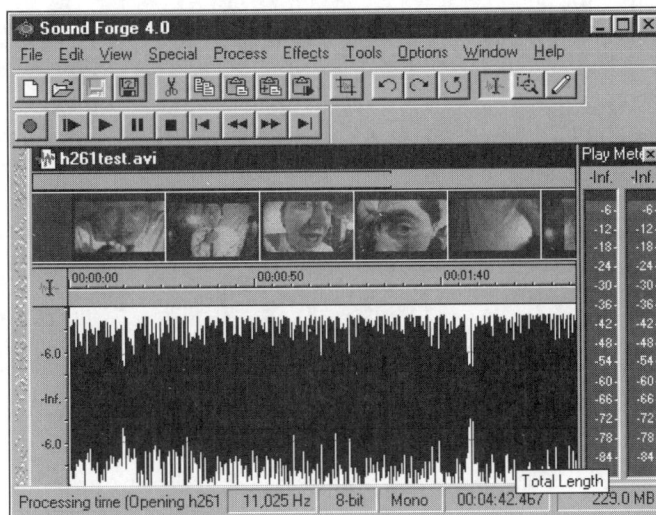

Figure 7.24 H261TEST.AVI opened for business.

that the audio frequencies are spread across as wide a band as possible without peaking. This may seem a wasted miracle for this particular movie, but it's always good practice to normalize any audio clip. Figure 7.25 shows Sound Forge's Normalization panel, which is invoked via the Normalize item in the Process menu.

3. To resample this audio track, select the Resample item from the Process menu. The dialog box in Figure 7.26 will appear. You can key in 8,000 directly or use the up and down arrows to the right of the edit field to change the existing value. If you need information about the rest of the controls in this dialog box (or any of Sound Forge's control panels), just click on the Help button. Sound Forge's help system is quite extensive.

4. With these two operations complete, we can now exit Sound Forge by doing a File|Save, then File|Exit (or just clicking on the top right corner and confirming that we want to save the AVI file with the edited audio track). Serious desktop producers will likely want to edit their movies and audio-only clips in other ways as well, which Sound Forge can do in spades.

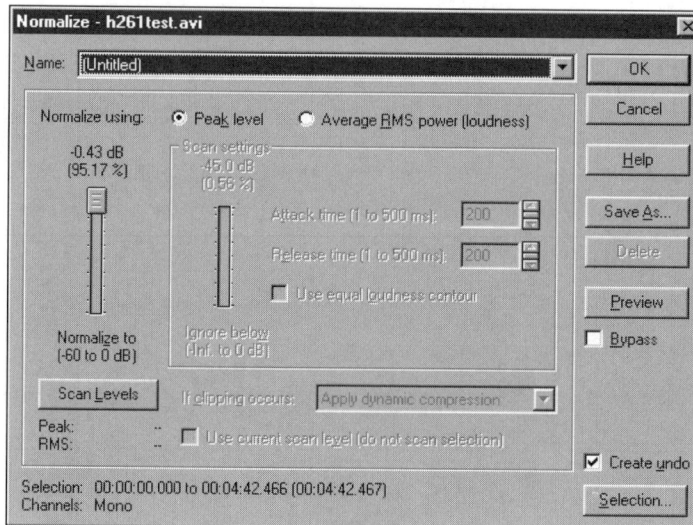

Figure 7.25 Normalizing H261TEST.AVI.

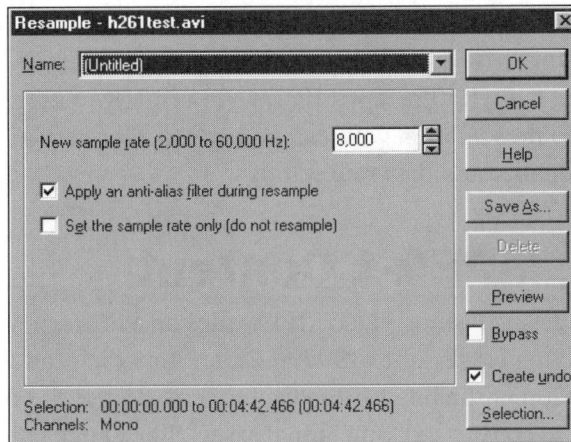

Figure 7.26 Resampling H261TEST.AVI to 8 kHz.

To make sure that a video compressor does the best possible job within the constraints of a specified data rate, some producers like to encode movies in Premiere without an audio track, then edit and attach the audio track after the video is compressed. Sound Forge is up to this task as well. Also note that, for quick and dirty jobs, the Windows 95 Sound Recorder allows you to save WAV files in some non-MPC formats (such as 8 kHz), as shown in Figure 7.27.

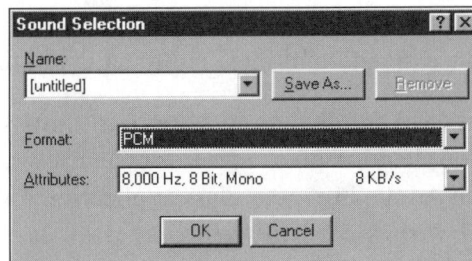

Figure 7.27 Resampling to 8kHz with the Windows Sound Recorder.

This movie is now ready for multicasting. You can make a Precept .SVR file for it (see chapter 6), play it with Precept's IP/TV Server, and receive it with Precept's IP/TV Viewer. If you are unsatisfied with the video presentation, you can go back to Premiere and experiment with the quality and data rate settings.

Producing MPEG-1 Content

Capturing desktop video MPEG files on a PC from video tape is still an evolving art. Prior to 1997, most multimedia production firms did not own top of the line MPEG capture boards, nor did they have a reliable way to convert existing digital assets (like QuickTime and AVI movies) to and from the MPEG file format. As noted earlier, see Chapter 1 for a more complete discussion of the various flavors of MPEG.

Both of the previous situations are now changing as industrial strength MPEG capture gear drops below the $10,000 price point and companies like Digigami (**www.digigami.com**), with its MegaPeg solution, bring to market good conversion utilities.

A good example of high-end hardware is FutureTel's PrimeView II board, a very high-quality MPEG encoding machine. Unlike with QuickTime and AVI, the PrimeView II's capture and compression are both done simultaneously in realtime, producing finished MPEG clips at the end of the capture session. Unfortunately, professional MPEG *editing* suites (like Premiere) have not fully converged on the PC desktop (in the estimation of most multimedia producers).

Of course, we are dealing in some fairly gross generalities here, but production demographics speak for themselves. Simply put, there is not yet an Adobe Premiere-class application for editing MPEG media captured with a card in the same class as the PrimeView II. As software-only MPEG playback proliferates, however, this situation should change dramatically.

Unfortunately, the current version of Precept's IP/TV software does not allow you to multicast native MPEG files, such as ones captured with the PrimeView II. Precept plans to offer this capability in the near future.

Other Tools

As most practitioners will testify, Windows software for multimedia production has improved faster than corresponding software on the Mac in the last few years. This is not surprising given the standardization of Video for Windows, QuickTime for Windows, and ActiveMovie in the market and in developer communities.

That being said, there are still some useful (if aging) tools out there—some used in areas other than desktop video production—that come in handy occasionally or just keep on giving. The balance of this chapter summarizes these additional tools.

VidEdit And VidCap

According to Microsoft, the Windows 3.1 (16-bit) versions of these two complementary programs are as old as the hills. But, while 32-bit versions exist, you can only get them by subscribing to the Microsoft Developer Network (MSDN) Level 2. Sources for the 16-bit apps include Microsoft's FTP site and the temporarily discontinued JumpStart CD-ROM, also published by Microsoft.

Next to Premiere, VIDCAP.EXE and VIDEDIT.EXE are probably the most widely-used programs for capturing and compressing video under Windows, despite the fact that many Mac developers have never heard of them. Some people prefer these apps just because they don't want to spend $500 or so for Premiere—a questionable motivation.

Many high-end Windows capture cards include proprietary capture programs as part of the package. If you can make the cards work with VidCap instead, you'll likely be less frustrated in the long run—assuming you are making Web, multicast, or CD-ROM movies and do not need to output to video tape.

VidEdit (VidCap's companion program) is vastly underrated. Hidden in VidEdit's modest user interface are facilities for cropping, scaling (resizing), creating palettes, replacing audio and video tracks, and importing/exporting other types of multimedia files (like bitmaps and FLC clips). Straight-ahead tasks, like compressing raw captures, are a snap after you do it a few times.

As noted earlier, relatively simple apps like VidEdit seem to only work with media files that conform to so-called MPC specifications—such as 8-bit/22.05 kHz/monaural audio attributes. In other words, a streaming media file encoded with, say, 8 kHz audio cannot be loaded or output by VidEdit.

Adobe Photoshop

Like Premiere, Photoshop is the reigning heavyweight in its field. Nearly any still image file that will decorate a Web page or be imported into a Premiere movie project can be processed with confidence in Photoshop, with either the Mac or Windows version. Photoshop is such a powerful program, in fact, that it can seem overwhelming at first. Once you get the hang of it, however, you'll get productive fast. For the record, Ulead's Photo Impact is already a close second on the Wintel side and coming on strong.

MoviePlayer And ConvertToMovie

MoviePlayer and ConvertToMovie are the simple movie playing and editing apps associated with the runtime version of QuickTime for the Mac. Clicking on a movie file in a Finder window will usually invoke MoviePlayer (if the movie is a MoviePlayer document according to its file type and creator tags).

With the 2.0 (and higher) version, you can obtain detailed information about the properties of a QuickTime clip; cut, copy, and paste frames; add and remove audio and video tracks; and save the clip for playback on the Microsoft Windows desktop.

ConvertToMovie is one of the least complicated ways to re-compress a QuickTime clip and can also be used for cropping, scaling, palette creation, and a few other tasks (like VidEdit on the Windows side). Unfortunately, ConvertToMovie is somewhat useless for anyone who uses Premiere on a regular basis.

MovieShop Vs. Movie Cleaner Pro

In the first golden era of QuickTime, not everybody had Premiere. Production often took the form of capture with MovieRecorder (now retired), rough edit with MoviePlayer, and final compression with a third-party app (written by George Cossey) called MovieShop.

Apple has alternately supported and back-pedaled MovieShop, seemingly based on their mood of the moment, but it remains a warhorse of the desktop video industry, especially for quarter-screen (and smaller) QuickTime clips. In the opinion of most producers, the best version is 1.14, if you can find a copy. A guide to using it effectively can be found in the book *How to Digitize Video*, ISBN: 0-471-01440-0.

Interestingly enough, and in spite of the long shadow cast by Premiere, a possibly worthy successor to MovieShop has appeared on the scene: Movie Cleaner Pro, developed by Terran Interactive, (408) 278-9026. This dedicated app has some advanced features that give it at least a temporary edge over similar features in Premiere, including high-quality smoothing and gamma filters, and the ability to have a guaranteed high-resolution last frame (great for movie credits).

SoundEdit16

Macromedia's SoundEdit16 is an audio file editor of almost the same class as the Windows app Sound Forge. Like Sound Forge, one of SoundEdit16's handier features is the ability to open a movie file and just work on its sound track, as opposed to stripping off the sound track beforehand.

All the essential functionality is there: down-sampling, normalization, EQ, noise reduction, etc. All the popular file formats are supported for importing and outputting. More sophisticated (and more expensive) Mac sound tools are available, but this is the one to start with. For more information, call Macromedia at (415) 252-2000.

DeBabelizer

The Swiss Army Knife of bitmapped graphics converters for the Mac, especially for batch operations. A Windows version is reported to be in development. Most multimedia producers depend on this program. Ignore it at your own risk. For more information, call Equilibrium Technologies at (415) 332-4343.

After Effects

Premiere on steroids—and at a commensurate price. After Effects is sworn at by people without the patience to learn its initially obtuse user interface and sworn by broadcast pros who know how to get great results from it. For more information, call Aldus at (206) 622-5500.

Cross-Platform Production Software

If you need to convert from QuickTime to AVI or vice versa, you can see why the point is made earlier that this is a tool-centric environment. A proven Windows program that converts without re-compression is TRMOOV.EXE, available at the Web site **www.downrecs.com**. On the Mac side, there is a pair of Microsoft apps (one for each conversion direction) that can be extracted from the file QTAVI.ZIP in the CompuServe forum WINMM, Library 4 (GO WINMM). These utilities are covered in more detail in Chapter 13.

Summary

What's worth remembering from this chapter? Two important points:

- In general, you can continue to capture and edit desktop video and audio with your existing multimedia production tools, then compress it to multicast format as the final step.

- MPEG is finally coming on strong. Some of the emerging streaming codecs are based on MPEG technology. As a desktop videographer, it is worth getting involved with the hardware and software used in MPEG movie production. By the time you read this, you should be able to multicast native MPEG files with Precept's IP/TV.

As you upgrade your Windows or Mac (or cross-platform) studio to accommodate the demands of multicast media preparation, you will likely find more and better applications that will save you time and effort. The ones presented in this chapter made their mark in the first wave of new media production but will continue to be useful for serious multicasters.

Chapter 8

- **Setting up for live multicasting**

- **Working with mobile multicast systems**

- **Maintaining a multicast production studio**

8

Live Multicasting And Maintaining A Production Studio

This chapter brings together several disparate though important areas of multicasting: live multicast transmissions, multicasting with mobile equipment (laptops, for instance), and maintaining a studio for producing multicast video content. If you plan to do any serious work in these areas, the material that follows will equip you with some basic knowledge and a solid working perspective.

As discussed in other chapters, so-called live multicasting is not limited to sending a realtime camera feed across a network. One of the beauties of software developed by companies like Precept and Starlight is the ability to stream video digitized in realtime from VCRs and other analog video equipment. In other words, it doesn't matter whether the analog video source is a camera or a video tape deck, as long as the capture card can digitize the analog video signal in realtime.

In the section that follows, we'll demonstrate a couple of live multicast sessions using Precept software's IP/TV Server and Viewer, using both a camera feed and an NTSC video signal from a consumer VCR. Starlight's solution is covered in Chapter 14.

Note! *This demonstration features IP/TV v1.5, still in beta when this book was written. The version of IP/TV on the companion CD-ROM is 1.1.*

Live Multicasting

IP/TV Server (v1.5 beta) basically supports two types of video capture cards: FutureTel and Video for Windows compatible—such as the Intel Smart Video Recorder Pro (ISVRP). This section covers operations on a machine using the FutureTel PrimeView II MPEG card. To expedite the following demo, we've already connected a VCR to our PrimeView board using composite video and the built-in audio jacks (as opposed to going through our PC's sound card).

Running The IP/TV Server With A VCR

The procedure here is actually quite similar to multicasting using a video camera, as you'll see in a moment. To begin, double click on the shortcut icon for the IP/TV Server or fire it up from the Start|Programs menu. The main UI appears as shown in Figure 8.1.

Note! *If you have a video capture card installed, a brief message confirming this will flash on your desktop as the IP/TV Server initializes. If you don't see this message, you should make sure your capture card is installed correctly and functioning normally with your favorite movie capture application.*

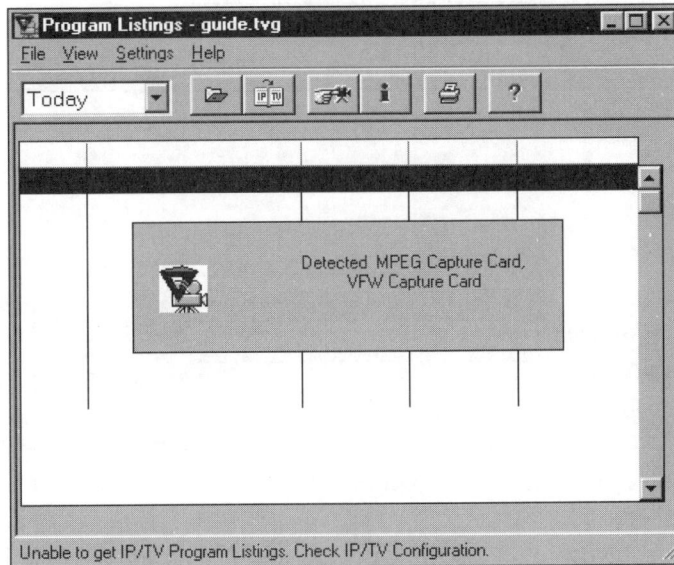

Figure 8.1 The main IP/TV Server interface.

Now, go ahead and execute the following steps:

1. From the File menu, select the Launch Session item, as shown in Figure 8.2.

2. The Precept IP/TV Server dialog box will appear, as shown in Figure 8.3.

3. In the Files Of Type combo box, select the Capture Session item, then click on the SAMPLE.CAP file that should appear by default in the main list box. These items are shown pre-selected in Figure 8.3.

Figure 8.2 Launching an IP/TV session.

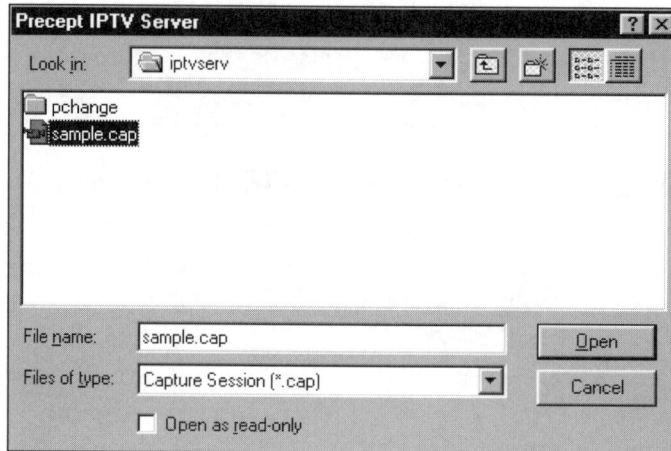

Figure 8.3   Selecting a session type.

4. Now, click on the Open button. A message box stating *Initializing Capture Card* should appear briefly, followed by the IP/TV MPEG Server panel (Figure 8.4). As noted in the bottom-right corner, a Live Capture Session is active (even though it is not previewed in the movie window).

5. Make sure a tape is playing in the VCR, then we'll take a look at what's being multicast to an IP/TV Viewer.

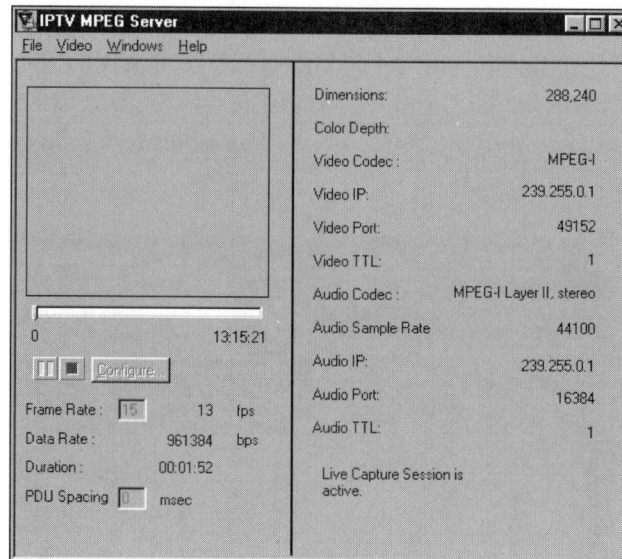

Figure 8.4   The IP/TV MPEG Server control panel.

Note! *Remember that, because multicasting is quite labor-intensive for the CPU, any user input (like clicking on menu items and performing subsequent actions) may adversely affect the Server's performance.*

Receiving A VCR Stream With The IP/TV Viewer

Now, let's fire up the Viewer on another machine (on the local LAN). Performing the following actions should tune in the stream from the VCR we just started multicasting live from the IP/TV Server. For the sake of this demonstration, the steps will be similar to those in the Viewer test drive in Chapter 6.

1. Double click on the IP/TV Viewer shortcut icon (or invoke it using Start Programs). As the Viewer application gets rolling, you will first see the splash panel, which will segue into the Program Listings user interface, shown in Figure 8.5.

Note! *If we were connected to a server that had a Program Guide available, we could retrieve it and populate the Viewer UI with scheduled programs. For now, all we want to do is see the live content that the IP/TV Server is multicasting.*

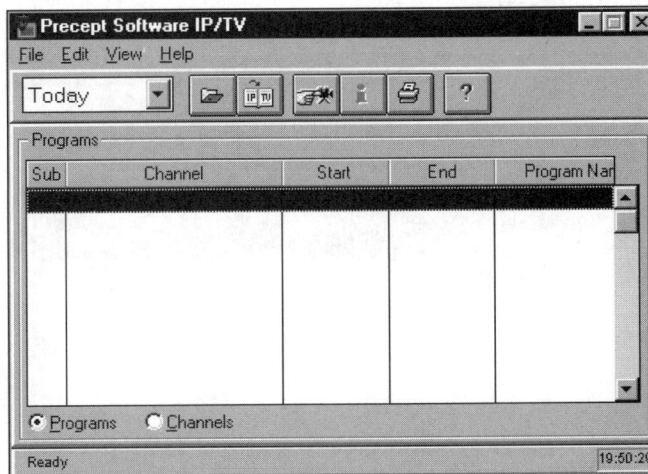

Figure 8.5 The IP/TV Viewer Program Guide.

2. From the File menu, select the Open item. Like in the test drive in Chapter 6, a File Open dialog box will appear asking you to select a file with an .SDP extension (see Figure 8.6). Again, this is a text file containing information concerning the movie about to be viewed.

3. As noted, the IP/TV Viewer comes with two sample SDP files, as shown in Figure 8.6. For this demo, choose the one named *SAMPLE.SDP*.

4. After a moment, the Viewer window shown in Figure 8.7 will come up, along with the live movie being multicast from the Server, complete with good quality audio (depending on the audio quality inherent in the movie itself).

As in the Viewer test drive, you might want to take a minute to play around with the controls in the Viewer window. As you'll see, these controls allow you to:

• Adjust the movie volume

• Scale the movie window size

• Toggle between color and black and white

• Start, stop, and pause the movie

And don't forget the IP/TV Viewer's more advanced features, as shown in Figure 8.8.

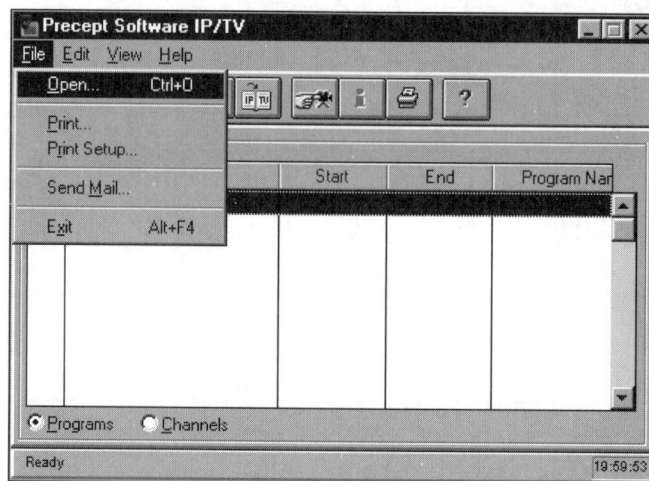

Figure 8.6 Selecting an SDP file.

Figure 8.7 Receiving the live (VCR-based) multicast movie.

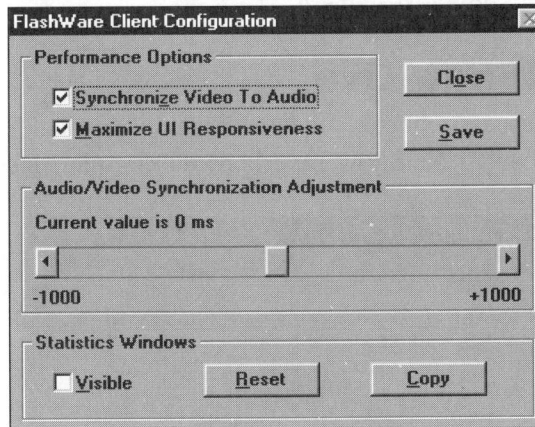

Figure 8.8 The IP/TV Viewer's advanced features.

It's worth repeating that if you have other clients on your LAN, you can run the IP/TV Viewer application and tune in the live multicast on those machines also, with the same level of performance for all (such is the beauty of multicasting). Assuming your systems are functioning smoothly, this is the basic live multicasting experience using Precept's IP/TV Server and Viewer, at least on a LAN.

Running The IP/TV Server With A Video Camera

To multicast a truly live video clip, simply substitute a video camera for the VCR used in the demonstration in the previous section. Of course, the video camera must have audio and video out jacks, which are not present on all consumer class camcorders. Most prosumer (and higher) video equipment, however, does have these features.

Assuming you're using a professional grade camera, possibly on a tripod, properly cabled to your capture card, with your talent/subject cued to start performing, you can execute Steps 1 through 4 presented in the Server/VCR section to start your genuinely live multicast.

With the live performance underway, you can inform your audience that it's time to tune in (assuming the event wasn't already scheduled) using Steps 1 through 4 in the Viewer/VCR demonstration presented earlier. Figure 8.9 shows a screen shot of a talking head multicast shot with a Sony Hi-8 camera.

NetShow Live

Because this chapter concerns live multicasting, it is worth mentioning Microsoft's NetShow Live here for completeness. As already noted,

Figure 8.9 A live multicast from a video camera.

however, the current version of NetShow Live only supports audio. Several demonstrations of multicasting stored audio are presented elsewhere in this book (for instance, in Chapter 6). For the latest information, you can always monitor the pages at **www.microsoft.com/netshow**.

Microsoft has staged some interesting events to date using this technology, both on the Internet and within their corporate enterprise, but how soon video will be supported is unclear as of the writing of this chapter. Fortunately, it will probably adhere closely to IP Multicast standards, based on Microsoft's positioning so far.

Mobile Systems

Being able to do a live multicast from a camera feed raises some interesting possibilities, and some even more interesting questions. In Chapter 17, for instance, there is coverage of a live MBone multicast called the Summit Of Hope. In this event, several world leaders were shot with video cameras, digitized in realtime, and routed through the MBone—all in realtime.

One of the key technical issues was how to get the video signal to the digitization site/MBone node. In at least one case, this was accomplished by microwaving the video signal from the camera several hundred miles to the MBone access point. In other words, it was easier to bring the analog video stream to the global multicast site than vice versa.

Non-MBone Mobility

So far, this discussion is based on the idea that you want to be the publisher, and that you want to do so on the MBone. If you only want to consume MBone multicasts, you should read Chapter 15. In general, your mobility will be a function of MBone ISP availability and the type of router you are using with your mobile system (it needs to support multicast protocols).

If you want to publish MBone content on an internetwork (as opposed to the MBone proper), your mobility will be limited by the availability (and compatability) of high speed communications lines (such as ISDN), as well as router technology. In other words, you may be bypassing the global Internet, but you may be limited by a whole new set of problems.

As you can see already, the issues surrounding mobile multicasting are complex and almost impossible to solve at this point—let alone put into the proper perspective. The best advice here may be to set these questions aside until you finish the later chapters in this book, then take them up again with a better understanding of the limits of this technology.

Maintaining A Multicast Production Studio

Setting up a facility for multicast media production is a lot like building a traditional multimedia studio. The decision to use Mac gear or PC equipment will likely be a function of the environment in which you are most comfortable, as opposed to the relative merits of either. If you've had positive experiences working on both platforms, you will probably incorporate elements of each, particularly if your media is cross-platform.

Because of market pressures, Mac developers are more likely to venture into the Windows world than vice versa. The fact remains, however, that experienced Windows-based media makers will still be lured by the top-notch digitization they can achieve with high-end Mac capture devices.

The Abstract System

In Chapter 5, we discussed an abstract media capture station composed of abstract components (see Figure 8.10). The idea was to visualize how those components work together (or limit each other) based on understanding the potential bottlenecks. When building your own Web media studio, you might consider using that abstract model as an overlay for the actual components you plan to integrate.

Regardless of your production platform (Mac or PC), there are some basic habits you should consider for the day-to-day operation of your computer systems and analog media hardware. These practices fall into two categories: technical and practical.

TECHNICAL SETUP RECOMMENDATIONS

These tips are based on several years of desktop video production experience and can save time when you need it most—such as when a deadline is looming.

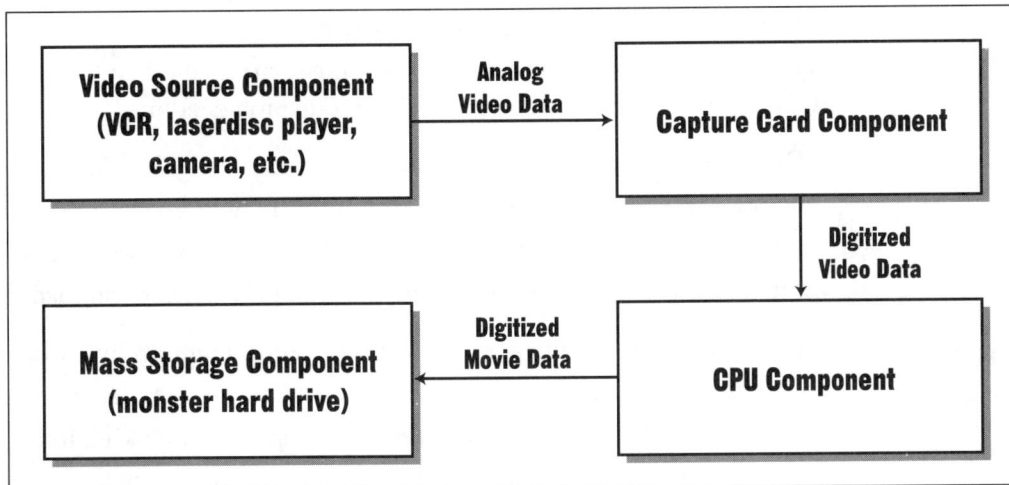

Figure 8.10 The abstract capture station.

- Number your SCSI devices in the order they are connected on your physical SCSI chain. For instance, make your external hard drive SCSI ID 1, the CD-ROM drive SCSI ID 2, your Jaz or Zip drive 3, and so on, assuming they are connected in that order.

- Consider your big, external hard drives as rapid deployment gear, ready for space-hungry raw captures at any given time. If you have both Mac and PC capture stations, keeping a big hard drive wiped clean between capture sessions will let you switch it between the two platforms with a minimum of overhead.

- While products like DeskLink and LapLink are fine for moving small files between computers without the overhead of a LAN, don't consider them for day-to-day transfers of movie files—especially raw movies. Serial port products just aren't fast enough compared to LANs and hard drive (or Jaz cartridge) swaps.

- For realtime editing with possibly hundreds of MBs worth of raw clips, burning those files to CD (to free up hard drive space) can backfire if your CD-ROM drive is too slow (under 4X). If you want fast previews and updates in your Premiere Construction window, plan on keeping your working clips on a hard disk—unless you have a speed-demon CD-ROM drive.

PRACTICAL SETUP RECOMMENDATIONS

Again, most of these tips are based on doing it wrong the first time and wasting time better spent on meeting a production deadline.

- Draw some stick diagrams of your work area on a yellow legal pad before shelling out for any new furniture. Include power and data cable paths in the sketches. Check with building authorities to make sure the existing circuitry can handle the increased electrical load.

- Use reinforced metal racks for all your equipment. Why torture expensive wood-grain tables and shelves with the inevitable wear and tear? Anthro carts (**www.anthro.com**) are worth looking into if you expect to move pieces of your studio around very much.

- Do you need a CD-ROM burner in your multicast media studio? The short answer is probably *yes*, if only for making archives and keeping clients happy. Burners are relatively cheap now, and the software that runs them has matured greatly.

- Give all your gear lots of space to breathe. In other words, only keep one or two components on each shelf, and ensure that there is air space between them. Temperature issues notwithstanding, you'll want continuous and convenient access to all cable connections (even if you don't think so now).

- Even if your work area is relatively small, leave adequate room behind your racks for going back there to re-cable and track down bad connections. You'll be glad you did.

- If your computers are of the desktop variety—as opposed to the tower models—don't pile peripheral gear on top of them (such as big hard drives or even monitors). If you do lots of production, you'll find yourself opening up your machines frequently to swap adapter cards, add RAM, and even upgrade Pentium chips. Few things are more grim than clearing heavily-wired components off your CPU when you need to re-terminate your SCSI adapter card—or watching the whole lot crash to the floor if the equipment was stacked carelessly.

- Color code your cables (don't laugh). Yellow is good for video, white for the left audio channel, and red for the right. If you can stand it, label each end of your serial, telephone, and SCSI cables with a strip of tape. Okay, laugh a little—but if you don't someone else might be laughing later.

- Use switch boxes as necessary (for at least audio and serial cables), but be careful how you arrange the wires. To prevent buzzing and general electrical interference, avoid coiling of data cables and having them in close proximity to power cables. Check out **www.vir.com/ cablek** for some ideas on this subject.

Building A Mac-based Web Media Studio

As of this writing, most professional Mac movie makers have invested in Power Macs as their workhorse CPUs. The standard 8100 is still somewhat common (with lots of extra RAM), but many media producers have by now invested into 9500—and beyond.

If you have a Quadra 840AV, or even a Quadra 950 that continues to make movies reliably, there is no reason to give it up. Because multicast clips easily may be less than quarter screen, new life can be breathed into many older Macs, at least for the time being. You probably wanted to use that new 950 to browse with anyway. Figure 8.11 shows the basic components of a multicast media production station, including two CPUs for LAN testing.

Building A PC-based Media Studio

Again, as of this writing, most professional Windows-based movie makers have invested in Pentiums (with lots of extra RAM) as their workhorse CPUs. Many are also running Windows NT. Like with Quadra-era Macs, if you have a 486 that keeps on giving (as in making movies reliably), there is no reason to retire it from show business.

Miscellaneous Equipment

Without a few boxes of loose cables, connectors, and adapters, you have no right to hang out your desktop media production shingle. Following is a short list of the types of spare parts you'll want to have handy. For brevity, it's expressed in techno-geek, but any Radio Shack salesperson will be able to help you without a fuss.

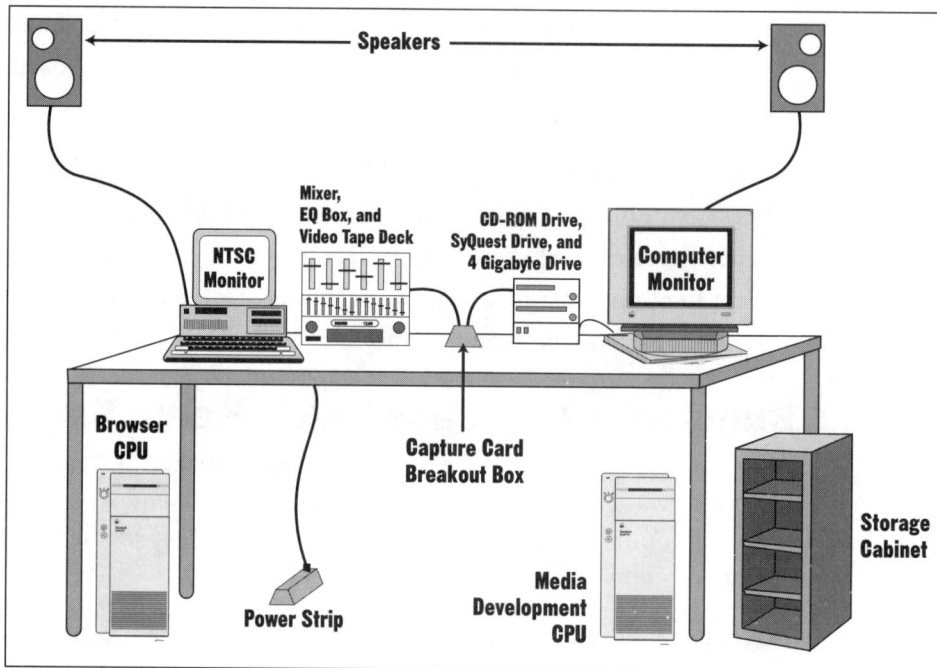

Figure 8.11 A multicast media production station.

And don't forget lots of blank video tapes, head cleaner tapes, extra batteries, a charger for your video camera, and a supply of blank CD-ROMs, if you decide to get a burner.

- Loose audio and composite video cables

- Loose S-video cables

- Loose SCSI cables with various SCSI connectors (SCSI 1, SCSI 2, and so forth)

- Loose modem and other RS-232 cables

- Y connectors

- RCA to phone jack (and plug) adapters

- RCA to mini phone jack (and plug) adapters

- Phone jack to mini phone jack (and plug) adapters

- BNC to RCA and BNC to phone jack connectors

And the list goes on. Imagine, you're on a deadline for the next morning with rented gear. Around midnight you determine that some re-cabling is necessary, but you've already used up your modest supply. Unfortunately, most Radio Shacks are not yet 24-hour stores. Who are you going to call? This stuff really happens.

Other miscellaneous items like microphones, headphones, and cheap analog audio components like mixers and EQ boxes will also come in handy sooner or later, as will rip-ties and other types of cable organizers. Don't forget a generous selection of tools either—like various gauges of screwdrivers and a pair of needle nose pliers.

Note! *It's worth mentioning video device control here, but the subject has become less crucial for producers of multimedia assets. If you need to control the operation of your video deck from your Mac or PC, you can get more information from Adobe Tech support or by searching on MCI device control at the Microsoft Web site.*

Video Equipment Issues

As for analog video equipment, the more work you do, the more you will handle content provided by unpredictable clients. Despite the changing aesthetic and quality issues, such content will often be in Betacam SP format. This can mean renting a Betacam deck, the cost of which should be passed through to the client, if possible.

These are big issues for small desktop media production shops. Beta decks are expensive and do not decrease in price over time at the same rate as personal computers. Buying one outright can seem non-cost efficient until, a year later, when you look at how all those rentals added up. If you have the vision to know you're going to be in business a year from now, buying a Beta deck on credit may be an acceptable risk.

Because this chapter is about setting up a media production studio, I thought you might want to get into a little more detail than a general overview. Therefore, the rest of the chapter is devoted to understanding less common (but potentially threatening) analog video problems and the technical standards for analog video equipment.

Time Base Correction

If you don't have a background in analog video, you may not recognize time base correction (TBC) problems when you first see them. Often they appear as a particularly jagged form of distortion, but sometimes there are related symptoms as well. Most Betacam decks have some type of TBC already built in. Some top drawer Hi-8 units also have them, but you'll need to consult the manual to be sure.

TBC troubles stem from a number of factors.

- Video tape performance is a function of the tape transport mechanism inside a deck (or camera). The precision-tooled components comprising the transport can malfunction and skew the timing processes involved in the generation of video signal. This results in so-called synchronization problems, which are common in Hi-8 and 8mm gear. One visible result, a wavering picture, is known as *flag-waving*.

- Sometimes analog color and brightness values don't translate efficiently to digital values. This happens frequently with NTSC signals (Never The Same Color, as video pros like to joke) and produces level and chroma noise problems. The visual effect is colors that are too hot and blurry.

Because consumer video gear is more tolerant of TBC problems than Mac and PC digitization equipment, distortion in your captured clips might not be evident on your NTSC monitor. The only good way to solve TBC problems is with a time base corrector. Most of the pro TBC products are standalone boxes, ranging in price from roughly $1,000 to $1,500, although TBC add-in cards are also available.

Key features to look for are:

- Infinite window memory. This is very important for Hi-8 and 8mm VTRs.

- Composite and S-video ins and outs.

- Processing amplifier controls (for adjusting color, intensity, and saturation).

- Frame synchronization, phase controls, dropout compensation, freeze frame, and remote control.

Dropout Problems

Dropout happens when particles of metal oxide are detached from the surface of a video tape. Because those particles contain video information, the resultant video image will contain speckles when you play the tape. Hi-8 tape is notorious for dropouts.

Two big causes of dropouts are:

- Tape cartridges are not conditioned properly and thus contain uneven and loose particles. Normal recording dislodges those bogus elements, resulting in lost video data (a.k.a. dropout). A good way to condition your tapes is to record onto them all the way through in one pass (without an incoming video signal) then rewind to the beginning. This also helps pack your tape by relieving tight winding patches introduced at the factory.

- Moisture seeps into recorded tapes and then evaporates. This produces rocky areas on the tape surface. Playing the tape makes the tape heads do further damage to the craggy surface.

There is not much you can do once the damage is done. Some analog gear contains dropout compensation circuitry, but no device can restore actual lost data. The best medicine is prevention: treat all your analog media with great care. In terms of everyday video problems, TBC and dropout are arguably the most common.

If you work exclusively with Beta quality tape, you may never have to deal with these problems because Beta decks and cameras normally prevent them from being introduced in the first place.

Transferring Film To Video

A whole separate industry exists for transferring Super 8 home movies to VHS cassettes (check out Video in the Yellow Pages). Expensive, dedicated machines do the transfers. Quality can vary greatly, depending on the experience of the technician.

If you have film you want to transfer to video, let a service bureau do it. Aiming a video camera at a film projected on a screen might work in a pinch, but the resultant video will flicker—just like computer screens or television monitors you see in TV programs.

When commercial movies are transferred to video for television broadcast, they are scanned frame by frame and stored digitally on D1 tape (or higher). Moving films to commercial laser discs is essentially the same process, but may not come up to broadcast standards.

A final process worth noting is 3/2 pull-down. You will likely hear this mentioned in technical deliberations concerning film-to-video transfer. 3/2 pull-down is basically a process in which 24 frames per second (film) are converted to 30 frames per second (video).

More On Video Decks

Of all the video gear connected to your workstation, the VTR is the most crucial for real production chores. For professional video work of any type, an industrial quality deck (at least S-video or Hi-8) is usually essential. If you haven't worked with such equipment before, it can be somewhat intimidating at first.

The remainder of this chapter provides a list of issues to consider when looking for a workhorse VTR. You might not want to walk into Circuit City and try to impress the salesperson with technical minutia, but it can be useful to know the right questions when someone tries to sell you a deck you don't know much about.

Tape Transport

The value of any video deck is a direct function of the quality of its tape transport mechanism. These mechanisms are extremely delicate and subject to malfunction if not treated right, especially in Hi-8, 8mm, and other compact gear. In general, the more expensive the deck, the more sophisticated the tape transport.

The apparatus that impels the transport system is the *servo motor*. The servo drives the fragile appliances that guide the tape through the transport mechanism. As the tape snakes through the system, it drags across the VTR's play and record heads, transferring analog video data (in either play or record mode).

Servos differ greatly in terms of precision. A common way to rate a servo motor is to determine the number of steps it performs in one rotation cycle. Because the servo drives the capstan, which indirectly drives the big cylinder that pulls the tape, more discrete steps means more control over positioning the tape.

In principle, the tape moves through the transport mechanism at a uniform velocity. This guarantees that the video signal stays synchronized. As noted earlier, all hell breaks loose when the tape speed is inconsistent. If you want accuracy to the frame in a VTR, you should get a deck with capstan override (ask the salesperson).

Tape Heads

An important difference between consumer and industrial video tape decks is that most industrial decks have heads that record video and audio simultaneously. They also usually have a flying erase head that erases the tape just prior to recording onto it.

Heads are usually grouped in twos or threes in industrial equipment. In Hi-8 and 8mm machines, however, tape head quantity is generally not as important as tape head width. In other words, the more your tape heads come into contact with the tape surface, the better the quality of the video (and audio).

In most decks, when the machine is not playing or recording, the tape remains in the cartridge (not in the transport system). Pushing the play or record button causes the transport assembly to go to work, pulling the tape out of the cartridge, laying it around the big tape cylinder, and then either playing or recording.

With a so-called full-load deck, the tape is kept in the transport mechanism between transport events (like play and record). The obvious benefits of this feature are faster response time when you push the play or record button, as well as increased stability of the image from when you push play until the tape is up to speed.

Other Video Issues

Some other VTR capabilities to research or ask about when shopping for a deck for your digitization station are:

- Signal to noise (S/N) ratio

- Chroma noise reduction (CNR)

- Time base correction

The S/N ratio gets more favorable as it increases. The official S/N ratios for most VTRs are posted in their manuals. Decent ratings for industrial decks start at about 40db. For broadcast equipment, S/N ratios shouldn't dip below 55db.

Simply stated, chroma noise degrades a video signal. Most industrial decks have built-in CNR, but it is worth asking about to be sure. Some chroma noise is inevitable. Certain manufacturers reduce it effectively, while others do not.

Time base correction is covered earlier in this chapter. Worth noting here is that few Hi-8 or 8mm decks have built-in TBC (unlike most Betacam decks, which do). Perhaps TBC high-quality circuitry will be added to video capture cards (or personal computers themselves) in the future.

Audio Features (In Video Decks)

Design differences abound among prosumer and industrial VTRs when it comes to recording audio. Linear decks allow audio tracks to be recorded without disrupting existing audio (and video) tracks. Nonlinear VTRs permit existing tracks to be overwritten. Also, understand that decks without a dedicated time code channel will use an audio track for recording time code (such as SMPTE).

Most desktop producers capture and compress clips with monaural sound, so this will probably not be a bottleneck. If you want to add additional audio tracks to your AVI or QuickTime movies, you will likely do it in a movie editing program such as Adobe Premiere.

Consumer Decks

There are far fewer technical decisions to make when shopping for a consumer-level VCR than when comparing industrial-grade VTR decks. If you need to postpone purchasing professional equipment, here are some things to think about in regard to off-the-rack VCRs:

- *Picture quality.* This is often a function by the number of heads in the tape transport mechanism. Four-head machines give significantly better performance than two-head VCRs.

- *Stereo versus monaural sound.* As noted earlier, not many of your Web clips will need stereo sound—at least not yet. Don't pay extra for it unless you plan to repurpose the VCR later (like in your home theater).

- *A/V in and out.* Some bargain-basement VCRs don't have these connector capabilities—just the straight coaxial cable jack. Remember to check for color-coded Video In/Video Out and Audio In/Audio Out RCA jacks (usually red and white or yellow and white) on the back of the VCR.

Summary

As shown in this chapter, live multicasting can mean different things to different people. To some, it can mean multicasting an event shot with a video camera and digitized with a PC capture board in realtime. To others, it may mean digitizing an analog tape in realtime (like for CD-ROM distribution) then multicasting that content across a network. Either way, live multicasting has a very significant future on the LAN and on the global Internet.

But don't forget video assets that are already digitized, or that need to be multicast from media such as CD-ROM. To create, edit, and archive digital media professionally, you'll need a full-featured desktop media studio. Following the advice presented in this chapter should help keep this process academic.

Chapter 9

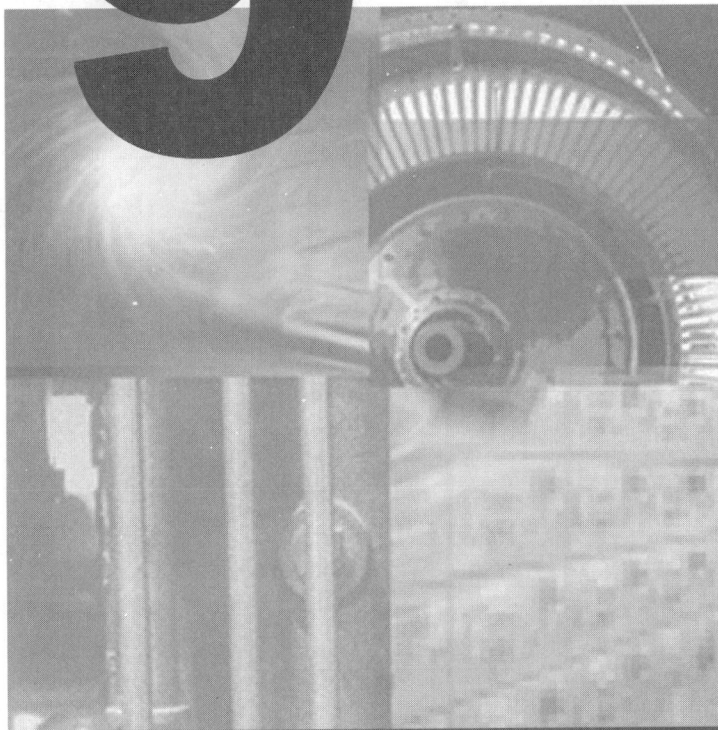

- **Playing multimedia files on a LAN**

- **Serving multimedia assets on LANs and WANs**

- **Understanding the role of an intranet**

Chapter 9

LAN-Based Video

Let's begin this chapter with some simple exercises. If you have a Windows 95 machine connected to a LAN, please step through the following procedure:

1. Right click on the My Computer icon (or whatever you've named your machine).

2. Click on the Map Network Drive menu item.

3. In the Map Network Drive dialog (shown in Figure 9.1), select an appropriate drive letter (let's say G:) in the drop-down list box, then fill in the complete path to a shared drive on a remote computer on your LAN that contains some movie files. For the sake of this exercise, these movies can be standard AVI, QuickTime, or MPEG format (as opposed to streaming movies).

4. Double click on My Computer to see the updated drive list.

5. Double click on G:, and navigate to the folder that contains the movies.

6. Double click on one of the movie files (let's call it mymovie.mpg, assuming it's a non-streaming MPEG file).

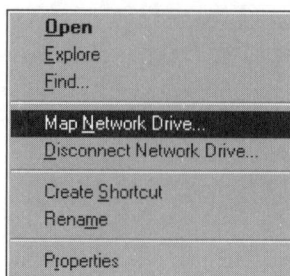

Figure 9.1 Mapping a network drive.

In a second or two, mymovie.mpg should start to play, just as if it resided on your local machine—with the following caveats:

- The proper movie playing software must be installed on your local machine (e.g. ActiveMovie).

- If the movie's data rate exceeds the bandwidth imposed by the network or other LAN traffic while the clip is rolling, playback performance will suffer. At best, this will be manifested by dropped frames and, at worst, audio breakup will occur.

- Other users on other LAN clients may or may not be able to play the movie at the same time, depending on a number of factors not worth going into here.

Setting A Bad Example

Crude as this exercise may be, it demonstrates a basic form of desktop video on the LAN. If you have read Chapter 1, you'll appreciate that it follows the video on demand model: Click on a movie, and it starts to play—right now, from the beginning.

Of course, mymovie.mpg is not a streaming video file, and this is where meaningful comparisons to the newer desktop video technologies start to fall apart. Because mymovie.mpg was specifically encoded for playback from CD-ROM or a local hard drive—as opposed to a LAN or a WAN—we are making our machines participate in a process most inelegant.

In other words, desktop video engines that play movies made for CD-ROM were not originally developed to play such movies over a network, even though we can make them do it, up to a point, as illustrated in the exercise just completed. While these engines (basically QuickTime and Video for Windows) have matured over the last few years, the real work involved in most network streaming solutions is done at the server level and with the help of the new generation of streaming codecs (see Figure 9.2).

Generally speaking, the reason we could get a movie playing in Exercise 1 is that the local machine was treating the clip on the remote computer just like a local file on a local drive—at a deep system level. Clearly, this is how things are supposed to happen in the world of PC networking, but it does make you appreciate the layers of software involved (and cooperating) here.

When QuickTime and Video for Windows were new on the scene (and many multimedia developers were dreaming up solutions in search of problems), this type of LAN-based desktop video delivery seemed almost viable for packaging into commercial products. Fortunately, some other approaches to desktop video on the LAN were also being developed at that time, most notably by Intel and Starlight Networks (as well as several others companies).

Before we look at those other approaches, let's run through one more example of basic-but-wrong-headed LAN video, just to make a point. This second exercise involves a remote client dialing in to a LAN—in effect, a WAN client (though not using traditional WAN protocols).

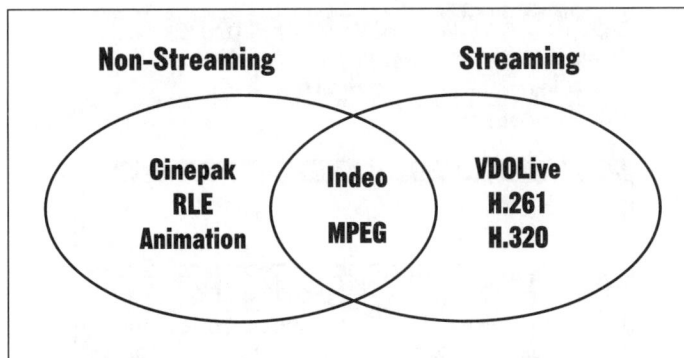

Non-Streaming   **Streaming**

Cinepak
RLE
Animation

Indeo

MPEG

VDOLive
H.261
H.320

Figure 9.2 Old versus new codecs.

Another Marginal Performance

Assuming you have access to both an NT 4.0 Server and a Windows 95 Workstation, both with 28.8 modems attached to separate phone lines, please execute the following two sets of instructions:

On Your Server

Let's get the server set up first. We'll add a New User for this exercise, configured for dial-in privileges.

1. Execute Start|Programs|Administrative Tools (Common)|User Manager for Domains (see Figure 9.3).

2. In the User Manager dialog box, select the New User menu item from the User menu (see Figure 9.4).

3. In the New User dialog box, fill in the fields as shown in Figure 9.5.

4. When all the information is entered, click on the Dialin button at the bottom of the dialog box.

5. In the Dialin Information dialog box, shown in Figure 9.6, put a check in the *Grant dialin permission to user* checkbox. Not that it matters for this exercise, but check the *No Call Back* radio button just to keep things simple.

6. Click on the OK button to exit the Dialin Information dialog box.

7. Click on the Add button to execute the add, and exit the New User dialog box.

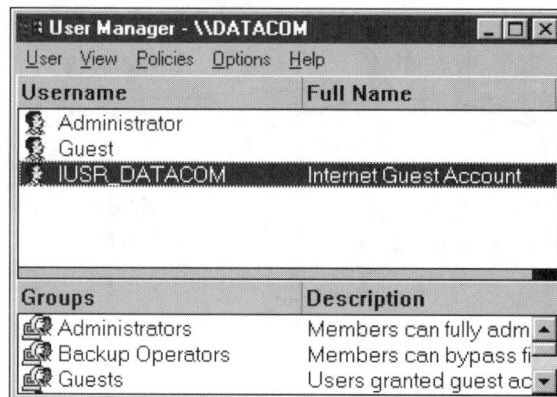

Figure 9.3 Invoking the User Manager.

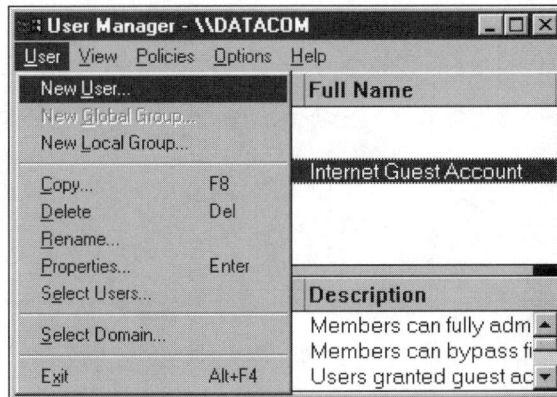

Figure 9.4 Adding a new user.

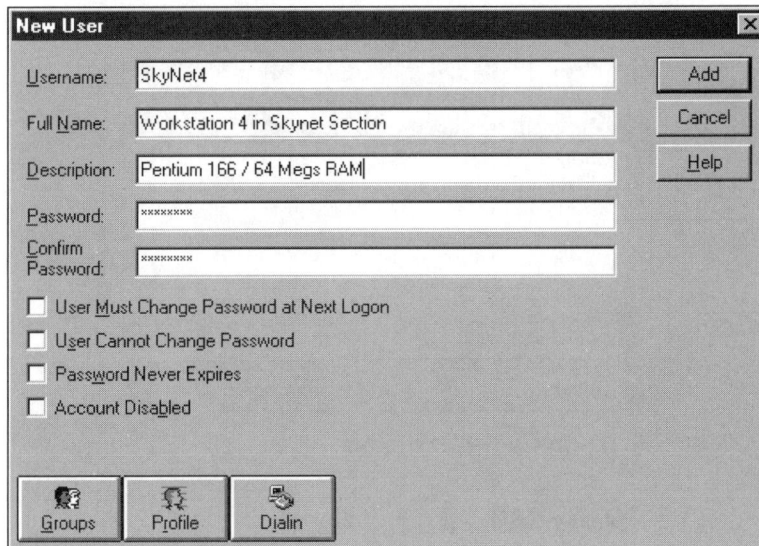

Figure 9.5 Configuring a dialin user.

8. Confirm that the new user shows up in the list of users (see Fig-ure 9.7).

9. Select Exit from the User menu to dismiss the User Manager dialog box.

Your server should now be ready to accept a call from the new user you have specified, and to accept that new user as an otherwise normal LAN client.

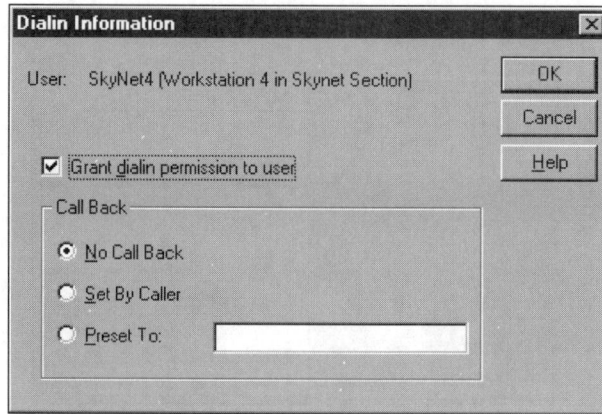

Figure 9.6 Granting the new user dialin permission.

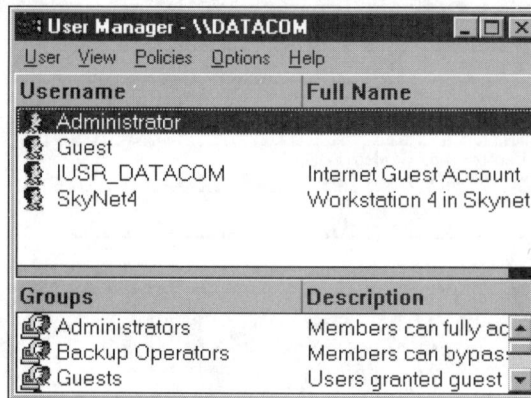

Figure 9.7 The new dialin user is official.

On Your Workstation

Now we'll set up the Workstation so it can call the Server directly. This can easily be deleted following the exercise.

1. Double click on the My Computer icon.

2. In the My Computer window, double click on the Dial-Up Networking folder (assuming you have already configured your machine for dial-up networking).

3. Double click on the Make New Connection item.

4. In the Make New Connection dialog, shown in Figure 9.8, fill in a name for your server (not the official name of the server, just a useful name for this connection item). For the sake of this example, let's use the name *Uncle Enzo*. If you have a modem installed, you should see it listed in this dialog box, as well.

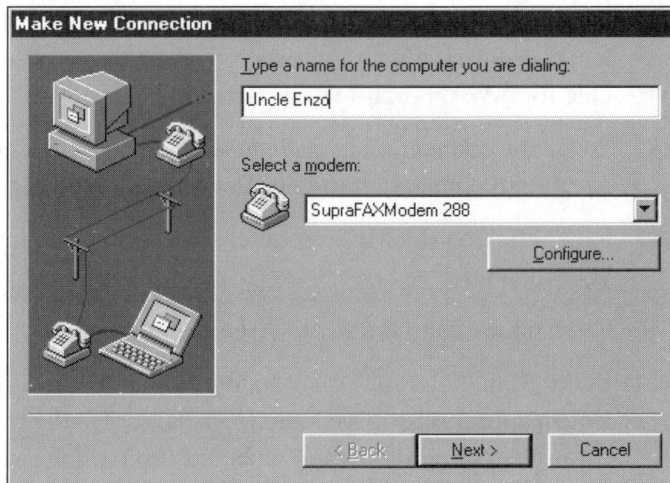

Figure 9.8 The Make New Connection dialog box.

5. Click on the Next button to show the entry fields for the phone number of your server, as shown in Figure 9.9. Enter the appropriate phone number.

6. Click on the Next button, then the Finish button in the following dialog box. There should now be a Uncle Enzo item in the Dial-Up Networking folder. If you wish, you can make a shortcut for quicker testing later.

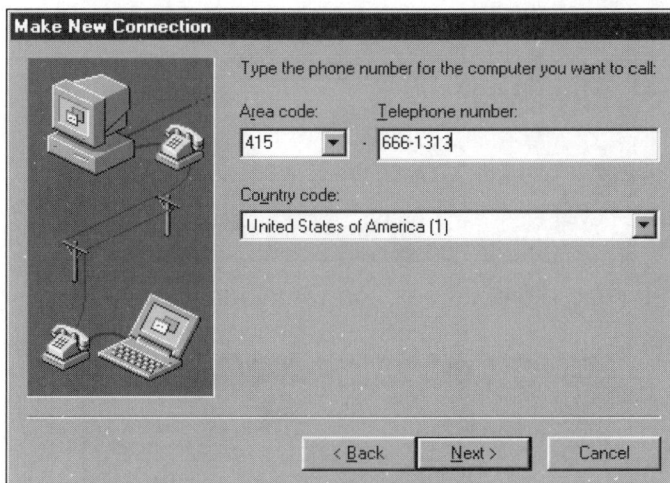

Figure 9.9 Entering the server's phone number.

7. Double click on the Uncle Enzo item (or its shortcut icon) to begin a dial-up session with your server (assuming it is set up and available for a WAN dial-up), as shown in Figure 9.10.

8. When the connection is made, it will look just like confirmation of a standard connection to your favorite ISP (see Figure 9.11).

9. Right click on the My Computer icon (or whatever you've named your machine).

10. Click on the Map Network Drive menu item.

11. In the Map Network Drive dialog box(shown in Figure 9.12), select an appropriate drive letter (let's say G:) in the combo box, then fill in the complete path to a shared drive on the server you have made the connection to. As in our previous exercise, this shared drive should have some movie files on it. Again, for the sake of this example, these movies should be standard AVI, QuickTime, or MPEG format (as opposed to streaming movies).

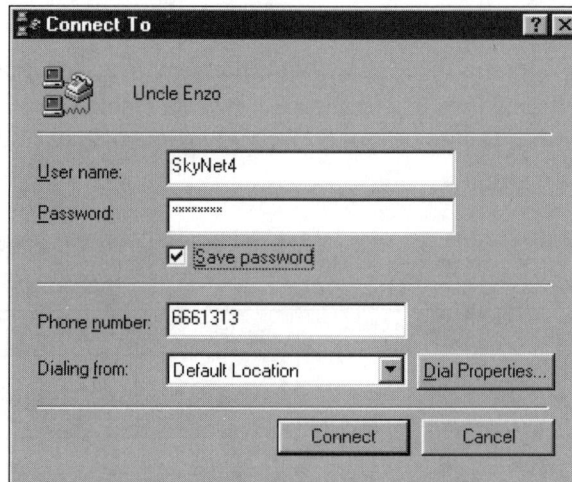

Figure 9.10   Starting a dial-up session with your server.

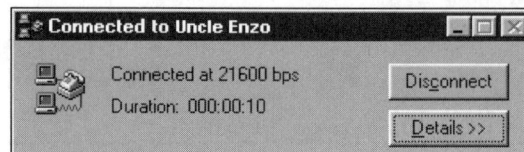

Figure 9.11   A confirmed server connection.

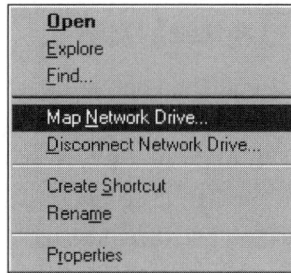

Figure 9.12 Mapping a network drive.

12. Double click on My Computer to see the updated drive list (along with, presumably, drive G:, the shared drive on the dialed-in server).

13. Double click on G:, and navigate to the folder that contains the movies.

14. Double click on one of the movie files (let's call it mymovie2.avi, assuming it's a non-streaming AVI file).

Here's where the bits can really hit the fan. At some point, depending on a number of factors, mymovie2.avi should start to play as if it resided on your local machine. Whether it continues to play with any kind of smoothness is up for grabs. Like in Exercise 1, we also have the following caveats:

• The appropriate movie playing software must be installed. In this case (AVI), support for the file format is built in.

• If the movie's data rate exceeds the bandwidth imposed by the dial-up connection and other LAN traffic while the clip is rolling, playback performance will suffer even more than in Exercise 1. At best, this will be manifested by dropped frames, and, at worst, a total collapse of the playback process will occur.

Establishing A Baseline

Why demonstrate such bad performance? Let's break the answer down. First, remember that the goal of this exercise was to make some particular points. The main point here is that context is everything. For instance, what if we had used two ISDN adapters instead of two 28.8 modems? Would the performance have been as good as in Exercise 1 (where all the computers were on the local LAN)? You'd have to try it to see. If the performance was as good, would you consider using that sort of connection in your business operations?

These questions beg further questions, such as:

- When does older movie playing software itself become a network video performance inhibitor?

- How and when should you upgrade your LAN cards, hubs, and cables?

- Which brand-name products are best for facilitating video on the LAN (and the WAN)?

- What types of benchmarking tools are available for testing LAN/ WAN throughput?

These are big, open ended issues, but they suggest the lack of mature standards (and the wealth of opportunity) on the current LAN-based video scene. Lots of intensive software development is going on in this arena, including work on multicasting products and standards, as we'll see in later chapters.

In effect, the results of Exercise 2 set a worst-case baseline for desktop video performance on a LAN. Let's distill those exercises by considering the following chain of reasoning:

- The simplest way to play a non-streaming desktop video movie is with the player program provided by the engine/codec developer (as with, for example, QuickTime).

- The simplest way to access a remote file on a normal LAN is to log on to its drive after that drive is shared by its local machine.

- The simplest way to become a LAN client via a modem connection, at least under Windows, is by dialing in using Dial-Up Networking/Remote Access.

What happens when you try to play a non-streaming, LAN-based movie by mixing all of these lowest-common-denominator techniques and environments together? Basically, the kind of behavior we saw in the two exercises. Is this still video on demand? Technically speaking, you bet. Is it commercially viable? Not even.

Early LAN-Based Video Streaming

With such a baseline in mind, it is now easy to see why certain forward-looking companies decided to develop streaming software for playing desktop video clips on networks. One of these pioneers was Starlight Networks (see Figure 9.13), a firm now heavily involved in multicasting technology (as described in Chapter 3).

In its initial solutions (circa 1992-93), Starlight enabled servers to continuously *broadcast* video data, as opposed to waiting for file transfer requests from users. Only a fraction of the network bandwidth was utilized by the broadcast, allowing other network traffic to flow normally. Lots of LAN clients could tune into such transmissions, as was often demonstrated by Starlight at trade shows during that period.

Figure 9.13   The Starlight home page.

One of Starlight's particular claims to fame was that they made their proprietary software work with existing consumer systems—as opposed to tweaked high-end machines. Also, the media they used were traditional CD-ROM movies, such as QuickTime clips (remember this was all being done on the LAN, not the WAN), so the visual quality was fairly high.

How Starlight Did It

The following strategies were used by Starlight in its first-generation software:

- Utilizing a proprietary streaming facility to give video data a higher priority than other LAN traffic and a guaranteed bandwidth allocation.

- Allowing a system to treat its SCSI hard disk as a customized hard drive array, for which no caching is necessary.

- Intercepting data as it arrived at a client machine, and then processing it more efficiently than other resident network drivers.

History has proven that Starlight had the right ideas at the right time, enough so that they are still at the forefront of the network media streaming industry. Because they are now involved in marrying these and other strategies to the TCP/IP and IP Multicast protocols (again, check out the section on them in Chapter 3), Starlight should be able to push its success even further.

Interestingly enough, Starlight is not in the codec business, streaming or otherwise (at least not as of this writing). What they are expert at is the network transport business, in which they develop so-called "middleware" to synchronize network media streams (as well as other types of time-based data) without affecting running applications and operating system components.

To recap their multicasting position from Chapter 3: "StarWorks-TV multicasting software provides 'one-to-many' multicasting services over your corporate enterprise network. Together, StarWorks-TV and a StarWorks video server provide integrated live and stored multicasts over standard Ethernet local area networks or Hughes DirectPCs for applications such as: distance learning, remote manufacturing process management, Wall Street live TV news for financial analysts/traders, security/surveillance systems, video conference multicasts, corporate communications, and emergency broadcasts."

The Intel/Turner Connection

Which brings us to Intel. Because they are not primarily a software vendor or a router manufacturer, Intel may seem an unlikely competitor for a company like Starlight in the network media game. However, Intel controls a powerful codec that could have an important future in multicasting and network streaming: Indeo.

In fact, back in the early 1990s, Indeo 3.1 was key to an Intel product known then as WorldView. Generally speaking, Intel had teamed up with Turner to provide a way for a Windows video server to:

• Receive a CNN broadcast (or any other type of NTSC video input).

• Capture and compress the broadcast in realtime.

• Transmit the digitized broadcast across a LAN using only a small portion of the total LAN bandwidth.

The capture device back then was a plain old Intel Smart Video Recorder, installed on the video server. The WorldView client software worked quite well indeed on generic 486 machines running Windows 3.1 and connected with generic network cabling.

What ever happened to WorldView? Perhaps, it was the victim of the Intel marketing machine. In any event, it seems to have vanished in the mists of time—although it was superior technology for its day and helped advance the cause of LAN-based desktop video in general.

In fact, WorldView (and Starlight's early solutions) were fairly ahead of their time in terms of establishing a model for broadcasting video (and other media) on a network. Both of them practiced a high level of bandwidth conservation while providing multimedia content to any client who chose to tune in. WorldView's user interface even had a marquee that announced upcoming events.

Did Intel use strategies similar to Starlight's? Perhaps, although WorldView was based on Indeo and Starlight's products were codec-independent. Both products, however, lacked an underlying presentation platform—such as a Web page—for displaying the video they were streaming against a standard backdrop.

In other words, what media streaming products needed back then (and still require today) is a stage. The bare-bones Windows or Mac desktop is not enough all by itself. Like any theatrical presentation, there needs to be a proscenium under which all the action takes place. Enter the World Wide Web.

What A Difference A Web Page Makes

Prior to the advent of the Web, and specifically the Web browser, there was no uniform, widely-accepted way to tune into some video on a network. As noted earlier, there were custom interfaces like Intel's WorldView and Starlight's StarWorks, but nothing for a third party developer to use when designing a generic new product.

Browsers like Netscape Navigator and Microsoft Internet Explorer have changed all that—both for the Internet and, maybe more importantly for LAN-based video, the intranet. As you are probably aware, many large companies—and smaller firms that can afford it—are constructing sophisticated internal PC networks using LAN wiring schemes and TCP/IP protocol.

These so-called intranets look and feel just like the global Internet when you traverse them with a Web browser. The good news is, generally speaking, things happen a lot faster. Email, FTP transactions, streaming media—all of these operations have much more bandwidth in which to perform. In fact, it kind of spoils you for the global Internet.

Even relatively smaller organizations can build very useful intranet sites for a small investment per machine (under $1,000) as compared to last-generation Client/Server standards. And don't be concerned that you're using a weak imitation of the global Internet as you cruise around your own (or someone else's) intranet. Plenty of Web developers are cashing in by working on intranet contracts.

The Intranet Players

Because desktop video on the LAN benefits greatly from playing on a Web page, it is worth covering some of the intranet server and Web site construction products currently available. As you gear up for multicasting, you will find that these platforms and tools will, in general, support that activity as well.

The main thing to keep in mind as you look over this material is that little of it may have real meaning for you unless you know exactly what you are looking for. But also remember that the complexity of these products doesn't come from their producers' imaginations. These features and differentiations are what real users really want, and are really buying.

SuiteSpot

SuiteSpot is the big ticket, ever expanding intranet management solution from Netscape (see Figure 9.14). Included in the package are such essentials as email and news modules, as well as a Yahoo-like directory and general site management services. But this is just scratching the surface, as you'll see.

SuiteSpot runs on Unix and Windows NT, and includes built-in support for Java, VRML, Shockwave, C, C++, PERL, and various brands of databases (such as Oracle and Sybase). Netscape has always been ahead of the curve in introducing new media-centric features to its browsers, so it makes sense to have SuiteSpot as your intranet server if you hope to fully exploit these features.

According to Netscape, SuiteSpot incorporates the following components (as of this writing). These components are expressed as servers, even though they are software modules—a common practice in the Windows NT world.

Figure 9.14 Netscape's SuiteSpot.

- *Enterprise Server*—The basic component for managing and publishing Web-based information.

- *Messaging Server*—Essentially a sophisticated email server.

- *Proxy Server*—Replicates and filters Web content. Replication enhances performance and cuts down on network traffic (shades of multicasting). Filtering (by user, document, and content type) makes for better security and allows administrators to ensure productive use of network resources.

- *Media Server*—According to Netscape, "Media Server's standards-based, high-quality audio streaming capabilities allow organizations to build audio-enabled Web sites, enhancing communication inside and outside of the organization." The company's intranet video streaming plans seem unclear at this point, according to available documentation.

- *Calendar Server*—Provides scheduling services for people, groups, and resources.

- *Collabra Server*—"A high-performance, open, and secure discussion server. Netscape Collabra Server makes collaboration and knowledge-sharing among teams of people inside and outside your organization easy, effective, and productive." Apparently, it does not include video conferencing.

- *Catalog Server*—A search engine (for the benefit of company personnel) for managing online catalogs of documents located on corporate intranets and the Internet.

- *Certificate Server*—"...a new class of software that enables organizations to issue, sign, and manage public-key certificates using Secure Sockets Layer (SSL) for secure, private commun-ication over the Internet or an intranet. It enables strong authen-tication and single user log-on that scales from intranets to the Internet."

- *Directory Server*—A solution for managing "white pages" information, such as names, email addresses, phone numbers, and certificates (built on the Internet directory protocol LDAP).

- *LiveWire Pro*—"Provides application developers the power to manage highly complex Web sites and deploy network-centric applications for intranets and the Internet. Includes an INFORMIX-OnLine Workgroup Database, and database connectivity for integration with existing databases such as Oracle, Informix, Sybase, or ODBC-enabled databases."

Netscape Gold

In a certain sense, Netscape Gold is just a superset of the standard issue Netscape Navigator. All the Gold product really adds is an HTML editor, but it is considered a very good one (see Figure 9.15). You can download Netscape Gold for free from the Netscape site (**www.netscape.com**). For some reason, many people seem to think the Gold version means it comes with a manual, and you have to pay for it.

The HTML editor is known for being very fast, and it integrates seamlessly with the Navigator browser. In other words, you can work on a Web page for a while, then switch to Navigator to see how the page will look live with just one or two clicks. (Note that you have to start Navigator first to get into the editor.)

The editor's UI is completely WYSIWYG, but, unfortunately, there is not as much support for multimedia file types as there is in other authoring products—even Internet Assistant. It's hard to know

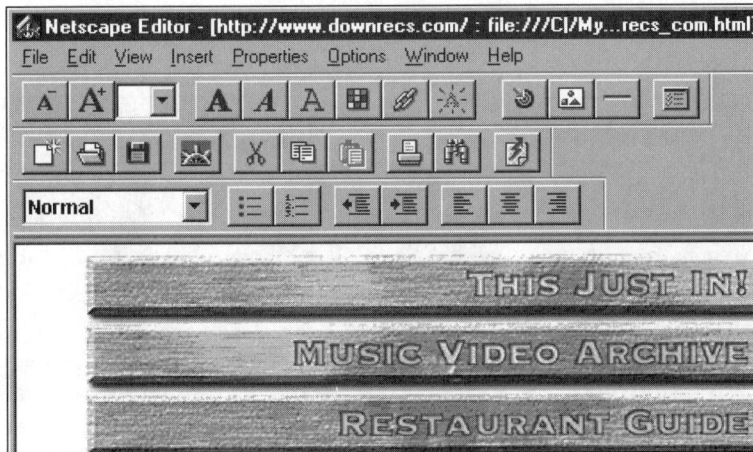

Figure 9.15 The Netscape Gold UI.

whether this is by design, because the rest of what the editor does works so well.

Some other drawbacks:

- No facility for form creation.

- No drag and drop support for some of the proprietary Netscape extensions.

- General lackluster feel until you appreciate its underlying power.

Oracle Universal Server

Oracle Universal Server sometimes feels like a more formidable product than SuiteSpot in the way that it's marketed, but both provide the same essential services for the other machines on their respective intranets. Web media developers should take note of the Oracle Video Option component (see Figure 9.16).

According to Oracle, "customers can embed compelling full-motion video into existing database applications, or develop new applications. Example applications include training-on-demand, corporate communication repositories, marketing information systems, multimedia product catalogs, and point-of-sale kiosks.

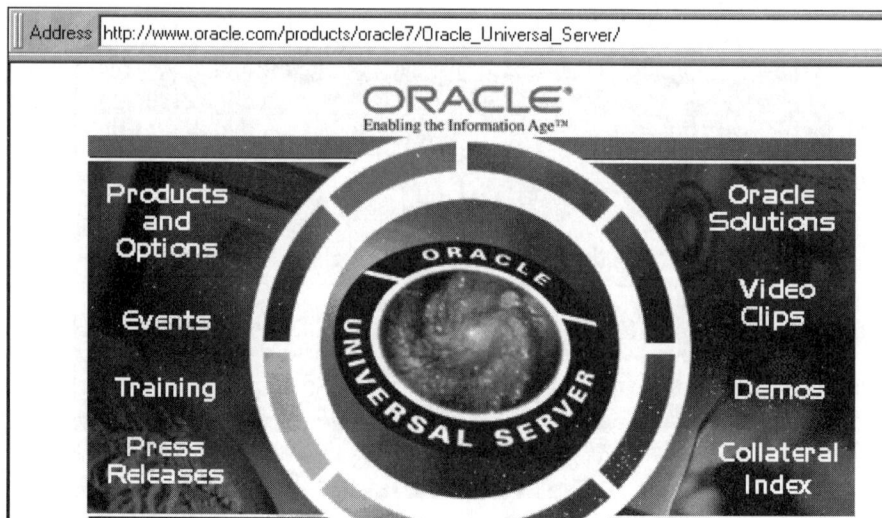

Figure 9.16 The Oracle Universal Server.

"To develop applications, customers can take advantage of a varied suite of application development tools. The Oracle Video Client component of the Oracle Video Option includes support of Oracle Media Objects, Oracle Power Objects, Oracle Forms, and Microsoft's Visual Basic. Through the client programming interface, it also supports other applications that can embed OLE Custom Extension (OCX)."

Originally targeted for Windows NT, Sunsoft Solaris and HP/UX (to run on HP9000 systems), this scaleable product reportedly leverages Oracle's database technology to organize video for efficient delivery across multiple types of networks. Naturally, lots more (and more timely) information can be obtained at **www.oracle.com**.

Starlight StarWorks

When this chapter was written, Starlight Networks was reportedly readying an NT-based video server solution for the intranet, scheduled to ship in the Fall of 1996 (see Figure 9.17). Starlight's current high-end networked video product, StarWorks, runs on various flavors of Unix. Starlight's Web site, **www.starlight.com**, has all the current details. See Chapter 3 for a description of Starlight's multicasting strategy.

Figure 9.17 Starlight Networks' StarWorks.

Microsoft Media Server

Finally, there is the Microsoft solution—at least in theory. When it was called Tiger, the available specs said the product was scaleable, NT-specific, and ran on clustered high-end PCs that functioned as a composite virtual server, with media data striped across both hard drives and the PCs themselves—quite an ambitious design.

The word now seems to be that the high performance part of the product is still called Tiger, but it is targeted specifically for hotel video systems (see Chapter 1) and the (admittedly fuzzier) home markets. The intranet part of the Microsoft Media Server is reportedly code-named Bengal.

Which brings us to Microsoft's BackOffice, a collection of intranet servers that goes head to head (often quite publicly) with Netscape's SuiteSpot (see Figure 9.18). The components of BackOffice (as of this writing) are:

- *Conference Server*—A scaleable solution for realtime communications. Allows you to launch conferencing applications, including NetMeeting, that support shared whiteboards, shared applications, chat, and IP phone applications. As noted in Chapter 3, NetMeeting does not yet support video conferencing.

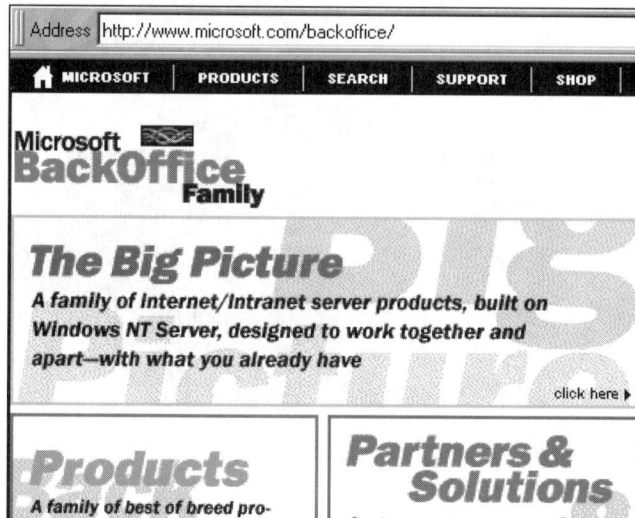

Figure 9.18 The BackOffice home page.

- *Content Replication System*—According to Microsoft, "A server system for Web publishers that provides a reliable, secure, and efficient way to move content across the Web and to central intranet servers." Sounds somewhat like SuiteSpot's (Netscape) Proxy Server, although Microsoft has its own Proxy Server, as noted.

- *Exchange Server*—Again according to Microsoft, "The only communication and collaboration server that embraces Internet standards and extends rich solutions to businesses of all sizes."

- *Merchant Server*—Simply put, provides a solution for customers who want to purchase products online.

- *Proxy Server*—More from Microsoft's literature: "The easiest way to provide fast and secure Internet access to every desktop in your organization."

- *SNA Server*—Integrates an organization's other existing networks with the Internet and the organization's intranet.

- SQL Server—A database server that works with Web-based databases (both Internet and intranet).

- *Systems Management Server*—"Centralized management for Windows-based systems, providing extensible hardware and software inventory, software distribution, and diagnostic services."

And don't forget Microsoft Windows NT Server, the bedrock for all the BackOffice components. The off-the-shelf version of NT Server 4.0 currently includes:

- *Internet Information Server (IIS)*—A simple but powerful tool for quickly constructing reliable Internet and intranet sites. Works with most video- and audio-on-demand products, such as VDOLive and RealAudio.

- *Index Server*—Provides search facilities to find documents and other types of files on your intranet or Internet sites.

- *FrontPage*—See the following section. Like IIS and Index Server, you can download FrontPage standalone from the Microsoft Web site.

FrontPage

This is Microsoft's lead product for Web-based (and intranet) publishing per se. As of this writing, it is still in beta, and it works pretty much as advertised (see Figure 9.19). Microsoft is pushing this product as both an authoring tool and a site management solution—specifically for non-programmers.

Just about everything in FrontPage is automated with templates and Microsoft-style wizards. Also, you can add sophisticated interactive features by dragging and dropping so-called WebBot components right onto your pages. Finally, FrontPage seems to be largely designed for workgroups—teams of people who like creating and managing big Web sites together. Check out the rest of the story at **www.microsoft.com/ frontpage**.

Internet Assistant

Internet Assistant (IA) is a free but powerful add-on to Microsoft Office components. For instance, if you are already a Word user, IA will let you create HTML pages almost as easily as standard Word documents. As you work, you can flip back and forth between Web Browse View and HTML View to see how your pages will look live.

Two versions of the product are currently available: 1.0z and 2.0z. Both support the English version of WinWord, as well as several European versions, and are available at **www.microsoft.com/msoffice/freestuf/**

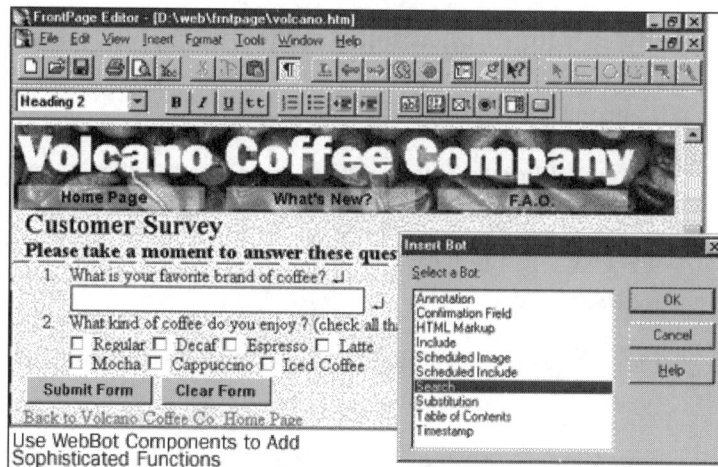

Figure 9.19 The Main FrontPage UI.

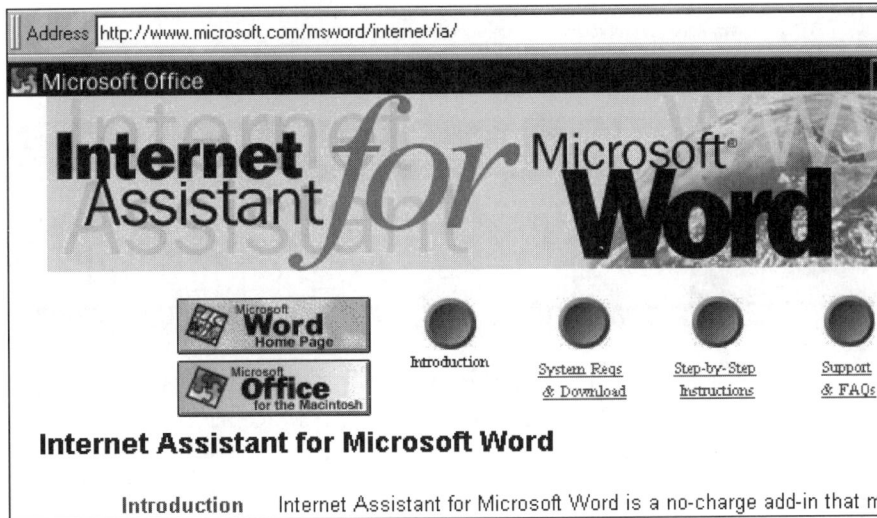

Figure 9.20 The Internet Assistant home page.

msword/download/ia. Other limitations are detailed at the Microsoft Web site, as shown in Figure 9.20.

Version 2.0z is much more powerful than 1.0z, but it only works—as of this writing—with Word for Windows 95 and Word for NT (English, Italian, German, and French editions). Most common extensions are supported, as well as the ones for the Microsoft Internet Explorer (both proprietary and HTML Level 2 standard).

Assuming you have Word for Windows 95 on your system, you might want to download and run the self-extracting IA installation program, followed by the standard Microsoft setup routine (all plain vanilla). You also might want to read the documentation on the Microsoft site just to give yourself a basic context.

PageMill/Site Mill

Adobe took an early lead in the Web-based authoring game with two key products: PageMill (for drag-and-drop Web page creation) and Site Mill (for Web site management). Both were designed for industrial strength Web site chores, although PageMill is a much more mature product at this point (see Figure 9.21). More information is available at **www.adobe.com/prodindex**.

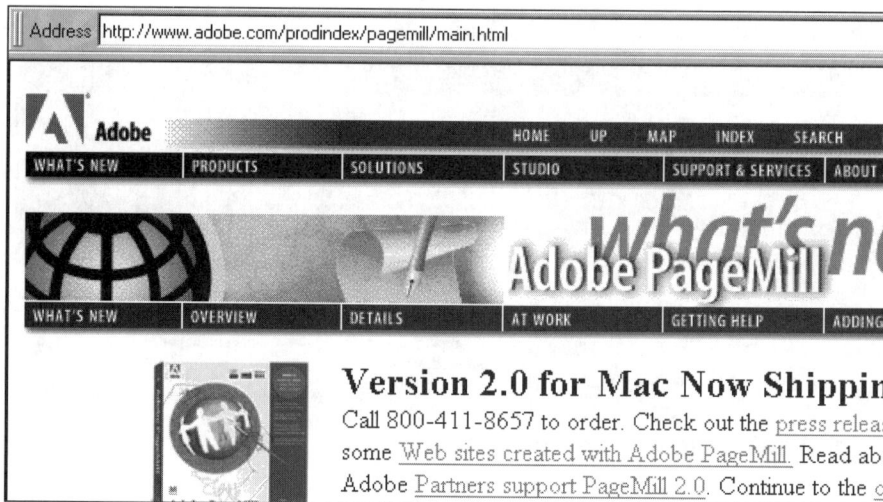

Figure 9.21 The PageMill home page.

WebAuthor

Like Microsoft's Internet Assistant, WebAuthor from QuarterDeck, Inc. is an add-in module for WinWord 6. Also like IA, it provides a custom View in Winword (like Normal, Outline, and Page Layout) where you get access to proprietary HTML functions. Figure 9.22 shows the WebAuthor home page.

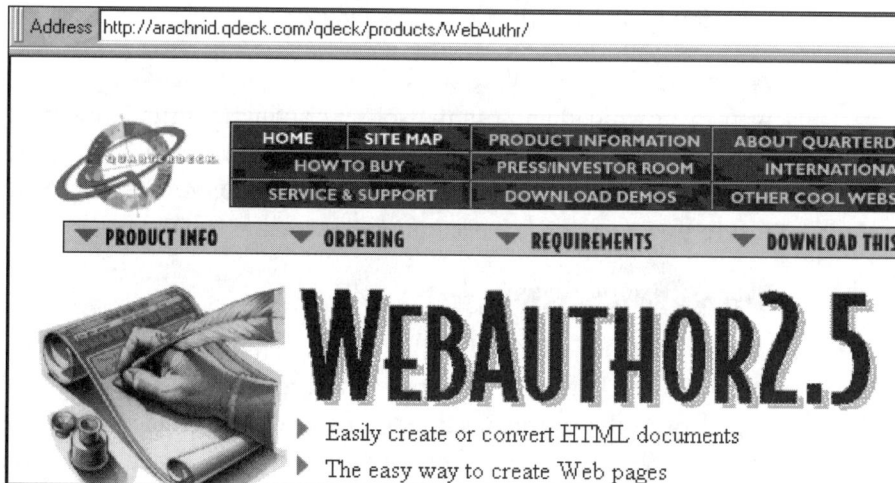

Figure 9.22 The WebAuthor home page.

Unlike Internet Assistant, WebAuthor is not free, although you can test drive it for a standard evaluation period. In fact, WebAuthor differs from Internet Assistant in many ways. For example, it actually manages two documents relative to your in-progress Web page (a separate HTML script and the underlying Word file).

If you go through Word's menus after WebAuthor is installed, you'll see a lot of new items. This is indicative of the level of power that WebAuthor gives you for authoring HTML pages. Unfortunately, it seems to have no special love for handling multimedia files. Some of the program's significant features are:

- An intelligent conversion facility for large existing WinWord and RTF files.

- Support for imagemap graphics (to some extent).

- Good support for tables and forms.

- Good support for hyperlinks.

- Good support for formatting individual elements of a document.

Because of its extensive use of Word macros, WebAuthor requires a relatively powerful machine. Consider at least a Pentium with 8 MB of memory if you want to work completely free of sluggishness. For more information, point your browser to **www.qdeck.com**.

Other Site Management Products

The previous list is certainly not exhaustive, and may well be a bit out of date by the time you read this. It does, however, highlight the major intranet players so far. As you can see, some reading between the lines is necessary to discern how these products handle desktop video—streaming and otherwise. If you go to the respective Web sites, you can usually find more complete information on how they deal with all forms of multimedia.

Some other products worth checking out:

- O'Reilly's WebSite at **www.ora.com**

- DeltaPoint's QuickSite at **www.deltapoint.com**

- Spider from Incontext at **www.incontext.com**

Dialing In To A Private Intranet

A good question at this point is whether you can dialin to a remote LAN (like in Exercise 2 at the beginning of this chapter), fire up your Web browser, and play some video stored on the remote server. The short answer had better be yes, and so it is (assuming you are using TCP/IP protocol).

Exercise 3 provides a brief tutorial:

1. Double click on the My Computer icon.

2. In the My Computer window, double click on the Dial-Up Networking folder (assuming you have already configured your machine for dial-up networking).

3. Double click on the Make New Connection item (assuming you didn't do Exercise 2 or don't yet have a favorite server configured to dial in to).

4. In the Make New Connection dialog box, shown in Figure 9.23, fill in a name for your server (not the official name of the server, just a useful name for this connection item). For the sake of this example, let's use the name *Uncle Enzo*. If you have a modem installed, you should see it listed in this dialog box, as well.

5. Click on the Next button to show the entry fields for the phone number of your server, as shown in Figure 9.24. Enter the appropriate phone number.

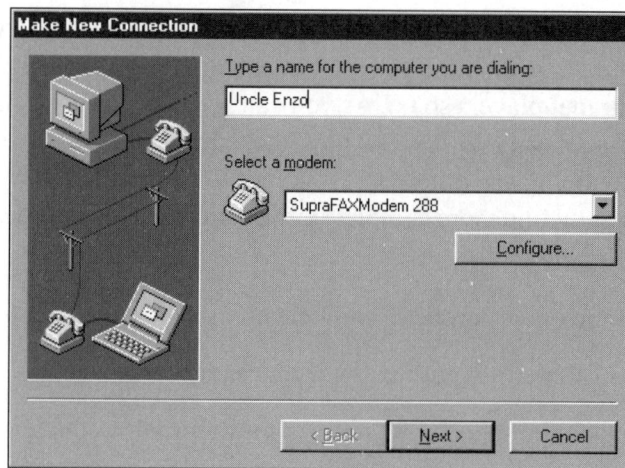

Figure 9.23 The Make New Connection dialog box.

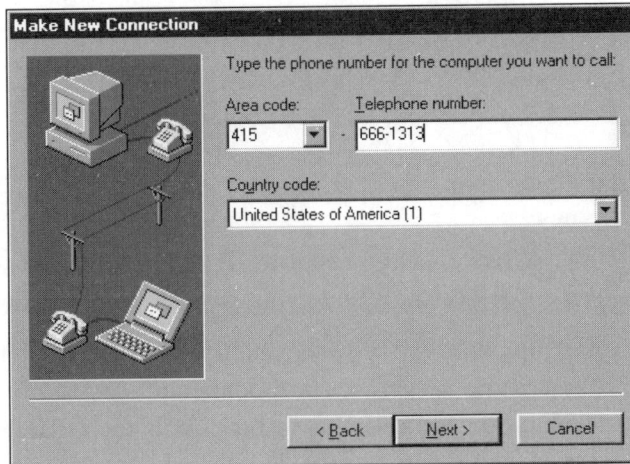

Figure 9.24 Entering the server's phone number.

6. Click on the Next button, then the Finish button in the following dialog box. There should now be a Uncle Enzo item in the Dial-Up Networking folder. If you wish, you can make a shortcut for quicker testing later.

7. Double click on the Uncle Enzo item (or its shortcut icon) to begin a dial-up session with your server (assuming it is set up and available for a WAN dial-up), as shown in Figure 9.25.

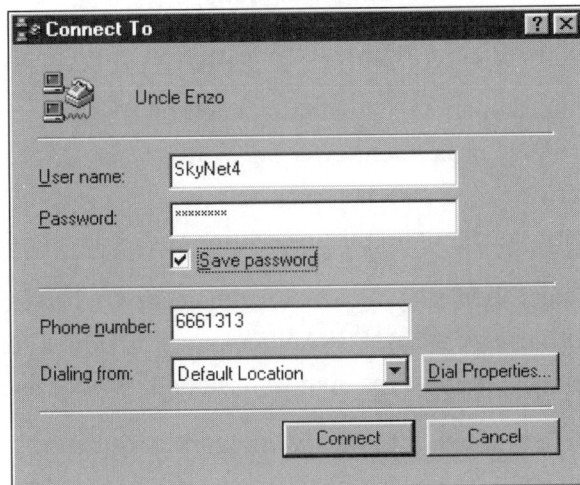

Figure 9.25 Starting a dial-up session with your server.

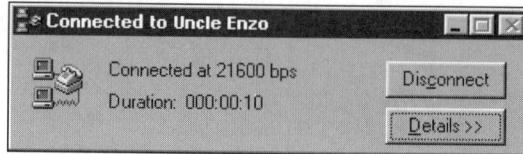

Figure 9.26 A confirmed server connection.

8. When the connection is made, it will look just like confirmation of a standard connection to your favorite ISP (see Figure 9.26).

9. Fire up your Web browser, and try surfing to the URL of the site on the remote server you are connected to—assuming the remote Webmaster has done his or her job. If the URL doesn't work, try the machine name or the TCP/IP address of the remote server, if the remote Webmaster will give them to you.

10. When your browser makes the connection, try playing some streaming video.

Summary

This chapter surveys the current state of desktop video on the LAN and, by extension, on the intranet. Because a dialin client is by definition a card-carrying member of any LAN, we needed to take that type of user into consideration, as well.

Here are four key concepts to learn from this chapter:

• You can play non-streaming video-on-demand clips without using a browser on a client desktop with a *local* LAN connection. While performance may be acceptable, too much bandwidth gets tied up. Plus, you can't do this in realtime with a standard Web browser.

• Forget about playing non-streaming clips (when using a 28.8 modem) with a remote LAN (WAN) connection, or just forget about playing non-streaming clips in most, if not all, WAN scenarios.

• On an intranet, things *should* work a lot better—although you will generally be consuming streaming video (on demand).

• As you'll see in following chapters, multicast video on the LAN/ WAN simplifies these issues substantially.

Chapter **10**

- **Understanding internetworks**

- **Defining basic multicast hardware: the ISDN router**

- **Designing a commercial internetwork application**

Chapter

10

Multicasting On Internetworks

In Chapter 5, we constructed a set of so-called *meta systems,* which we used to view multicast systems abstractly. This made it easier to look at each component of a given meta system in context. Moreover, it helped us to understand a component's role in a complete system.

For instance, we identified the role of the Network Adapter Card as the abstract component that connects the CPU to the Network Router (at least in a standard Wintel box). If we know the limitations (such as last year's bandwidth) of a real piece of hardware used to fill a particular role in a real system, we know where to start looking for potential bottlenecks (see Figure 10.1). That's the advantage of our meta system and of thinking abstractly about networking in general.

You'll recall that at least one of the meta systems in Chapter 5 was a model for connecting to a private multicasting network (as opposed to the global Internet) with a dial-up link. In fact, it was suggested that such dial-up links—specifically router-to-router links—may be the next step in the multicast

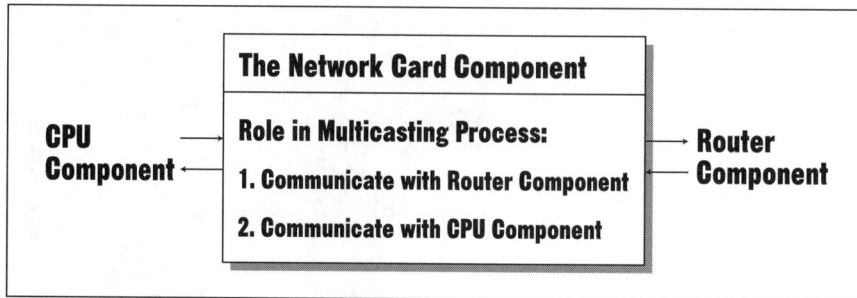

Figure 10.1   The role of the Network Adapter Card.

revolution, unless the routing structure of the global Internet (with its multicast islands) undergoes a sea change in the near future. The local area network is, of course, the first step in the multicast revolution.

In this chapter, we'll take a general look at the issues surrounding router-to-private network connectivity, getting into specifics where necessary. To make things interesting, we'll construct a scenario for commercial use of private LAN multicasting, based on software development projects known to be underway. But first, we need a firmer grounding in the general world of WANs (especially off-the-rack technology) and so-called *internetworking*—if only to illustrate the current limitations of multicast networks (as of Fall 1996).

Internetworking

The *internetworking* buzzword is a combination of *inter* and *networking*, not *Internet* and *working*. It's a broad term, but it looks great on book jackets and in corporate white papers. Basically, internetworking means tying networks (LANs, mostly) together with routers, bridges, and other similar types of equipment. You could argue that dialing into your ISP with a 28.8 modem is also a form of internetworking, but you'd be straining the definition on several fronts. As you may know, the global Internet itself is the mother of all internetworks.

Simply stated, full-on multicasting only works in certain types of internetworking scenarios (at least for now). We keep coming back to this idea from different perspectives, but that just means it's a major issue. The goal of this chapter is to isolate the networked environments where true multicasting works by describing and discarding the environments where it doesn't work.

When we have boiled off the noise, we'll flesh out a real-life model and talk about where breakthroughs may happen in the future. As you'll see, the bottom line is that an ISDN router is your current best bet for consuming multicasts on internetworks. Sure, this situation will change as communications technology improves and vendors package that technology into billable services (which is already happening). But ISDN and affordable ISDN routers are here now, and it all works.

> **Note!** *For the rest of this chapter, we'll use the word subnet instead of LAN. You've probably seen this term when installing TCP/IP drivers, and it has generally the same meaning in that context as well. So from now on, subnet = self-contained LAN (remote clients not included).*

Forget 28.8

At the beginning of Chapter 9, we ran through a few quick examples to make some basically negative points about trying to do internetworking with 28.8 modems. For the record, those examples used nonstreaming video clips to make their points. If you really want to see for yourself whether video streaming makes a difference in 28.8 land, try the following test:

1. Go to the VDOLive Web site (**www.vdolive.com**), and download the Personal Server software.

2. Install the VDO Personal Server on the server machine used for the examples in Chapter 9. Make a VDO-encoded movie, and compose a Web page for playing the movie (see Figure 10.2). Add that Web page and the movie to the collection of documents and media already handled by your Web server.

3. Call your server from a separate machine with a 28.8 modem and a Web browser installed (presumably the same machine used in the Chapter 9 examples). Navigate to the VDO test page, and play the streaming video clip created in Step 2.

The result? As they say in show business, the production closed out of town. Clearly, this is a lot of trouble just to prove a point, but it

Figure 10.2 A Web page for serving a VDO clip with a 28.8 modem.

should convince you once and for all that things need to be taken to the next level in terms of data transfer rates. If you've got the patience, you could even try this 28.8-to-28.8 test with Microsoft's NetShow On Demand, but you will see the same—or worse—results (see Figure 10.3).

The reason we need to kick 28.8 connections out of the multicasting bar is that such transmission speeds just aren't viable when connecting subnets for multicasting, or for any type of internetworking when you get right down to it. A 28.8 modem is perfectly fine for someone dial-

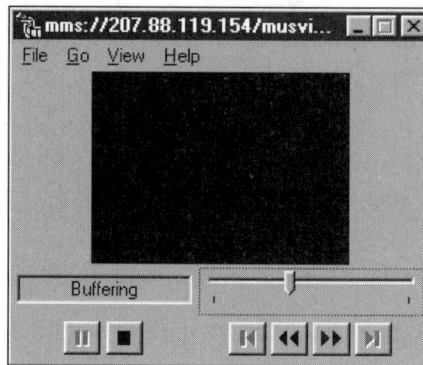

Figure 10.3 Bringing NetShow On Demand to its knees with 28.8 modems.

ing in to the office server from the road, or for connecting to AOL from home, but serious internetworking (subnet-to-subnet) simply needs a wider data pipe—like ISDN.

Before laying the groundwork for discussing the PC-to-ISDN connection, let's preview what's in the next few pages. What we want to do is distill the least exotic common ground among three converging planes:

1. Data transmission technologies

2. Switching/routing hardware

3. PC operating systems

Figure 10.4 illustrates this concept. As you can see, the common patch within reach of the average independent Web developer is the ISDN Router for Windows or the Mac. Of course, the deeper your pockets, the bigger the common ground becomes. Well-heeled Webmasters are already playing with Borg-level routers, as well as ATM and Frame Relay data transmission standards.

The ISDN Angle

Because this chapter is about general issues in internetworking, as opposed to configuring *specific clients* for multicast reception (covered

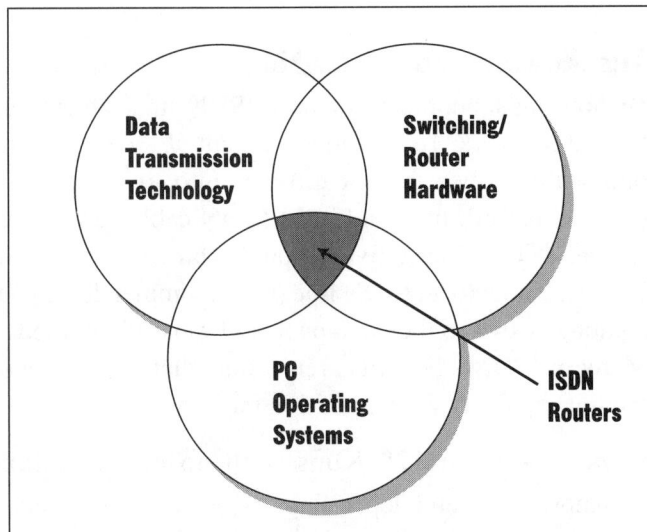

Figure 10.4   Converging on the ISDN router.

in upcoming chapters), we can take the 30,000-foot view concerning the three converging planes. Remember that we have isolated the ISDN router as the weapon of choice for accessing multicasts on remote subnets. Let's now look at the ISDN side of this generic hardware.

Like the consumer VCR, ISDN has had a long latency period. Unfortunately, that latency period was also a time of frustration for many ISDN early adopters, arguably due to a laissez-faire attitude on the part of ISDN service providers (big phone companies). As a result, ISDN has a somewhat tarnished image. For newcomers, however, there will still be a honeymoon period. And, now that there is starting to be a mass market demand for ISDN due to the Internet, big phone companies are starting to get off their dimes in terms of providing decent ISDN service to average consumers.

Note! *Also prodding big phone companies is the specter of new, rival transmission solutions like ADSL and satellite downlinking, like with DirecPC (noted in earlier chapters). The difference is that ISDN is already field tested and ready for full deployment—if the phone companies and ISDN Internet access providers can keep up with the demand.*

The Advantages Of ISDN

By now, most people know what ISDN stands for: Integrated Services Digital Network. To be honest, it's not *physically* digital—like in fiber optic cables—because it can function over most regular phone lines. (For the record, new and rural ISDN cables are usually thicker than regular POTS lines.) Even though you can't hear a dial tone if you attach a phone to an ISDN line (not recommended), you can still attach a phone or two to the back panels of most ISDN modems and routers. Many of ISDN's benefits aren't immediately apparent until you stack them up against the competition (such as it is):

- *Speed*—Up to 128 Kbps with no compression. With 4-to-1 compression (and depending on the degree to which your particular data can be compressed), this number can go up to 512 Kbps.

- *Multitasking*—In other words, you can order a pizza from Uncle Enzo with a telephone connected to one of your ISDN adapter's B Channels (assuming you have two) while you download a QuickTime movie. After you hang up, the adapter will automatically resume full bore operation.

- *Reliability*—According to ATT, ISDN is substantially more reliable than POTS. Of course, ATT wants to sell ISDN lines and services.

- *Relative Cost Effectiveness*—Depending on where you are in the world (and how much you use your ISDN line), ISDN service normally runs between $30 and $75 per month, exclusive of installation charges.

- *Installed Foundation*—As noted earlier, ISDN works on most regular copper phone lines.

- *Large Scale Connectivity*—Most phone companies are already rewired for ISDN, especially the big-city ones. Consequently, you can originate an ISDN call in San Francisco and expect that it will be answered on an ISDN line in Paris.

THE FORCES AT WORK

As noted previously, interest in the World Wide Web is at the heart of the ISDN renaissance. The bad news is that this situation has joined mismatched partners: the PC world and the telecommunications industry. Fortunately, this is a better combination than the marriage of PCs and Hollywood.

Still, all is not running at peak efficiency. For instance, I got an ISDN line from Pacific Bell in March of 1996 with the idea (if not the promise) that Pac Bell Internet access would be available on that line in a couple of months. Finally, in late Fall of 1996, I got the Pac Bell ISDN Internet service after surviving marginal ISDN ISP service from a number of overburdened independent firms.

Note! *If you surf to **www.thelist.com**, you can get a breakdown on the services, ISDN and otherwise, offered by a wide variety of ISPs (see Figure 10.5).*

Figure 10.5 A view of **www.thelist.com**.

Once I received one-stop shopping, I still wasn't 100 percent satisfied with the quality of the service, even though the tech support people were extremely courteous. Finally, when I got my first Ascend Pipeline 25 router, I discovered that Pac Bell didn't then offer static IP address assignment (which is still essential for routing as of this writing).

Ultimately, I found an aggressive, larger independent ISP that did offer routing with my ISDN Internet access (the line is still switched by Pac Bell). So far, the service has been excellent, especially for multicasting, using even my original Pipeline 25.

In general, the reason for the friction between the telco world and the PC industry is that the PC industry is much more adaptive to changing trends and market pressures. As new types of routers and ISDN adapters are manufactured by firms from the PC sector, the service providers (telcos) will have less control over how those services (ISDN specifically) are used. Add this to their relative lethargy, and, well, you get the idea.

THE TELECOMMUNICATIONS ACT OF 1996

As if the previous situation wasn't sticky enough, there are even bigger forces at work in the ISDN arena—and beyond. The Telecommunications Act Of 1996 struck down a lot of the regulations controlling the radio, television, cable, telecom, and data processing industries. In effect, the message was: Let the most competitive high-tech company win.

On the telecom front, things haven't been this much fun since congress fragmented AT&T in 1984. Under the new rules, local and regional telcos are essentially free to merge (with government approval, of course) and do business in each other's sandboxes. What does this mean for multicasters and Joe consumer? Hopefully, lower ISDN rates all around—as well as cheaper phone service in general.

ISDN And Windows 95

Compared to other data transmission technologies, ISDN is predisposed to deliver high performance in so-called client/server environments, specifically those involving remote access. On the Wintel PC side, Windows 95 is the first OS that has acceptable networking support built in. Not surprisingly, ISDN is also supported natively, to some extent (see Figure 10.6). Windows NT, of course, takes this all a lot further.

Unfortunately, the current version of Windows 95 does not support the type of routing support needed for multicasting in its remote access components (specifically Dial-up Networking). This is true for all data transmission modes, including ISDN. As we have seen, you can certainly do multicasting with Windows 95, but just not with Windows 95 Dial-up Networking.

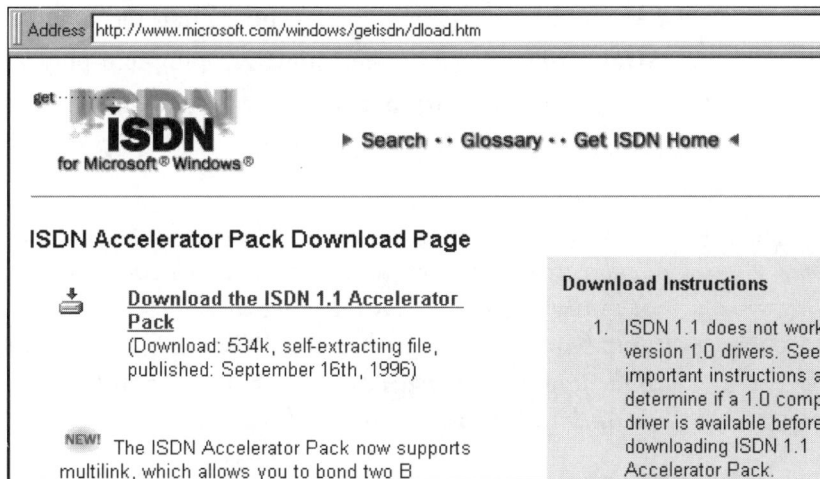

Figure 10.6 ISDN support in Windows 95.

For the record, Windows 95 includes a number of facilities for integrating ISDN under stable conditions. Here's a quick rundown:

- *Speedier Serial Communications*—Windows 3.1 limited serial communications to 19,200 bps (which is why you see that number so often when configuring Windows communications software). Third-party software allows you to surf the Web in Windows 3.1 at 28.8 Kbps with your 28.8 modem. Under Windows 95, serial communications can go as high as 921,600 bps (assuming you have a modern UART chip). This allows ISDN adapters, such as Motorola's BitSUFR Pro, to connect directly to your serial port.

- *Native TCP/IP Support*—Under Windows 3.1, you needed a third-party TCP/IP stack to surf the Web (this was prior to the days of the Microsoft Internet Explorer). Favorites of the time were the free Trumpet product and the pioneering Chameleon solution from NetManage. Under Windows 95, a Microsoft TCP/IP stack gets installed at setup, or the user can always add it later.

- *Plug-and-Play Capability*—The value of this feature is often less clear to the average user, but it relies on cooperation between hardware vendors and Microsoft (with Microsoft calling the shots, as usual). As ISDN hardware proliferates, however, plug-and-play will likely assume greater importance because everyone wants to keep configuration problems to a minimum.

Note! *If you're wondering if you should use Microsoft's ISDN Accelerator Pack, the word seems to be that you may not really need it, essentially because the current version limits bandwidth to only one B Channel. Dan Kegel's ISDN page (**www.isdn.ocn/dank /isdn/isdn.html**) likely has updated information on this issue.*

ISDN And Windows NT

For the purposes of this ISDN-based discussion, we can talk about NT 4.0 Server and NT 4.0 Workstation as if they were the same thing. When it comes to internetworking, perhaps the biggest difference between Windows 95 and NT 4.0 is that NT implements remote access as an official NT service: Remote Access Service, or RAS (pronounced RAZZ by Microsoft tech support). There is still Dial-up Networking in NT, like in Windows 95, but RAS is a lot more sophisticated than the standard Windows 95 network driver installation and configuration.

ISDN is supported under Windows NT as follows:

- First, all the ISDN advantages listed for Windows 95 are enjoyed under NT.

- Next, because Windows NT 4.0 Server sees a RAS NT client as a completely local entity (as opposed to how Windows 95 handles remote clients), operation is a lot more streamlined internally, especially for ISDN connections (see Figure 10.7).

- Finally, under RAS, there are specific settings for ISDN connections, as you'll see at NT RAS installation time.

Remember that if you go with a RAS/ISDN connection to your NT Server, the only way a client can log in remotely is if that client also has ISDN service. In other words, they can't call your ISDN number with a standard POTS modem (unless you have a POTS modem attached to one of the B Channel ports on your ISDN adapter or ISDN router).

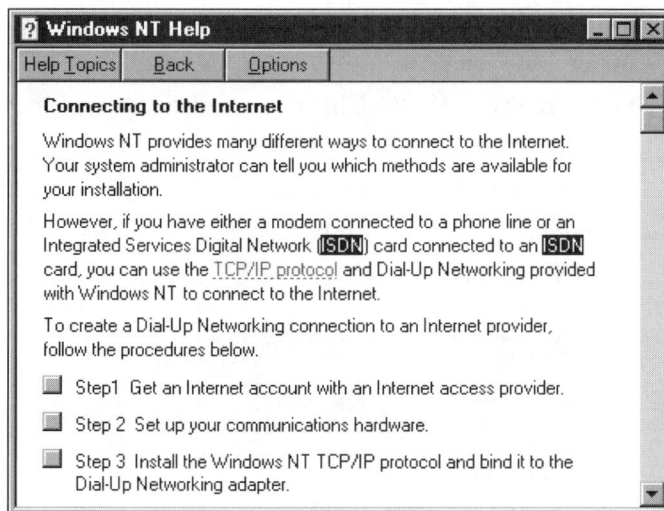

Figure 10.7 ISDN support in Windows NT 4.0.

ISDN And The Mac

At the System 7.5.5 level, Apple's new Open Transport software appears to offer specific support for ISDN connectivity (as in special control panels). In general, most ISDN adapters (like the BitSURFR Pro) and ISDN routers can be configured to work with Macs just as easily as with Wintel machines. Searching on ISDN at Apple's Web site (**www.apple.com**) will always yield timely information on this subject, as will downloading and reading the documentation for the new System 7.5.5 components.

Serial Port ISDN Connections

Because we're more interested in ISDN routers, we won't dwell on serial connections, but a brief discussion will help fill in the big picture of PC-to-ISDN connectivity in general. Here are some important points to remember:

• ISDN modems (a common name for ISDN devices that get connected to PC serial ports) are generally easier to install and maintain than other types of ISDN gear, assuming you're running under Windows 95 (as opposed to Windows 3.1). Also, like with 28.8 modems, you can usually swap ISDN modems back and forth between Macs and Wintel machines.

• Because PC serial communications are asynchronous, there is an upper limit on data transfer speeds through a PC's buit-in serial port, even with ISDN. This limit is effectively somewhere between 92 Kbps and 115 Kbps, depending on a variety of system-level factors, which is why you may often see a dialog reporting *Connected at 115200 bps* (see Figure 10.8) when using, say, a BitSURFR Pro with two active B Channels.

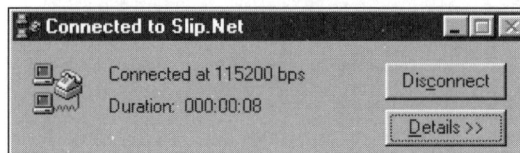

Figure 10.8 Slowdown at the serial ISDN corral.

ISDN Adapter Cards

ISDN adapter cards usually fit in ISA slots in Wintel boxes, but there are PCI ISDN cards out there also, for both Macs and PCs (as well as NuBus ISDN adapters for Macs). In a generic sense, these card-based solutions are more like external ISDN modems than the ISDN routers we'll discuss next. The facts about ISDN adapter cards worth remembering are:

- No serial port speed limits. Because such adapter cards plug right into the system bus, the bottleneck is now the ISDN line. Even ISA— the slowest PC systems bus—transfers data at roughly 5,000 Kbps (50 times that of a 100 Kbps ISDN connection).

- Setup and operation under Windows 95 and Windows NT is normally quite straightforward. These platforms actually tend to treat ISDN adapter boards as *network* cards, at least when it comes to installing drivers. Of course, your mileage may vary here, and pre-sales research is highly recommended.

ISDN Routers

Now, to the heart of the matter. The goal of the prior page or two was to establish that ISDN connectivity is mature and generally accepted in the Wintel and Macintosh environments. The aim of the next few pages is to illustrate that the ISDN *router* is the device that will usher in the first great era of reliable (and enjoyable) multicasting for Mac and PC media consumers.

As it turns out, ISDN routers are nothing new. What *is* new are the relatively inexpensive and easy-to-use ISDN routers for the PC—and it's only going to get better. Remember in our discussion of multicasting meta systems, we noted that the router component was not a brand new abstraction, just new to abstract PC systems.

General Issues

Routers are the glue that makes internetworking possible. ISDN routers can be considered heavy hitters in this ball game for at least one compelling reason: ISDN itself forms a homogenous wide area network (WAN). Take a second to let this sink in. The protocol is mature, widely implemented, and clearly, cross-platform.

Also consider that ISDN depends on Ethernet technology to link the computers on a given subnet (LAN). Routers are Ethernet-compliant mechanisms, so there is a high degree of harmony among all these basic elements (see Figure 10.9). As noted earlier, routers differ from bridges in their ability to actually route data packets based on their destination addresses. (Bridges essentially transfer data between subnets regardless of protocol and routing information.)

On PCs running Windows 95 and NT, if you are using a router, you can dispense with Dial-up Networking altogether. In general, all you have to do is fire up an Internet application (such as your favorite Web browser), and the router makes a connection to the Internet automatically. Same goes for the Mac. When you get right down to it, buying an ISDN router for your LAN is cheaper than purchasing a separate ISDN modem for each of several machines on that LAN—plus, you are assured of being multicast capable (assuming that router specifically supports IP multicast).

Leading Vendors

In Chapter 3, we roughly surveyed the players in the emerging multicasting hardware market (Cisco, Ascend, etc.). This market is finally on the way to becoming congruent with the router market in general. For Web developers, the most interesting segment of this market is where ISDN router vendors dwell.

The reason we make so many references to Ascend products (like the Pipeline 25) is that Ascend is the market leader in the ISDN router segment. Other players include Cisco and, in particular, Farralon Computing (with its Netopia product). Currently, not all these products ship

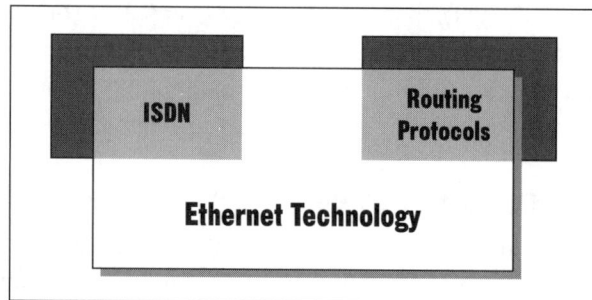

Figure 10.9 The relationships among ISDN, Ethernet, and routing technologies.

with drivers that enable them for multicasting. The Ascend and Cisco products definitely do, which is why we've concentrated on them. If you're interested in a competing product, make sure that it specifically supports multicasting.

Static Vs. Dynamic IP Addresses

One of the evolving issues in multicasting—and internetworking in general—is using static versus Dynamic IP addressing. Earlier in this book, we stressed that static IP addressing was essential for the kind of routing that supports multicasting, but that situation may be in flux by the time this book is published.

The bottom line here seems to be that static IP addresses will continue to work well for multicasting, while dynamic address allocation will be phased in as ISPs get their services in order. Because this is a key concept in the field of multicasting, lets look at it a bit more closely.

THE OLD WAY

Traditionally (as such traditions go), if you wanted to connect your subnet to the global Internet, your ISP needed to assign you a static IP address for every device on your subnet (including your router). A subnet mask was also required to be assigned, which basically identified the LAN as a separate entity apart from the individual machines.

Even though the pool of IP numbers available to humanity is huge (arguably from 0 to 999,999,999,999), it is nevertheless finite. Moreover, it is substantially less than one trillion, based on general usage conventions. Consequently, ISPs have become sensitive about offering ISDN accounts with static IP numbers from their finite pools, often exacting a premium when doing so.

THE NEW WAY

In response to the situation described, dynamic IP assignment is beginning to proliferate in the ISDN router world. In this new environment, you can connect your subnet to the global Internet using a temporary IP address allocated by your ISP for the duration of your connection session—just like logging on to an ISP as an individual user with a modem (as shown in Figure 10.10).

Will this new dynamic environment specifically support multicasting (as well as ISDN routers in general)? Not enough ISPs have adopted

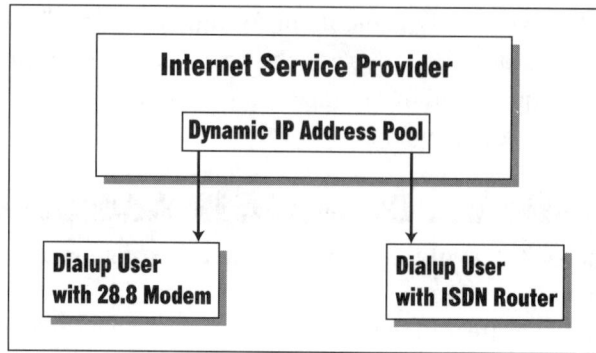

Figure 10.10 The new breed—dynamic IP assignment for LAN connections.

this level of service to predict with authority. The bright side (if there is a dark side) is that static IP address assignment will probably continue on its merry way—at least until everything works on a dynamic basis.

Welcome To The New World

Are you ready to get an ISDN router yet? Once you get one installed, and go with the ISP that best serves your internetworking needs, you may wonder why you even considered an ISDN modem or internal ISA adapter card for global Internet access. If you have multiple computers on your subnet (connected with Ethernet cabling), you will be even more satisfied in the long run—even if you don't wind up doing much multicasting.

Hopefully, however, you now have good reason to consider an ISDN router as the basic but highly capable gear for connecting your subnet to another remote subnet for the express purposes of consuming multicast content. If so, Chapters 11 and 12 provide information on how to put an actual ISDN router to work. In the meantime, let's take a quick look at what some experts think is ISDN/Ethernet's logical successor in the not-too-distant future.

Beyond ISDN

The acronym about to be uttered is ATM, which stands for Asynchronous Transfer Mode. Right off the bat, it's too complex a subject to get a complete fix on in a page or two. However, it can be put into meaningful perspective relative to ISDN and Ethernet.

Of course, people close to a given technology will want to pick apart any encapsulation by an outsider, so independent research on all ATM-related subjects is certainly encouraged. That being said, here are some important things to remember about ATM for your next industry cocktail party:

- ATM already exists and is a growing part of the communications infrastructure (see Figure 10.11).

- ATM began as a telecom technology (like ISDN), even though it now competes squarely with Ethernet (and so-called Fast Ethernet) technology in the PC internetworking world.

- Among the next generation broadband transmission candidates (like Frame Relay), ATM is considered superior, even though it does have significant limitations.

- Past ATM, there is wide open space, at least in practical terms. In other words, the existing communication standards continuum pretty much ends with ATM at the high end.

- Brand new standards may yet be invented, but none seem to be on the near horizon, aside from supercharged versions of existing standards (such as so-called gigabyte Ethernet).

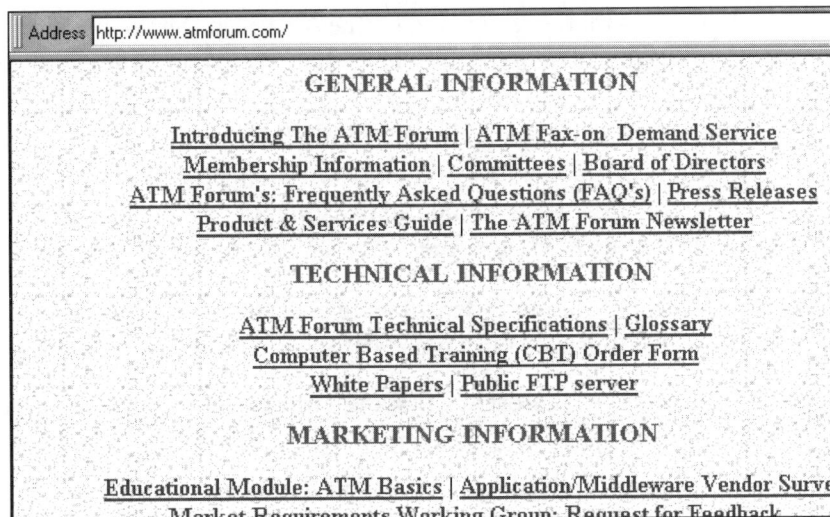

Address http://www.atmforum.com/

GENERAL INFORMATION

Introducing The ATM Forum | ATM Fax-on Demand Service
Membership Information | Committees | Board of Directors
ATM Forum's: Frequently Asked Questions (FAQ's) | Press Releases
Product & Services Guide | The ATM Forum Newsletter

TECHNICAL INFORMATION

ATM Forum Technical Specifications | Glossary
Computer Based Training (CBT) Order Form
White Papers | Public FTP server

MARKETING INFORMATION

Educational Module: ATM Basics | Application/Middleware Vendor Surve
Market Requirements Working Group: Request for Feedback

Figure 10.11 The role of ATM in broadband telecommunications.

- Because ATM may one day supersede today's ISDN/Ethernet data communications standards, it must grandfather existing IP routing and addressing (and presumably multicasting) conventions.

Although this bulleted list places ATM in a somewhat meaningful context, it obviously doesn't explain what ATM is technically. As an aspiring multicaster, you might only need to know that ATM is out there and coming on strong as the underlying fabric of the Internet.

You can certainly educate yourself on ATM technology to a high degree, but, unless you work for a company like Sprint or MCI, you might not get to use that knowledge in any kind of production capacity for another year or two.

Real Life Internetwork Multicasting

Because this chapter concerns general issues involved in internetworking, let's construct a lifelike multicast scenario that makes use of existing equipment. The following example is loosely based on a project known to be in development, but it is generic enough not to tread on anyone's proprietary technology or product idea. Essentially, it is an exercise in systems integration.

An Interactive Infomercial

Let's say a market executive for the American Bar Association wants to put together a seminar in which three well-known legal experts will communicate directly to a select group of attorneys regarding some important new legislation. Assuming most parties concerned are tired of air travel and far away hotels (even when on expense accounts), how can internetworking—and multicasting, in particular—be used to pull off a high-tech but non-geeky version of such an event?

A possible solution is described in executed form in the following text (and also illustrated in Figure 10.12). First, the basic setup:

- Roughly 100 attorneys (paying customers) in a given metropolitan area travel to a downtown hotel and gather in a high tech conference hall with multiple ISDN (or better) lines constituting the room's electronic plumbing.

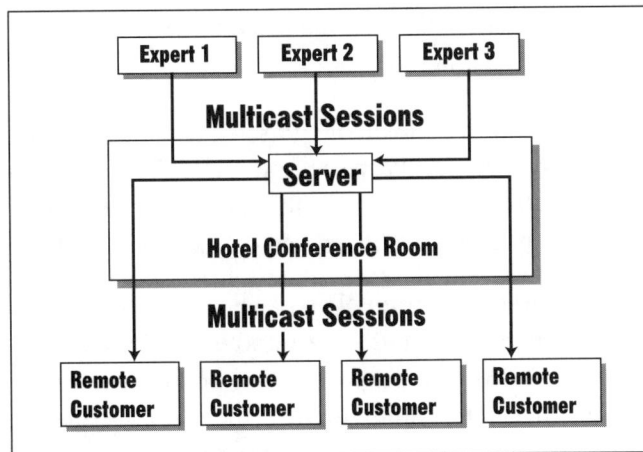

Figure 10.12 A schematic for this event.

- A subnet is set up in the conference room, with an NT server connected via an ISDN router/switch to the ISDN (or better) telco line(s). An NT client machine, operated by a moderator, is connected to the server via Ethernet cable. A suitably-sized monitor is placed in the conference hall so that all the attendees can see it comfortably.

- Other conference rooms may be set up similarly in other metro areas, depending on the scope of the overall event and the topology of the overall internetwork.

- Back in their offices, the three legal experts face video cameras connected to NT machines (self contained subnets) supplied by the marketing executive. These NT machines are connected to ISDN routers which have dialed in to the servers in the main conference room participating in the event. If an expert didn't already have ISDN service at his or her office, it was arranged by the marketing executive.

- An audio bridge is set up so that the moderator in each hotel conference room is connected to each remote expert via an open POTS line.

- Interested attorneys (more paying customers) who couldn't travel to the hotel conference room in one of the participating metro areas may be supplied with multicast addresses to tune to, assuming they have ISDN routers and lines and the router/switch at the conference's

HQ can handle the volume of calls. They also have dialin access to the POTS audio bridge.

Before the show officially begins, the experts turn on their cameras and initiate live multicasts on separate Class D IP addresses. This is coordinated by the moderator via the audio bridge. None of the audience members hear what's being said on the audio bridge.

The moderator has three Web pages loaded on his desktop, each with a window tuned to one of the remote multicasts from the experts (remember, this is also happening on a private internetwork—not the global Internet). Depending on how the script for the event is organized, the moderator is able to switch among the three pages and display the video window.

It's Show Time

The moderator starts the conference, makes introductory remarks, and then turns the show over to each expert in turn. The experts deliver their speeches in order, appearing as fluid quarter-screen video clips (with unbroken sound tracks) on the desktop of the big monitor in the conference room (as shown in Figure 10.13). The remote audience members consume the multicasts but don't see the moderator (at least not in this event).

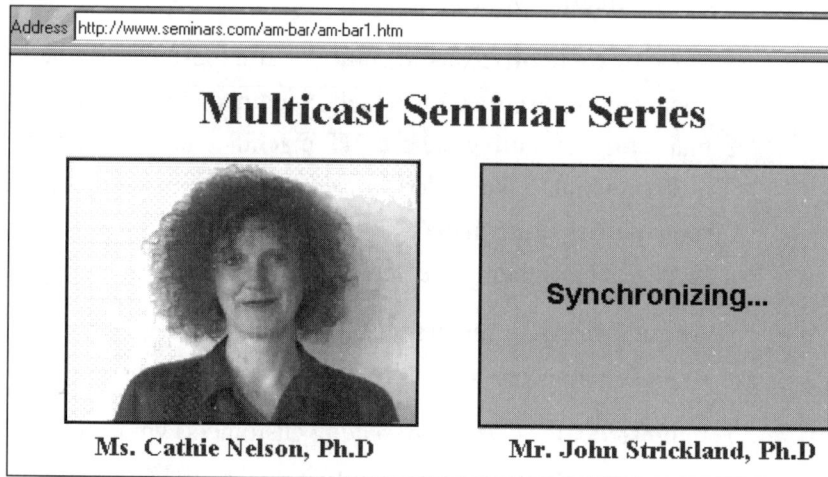

Figure 10.13 What the audience sees.

Following the prepared presentations, the legal experts endure a Q&A session from the audience, with questions supplied to them by the monitor over the audio bridge and answers delivered back to the audience over the multicast channels. When the questions run out (or the allotted time is up), the conference is over, and the experts end their multicasts.

Breaking It Down

Can all of this really be done with existing hardware and software? The answer is yes, based on the types of products discussed in this chapter. Here's a quick breakdown:

- Software: NT Server 4.0, Netscape Navigator, and Precept's Netscape plug-in. Depending on how the remote audience members get their transmissions, some custom internetwork software may be required.

- Hardware: High-end Wintel boxes, medium to low-end ISDN routers, and at least one ISDN router/switch (for multiple incoming lines).

- Peripherals: Video cameras (with adequate microphones), audio bridge connections, and big screen monitors.

This example just scratches the surface of the commercial uses to which private subnet multicasting will ultimately be put. As affordable, off-the-rack ISDN routers take the place of modems, scenarios like the one described will likely become commonplace.

Summary

The purpose of this chapter is to identify the ISDN router as the lowest common denominator for consuming or delivering a multicast on a private network. The facts used to make this case are:

- ISDN is a mature data transmission standard, which means it is stable and well-integrated on the PC and the Mac, and it provides a wide enough data pipe to facilitate good quality media presentation.

- Routing is essential for multicasting, whether based on static or dynamic IP addresses.

- ISDN routers per se are now affordable and reliable enough to invest in without hesitation. Just remember to confirm that the model you want supports multicasting.

Chapter

11

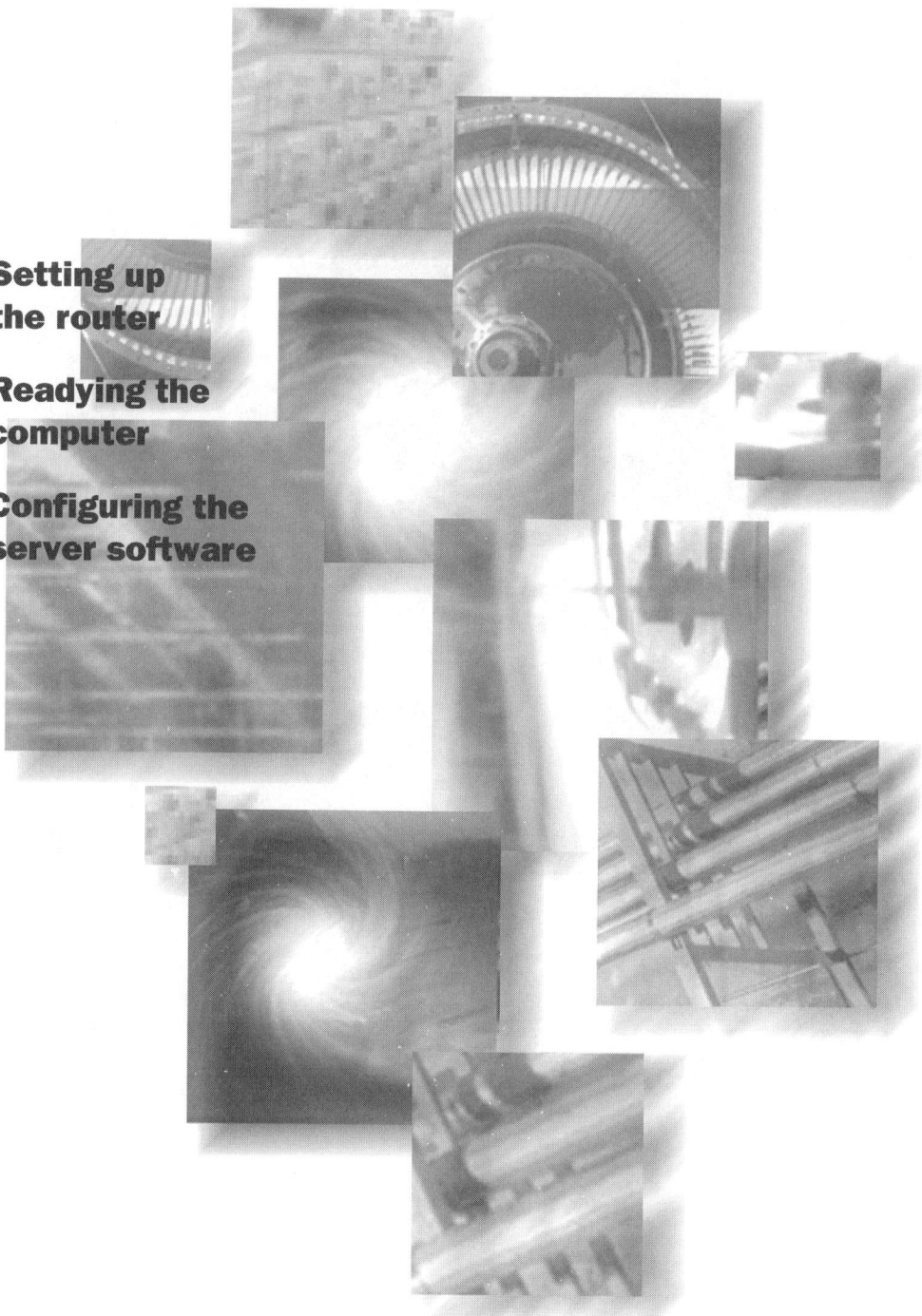

- **Setting up the router**

- **Readying the computer**

- **Configuring the server software**

11

Configuring A Private LAN Server For Multicasting

This chapter addresses the details of configuring an NT 4.0 server for multicasting video to internetworked clients. As noted in previous chapters, until NT is ready to support full-on MBone multicasting (which may be as soon as the first half of 1997), remote LAN multicasting will be the best we can expect from NT, aside from multicasting to *local* LAN clients.

On the Mac side, MBone and internetworked server technology seems to be even further behind (judging by the products available), but perhaps Apple will enjoy success in the multicast server arena once the NeXT OS is successfully transplanted to the PowerMac hardware line. Regardless of the operating system, there is still a tremendous potential for multicasting in private network environments.

Let's break our NT 4.0 server configuration process into three principal pieces so we can address each individually:

- Setting up the router

- Readying the computer

- Configuring the multicasting software

We'll execute each of these task groups in order, with the goal of bringing our multicasting server online, ready to take calls from preauthorized, dialin clients (via ISDN) and serve them multicast streams. In Chapter 12, we'll actually do the dial-ins, once we have set up the remote client machines.

Remember that this is not going to be a Web *surfing* experience for multicast clients. As you'll see in a minute, internetworking servers must know about potential dialin clients in advance, just like on a plain old LAN. Similarly, a dialin client must be configured for a pre-authorized relationship with the server it plans to receive multicasts from, again like on a regular local subnet. This is not because of baggage imposed by multicasting. Rather, it has to do with how routers work and how ISDN calls are made, as well as with how TCP/IP and other protocols are working at the system level on your computer.

Setting Up The Router

This is the hardest part, at least the first time you attempt it. Right up front you should be prepared to spend some time on the phone with your ISP and tech support at your router's manufacturer, unless you just plain get lucky. Once you do get your router working (on both the server and client side), modifying the settings to add more registered clients is generally much easier. But again, be prepared for some frustration at first.

Note! *You might want to make some calls to tech support and your ISP before you sit down to do the dirty work, just to get a sense of how they will be positioned to help you. Also, reading the router manuals in advance (no way!) can help you get familiar with the user interface for configuring the router.*

In prior chapters, we noted that Ascend is considered the leader in the ISDN Router market segment. As it turns out, Cisco Systems currently holds the lead in the multicast firmware (software stored in a router's ROM and flash memory) department. Because Cisco is a leader in ISDN router hardware (even though they are essentially a software company), the equipment used in this chapter is the Cisco 2524 router (under $1,000 retail).

Good as Cisco equipment is, there is one drawback, at least for the 2524: Configuration must be handled from a command line interface, at least on the Wintel side (other Cisco routers use menu-driven and graphical interfaces). As routers proliferate in general, we will likely see GUIs solve this temporary inconvenience for all router product lines.

In the meantime, the most common way to communicate with the Cisco 2524 from a command line is via a serial cable between your PC's serial port and the console jack on the back of the router. Note that the console jack needs an RJ45 plug, which is generally a specialty item for most serial cables, but not hard to find at Radio Shack or have custom made.

Assuming you have your serial connection in place and have your ISDN line plugged into the back of the Cisco 2524 (see Figure 11.1), as well as a connection to your NT machine's network card, you are now ready to initiate a serial communications session. A good tool for this purpose is the Hyperterminal utility that comes with NT Server (Start|Programs|Accessories|Hyperterminal).

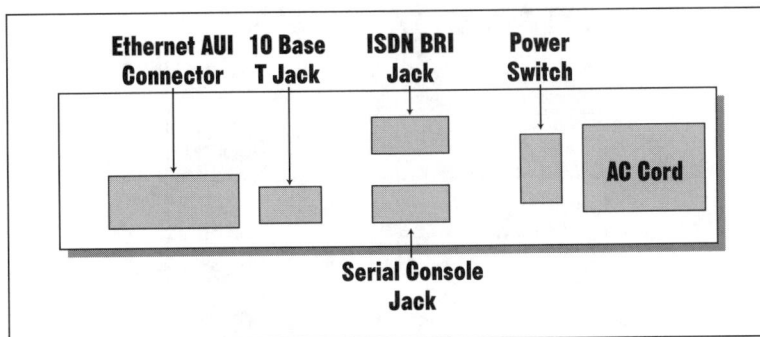

Figure 11.1 The back panel of the Cisco 2524 router.

Note! *Many routers are sensitive to ISDN switch types. For instance, because the ISDN provider in this case employs an NT-1 switch, our router specifically needs an ISDN interface (a.k.a. BRI) that supports it. The 2524 used in this example has a label next to the ISDN jack that reads: ISDN-BRI with NT1.*

Configuring Your Router With Hyperterminal

If you haven't used Hyperterminal before, here's a short list of steps to get it talking to your router.

1. Executing Hyperterminal the first time brings up the window shown in Figure 11.2.

2. Key in a name for this connection, in this case *Cisco 2524*, then click on OK. The panel shown in Figure 11.3 will appear next. Note the COM2 setting in the Connect Using combo box, which has caused the other controls to be grayed out. If you have any modems installed, they will also be listed in the Connect Using combo box. (Note that COM2 appears here because we have previously installed it using the modem applet in the NT Control Panel.) With COM2 selected, click on the OK button.

3. The dialog box in Figure 11.4 now appears. The settings shown are correct. Click on OK to continue.

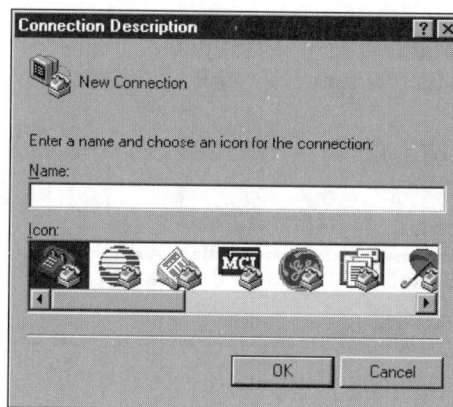

Figure 11.2   Launching Hyperterminal.

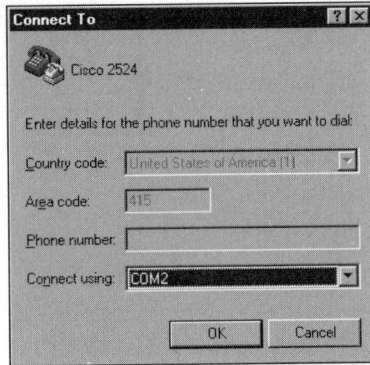

Figure 11.3 Hyperterminal's *Connect To* dialog box.

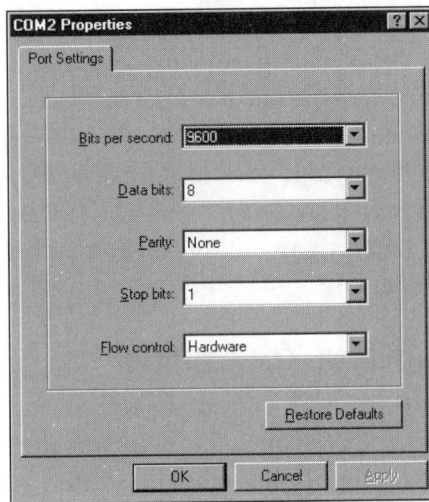

Figure 11.4 Hyperterminal's *Port Settings* dialog box.

If a serial port communications session has been successfully initiated, you will see the window shown in Figure 11.5 (with the status shown as Connected in the bottom left corner).

Note! *Depending on what state your router is in, you might just see a blinking cursor in the top left corner of the window. Pressing your Enter key a few times should get you to the command prompt shown in the illustration—depending on whether the router is properly configured yet.*

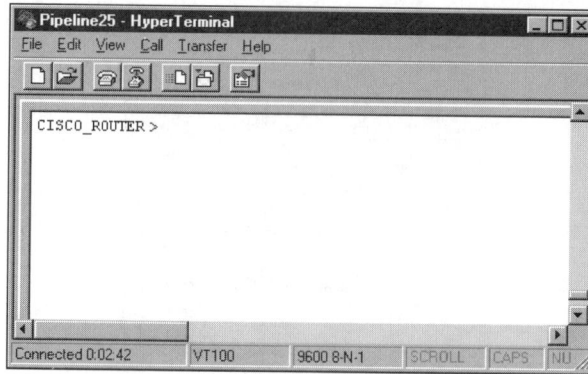

Figure 11.5 Hyperterminal's main operating window.

Now comes the challenging part. To keep things organized, we'll first configure our router to connect to our regular ISP so that our NT machine can receive normal Internet access service (at ISDN router speeds). Once we can do this, we'll reconfigure the router to work with our NT machine so that they effectively assume the role of an ISP—for multicasting purposes. The NT machine will still be functioning as an internetworking NT Server, but dialin clients will see it as just another ISP.

Connecting To An ISP

As you work with Cisco routing equipment, you'll find yourself becoming intimately acquainted with so called *config* files. You won't normally find config files stored on Cisco setup disks, but rather created from blocks of text cut and pasted from the UI of the serial communications program (such as Hyperterminal) used to talk to a router.

If you deal with Cisco tech support, they will probably ask you to email your config file at some point if they can't quickly solve your problem. One of the nice things about Cisco technology is that it is highly scalable—in other words, config files are useable up and down the product line. Older versions of the firmware might not support the same config file commands as newer versions, but that's normal. Not all router manufacturers embrace such scalability.

CONFIG FILE OVERVIEW

Listing 11.1 shows a config file that successfully connects a Cisco 2524 ISDN Router to an ISP. The entries in this config file do not represent the full range of entry types available, but most of the important ones are shown. We'll go over each of them separately in a moment (note that there are no multicast entries yet).

LISTING 11.1   A SIMPLE CISCO CONFIG FILE.

```
Current configuration:
!
version 11.0
service password-encryption
service udp-small-servers
service tcp-small-servers
!
hostname CISCO_ROUTER
!
enable secret 5 $1$TzOH$.8C63nkaFT5oWJmgtAeNX.
enable password 7 071F205F5D1E161713
!
username INX-12456 password 7 0009182E1C5A0D0457
username SanFrancisc01-M1 password 7 151F00241C2B2D2670
isdn switch-type basic-ni1
!
interface Ethernet0
 ip address 207.88.XXX.XXX 255.255.255.XXX
!
interface Serial0
 no ip address
 shutdown
!
interface BRI0
 ip unnumbered Ethernet0
 encapsulation ppp
 isdn spid1 415399162400
 isdn spid2 415399993400
 dialer idle-timeout 60
 dialer wait-for-carrier-time 60
 dialer map ip 205.158.3.52 name SanFrancisco01-M1 broadcast
14155362822
 dialer hold-queue 100
 dialer-group 1
 no fair-queue
 ppp multilink
 ppp pap sent-username INX-12456 password 7 141A192314052C297C
!
ip domain-name downrecs.xo.com
ip name-server 205.158.3.50
ip name-server 199.2.14.10
ip route 0.0.0.0 0.0.0.0 205.158.3.52
ip route 205.158.3.52 255.255.255.255 BRI0
```

```
snmp-server community public RO
dialer-list 1 protocol ip permit
!
line con 0
 exec-timeout 0 0
line aux 0
 transport input all
line vty 0 4
 password 7 1401061B0D17393C2B3A37
 login
!
end
```

We'll examine the individual entries in Listing 11.1 in a moment. If you are setting up an ISDN router for the first time, you likely switched to an IISP (ISDN Internet Service Provider). If so, you were probably given a list of ISDN connection settings. A quick browse of Listing 11.1 offers at least some idea of how these settings will be used. As we work through the salient entries in this listing, we'll coordinate specific configuration entries with the ISDN connection data provided by a generic IISP.

Depending on where you got your Cisco router, it may or may not already have a valid configuration profile. The 2524 model used in this example came as a loaner from a networking company but had to be reconfigured from scratch nevertheless. As with machine code in general, it's always a good idea to get rid of as much nonessential verbiage as possible.

Note! *Of course, Cisco provides ample documentation for all of its hardware products. The newer documentation comes on CD-ROM in hypertext format and walks you through configuration details with hardly any trouble at all. Also, their technical support people are courteous and well-trained. Cisco's general number, which takes you to tech support, is 408-525-4000.*

Config File Details

The following are the configuration details for this example. To change a Cisco configuration entry from the command line, you first need to know how to navigate the levels of the interface. While it may seem confusing at first, a little practice can make you comfortable fairly quickly—as long as you understand at which level you're working. Some basic navigation and configuration commands will be shown next.

Let's return to Hyperterminal's main operating window, last seen in Figure 11.5. To get started, we'll key in the following commands (as shown in Figure 11.6):

1. *enable* (or *en*), then press the Enter key.

2. *xxxxxx* (the password, whatever it is), then press the Enter key (Note: Password characters do not echo).

3. *config t*, then press the Enter key.

We're now enabled for configuration. As promised, we'll now look at the relevant entries in order.

- *hostname*—This is the name you assign to your router (and which appears at the command prompt), in this case CISCO_ROUTER. To make this entry, type *hostname CISCO_ROUTER* (or whatever you want to name your router), then press the Enter key. (Note: All further entries should be followed by a carriage return.)

- *username*—This is your user name, as assigned by your ISP. In this example, it is *INX-12456*. The password assigned by your ISP should also be entered here. To make this entry, type *username INX-12456 password xxxxxxx* (or whatever user name and password were assigned by your ISP).

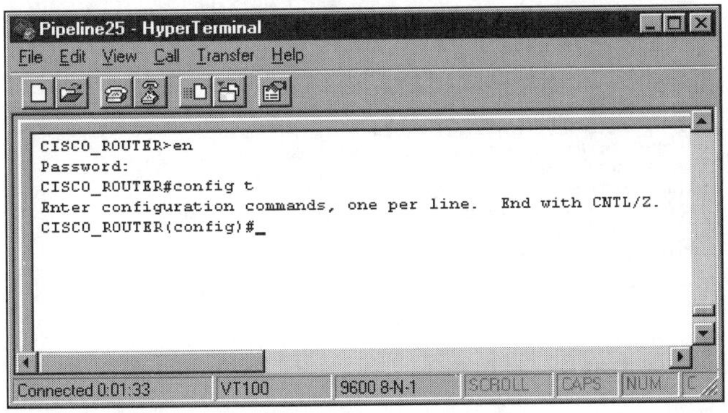

Figure 11.6 Putting a Cisco router in configuration mode.

As it turns out, the way the ISP used in this example works, we also need to add a *username* and *password* entry for the remote name assigned by that ISP—in this case, *SanFrancisc01-M1*. Your ISP will be able to help you figure this out if they are familiar with Cisco routers, which they should be.

- *isdn switch-type*—This is the type of switch used by your ISDN line provider (such as Pacific Bell). To make this entry, we enter *isdn switch-type basic ni1*. Figure 11.7 shows our progress so far. To save these entries, enter *Ctrl-Z* followed by *write* (or *wr*). If we turned our router off now, our work to this point would be preserved.

- *interface Ethernet0*—Now for some more sophisticated entries. To re-enter configuration mode, type *config t*, followed by *int Ethernet0*. Next, enter the static IP address your ISP gave you for your router, including the subnet mask. In this case, the entry is *ip address 207.88.XXX.XXX 255.255.255.XXX* (Xs used for security).

- *interface BRI0*—This concerns the router's ISDN port. As shown in Listing 11.1, there are 12 entries that make this example work successfully. To get to the BRI0 interface, enter *int BRI0*. Now, you can make each entry just as it looks in Listing 11.1. The only exception is the last one, *ppp pap sent-username INX-12456 password 7 141A....*

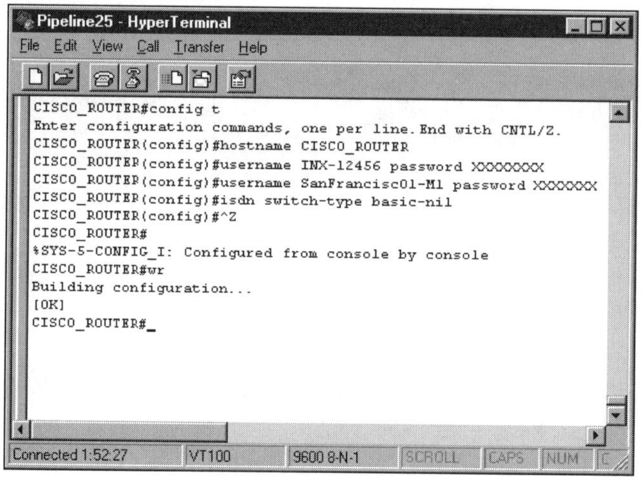

```
CISCO_ROUTER#config t
Enter configuration commands, one per line. End with CNTL/Z.
CISCO_ROUTER(config)#hostname CISCO_ROUTER
CISCO_ROUTER(config)#username INX-12456 password XXXXXXXX
CISCO_ROUTER(config)#username SanFrancisc01-M1 password XXXXXXXX
CISCO_ROUTER(config)#isdn switch-type basic-ni1
CISCO_ROUTER(config)#^Z
CISCO_ROUTER#
%SYS-5-CONFIG_I: Configured from console by console
CISCO_ROUTER#wr
Building configuration...
[OK]
CISCO_ROUTER#_
```

Figure 11.7 Entering configuration commands.

This is a special case due to the requirements of the ISP used in this example. A more common version of this entry is *ppp auth pap*. (Your ISP should be able to steer you straight here, as well.) Again, to save your configuration work so far, enter *Ctrl-Z* plus *wr*.

Note! *The character strings following password in Listing 11.1 are not the actual passwords assigned by our ISP. They are random character strings generated by the router when we instructed it to show us its current configuration. This is done by entering the command write t (or wr t).*

- *ip route*—Now, let's put in some IP routing information. Because the configuration we are building now will just be used to connect to our ISP, we only need two *ip route* statements (as indicated in Listing 11.1). These two statements reflect our ISP's own IP address and subnet mask (as provided by our ISP). Later in this chapter, we'll add additional *ip route* statements for our multicast server's prospective clients. Don't forget to first enter *config t* before typing in your *ip route* statements (getting the hang of this yet?).

- *ip name-server*—If your ISP gave you IP addresses for its name servers (primary and secondary DNS data), you can make these entries the *ip name-server* commands, also shown in Listing 11.1. Don't forget to enter *Ctrl-Z* and *wr* when you're done. To see if all of the configuration data you've entered has found its mark, enter *wr t*, and examine the result. It should look a lot like Listing 11.1. If your ISP provided data that doesn't correspond to any of the configuration entries, ask their help, or contact Cisco tech support.

TESTING THE CONFIGURATION

Assuming your configuration is finally ready for action, you can try pinging your ISP from the command line. Figure 11.8 shows the kind of messages you should see if things are working optimally. If they're not, don't be discouraged. As noted earlier, router configuration is one of the hardest parts of getting started with multicasting.

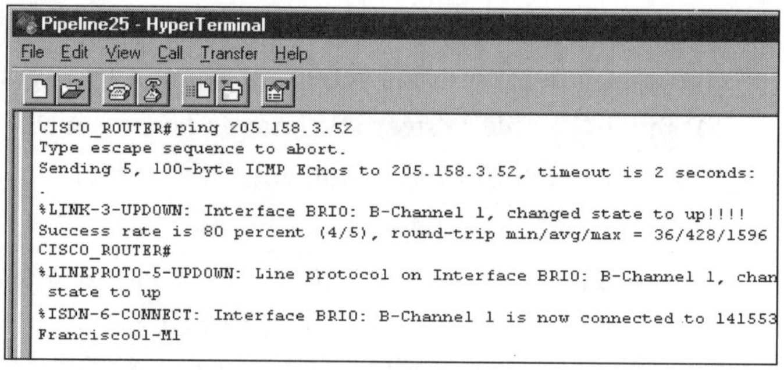

Figure 11.8 Router lift-off.

Sometimes, a minimal amount of config file tweaking can get you to the promised land, but, more often than not, you will spend a fair amount of time on the phone with tech support. Don't be surprised if your ISP throws you on the mercy of Cisco (or whoever manufactured your router hardware) after a few questions.

Note! *For the record, the ppp pap sent-username entry in Listing 11.1 caused no end of trouble when getting this example to work. Both the ISP and Cisco tech support were conferenced in, and lots of trial and error was necessary to get things sorted out. Once everything was sorted out, however, the router worked great.*

With your router up and talking to your ISP, go ahead and invoke your Web browser, email application, and whatever other Internet programs you normally run. When you're satisfied that all applications and services are functioning smoothly, we can move on to the next section.

Assuming The ISP Position

As explained earlier, our first goal in this chapter was to connect to an ISP using a bare bones config file with our Cisco 2524 router. With this accomplished, we're now ready to enhance our configuration to:

- enable multicasting.

- accommodate multiple dialin clients who want to receive multicasts.

In effect, this configuration enhancement will allow us to assume the role of an ISP (albeit, a very modest one). As you'll see in moment, we only need to add several additional entries to the configuration represented by Listing 11.1 to enable multicasting capability. Likewise, for multiple client accommodation.

Listing 11.2 shows our enhanced config file in its entirety. Give it a quick read-through, then we'll discuss each of the new elements in detail.

LISTING 11.2 A MULTICAST-ENABLED CISCO CONFIG FILE.

```
Current configuration:
!
version 11.0
service password-encryption
service udp-small-servers
service tcp-small-servers
!
hostname CISCO_ROUTER
!
enable secret 5 $1$TzOH$.8C63nkaFT5oWJmgtAeNX.
enable password 7 071F205F5D1E161713
!
username INX-12456 password 7 0009182E1C5A0D0457
username SanFrancisc01-M1 password 7 151F00241C2B2D2670
username Client1 password xxxxxxxx
username Clinet2 password xxxxxxxx
username Client3 password xxxxxxxx
isdn switch-type basic-ni1
ip multicast-routing
!
interface Ethernet0
 ip address 207.88.XXX.XXX 255.255.255.XXX
 ip pim dense-mode
!
interface Serial0
 no ip address
 shutdown
!
interface BRI0
 ip unnumbered Ethernet0
 encapsulation ppp
 isdn spid1 415399162400
 isdn spid2 415399993400
 dialer idle-timeout 60
 dialer wait-for-carrier-time 60
 dialer map ip 205.158.3.52 name SanFrancisco01-M1 broadcast
14155362822
 dialer hold-queue 100
```

```
dialer-group 1
no fair-queue
ppp multilink
ppp pap sent-username INX-12456 password 7 141A192314052C297C
!
ip domain-name downrecs.xo.com
ip name-server 205.158.3.50
ip name-server 199.2.14.10
!
ip route 0.0.0.0 0.0.0.0 205.158.3.52
ip route 205.158.3.52 255.255.255.255 BRI0
ip route X.X.X.X X.X.X.X XXX.XXX.XXX.XXX
ip route XXX.XXX.XXX.XXX 255.255.255.255 BRI0
ip route X.X.X.X X.X.X.X XXX.XXX.XXX.XXX
ip route XXX.XXX.XXX.XXX 255.255.255.255 BRI0
!
snmp-server community public RO
dialer-list 1 protocol ip permit
!
line con 0
 exec-timeout 0 0
line aux 0
 transport input all
line vty 0 4
 password 7 1401061B0D17393C2B3A37
 login
!
end
```

In Listing 11.3, you can see the code blocks where all of the action takes place (which are taken out of context for demonstration purposes). The entries in boldface are new and most worthy of our attention. Obviously, the bolded username and ip route entries are merely placeholders, but they show where new clients and their IP routing addresses would be registered.

LISTING 11.3 WHERE THE ACTION IS.

```
username INX-12456 password 7 0009182E1C5A0D0457
username SanFrancisc01-M1 password 7 151F00241C2B2D2670
username Client1 password xxxxxxxx
username Clinet2 password xxxxxxxx
username Client3 password xxxxxxxx
isdn switch-type basic-ni1
ip multicast-routing
!
interface Ethernet0
 ip address 207.88.XXX.XXX 255.255.255.XXX
```

```
ip pim dense-mode
!
ip route 0.0.0.0 0.0.0.0 205.158.3.52
ip route 205.158.3.52 255.255.255.255 BRI0
ip route X.X.X.X X.X.X.X XXX.XXX.XXX.XXX
ip route XXX.XXX.XXX.XXX 255.255.255.255 BRI0
ip route X.X.X.X X.X.X.X XXX.XXX.XXX.XXX
ip route XXX.XXX.XXX.XXX 255.255.255.255 BRI0
```

The most obvious new entry here is *ip multicast-routing*. This can be added as we did earlier for the bare bones config file. Assuming you're at the HOST_NAME prompt (depending on your host name) using Hyperterminal, key in the following commands, as shown in Figure 11.9:

1. *enable* (or *en*)

2. *xxxxxx* (your password, whatever it is)

3. *config t*

4. At the (config) # prompt, enter *ip multicast-routing*

5. Still at the (config) # prompt, enter any new client username data

6. Still at the (config) # prompt, enter any new ip route statements

7. Still at the (config) # prompt, enter *int Ethernet0*

8. At the (config-if) # prompt, enter *ip pim dense-mode*

9. Still at the (config-if) # prompt, enter *Ctrl-Z*

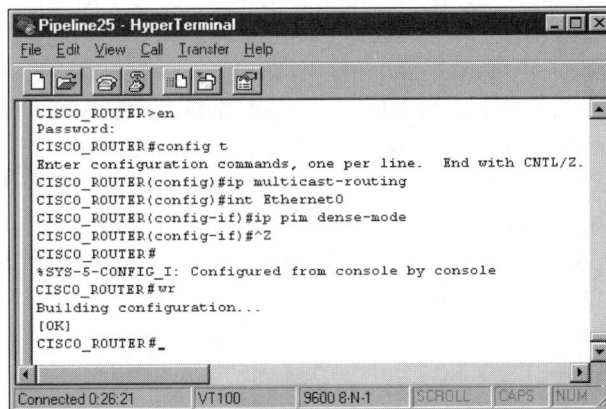

Figure 11.9 Enabling multicasting and multiple dialin clients.

10. Back at the HOST-NAME # prompt, enter *write* (or *wr t* to view the current configuration) to save your work

This completes the minimal amount of work needed to configure a Cisco router for multicasting. Note the word *minimal*. As you get more familiar with Cisco software and routing technology in general, you'll see that we're just scratching the surface here.

For instance, it's possible to set up a tunnel (covered in later chapters) at the command line with statements similar to the ones we just issued. Also, many other parameters specifying router behavior may be designated here. Entering *?* at different levels of the command line interface will give you a good sense of this complexity.

> ***Note!*** *Instead of issuing a whole series of individual ip route commands, you can use router rip as a blanket protocol to cover your dialin clients and their IP routing addresses (similar in concept to how the DCHP Server saves work under NT). While this seems handy, it does carry some performance issues best explained by Cisco tech support. Listing 11.4 shows the router rip syntax.*

LISTING 11.4 IMPLEMENTING ROUTER RIP.

```
router rip
 network XXX.XXX.XXX.XXX
```

If you wanted to at this point, you could fire up an application like Precept's IP/TV Server, get some multicast content rolling, then invite a client to dial in and enjoy the show. While Chapter 6 covered doing this on a completely local subnet, the beauty of solutions like Precept's is that it should make no difference whether the client is local or remote, as long as enough bandwidth exists—which should be the case using the Cisco ISDN router we have just configured. Later in this chapter, we'll install Precept's Program Guide software to give dialin clients some viewing choices.

Readying The Computer

From a hardware perspective, there is not much exotic activity necessary for setting up a desktop computer as an internetworking multicast server, outside of making sure it meets the minimum performance standards required by the networking/multicasting software you'll be using.

As noted in Chapter 6, Precept's IP/TV Server requirements for NT are as follows:

- a Pentium 90 (or greater) machine

- at least 16 MB of RAM (32 MB recommended)

Of course, a blazing network adapter card and Fast/Wide SCSI hard drives certainly don't hurt either. In short, whatever you can do to supercharge your server hardware (within reason) will likely yield quantifiable performance results when it comes to your remote clients receiving good multimedia presentations—just like with digital video and audio on the local desktop.

Configuring The Server Software

If you took the complete multicast test drive described in Chapter 6, you've already got the necessary Precept IP/TV Server software installed. If you want to make life easier for your clients, however, you might want to show them a listing of scheduled multicasts. Fortunately, Precept has just released their Program Guide for NT—implemented as a server-side Web application/NT service. The Precept Program Guide came out for Unix machines first.

Unfortunately, the Program Guide is not currently available on an evaluation basis. When you're ready to invest in Precept's overall solution, they sell you the Program Guide for $995. In any case, we'll demonstrate the facility now.

The Precept Program Guide

Downloading and installing the NT version of the Program Guide (for Microsoft Internet Information Server) is straightforward. In essence, it is a collection of Perl scripts and the previously mentioned NT Service. When the Program Guide is running in Channel View mode on a Precept Server, an IP/TV client machine sees the window shown in Figure 11.10.

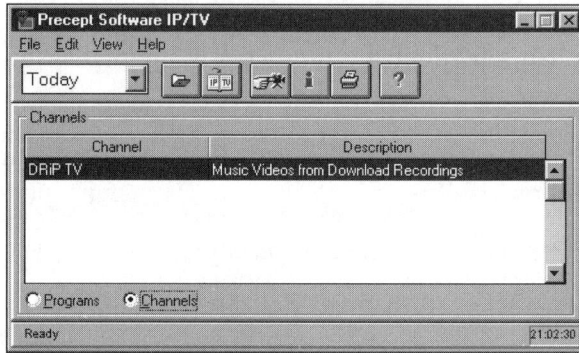

Figure 11.10   The IP/TV Program Guide UI (Channel View).

Note! *Perl5 for NT is currently distributed by Precept along with the IP/TV Program Guide.*

The Program Guide is designed to let an IP/TV Server administrator add and modify information from a Web page. Among other benefits, this allows an administrator to change a given program schedule remotely. When changes are committed, the Perl scripts installed on the IP/TV Server process the new data and update the Program Guide dynamically. Interested clients see the new data when they click on View|Refresh Listing from the IP/TV View main menu (see Figure 11.11).

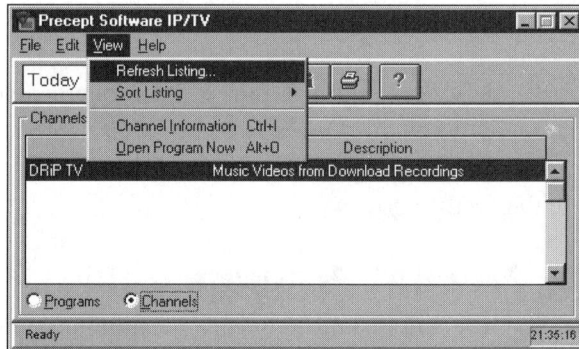

Figure 11.11   Refreshing the program listing.

MANAGING THE PROGRAM GUIDE

To give interested parties a sense of how the Program Guide is configured on the Server side, here is a basic management recipe:

1. Fire up your favorite Web browser.

2. Point your browser to **http://<NT_Web_server_name>/ scripts/ iptv/ iptvman.pl**, which brings up the page shown in Figure 11.12.

3. Click on the Preferences button. The page that comes up next is somewhat lengthy, but the fragment shown in Figure 11.13 suggests the kind of control it provides.

4. Click on the Channels button to set up some channel-level program organization, as shown in Figure 11.14.

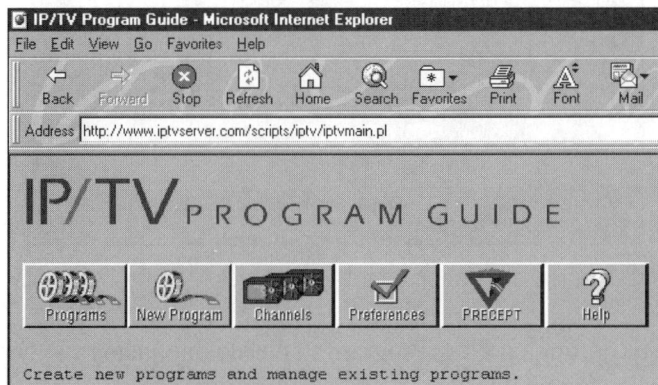

Figure 11.12 The Program Guide home page.

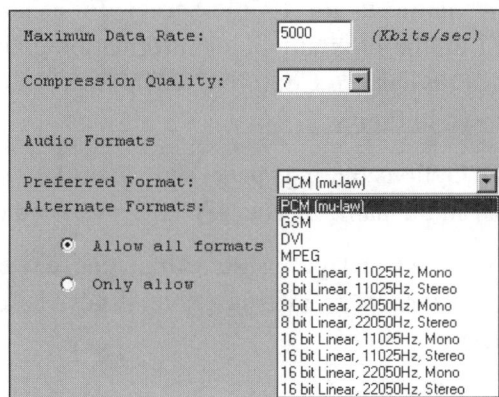

Figure 11.13 Setting the Program Guide preferences.

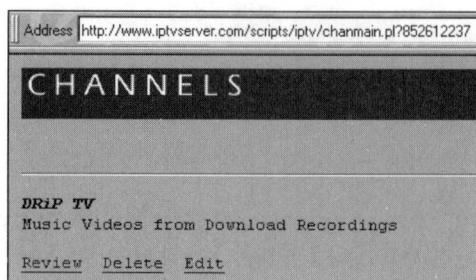

Figure 11.14 Setting the Program Guide preferences.

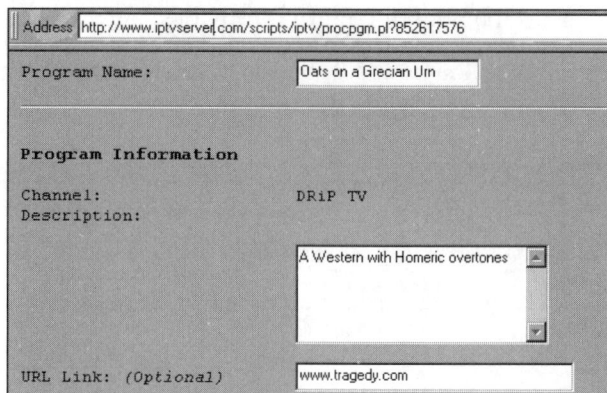

Figure 11.15 Defining a new program.

5. Click on New Program to define one, using the controls shown in Figure 11.15.

6. With an entry or two in your Program Guide, you can now see if it's visible to the IP/TV Server. First, start the IP/TV Server and let the Program Guide information come up naturally. Then, click on Options|Configure IP/TV Server from the main menu, as shown in Figure 11.16.

7. The Options Settings panel shown in Figure 11.17 comes up next. Key in the name of your IP/TV Server, and click on OK.

8. If you click on Options|Refresh Listing, any entries you added back at the Web page interface should now be displayed (see Figure 11.18).

This brings us to a point where we can test the IP/TV Program Viewer locally, although when a remote client (with an ISDN Router) dials in, that client should have the exact same experience once it is an active member of our multicasting WAN.

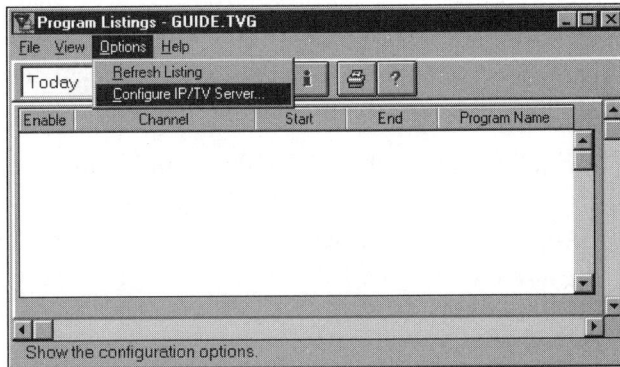

Figure 11.16 The IP/TV Server Options menu.

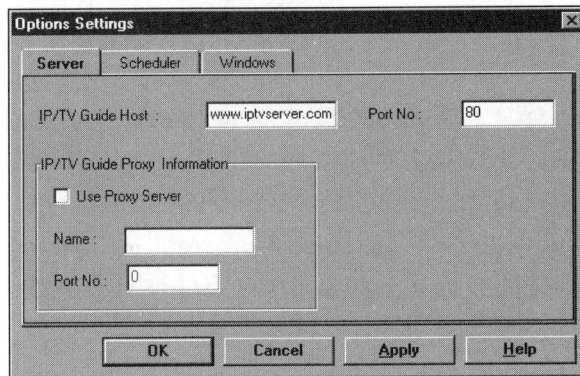

Figure 11.17 Setting the IP/TV Server Options.

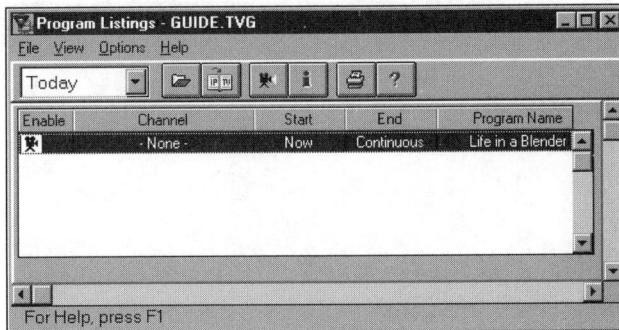

Figure 11.18 Refreshing the Program List.

A Local/Remote IP/TV Session

Regardless of whether you're testing with a local client or a dialin remote client, take a walk through the following steps:

1. Highlight one of the entries shown in Figure 11.18 (assuming you followed the recipe successfully up to that point), then click on the projector icon to subscribe to that entry (or right click on the entry to turn it on or off). The familiar dialog box shown in Figure 11.19 will appear.

2. If the movie being served does not start playing automatically, click on the green arrow to get it rolling. Minimize this window if you wish to keep your server desktop uncluttered.

3. Go to the test client machine (either local or remote), and invoke the IP/TV viewer. The window shown in Figure 11.10 should appear. Click on Edit|Settings to bring up the panel shown in Figure 11.20. Enter the name of your IP/TV server in the appropriate control, as shown, then click on OK.

4. If you don't see current program information like that shown in Figure 11.18, click on View|Refresh Listing from the IP/TV View main menu (shown in Figure 11.11).

5. Double click on the program item and the presentation should commence in a separate window, as show in Figure 11.21.

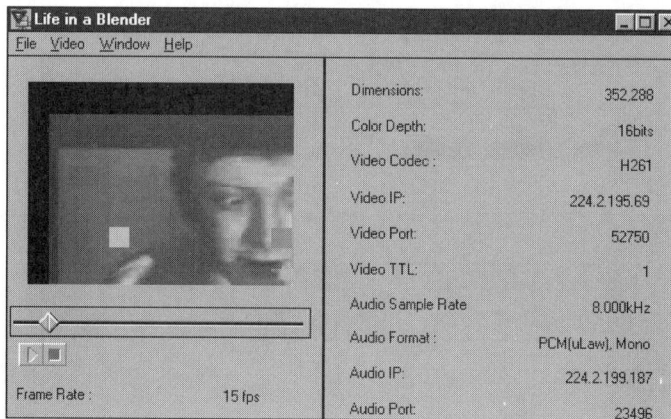

Figure 11.19 Starting the music.

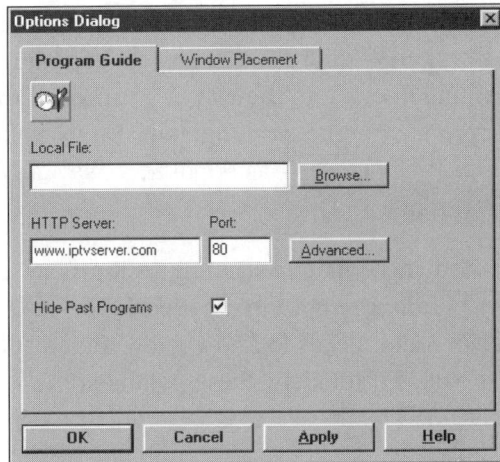

Figure 11.20 The Options dialog box.

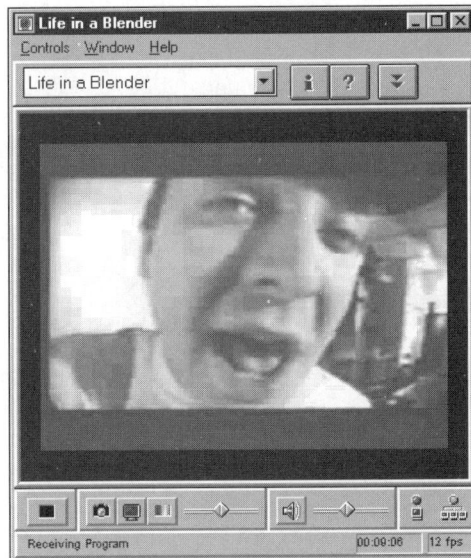

Figure 11.21 The movie playing on the test client.

Summary

If you take the time to organize your internetworking server setup into phases devoted to router configuration, CPU issues, and server software (for multicasting) installation, you should be able to get your server machine online in a way that makes the most sense conceptually.

Again, be prepared to spend the most time getting your ISDN router working properly—and don't be shy about getting tech support as soon as something doesn't go the way it's supposed to. Also, keep in mind that, for private internetworking, your ISDN router can only be called by another ISDN router—as opposed to, say, a 28.8 modem or even a T1 (serial) router.

Finally, remember that connecting to a private LAN is not like Web surfing. To join a remote internetwork, the LAN you're calling with your ISDN router needs to know a few things about you before it will welcome you. Fortunately, these details are few enough that this is a relatively small issue.

Chapter 12

- **Setting up the router**

- **Readying the computer**

- **Configuring the client software**

Chapter
12

Configuring A Remote Client For WAN Multicasts

As in Chapter 11, this chapter concerns itself with the details of preparing a system to engage in multicasting. Unlike Chapter 11, this time we'll work from the internetworked *client* perspective. For the record, specially-configured NT machines with high-end routers can actually receive *MBone* transmissions. Unfortunately, such specialized configurations are beyond the scope of this book.

As already noted, the hardest part of being an internetworked client can be getting served the first time. This is mainly due to problems most people experience in getting their routers and ISDN connections sorted out properly. We'll walk through all of the steps of getting your hardware working, then I'll document how to add data to your client configuration files so that you can connect to cooperative multicasting servers at will.

We'll partition the process into the following three main areas to keep things as clear and modular as possible:

- Setting up the router.

- Readying the computer.

- Configuring the client multicasting software.

We'll tackle each of these areas in sequence, with the objective of connecting to a multicasting server to receive an IP/TV video stream after selecting that stream from the IP/TV Program Guide. We'll also describe how to do the same using Microsoft NetShow software.

Again, bear in mind that this is not really analogous to Web surfing. Internetworked servers and clients do not normally operate on an anonymous basis, as do the legions of PCs and Macs that surf the World Wide Web. If you have enough server entries in your routing table, you may be able to jump around among several server links, but it's not like pointing and clicking on Web page hotspots and going somewhere brand new.

As noted, this is not because of how multicasting works. The limitations lie in the nature of ISDN, TCP/IP routing, and PC-based client/server technology, in general. It's hard to say whether these bottlenecks (if you can call them that) will clear up any time soon. Because private LAN internetworking is essentially a special case of Internet connectivity, MBone issues may take precedence in the short run.

Setting Up The Router

Let's start from rock bottom. The first major premise is that you already have the following items:

1. An off-the-rack desktop computer with a good quality network card—in this case, a mid-range (P90) or better Pentium running Windows 95 or NT 4.0.

2. A dedicated ISDN line—2 channel (128 Kbps) preferred.

3. Some decent multicasting software—for this demo, Precept's IP/TV Viewer.

4. A multicast-capable router—in this case, the Cisco 2524, although products from Ascend, Farallon, and others will likely be good candidates by the time you read this.

5. A multicasting server to call. The catch here is that the server must receive the call on an ISDN line (remember, we are not communicating via the Internet in this demonstration).

Remember the meta systems introduced in Chapter 5? The previous list contains all the components required for the Multicast Consumer model, and Figure 12.1 displays the Multicast Consumer meta system. Here, the ISP role is now played by our multicasting server. If you feel any fuzziness with this concept, you might want to review the other models described in Chapter 5 as well.

Assuming the big picture is clear for now, let's get into the configuration details. Our second major premise is that you're eager to proceed, willing to get your hands dirty, and able to deal with a certain amount of frustration in the early going. Some people may want to put on a pot of herbal tea and some classical music at this point.

As noted earlier, the router in question is the Cisco 2524, although the configuration profile we'll be editing is a standard text stream that works in routers up and down the Cisco product line. This text stream is normally referred to by Cisco customers and tech support personnel as the router's *config file*, because it can be cut and pasted into an ASCII text file if necessary. Pasting your config file into an ASCII text file enables you to email the file to tech support for review if they can't solve your problems by phone.

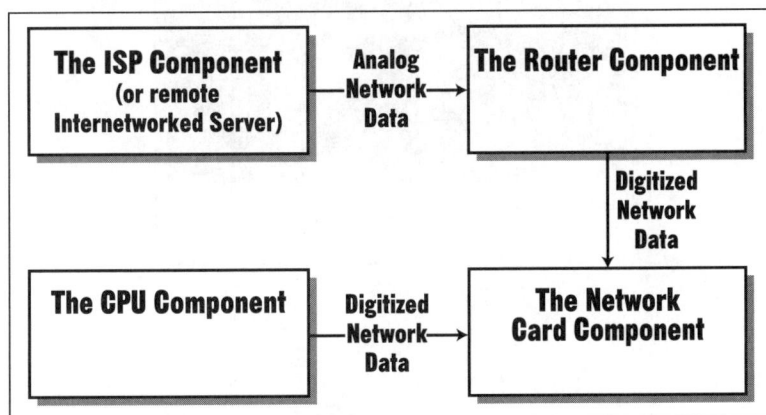

Figure 12.1 The Multicast Consumer meta system.

Remember that you'll be dialing another computer, as opposed to your commercial ISP. Consequently, calling your ISP's technical support desk (recommended at this point in Chapter 11 to get an advance sense of their knowledge level) isn't really necessary. You might, however, want to keep the router manufacturer's tech support number handy.

Chapter 11 presented a recipe for editing Cisco config files using the HyperTerminal program that comes with Windows 95 and NT (via a direct serial connection from COM1 or COM2 to the router). For variety, we'll edit the config files discussed in this chapter on a Mac (also with a serial connection). Your favorite terminal program will likely do nicely, although in this example, we'll use the excellent shareware app Black Night (see Figure 12.2), available at **www.shareware.com**.

Configuring Your Router With Black Night

Even though we'll consume multicast streams on a Wintel desktop, we can still talk to our router component with a Mac—or with any other machine sporting a serial port. If we were using a Mac to receive multicasts with this router, we could configure the router on the same Mac with a terminal program like Black Night. This is analogous to using HyperTerminal on the same Wintel machine running the IP/TV Server in Chapter 11.

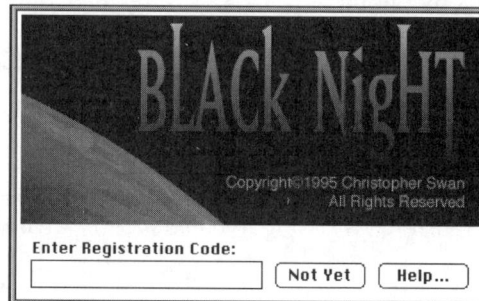

Figure 12.2 Launching Black Night.

Note! *Many routers let you Telnet into them to perform configurations rather than going in via a serial port. While this is a bit more elegant, it requires you to know the IP address of the router in advance.*

If you haven't used Black Night before, here's the simple formula to get it talking to your router:

1. Click on the Not Yet button shown in Figure 12.2 if you're not ready to register just yet (otherwise, complete the registration process). A window with a black background will open.

2. Click on the Connect item in the Session menu. A short tone will play, indicating you're connected. Tap your Enter key to see the prompt shown in Figure 12.3. This router's hostname is INX-12456.

3. If you wish, you can save this session by clicking on Save As in the File menu, which brings up the dialog shown in Figure 12.4.

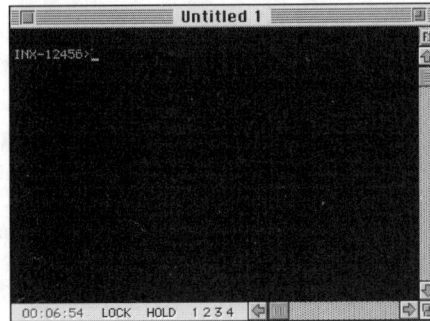

Figure 12.3 Connecting to the router.

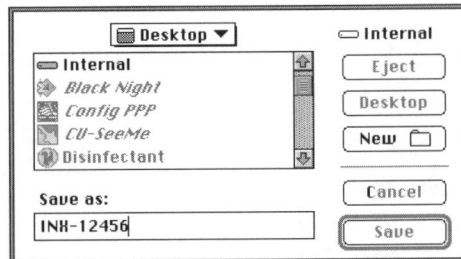

Figure 12.4 Black Night's Save As dialog box.

If you followed the plan in Chapter 11, you'll already be familiar with what procedures come next:

1. For overall clarity, we'll start with a config file that simply connects our router to our regular ISP. This will allow our system normal Internet access (at ISDN router speeds).

2. Next, we'll add sample entries to the config file so that our router can connect to at least one sample server.

In Procedure 2, we'll also add the entries that make our router multicast-capable. For logistical reasons, the sample server entries will not reflect WAN ports on actual private networks. We will, however, make one of the server entries agree with a client entry specified in the server config file shown in Chapter 11.

Connecting To An ISP

As noted, the more you work with Cisco equipment, the better you'll become at editing config files. It can seem very frustrating at first, especially if you're working at the command line, but this is money in the bank for serious multicasters. Again, if you deal with Cisco tech support, they will probably ask you to email your config file at some point if they can't quickly solve your problem.

CONFIG FILE OVERVIEW

Listing 12.1 is a Cisco config file that connects a 2524 ISDN Router to an ISP. Note that the entries shown do not reflect all the configurable parameters. Also note that no multicast parameters are specified yet, and that certain digits are replaced with Xs for security reasons. We'll address the entries individually in a moment.

LISTING 12.1 A SIMPLE CISCO CONFIG FILE.

```
Current configuration:
!
version 11.0
service password-encryption
service udp-small-servers
service tcp-small-servers
!
hostname INX-12456
!
enable secret 5 $1$TzOH$.8C63nkaFT5oWJmgtAeNX.
enable password 7 071F205F5D1E161713
!
```

```
username XXX-XXXXX password 7 0009182E1C5A0D0457
username SanFrancisc01-M1 password 7 151F00241C2B2D2670
isdn switch-type basic-ni1
!
interface Ethernet0
 ip address 207.88.XXX.XXX 255.255.255.XXX
!
interface Serial0
 no ip address
 shutdown
!
interface BRI0
 ip unnumbered Ethernet0
 encapsulation ppp
 isdn spid1 415399XXXX00
 isdn spid2 415399XXXX00
 dialer idle-timeout 60
 dialer wait-for-carrier-time 60
 dialer map ip 205.158.3.52 name SanFrancisco01-M1 broadcast
14155362822
 dialer hold-queue 100
 dialer-group 1
 no fair-queue
 ppp multilink
 ppp pap sent-username XXX-XXXXX password 7 141A192314052C297C
!
ip domain-name downrecs.xo.com
ip name-server 205.158.3.50
ip name-server 199.2.14.10
ip route 0.0.0.0 0.0.0.0 205.158.3.52
ip route 205.158.3.52 255.255.255.255 BRI0
snmp-server community public RO
dialer-list 1 protocol ip permit
!
line con 0
 exec-timeout 0 0
line aux 0
 transport input all
line vty 0 4
 password 7 1401061B0D17393C2B3A37
 login
!
end
```

As explained in Chapter 11, if you are installing an ISDN router from
scratch, you may have switched from a standard 28.8 ISP to an ISDN
ISP. If you did, you were likely provided with a ledger of connection
details. As we review the entries in Listing 12.1, we'll resolve them
with the ISDN connection setting provided by a generic ISDN ISP.

If your router already has a working config file, you may want to erase as much of it as possible so that you are working with a relatively clean slate. Of course, it will be hard to tell what's important at the beginning, but bear in mind that if a certain parameter is not specified in a Cisco config file, the default value for that entry is generally in force. In other words, just because an entry is missing from the config list doesn't mean it doesn't have a value assigned.

Note! *Once again, Cisco provides ample documentation for all of its hardware products. The newer documentation comes on CD-ROM in hypertext format, and walks you through configuration details with hardly any trouble at all. Also, its technical support people are courteous and well-trained. Cisco's general number, which takes you to tech support, is 408-525-4000.*

CONFIG FILE DETAILS

Following is a discussion of the individual configuration entries for this particular demonstration (simply connecting to an ISP). As shown in Chapter 11, editing a Cisco config file from the command line with confidence requires some basic navigation skills, which we'll cover here as well. The process is essentially the same regardless of the type of terminal program you're using (HyperTerminal, Black Night, and so on).

Let's revisit Black Night's main UI, last seen in Figure 12.3. To get started, we'll key in the following commands (as shown in Figure 12.5):

1. *enable* (or *en*), then press the Enter key.

2. *xxxxxx* (the password, whatever it is), then press the Enter key. (Note: password characters do not echo.)

3. *config t*, then press the Enter key.

With configuration mode thus enabled, we can now address the individual entries.

- *hostname*—This is the name you assign to your router (and which appears at the command prompt), in this case INX-12456. To make this entry, enter *hostname INX-12456* (or whatever you want to name

```
                    INH-12456
INX-12456>en
Password:
INX-12456#config t
Enter configuration commands, one per line.  End with CNTL/Z.
INX-12456(config)#




00:40:08  LOCK  HOLD  1 2 3 4
```

Figure 12.5 Putting a Cisco router in configuration mode with Black Night.

your router), then press the Enter key. (Note: All further entries should be followed by tapping the Enter key.)

- *username*—This is your username, as assigned by your ISP. In this example, it is XXX-XXXXX for security purposes. The password assigned by your ISP should also be entered here. To make this entry, type *username XXX-XXXXX password xxxxxxx* (using the real user name and password assigned by your ISP).

  As it turns out, the way the ISP used in this example works, we also need to add a *username* and *password* entry for the remote name assigned by the ISP—in this case, SanFrancisc01-M1. Your ISP will be able to help you figure this out if it is familiar with Cisco routers—which it should be.

- *isdn switch-type*—This is the type of switch used by your ISDN line provider (such as Pacific Bell). To make this entry, we enter *isdn switch-type basic ni1*. Figure 12.6 shows our progress so far. To save these entries, press Ctrl+Z, then enter *write* (or *wr*). If we turned our router off now, our work to this point would be preserved.

Note! *Some people prefer to enter wr mem (as opposed to just wr) to absolutely guarantee their edits are saved.*

- *interface Ethernet0*—Now for some more sophisticated entries. To reenter configuration mode, enter *config t*, followed by *int Ethernet0*. Next, enter the static IP address your ISP gave you for your router,

Figure 12.6 Editing the config profile.

including the subnet mask. In this case, the entry is *ip address 207.88.XXX.XXX 255.255.255.XXX* (Xs are used for security purposes).

- *interface BRI0*—This concerns the router's ISDN port. As shown in Listing 12.1, there are 12 entries that make this example work successfully. To get to the BRI0 interface, enter *int BRI0*. Now you can make each entry just as it looks in Listing 12.1. The only exception is the last one, *ppp pap sent-username XXX-XXXXX password 7 141A....* This is a special case due to the requirements of the ISP used in this example. A more common version of this entry is *ppp auth pap*. (Your ISP should be able to steer you straight here, as well.) Again, to save your configuration work so far, press Ctrl+Z and enter *wr*.

> **Note!** *The character strings following **password** in Listing 12.1 are not the actual passwords assigned by our ISP. They are random character strings generated by the router when we instructed it to show us its current configuration. This is also done by entering the command show config.*

- *ip route*—Now, let's put in some IP routing information. Because the configuration we are currently building will just be used to connect to our ISP, we only need two **ip route** statements (as indicated in Listing 12.1). These two statements reflect our ISP's own IP address and subnet mask (as provided by our ISP). Later in this chapter, we'll add additional **ip route** statements for our prospective multicast servers. Don't forget to first enter *config t* before entering your **ip route** statements.

- *ip name-server*—If your ISP gave you IP addresses for its name servers (primary and secondary DNS data), you can make these entries the **ip name-server** commands, also shown in Listing 12.1. Don't forget to press Ctrl+Z and enter *wr* when you're done. To see if all of the configuration data you've entered has found its mark, enter *wr t*, and examine the results. It should look a lot like Listing 12.1. If your ISP provided data that doesn't correspond to any of the configuration entries, ask its help or contact Cisco tech support.

TESTING THE CONFIGURATION

Assuming your config profile is now ready for prime time, try pinging your ISP from the command line. Figure 12.7 shows part of the message flow you'll probably see if things proceed normally. If you get error messages, don't be discouraged. As noted earlier, router setup is one of the hardest parts of configuring a multicast client—if not *the* hardest.

As noted in Chapter 11, sometimes just a small bit of super-tuning is all it takes to get your config file running on all cylinders. Often, however, new multicasters (and multicast consumers) spend a good deal of time calling tech support. In fact, don't be surprised if your otherwise friendly ISP immediately sics you on you router manufacturer (in this case, Cisco).

With your router now able to talk to your ISP, try running a Web browser and some other Internet applications (email, FTP, and so on). When you're satisfied that they all work like they did prior to using your ISDN

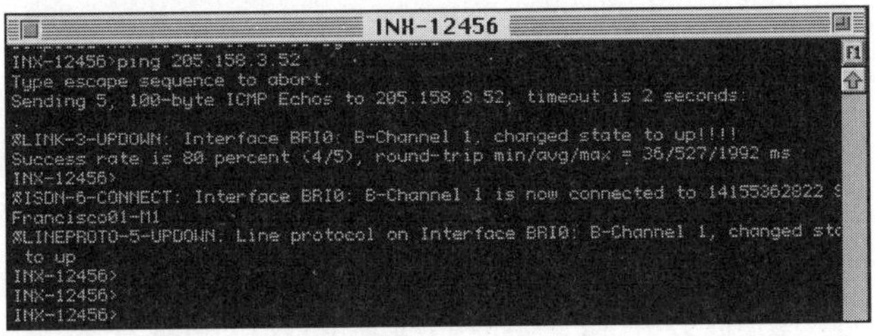

Figure 12.7 Houston, we have liftoff!

router, we'll move on to the next section. You should find all your Internet apps working much better, assuming you were using a 28.8 Kpbs modem previously.

Note! *You'll probably have to reset the IP addresses, domain names, and related values in the Windows Network Applet for all the machines on your LAN that need to connect to the Internet. For completeness, we'll cover this later in the section titled "Readying The Computer."*

Connecting To An Internetworked Multicast Server

Our first goal in this chapter was to connect to an ISP using a bare-bones config file with our Cisco 2524 router. With that accomplished, we're now ready to enhance our configuration to:

• enable multicasting.

• connect to multiple dialin servers from whom we want to receive multicasts.

As shown in Listing 12.2, only a few additional entries are needed by the configuration represented in Listing 12.1 to enable multicasting capability. Likewise, for multiple server accommodation. Listing 12.2 shows our enhanced config file in its entirety. Give it a quick read-through, then we'll look at each of the new entries in context.

LISTING 12.2 A MULTICAST-ENABLED CISCO CONFIG FILE.

```
Current configuration:
!
version 11.0
service password-encryption
service udp-small-servers
service tcp-small-servers
!
hostname INX-12456
!
enable secret 5 $1$TzOH$.8C63nkaFT5oWJmgtAeNX.
enable password 7 071F205F5D1E161713
!
username XXX-XXXXX password 7 0009182E1C5A0D0457
username SanFrancisc01-M1 password 7 151F00241C2B2D2670
```

```
username Server1 password XXXXXX
username Server2 password XXXXXX
username Server3 password XXXXXX
isdn switch-type basic-ni1
ip multicast-routing
!
interface Ethernet0
 ip address 207.88.XXX.XXX 255.255.255.XXX
 ip pim dense-mode
!
interface Serial0
 no ip address
 shutdown
!
interface BRI0
 ip unnumbered Ethernet0
 encapsulation ppp
 isdn spid1 415399XXXX00
 isdn spid2 415399XXXX00
 dialer idle-timeout 60
 dialer wait-for-carrier-time 60
 dialer map ip 205.158.3.52 name SanFrancisco01-M1 broadcast
14155362822
 dialer map ip 0000.0000.0000.0000 name Server1 broadcast
14155551212
 dialer map ip 0000.0000.0000.0000 name Server2 broadcast
14155551212
 dialer map ip 0000.0000.0000.0000 name Server3 broadcast
14155551212
 dialer hold-queue 100
 dialer-group 1
 no fair-queue
 ppp multilink
 ppp auth pap
!
ip domain-name downrecs.xo.com
ip name-server 205.158.3.50
ip name-server 199.2.14.10
!
ip route 0.0.0.0 0.0.0.0 205.158.3.52
ip route 205.158.3.52 255.255.255.255 BRI0
ip route X.X.X.X X.X.X.X XXX.XXX.XXX.XXX
ip route XXX.XXX.XXX.XXX 255.255.255.255 BRI0
ip route X.X.X.X X.X.X.X XXX.XXX.XXX.XXX
ip route XXX.XXX.XXX.XXX 255.255.255.255 BRI0
!
snmp-server community public RO
dialer-list 1 protocol ip permit
!
```

```
line con 0
 exec-timeout 0 0
line aux 0
 transport input all
line vty 0 4
 password 7 1401061B0D17393C2B3A37
 login
!
end
```

The new entries (shown in boldface) are broken out in the code blocks shown in Listing 12.3. Obviously, the bolded **username**, **dialer map**, and **ip route** entries are merely placeholders, but they show where new servers and their IP routing addresses would be registered (in similar fashion to the previous ISP entries). Note that the authentication entry has changed completely, from **ppp pap sent-username** to **ppp auth pap**, although some configuration scenarios may require using **chap** instead of **pap**. Also note that some people like to add the setting *speed 56* to the *dialer map* entry (to ensure broader compatibility among connected routers), as in the syntax:

```
dialer map ip 205.158.3.52 name SanFrancisco01-M1 speed 56
broadcast 14155362822
```

LISTING 12.3 THE HEAVY-LIFTING AREA.

```
username XXX-XXXXX password 7 0009182E1C5A0D0457
username SanFrancisc01-M1 password 7 151F00241C2B2D2670
username Server1 password XXXXXX
username Server2 password XXXXXX
username Server3 password XXXXXX
isdn switch-type basic-ni1
ip multicast-routing
!
interface Ethernet0
 ip address 207.88.XXX.XXX 255.255.255.XXX
 ip pim dense-mode
!
interface BRI0
 ...
 dialer map ip 0000.0000.0000.0000 name Server1 broadcast
14155551212
 dialer map ip 0000.0000.0000.0000 name Server2 broadcast
14155551212
 dialer map ip 0000.0000.0000.0000 name Server3 broadcast
14155551212
 ...
```

```
    ppp auth pap
    !
ip route 0.0.0.0 0.0.0.0 205.158.3.52
ip route 205.158.3.52 255.255.255.255 BRI0
ip route X.X.X.X X.X.X.X XXX.XXX.XXX.XXX
ip route XXX.XXX.XXX.XXX 255.255.255.255 BRI0
ip route X.X.X.X X.X.X.X XXX.XXX.XXX.XXX
ip route XXX.XXX.XXX.XXX 255.255.255.255 BRI0
ip route X.X.X.X X.X.X.X XXX.XXX.XXX.XXX
ip route XXX.XXX.XXX.XXX 255.255.255.255 BRI0
```

The most obvious new entry here is **ip multicast-routing**. This can be added in the same manner we added it earlier in the bare-bones config file. Assuming you're at the HOST_NAME prompt (depending on your host name) using Black Night, key in the following commands (as shown in Figure 12.8):

1. *enable* (or *en*).

2. *xxxxxx* (your password, whatever it is).

3. *config t.*

4. At the (config) # prompt, enter *ip multicast-routing*.

5. Still at the (config) # prompt, enter any new server username data.

6. Still at the (config) # prompt, enter any new ip route statements.

7. Still at the (config) # prompt, enter int *Ethernet0*.

8. At the (config-if) # prompt, enter ip *pim dense-mod*e.

9. Still at the (config-if) # prompt, press Ctrl+Z.

10. Back at the HOST_NAME # prompt, enter *write* (or *wr t* to view the whole current configuration) to save your work.

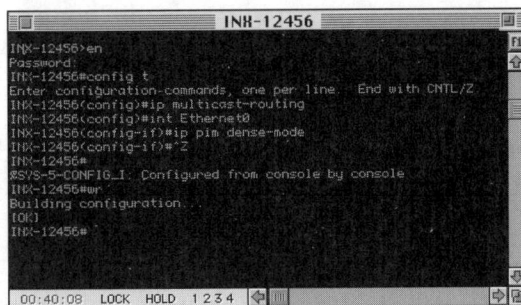

Figure 12.8 Enabling multicasting and multiple dialin servers.

Like in Chapter 11, this is the essential task list for configuring a Cisco router for multicasting mode. As you become more acquainted with Cisco equipment and routing technology in general, you'll see that we're just scratching the surface here in terms of utilizing complex config files. Also, these are not prescribed settings. Your final config file may look somewhat different by the time you are consistently dialing in stable multicasts.

For instance, it's possible to set up a tunnel (covered in later chapters) at the command line with statements similar to the ones we just issued. Also, many other parameters specifying router behavior may be designated here. Entering *?* at different levels of the command line interface will give you a good sense of this complexity.

Note! *Instead of issuing a whole series of individual **ip route** commands, you can often use router rip as a blanket protocol to cover your dialin servers and their IP routing addresses. While this seems handy, it does carry some performance issues best explained by Cisco tech support. Listing 12.4 shows the router rip syntax.*

LISTING 12.4 IMPLEMENTING ROUTER RIP.

```
router rip
 network XXX.XXX.XXX.XXX
```

Troubleshooting

In a perfect world, with the changes detailed earlier in this chapter made to your router (and your computer readied in the ways described in the next sections), you could launch an application like Precept's IP/TV Viewer, know that your router was dialing a remote server with an IP/TV Program Guide and IP/TV Server programming available, then choose the multicast you wanted to consume.

The reality is that you'll probably have to spend some time troubleshooting, even before the first remote multicast starts playing on your desktop. The best way to troubleshoot your setup is to find someone at a remote location—with an ISDN line and a multicast router—who is willing to take the time to get the packets flowing.

Probably the most common type of problems you'll encounter will be ISDN and Ethernet (addressed in the *interface BRI0* and *interface Ethernet0* sections of the config files shown in Listings 12.1 and 12.2). The worst offenders in the ISDN category likely will be your dialer-map and authorization (PAP, CHAP, and so on) entries. Unfortunately, most of these problems will only be solved by trial and error—hopefully based on wisdom gained by reading the documentation and consulting tech support personnel.

For example, you may not need an authorization entry if you're connecting to a dedicated remote server other than your ISP. Similarly, you may be able to dispense with certain passwords if the servers you wish to connect to don't require them (based on *their* config files).

Finally, keep in mind that, despite the rapid growth of ISDN in the home and small business markets, large corporations usually use bigger pipes (like T1 lines). Consequently, you'll likely be unable to test with people at large corporations unless they've gone to the trouble of putting ISDN ports on their LAN/WANs.

Readying The Computer

As on the server side, there is not much exotic activity required for installing a desktop (or laptop) computer as an internetworked multicast client—outside of making sure it meets the basic performance criteria required by the networking/multicasting software it will be running.

For instance (as noted in Chapter 6), Precept's IP/TV Viewer requirements are as follows:

- a Pentium 90 MHz (or greater) machine.

- at least 8 MB of RAM for Windows 95.

- at least 16 MB of RAM for Windows NT.

Of course, a fast network adapter card and high-end SCSI hard drives will increase performance also, but these are generally more important on the multicast server side. Still, it's worth noting that whatever you can do to upgrade your hardware will contribute to overall performance when it comes to receiving and playing multimedia streams—just like with digital video and audio on the local desktop.

Configuring The Network Applet

As noted earlier, setting up a router on a local subnet usually involves making changes to the values held in the Control Panel Network Applets of your local machines. Figure 12.9 shows where to start making these changes after executing Start|Settings|Control Panel|Network, then choosing Properties for the network adapter for a particular machine.

The gateway address is the IP address of your router. If your ISDN ISP assigned you a static address for your router, it should have also assigned you at least one other static IP number for at least one computer on your LAN. Depending on the scope of your ISDN service contract, you'll need to change the Network Applets for all your Wintel machines that need Internet access and were allocated new IP addresses by your ISP.

Configuring Mac Clients

One of the nice things about Windows NT is how well it accommodates Macintosh clients as full-on members of a given local subnet. The same applies for remote Macs seeking admittance to an NT LAN, assuming the NT server has been set up correctly (an easy task).

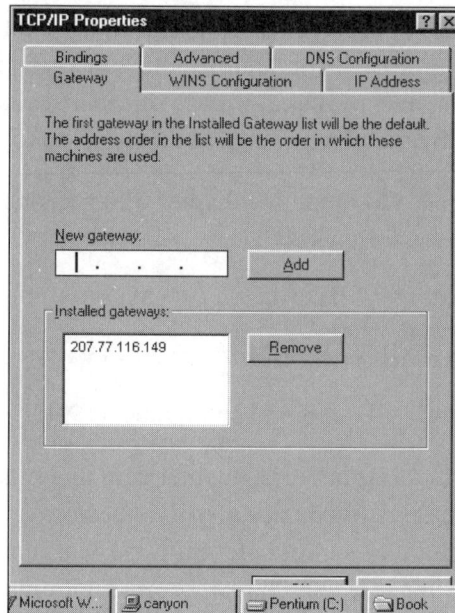

Figure 12.9 Configuring the Windows Network Applet.

With this foundation in place, successful multicast consumption on an internetworked Mac is generally a function of configuring the router correctly (especially the ISDN interface), just like on the Windows side. When Macs get more sophisticated at *serving* multicast content, there will be more Mac-related internetworking issues to deal with. Chapter 13 presents some cross-platform scenarios for receiving IP/TV and NetShow multicasts on the Mac

Configuring The Client Software

Assuming you know the addresses of some multicast servers on some remote subnets callable by your router (and you've got all the bugs worked out of your connection processes), you should be able to receive media streams from them with a minimal amount of application configuration. The balance of this chapter will present the steps involved in using the player apps for Precept's IP/TV and Microsoft's NetShow.

Precept's IP/TV

If you took the multicast test drive in Chapter 6, you've already got the necessary Precept IP/TV Viewer software installed. To pull in a program from a remote IP/TV server, execute the following sequence. The overall effect should feel just like consuming the same multicast on a local subnet. Because you'll be connected via a direct ISDN link (as opposed to over the Internet), overall performance should be quite acceptable.

1. Invoke the IP/TV viewer. Click on Edit|Settings to bring up the panel shown in Figure 12.10. Enter the name of your IP/TV server in the appropriate control, as shown, then click on OK.

2. If you don't see the expected program information, click on View|Refresh Listing from the IP/TV View main menu.

3. Double click on the program item, and the presentation should commence in a separate window, as show in Figure 12.11.

Microsoft NetShow

The drill for testing NetShow viewer apps on an internetworked client is essentially the same as for IP/TV, for both the Live component and the NetShow On Demand application. Again, as with the Precept

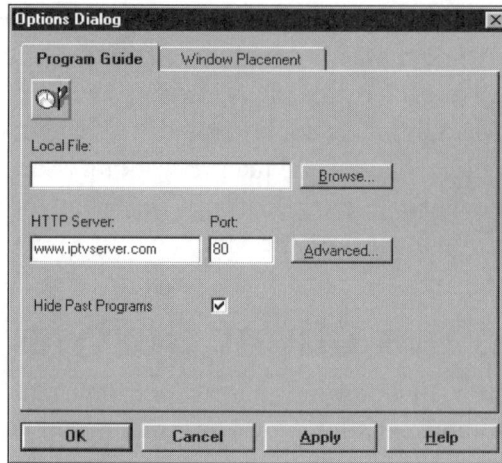

Figure 12.10 The Options dialog box.

Figure 12.11 A remote multicast in progress.

solution, consuming NetShow content remotely should feel almost like it does on a local subnet.

Assuming your router is connected to a LAN on which a NetShow server is pumping out multicast content, you should be able to successfully repeat the test drive described in Chapter 6—only this time with your media stream coming in over your ISDN line.

Summary

As in Chapter 11, if you break down your remote client setup into task groups for router configuration, CPU tuning, and multicast software testing, you can get your client machine online in a way that makes the most sense conceptually. Once again, be prepared to spend the most time getting your ISDN router working properly—especially the ISDN interface itself.

Finally, keep in mind that joining a nonlocal subnet is not like surfing the Web. To become a member of a remote internetwork, the server you're dialing into with your ISDN router must know about you in advance. Once you have the proper clearance, however, you should be able to enjoy remote multicasts with little additional trouble.

Chapter 13

- **Defining the new cross-platform landscape**

- **Testing Wintel servers with Mac clients**

- **Mastering cross-platform content production**

13

Cross-Platform Issues In Multicasting

Each major PC platform (Wintel, Macintosh, Sun, and so on) has evolving solutions for delivering and presenting multicast content. Not all of these platform-specific solutions are equally mature, but it's a fair generalization nonetheless.

Fortunately, working with cross-platform media assets is now a much easier task (and a much easier process to understand) than during the first great CD-ROM era. As one New York City-based developer observed recently, "The only cross-platform problem I have now is changing to the A train at 59th Street."

That Was Then

Originally, cross-platform issues for desktop multimedia producers could be broken down into two principal categories:

- Making media files (such as QuickTime movies) playable on both Macs and Windows machines.

- Making media transport mechanisms (such as CD-ROM disks) compatible with peripheral hardware devices (such as CD-ROM drives) on both Macs and Windows machines.

There were other considerations as well, such as whether program code could somehow be made cross-platform, but publishers usually included two copies of their programs (i.e., separate Mac and Windows executables on the same CD-ROM) that performed, as similar to each other as possible, on their respective platforms.

CD-ROM publishers were keen to master these cross-platform issues because they didn't want to produce extra copies of multi-megabyte media assets to satisfy both Mac and Windows markets. In other words, if you could produce a single CD-ROM that a user could put into either a Mac or a Wintel box, and that CD-ROM could deliver the same media files (again, usually flattened QuickTime movies) in either environment, you could consider yourself a cross-platform king.

This Is Now

As multimedia takes to the networks (and the global Internet), new cross-platform issues are surfacing. As noted, these issues are not as frustrating as the original ones faced by content developers in the early 1990s. But they do have implications when it comes to how day-to-day work gets done.

In an abstract sense, the network router has taken the place of the CD-ROM drive (see Figure 13.1). Multimedia assets still must be playable on multiple target platforms to reach the largest possible audience, but there are no longer problems associated with storage device formats (like ISO versus Apple HFS). In essence, cross-platform problems on networks (and internetworks) now stem almost entirely from software circumstances.

For example, what prevents an incoming media stream originating on a Windows NT Server from playing on a Macintosh client? Not the network itself, or even the Mac's router or modem. If appropriate application and system software is installed on the Mac client, and the

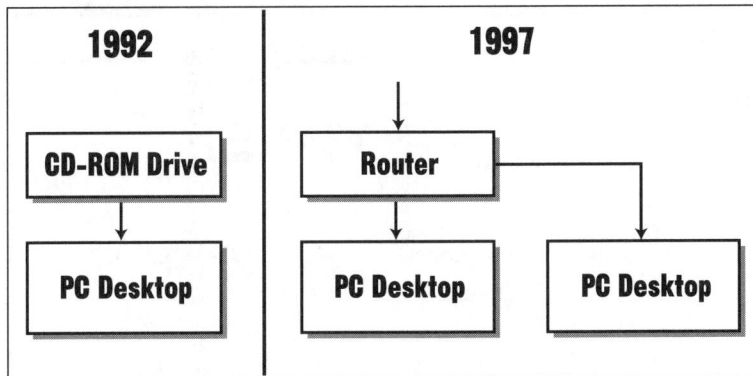

Figure 13.1 The new face of mass storage.

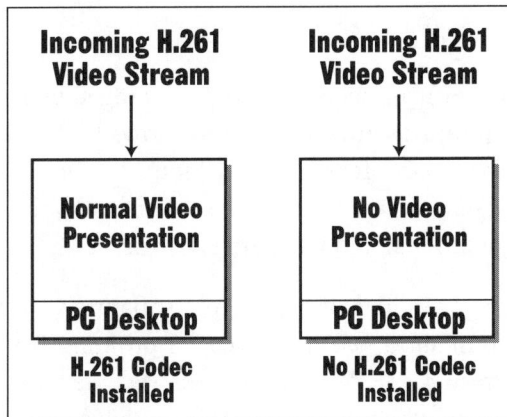

Figure 13.2 How cool are your codecs?

incoming media stream is compressed with a compatible codec, that stream should play just fine (see Figure 13.2).

This chapter looks at ways to solve the remaining cross-platform problems likely to be faced by multicast content developers. As just noted, these problems arise mainly from compressor mismatches and system-level incompatibilities, such as whether a given OS is (or can be made) multicast-capable.

Receiving Multicasts On The Mac

Back in Chapter 2, we spent several pages discussing Apple's QuickTime Conferencing (QTC) technology (see Figure 13.3). While the focus in

Figure 13.3 The QTC home page.

that chapter is on the video conferencing side of QTC, the literature at **http://qtc.quicktime.apple.com** shows that QTC is certainly not limited to video conferencing. In fact, like QuickTime itself, QTC is a highly sophisticated piece of system software that has applications throughout local and wide area networks.

You can get an idea of QTC's robust nature with the following demonstration. In short, we'll multicast a program from an NT 4.0 machine using Precept's IP/TV Server. We'll receive it on a local network with a Power Mac using a special MBone viewer application that leverages off the QTC system software.

Starting The IP/TV Server

As noted in Chapter 11, Precept's Program Guide is the preferred way to schedule multicasts from an IP/TV Server. However, only Program Guide-aware applications (such as the IP/TV Viewer) can use the Guide to tune in multicasts. Consequently, we'll launch a multicast manually like we did in the test drive demo in Chapter 6.

Here are the steps:

1. Invoke the IP/TV Server application.

2. From the File menu, click on the Launch Session item, as shown in Figure 13.4.

3. In the File Open dialog, click on an appropriate SVR file, as shown in Figure 13.5.

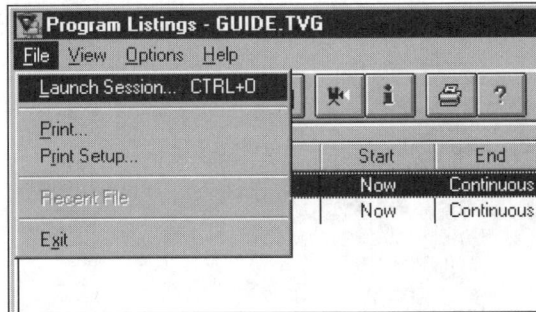

Figure 13.4 Launching a multicast session.

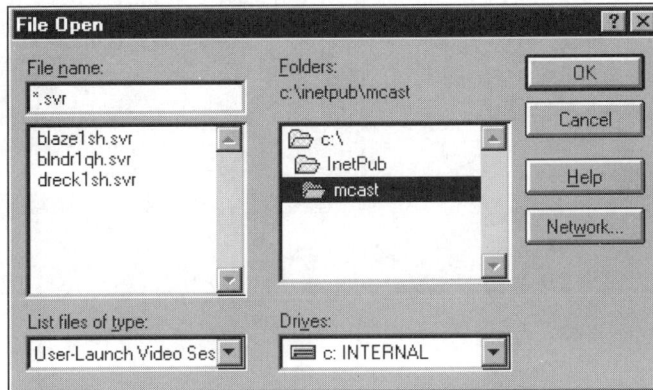

Figure 13.5 Selecting an SVR file.

> *Note!* The SVR file selected in Figure 13.5 was encoded with Precept's H.261 compressor using Premiere for Windows 4.2—a process detailed in Chapter 7. The point of this demonstration is to show that this compressor is specifically supported by the current release of QuickTime TV, as we'll see in a moment.*

4. After the appropriate SVR file is selected, the control panel shown in Figure 13.6 will appear.

5. Click on the green forward arrow under the left edge of the movie window to start the multicast movie. (If you wish to stop the multicast, click on the red square.) If you want to check that the multicast is proceeding normally, you can invoke the IP/TV Viewer on a Windows client on your local subnet and tune it in—with no effect on the movie's performance for other clients, naturally.

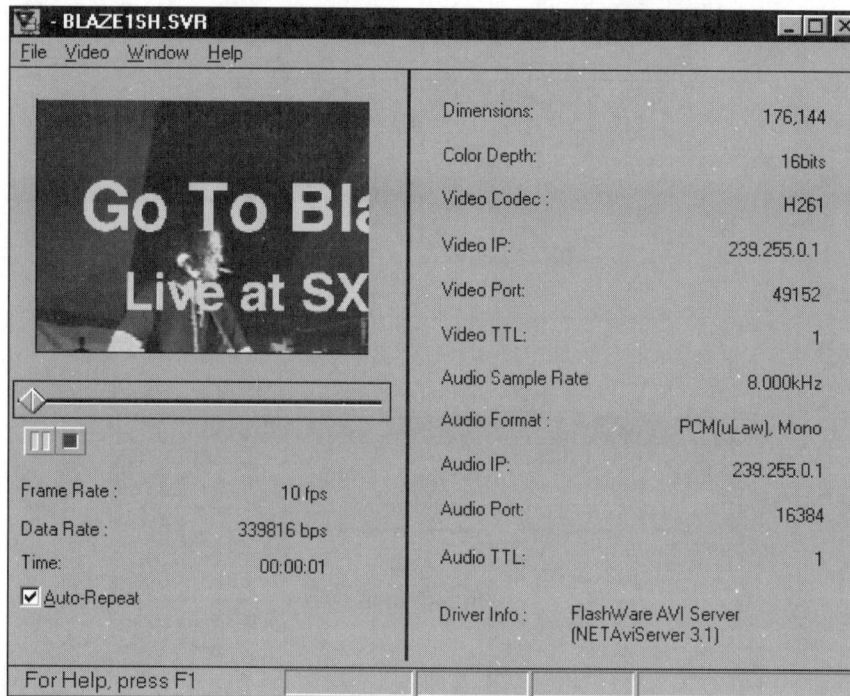

Figure 13.6 The IP/TV server control panel.

6. Until the Mac client is up and running, it's okay to leave the IP/TV Server apparently multicasting into space—it's the server's natural state anyway if it's a dedicated IP/TV station.

Setting Up The Mac Client

In the literature concerning QuickTime Conferencing, Apple advises QTC as strictly a Power Mac solution. For the record, you can install almost all of the QTC software on a 68 K machine (such as a Quadra 650) and receive audio multicasts, but it's not really worth the effort in the long run. What normally won't install on a 68 K system is Apple's H.261 codec, which handles video decompression.

As noted in Chapter 2, if you obtain the multicast software available at Apple's QTC Web site, you'll need to make sure you're using at least MacOS version 7.5.3 (7.5.5 preferred), along with Open Transport version 1.1.1. As usual, be aware that these requirements may change yet again by the time this book is published.

Assuming you've got the essential QTC components installed, there is one more piece to procure: the so-called QuickTime TV RTP Client (a.k.a. MBone TV). You can get this application at **http://qtc.quick time.apple.com/qttv/qttv.rtp.html**, as shown in Figure 13.7.

Installing the MBone TV application is straightforward. Once that task is complete, you are ready to receive a multicast from your NT machine running the IP/TV Server. Here are the steps:

1. On your Power Mac, double click on the MBone TV icon in your QuickTime Conferencing group (see Figure 13.8).

2. As the program starts executing, a splash screen will appear briefly, but the main UI consists of just a few menu items.

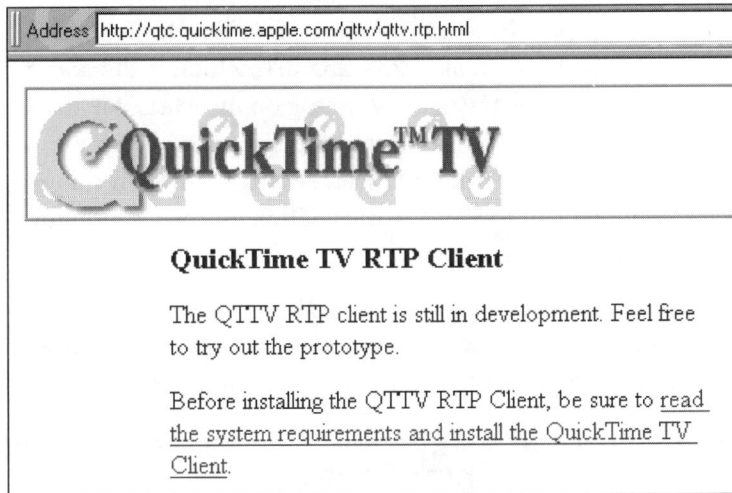

Figure 13.7   Where to get the MBone TV client.

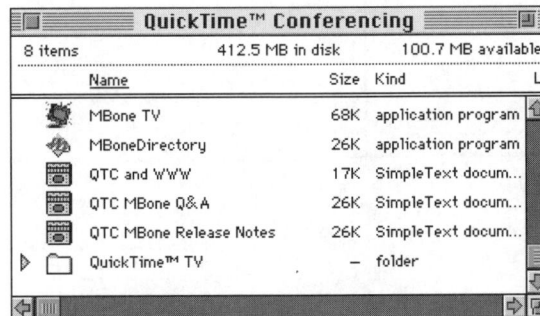

Figure 13.8   Where MBone TV normally installs itself.

3. In MBone TV's File menu, click on the Watch Broadcast item, which brings up the Browse The MBone panel shown in Figure 13.9. Because we are mixing technologies here, don't expect to see anything in MBone TV's Session List column.

Note! *This MBone TV application can actually be used to view bona fide MBone multicasts, as opposed to the local subnet multicast we're performing here.*

4. Now the low-tech part. First, check the Video checkbox in the lower left corner of the panel. Then click on the Type-In button, which brings up the small dialog shown in Figure 13.10. What we need to do now is go back to our IP/TV Server and take a look at the panel shown in Figure 13.6. You'll see that, in this case, the Video IP address is 239.255.0.1, which is the address we need to enter in the MBone TV dialog on the Mac. We also need to do the same thing for the Port number. For this example, we don't need to change the default TTL setting (although this is an important number in the real world). Click on the Okay button when these numbers are entered.

5. If the QTC software can handle the codec of our incoming multicast video stream, we should see the window shown in Figure 13.11. If not, MBone TV will put up the panel in Figure 13.12.

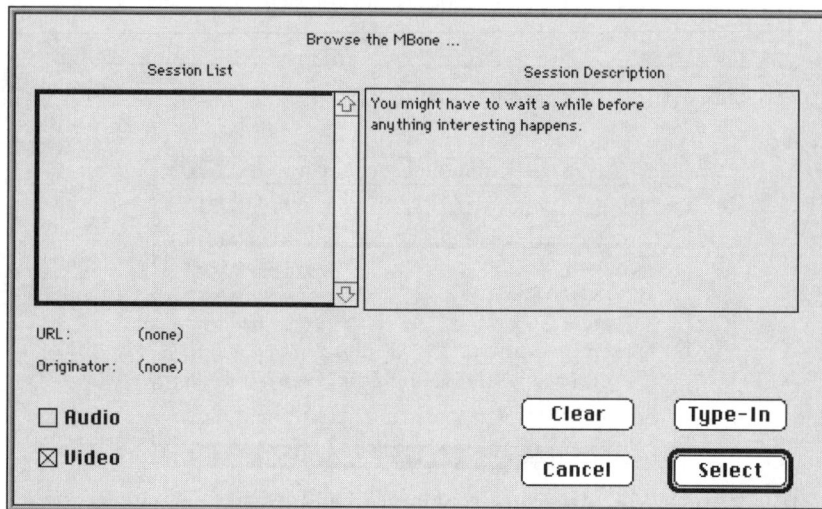

Figure 13.9 A Mac MBone program guide (with no program listings).

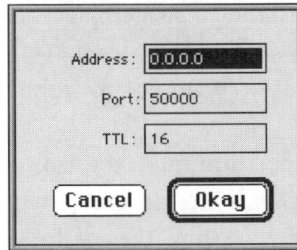

Figure 13.10   Setting up to receive video.

Figure 13.11   Receiving the IP/TV video stream.

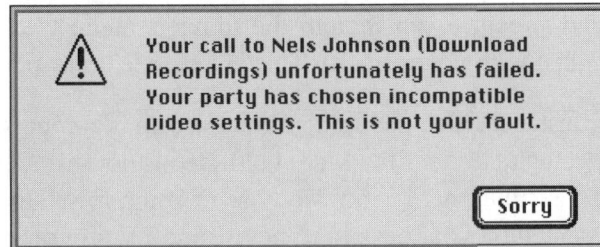

Figure 13.12   The result of an incompatible codec.

6. To tune in our movie's audio track, we need to repeat Steps 3 and 4, but this time check the Audio checkbox and fill in the Audio IP address and Port number shown on the IP/TV Server control panel—in this case 239.255.0.1 and 16384, respectively. Due to the pre-released nature of this MBone TV application, the audio presentation is handled via a separate movie controller bar, as shown in Figure 13.13.

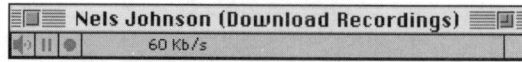

Figure 13.13 Receiving the IP/TV audio stream.

If you actually perform this exercise, you should take a moment to try out the controls (volume, start/stop, record) in the QTC movie controller bar to get a feel for how they differ from the controls in the standard QuickTime movie controller bar. Don't be surprised if the frame rate is substantially less than what is achieved by a Windows IP/TV client playing the same movie (on the same subnet).

Note! *If you're wondering about QTC for Windows, it is currently still in development. Check Apple's Web site frequently for late breaking developments on this front.*

Remember, this is essentially a proof-of-concept example. It does, however, set the stage for additional cross-platform experiments (which we'll get to in a moment). The thing to take away from this particular cross-platform demonstration is underscored by the message box shown in Figure 13.12: *Your party has chosen incompatible video settings.*

What this message boils down to is that your Mac doesn't have the right video decompressor installed to decode the incoming multicast video stream (even though the movie's audio track may have been handled with no problem). This is a classic cross-platform dilemma.

For instance, if an incoming movie stream is compressed with Indeo (a codec available for the Mac) but Indeo is not installed on your receiving machine, there is no way you're going to see the incoming video presented on your desktop. The MBone TV program is kind enough to give us a dialog to this effect—sometimes you just get a blank box or no video frame at all.

More Fun On The Mac

We gave Microsoft NetShow equal time in Chapter 6, so let's do the same here. We'll use NetShow's *Live* component to serve the content because it specifically supports the IP multicast standard—as opposed to NetShow On Demand, which uses a proprietary unicast protocol. Unfortunately, NetShow Live only works with multicast audio, at least for now.

On the receiving end, we'll once again use the Mac and the QTC/MBone TV combination. To keep things consistent, the audio file will be the sound track from the H.261 movie we used in the prior demo. Note that the H.261 video track has no bearing on the encoding nature of the audio track.

PREPARING THE AUDIO FILE

We'll use Premiere for Windows 4.2 for this task. Our goal is to simply create a test audio file with appropriate attributes for multicasting. Here's the drill:

1. Fire up Premiere and import the file used in the prior demo (see Chapter 7 for complete illustrations concerning working with movie files using Premiere 4.2).

2. Drag the movie from the Project window to the Construction window.

3. Double click on the audio track. The Waveform window shown in Figure 13.14 will appear.

4. Select File|Export|Waveform from Premiere's main menu, which brings up the dialog shown in Figure 13.15.

5. Key in a name for the audio file, set its attributes as low as possible, then save the file. Figure 13.15 shows these entries already made.

6. Close Premiere.

7. As you may have noticed, Premiere only gave us MPC values for File Save attributes even though the sound track of the movie we opened had an 8 kHz sample rate. To reset this value, we can use

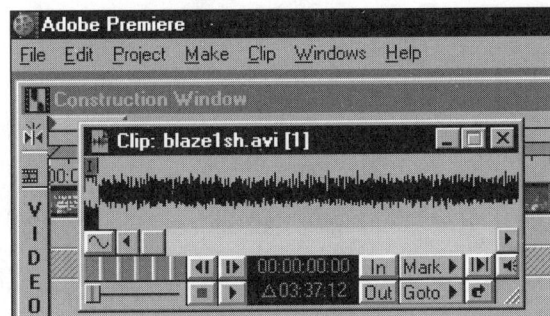

Figure 13.14 A Premiere audio clip window.

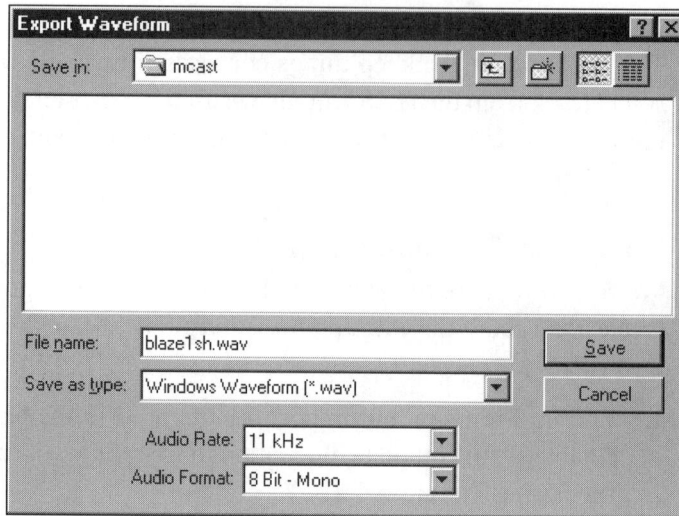

Figure 13.15 Saving off the WAV file.

the Windows 95 Sound Recorder, runnable by clicking on Start|Run, then browsing to SOUNDREC.EXE in your Windows directory.

8. Using Sound Recorder's UI, do a File|Open, and load the WAV file saved off in Premiere (see Figure 13.16).

9. Select File|Save As. When the Save As dialog appears, click on the Change button in the bottom right corner.

10. In the Sound Selection panel (shown in Figure 13.17), select the 8.000 kHz, 8 bit, mono setting in the Attributes control, then click on OK. (You can also get to this panel via File|Properties.)

11. Complete the Save As operation by saving the file under its original name, then exit Sound Recorder. We are now ready to multicast this file with NetShow Live.

Figure 13.16 Loading the WAV file in the Windows Sound Recorder.

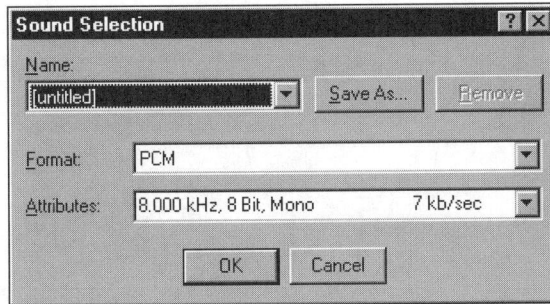

Figure 13.17 Changing the audio attributes.

Note! *If you are a Sound Forge user, you can open an AVI movie and save off the WAV audio file with an 8-bit sampling rate in one step—as opposed to the two-program process detailed earlier.*

SERVING THE NETSHOW MULTICAST

Now we can engage NetShow Live, as follows:

1. From the NT 4.0 Server desktop, click on Start|Programs|Microsoft NetShow|Live Administrator, which brings up the dialog shown in Figure 13.18.

2. Select File|New Session|Audio|WAV File to bring up the WAV File Session dialog shown in Figure 13.19 (with the appropriate entries already filled in). Fill in the data, and click on OK. Go ahead and use the defaults for the IP Address and Port number.

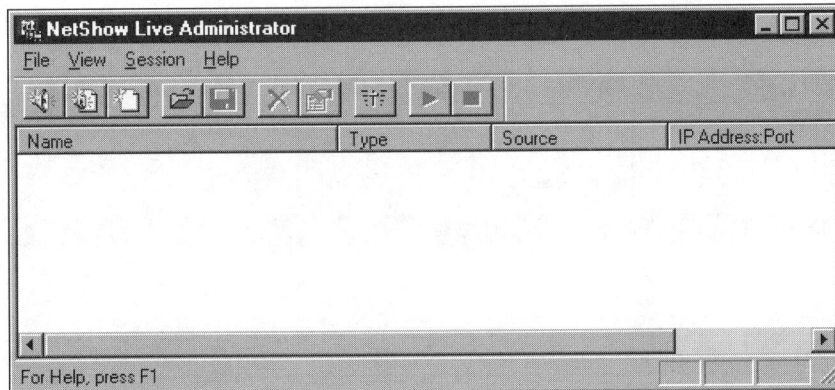

Figure 13.18 The main NetShow Live Administrator UI.

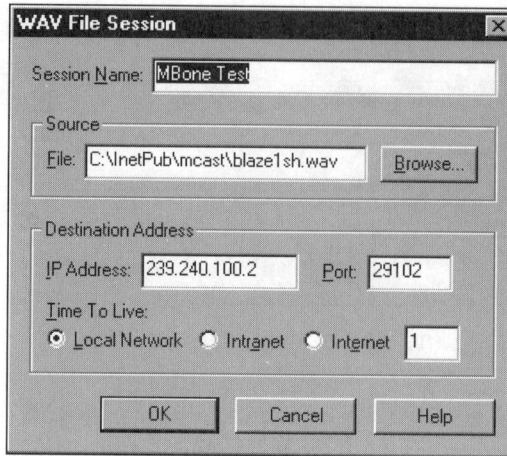

Figure 13.19 The WAV File Session dialog.

3. The NetShow Live Administrator window should now look like Figure 13.20. Go ahead and click on the black forward arrow control to start the audio file playing.

Our NetShow Server is now blasting the WAV file out to the IP multicast address specified in Figure 13.19. Let's go to the Mac to tune it in.

RECEIVING THE NETSHOW MULTICAST

This part of the demo is just like the IP/TV example.

1. Double click on the MBone TV icon in the QuickTime Conferencing folder.

2. In MBone TV's File menu, click on the Watch Broadcast item, which brings up the Browse The MBone panel shown earlier in

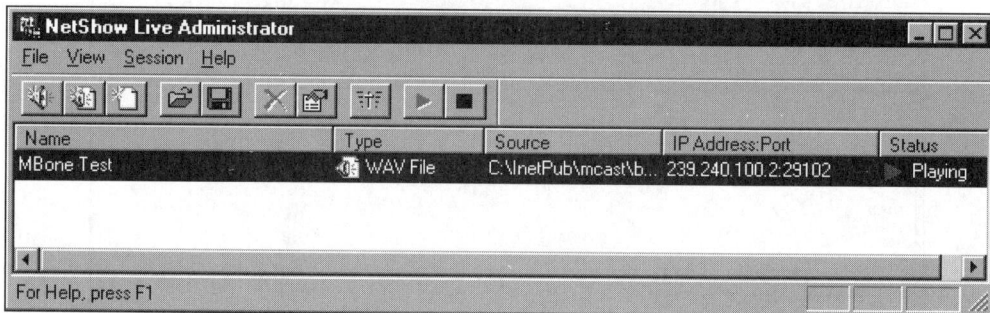

Figure 13.20 Starting the multicast.

Figure 13.9. Again, because we are mixing technologies here, don't expect to see anything in MBone TV's Session List column.

3. Check the Audio checkbox, then click on the Type In button. Fill in the Audio IP address and Port number shown in the NetShow Live Administrator window—in this case 239.240.100.2 and 29102, respectively.

4. Don't be surprised if the audio quality is a bit hinkier than in the IP/TV example, depending on the maturity of your versions of NetShow and QuickTime TV. Figure 13.21 shows the modest UI that should be on your Mac desktop as you receive the audio multicast.

5. If you wish, click on the red button on the movie controller bar. This will record the stream as a QuickTime sound-only movie on your Mac in realtime. The recorded movie will be placed on your Mac desktop.

If you perform either of these demonstrations, you'll see there are few barriers to cross-platform multicasting from a network transport perspective—save for the current immaturity of the desktop internetworking software, both at the system and application level.

In fact, if you paid close attention in the first example, you noticed that we were multicasting an H.261 video stream from an AVI file residing on a Wintel machine and playing that stream on a Mac that had an H.261 decompressor installed as a QuickTime component. Quite an interesting concept if you've spent the last few years pressing hybrid CD-ROMs.

Note! *You may be wondering if you can use CU-SeeMe or RealAudio to receive video and audio multicasts because they are billed as multicast-enabled products. The short answer is no. These two solutions use so-called application level (usually proprietary) multicasting, not true IP multicast protocols. Try them if you wish, but don't be surprised if you don't receive any standards-based multicasts—like the ones served by Precept's IP/TV.*

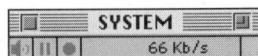

Figure 13.21   The QTC movie controller bar linked to the NetShow stream.

Mastering Cross-Platform Content Production

Regardless of the problems solved by delivering content on a network (as opposed to using mass storage devices), issues still remain for streaming media producers who like to capture and edit video and audio on one platform (such as a Mac) but need to compress and deliver (or just deliver) their finished clips on another, such as a Wintel box.

As noted in Chapter 7, you can bring a raw flattened QuickTime movie (digitized on a Mac) to a Windows machine for editing and compressing with Premiere 4.2. But, what if you want to edit and compress an existing raw AVI file on a Mac, especially a PowerMac with a 200 MHz or faster processor? The balance of this chapter presents ways to convert among the common video file formats for producers preparing media assets on their platforms of choice.

Converting On The Mac: QuickTime To AVI—Uncompressed Source

The first rule of thumb is to always perform conversions on files that are as uncompressed as possible. Because this example begins on the Mac, the appropriate uncompressed format is the QuickTime *None* codec. Starting with movies already compressed (with the Cinepak codec, for example) requires a different strategy, which is detailed later in this chapter.

If you grab video on the Mac with a board that saves raw captures in MJPEG, you can convert those clips to None in Mac Premiere with no loss of quality (although you could need up to 8 or 10 times as much hard disk storage space as the MJPEG files require). *None* essentially means straight RGB encoding with no effective data loss. Premiere for Windows 4.2 now uses this term also.

Note! *Speaking of hard drives, you're going to need a way to transport the converted movie file to your target Windows environment. If you're not using a LAN, plugging and playing mass storage devices (gig and larger hard drives, Jaz drives, and so on) can be quite acceptable in this context—as long as you manage them carefully and intelligently.*

Assuming you have a None-encoded QuickTime file ready to go on your Mac, the next task is to convert it to an AVI file. The Microsoft Macintosh program VFW Converter is custom-made for this purpose. You can download this program (as part of a StuffIt archive named QTAVI.SIT) from CompuServe's Windows Multimedia forum (GO WINMM).

While QTAVI.SIT was rumored to be on Microsoft's Web site at one time, recent searches have not produced results (although it is worth checking from time to time). This software was also included in the original Video for Windows developer's package.

Here's how to use the VFW Converter:

1. Double click on the program on your Mac desktop. The main user interface will appear, as shown in Figure 13.22.

2. Click on the Open Source button to invoke the File Selection dialog, then navigate to the directory that contains your source QuickTime movies (see Figure 13.23).

3. Back in the main UI, click on Open Destination to navigate to the target drive and directory. Then click on the Convert button. The dialog shown in Figure 13.24 will appear.

4. Enter the target file name in the Destination File Name field (if you want it to be different from the default).

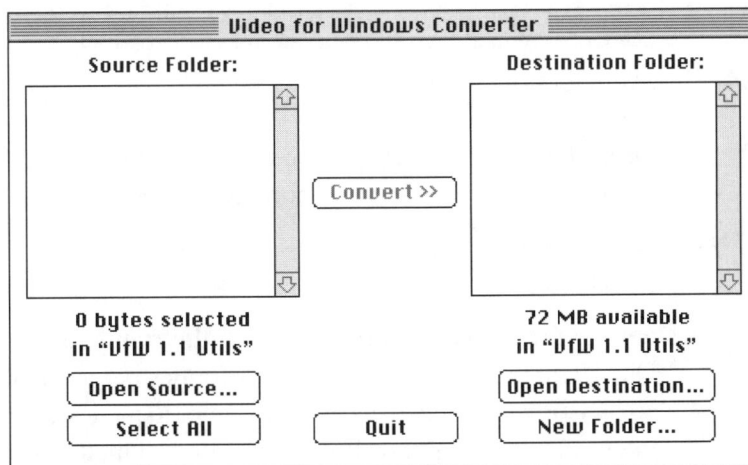

Figure 13.22 The VFW Converter main UI.

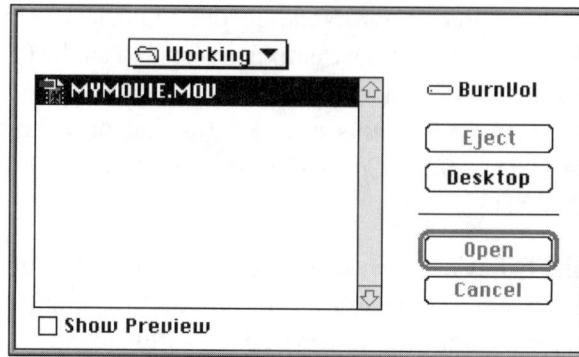

Figure 13.23 Selecting a source movie.

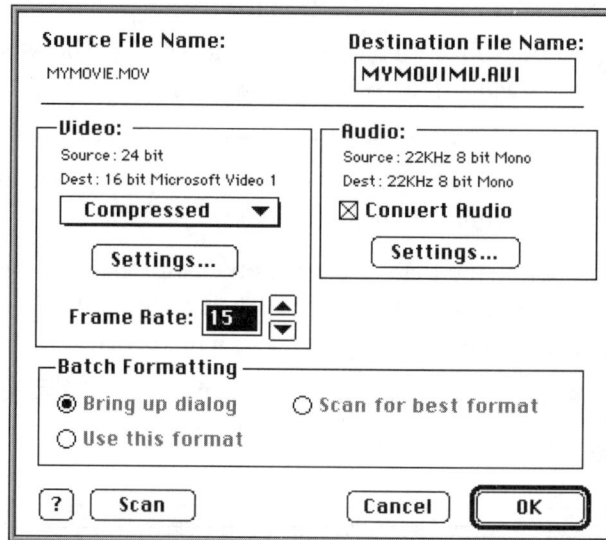

Figure 13.24 The Conversion window.

5. Drop down the top combo box in the Video group, and select Uncompressed. This is an important step (see Figure 13.25).

6. Drop down the bottom combo box in the Video group, and select 24 bit (see Figure 13.26).

7. Set the Frame Rate control to match the frame rate in the source QuickTime movie (for instance, 15 frames per second). Note that VFW Converter preserves the key frame frequency from the source to the target. In this case, however, it doesn't matter because all the target movie's frames are key frames (because the clip is uncompressed).

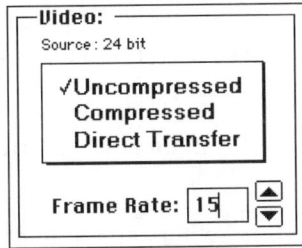

Figure 13.25 Selecting the Uncompressed option.

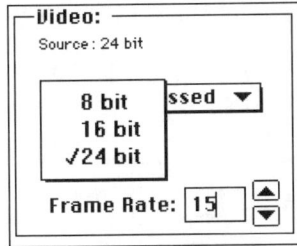

Figure 13.26 Selecting the target bit depth.

Converting On The Mac: AVI To QuickTime—Uncompressed Source

Continuing with the idea that working with uncompressed source movies is always preferable, let's now take a look at VFW Converter's companion program: AVI to QT Utility (another Microsoft product). This application is included in the same Mac StuffIt archive (QTAVI.SIT) that contains VFW Converter (when you download the archive from CompuServe). Also included is a file for your Mac's system folder named *Windows Compressors*, which needs to be installed when using the AVI to QT Utility.

Our goal is to derive an uncompressed (again, the None codec) QuickTime movie that we can process and compress just like any other raw QuickTime clip. To be honest, the AVI to QT Utility seems to be slightly less reliable than the VFW Converter, but it is regularly used for professional multimedia production.

Here's the blow-by-blow:

1. Get the uncompressed AVI file onto your Mac, either via a LAN or by connecting an external hard drive that has the file on it. The

codec type of the file will appear to VidEdit as *Full Frames (Uncompressed)* and to Premiere for Windows 4.2 as *None*.

2. Launch the AVI to QT Utility by clicking on its icon on your Mac desktop. Its main user interface will appear, as shown in Figure 13.27.

3. Navigate to the directory containing your source file using the drop-down combo box in the upper left of the UI. Double click on the source file (or highlight it, and click on the Add button) to move it into the Files To Convert list box (see Figure 13.28).

4. When all the clips you want to process are added to the Files To Convert list, click on the Convert button.

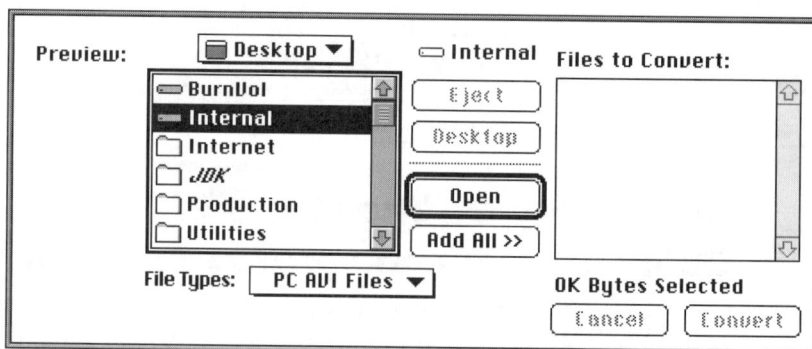

Figure 13.27   The AVI to QT Utility main UI.

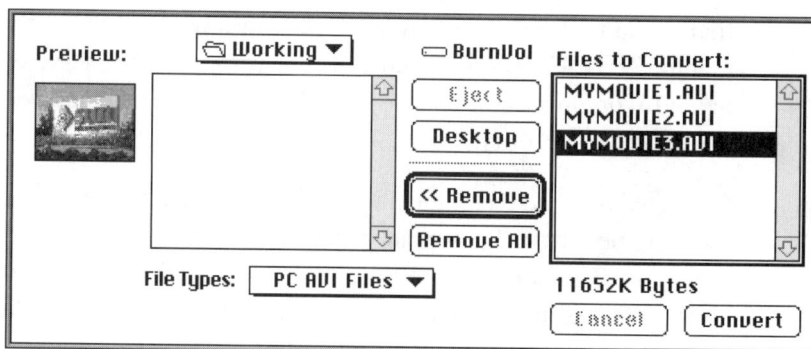

Figure 13.28   Selecting the source file.

5. In the dialog box that comes up next, do the following:

   a. Navigate to the destination folder for the converted clip(s).

   b. Check the radio button labeled *Save Self-Contained Movie*. Checking the other radio button, *Save Normally (Dependency To AVI File)*, does just that. It creates a pilot QuickTime clip that refers to the source AVI file for the movie data at playback time.

   c. Click on the Open button.

6. As the conversion proceeds, a progress bar will follow the action in a separate dialog.

7. When the conversion is complete, open the file in the QuickTime Movie Player. Check to see that the converted clip is well-formed by playing it and checking its attributes in Movie Player's various movie information menus (see Figure 13.29).

8. As a final precaution, do a Save As on the file from Movie Player. This will ensure audio chunks are interleaved correctly and enforce healthy movie data organization. Remember to flatten the movie when you do the Save As (see Figure 13.30).

Note! *To switch to another codec, you must have the Windows Compressors System Extension installed. This file is included in the QTAVI.SIT archive along with the VFW Converter and AVI to QT Utility.*

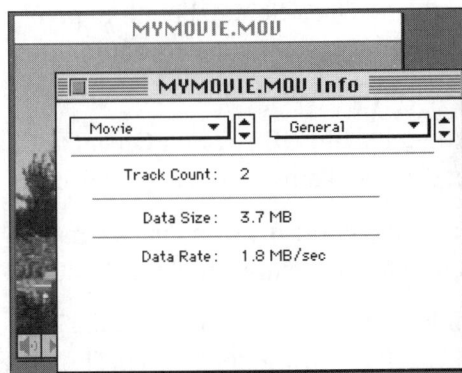

Figure 13.29 Confirming proper conversion.

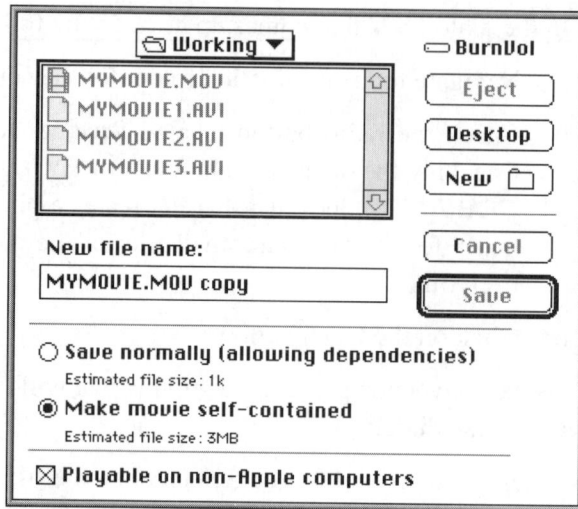

Figure 13.30 Flattening the movie while Saving As.

Converting On The Mac: QuickTime To AVI—Compressed Source

If you must convert starting with a compressed movie, VFW Converter can still do the job, but you need to watch out for a few things along the way. We'll point those out as we go through the following steps. This example assumes the source QuickTime movie is encoded with the Cinepak compressor.

1. Double click on VFW Converter on your Mac desktop. The main UI will appear.

2. Click on the Open Source button to invoke the File Selection dialog, then navigate to the directory that contains your source QuickTime movie(s).

3. Back in the main UI, click on Open Destination to navigate to the target drive and directory. Then click on the Convert button.

4. Enter the target file name in the Destination File Name field (if you want it to be different from the default).

5. Drop down the top combo box in the Video group, and select Direct Transfer (see Figure 13.31). This means we want the target movie to be encoded with Cinepak, just like the source. If you select the Compressed option, you can convert your source movie to a QuickTime file encoded with a non-Cinepak compressor—such

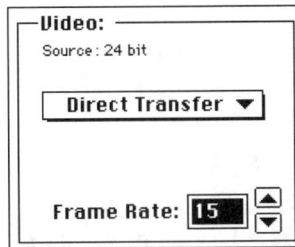

Figure 13.31 Selecting the Direct Transfer option.

as Video 1. This would take longer than a direct transfer because the clip would be physically recompressed. The best way to work around this is to do a Save As on the converted AVI file in VidEdit with a one-to-one interleave ratio, but with No Recompression selected in the compression options list box.

6. Set the Frame Rate control to match the frame rate in the source QuickTime movie (for instance, 15 frames per second). Again, note that VFW Converter preserves the key frame frequency from the source to the target. Also as previously noted, VFW Converter does not adjust the audio/video interleave in the target AVI movie. This is significant because AVI movies generally perform best when the AV interleave ratio is one-to-one. The standard QuickTime interleave factor is a half-second of audio to a half-second of video. This means that if a QuickTime movie's frame rate is 10 frames per second there will 5 be video frames together before there is any audio data. See Figure 13.32.

7. Check the Convert Audio checkbox. If you need to resample the audio track, click on the Settings button in the Audio group, and choose a new sample size and rate from the controls in the resultant Audio Settings dialog.

8. When you have everything calibrated, click on the OK button. A dialog with a progress bar will appear, showing you the relative time remaining in the conversion process. Because our target codec is the same as the source, this process should move right along.

9. The converted file can now be read by a Windows machine (at least Windows 95 or Windows 3.1 with Video for Windows installed) as long as the appropriate decompressor is present—in this case Cinepak. Assuming the converted file is on a DOS formatted external drive that you can plug into your DOS SCSI chain, do this now.

(Frames)

A u d i o	V i d e o	A u d i o	V i d e o	A u d i o	V i d e o	A u d i o	V i d e o	A u d i o	V i d e o	A u d i o	V i d e o	A u d i o	V i d e o	A u d i o	V i d e o	A u d i o	V i d e o

Optimal AVI Interleave

(Frames)						(Frames)				

1/2 second of Audio	V i d e o	V i d e o	V i d e o	V i d e o	V i d e o	1/2 second of Audio	V i d e o	V i d e o	V i d e o	V i d e o	V i d e o

Standard QuickTime Interleave

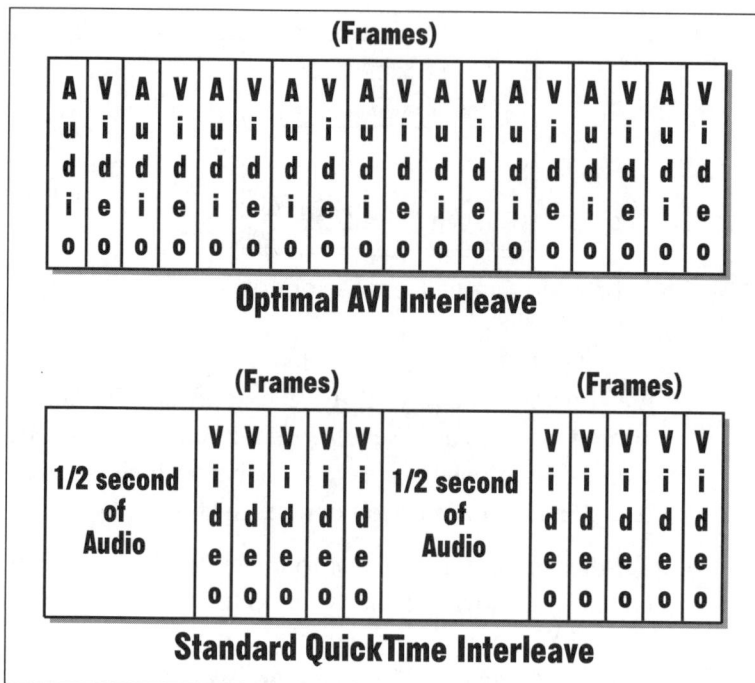

Figure 13.32   QuickTime versus AVI audio interleaving.

10. From your Windows desktop, launch the Media Player and test the converted clip. As noted previously, you may want to open it in VidEdit and re-save it to ensure one-to-one AV interleaving.

Note!   *While both the AVI to QT Utility and the VFW Converter do well with Cinepak and uncompressed movies, Intel's Indeo can be another story. Intel has a free (Windows-based) converter for Indeo files, and also a white paper on cross-platform development with Indeo, both of which are available on their Web site (www.intel.com).*

Converting On The Mac: AVI To QuickTime—Compressed Source

Of the four main methods for employing the VFW Converter/AVI to QT Utility combination, the one that follows is likely the one you'll use the least. Still, it does merit some attention if you don't want to capture on the Macintosh.

Our goal is simpler than when working with an uncompressed AVI source file. All we want is a compressed QuickTime movie that will play well on the Mac desktop. Again, the AVI to QT Utility sometimes seems a little less stable than the VFW Converter application, but it is definitely worth getting to know.

The steps for using the AVI to QT Utility when the source movie is already compressed are as follows:

1. Get the compressed AVI file onto your Mac (either via an LAN or external hard drive).

2. Launch the AVI to QT Utility. Its main user interface will appear, as shown in Figure 13.33.

3. Navigate to the directory containing your source file using the drop-down combo box in the upper left of the UI. Double click on the file you want converted in the current source directory to move it into the Files To Convert list box. You can see the first frame of a potential source movie if you highlight it in the Source Directory list.

4. When all the clips you want to process are added to the Files To Convert list, click on the Convert button.

5. In the next dialog, do the following:

   a. Navigate to the destination folder for the converted clip(s).

   b. Check the radio button labeled *Save Self-Contained Movie*.

   c. Click on the Open button.

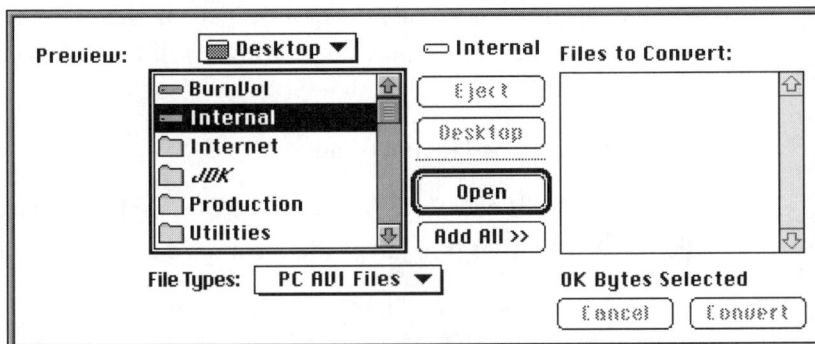

Figure 13.33 The AVI to QT Utility's main UI.

As noted earlier, checking the radio button labeled *Save Normally (Dependency To AVI File)* creates a pilot QuickTime clip that refers to the source AVI file for the actual movie data at playback time—a very Mac-centric idea.

While elegant in design, this facility is mainly used to view the contents of an AVI file if there is no other way to play it. Few, if any, commercial Macintosh products have been released that use this approach to playing movies.

6. As the conversion proceeds, a progress bar will follow the action in a separate dialog.

7. When the conversion is complete, open the file in the QuickTime Movie Player. Check to see that the converted clip is well formed by playing it and checking its attributes in Movie Player's various movie information menus.

8. As a final precaution, do a Save As on the file from Movie Player. This will ensure audio chunks are interleaved correctly and enforce healthy movie data organization. Remember to flatten the movie when you do the Save As.

TRMOOV

TRMOOV.EXE is a Windows application for converting back and forth between the QuickTime for Windows file format and the Video for Windows (AVI) file format without recompression. A copy of TRMOOV is included on the CD-ROM that comes with this book.

TRMOOV is specifically designed to convert movie files that have the same source and target codec. For instance, if the source file is a QuickTime Cinepak movie, the target movie will be a Video for Windows Cinepak movie.

Two other features of TRMOOV are:

- Conversion back and forth between QTW sound-only movies and Microsoft WAV files (the target file must have the .WAV extension).

- Batch mode conversions. TRMOOV takes command line arguments, so a Test Basic-style script can be constructed using multiple **run** statements. For example:

```
RUN "TRMOOV.EXE MOVIE1.MOV MOVIE1.AVI"
RUN "TRMOOV.EXE MOVIE2.MOV MOVIE2.AVI"
```

```
RUN "TRMOOV.EXE MOVIE3.MOV MOVIE3.AVI"
RUN "TRMOOV.EXE MOVIE4.MOV MOVIE4.AVI"
(more lines in script)
```

Following are the steps involved in running TRMOOV. Note that TRMOOV is also available on the Web site **www.downrecs.com**, along with some additional information concerning its redistribution policy.

1. Start the program from your Windows 3.1 or Windows 95 desktop. Its main user interface will appear, as shown in Figure 13.34.

2. Click on the Browse button opposite the Source Movie text field, then navigate (via the File Selection dialog) to the movie you want to convert as shown in Figure 13.35. The first frame of the movie should appear in the window in the middle of the UI.

3. Click on the Browse button opposite the Target Movie text field, navigate to the directory for the converted movie, and name the clip in the text field.

4. Click on the Start button. A progress bar will track the relative time left until the conversion is complete.

KNOWN RESTRICTIONS OF TRMOOV

When going from QTW to VFW, make sure your source movie's audio sampling rate is MPC (11.025 kHz, 22.05 kHz, 44.1 kHz, and so on).

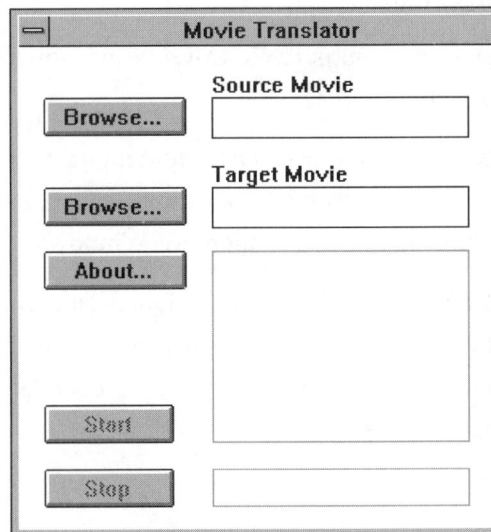

Figure 13.34 TRMOOV's main UI.

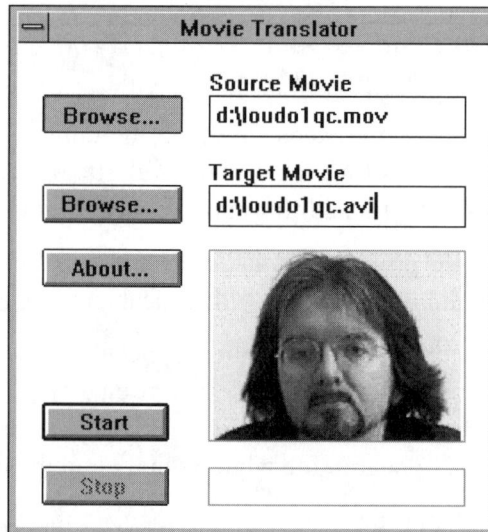

Figure 13.35 Selecting a source movie.

The current version of TRMOOV preserves the source movie's sampling rate, and some Windows sound cards do not handle Mac audio rates (such as 22.254) very well.

Other caveats include:

- If your source movie has a palette attached, it may not be present in the target movie.

- Longer movies output by TRMOOV may lose their audio/video synch after several minutes.

- For added quality assurance, remember to open and resave (with Movie Player) any QuickTime movie encoded on the Windows side—even clips output by Premiere for Windows.

- Neither Video for Windows nor QuickTime for Windows needs to be installed for TRMOOV to perform a conversion. Playback of the converted movie, however, requires installation of the appropriate software—either VFW or QTW.

Summary

It's hard to know how much emphasis to place on cross-platform issues in the emerging multicast environment, but the issues are certainly worthy of discussion. As this chapter explains, most cross-platform problems will come up in the content production phase, as opposed to the actual content multicasting phase.

Still, if some member of your audience can't receive your Wintel-based multicast because he or she is missing a crucial codec on their Mac, it will behoove you to know how to get to the root of the problem quickly. Clearly, having as much cross-platform hardware in your testing lab as possible can help you spot such vulnerabilities in advance.

Chapter 14

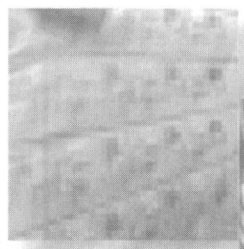

- **Installing the StarCast software suite**

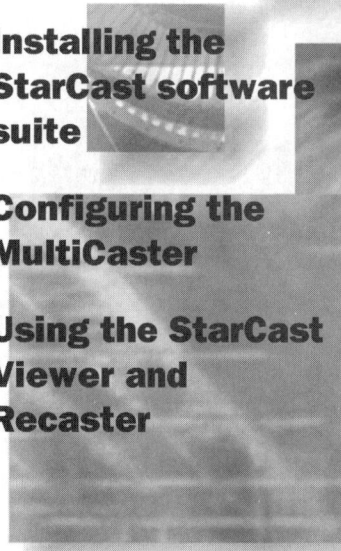

- **Configuring the MultiCaster**

- **Using the StarCast Viewer and Recaster**

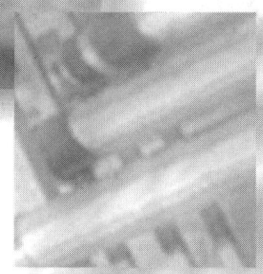

Chapter 14

Multicasting With StarCast

This chapter is about a new software suite that was just becoming available as this book was being written: StarCast, from Starlight Networks (see Figure 14.1). As you might have read in other chapters, Starlight was a pioneering force in network-based video. They have now leveraged their original technology with TCP/IP and multicast underpinnings to create products that compete with solutions from players like Precept and Microsoft.

In the same manner we walked through installing multicast software in Chapter 6, we'll walk through the installation of the StarCast software suite. Then, we'll take it for a test drive. Both the StarCast MultiCaster and the StarCast Viewer are currently supported on Windows 95. Starlight is still working on making the entire suite available as a Windows NT solution.

Installing StarCast

StarCast is currently distributed as a shrink-wrapped, off-the-shelf retail product (as opposed to being available via the Web). If the distribution model changes, this will likely be reflected on Starlight's Web site at **www.starlight.com**.

Figure 14.1   Presenting StarCast.

If you need other information about StarCast (or any other Starlight product), marketing contact data is readily available at their site.

The setup scenarios that follow are based on installation from floppies included in the shrink-wrapped retail version of the StarCast products, specifically the MultiCaster and Viewer applications. The StarCast suite also includes a product called the Recaster, the operation of which is described later in this chapter.

Note!   *Because StarCast relies on Microsoft's ActiveMovie technology, you'll need to make sure ActiveMovie is installed on your Windows 95 system prior to installing any of the StarCast software. In the version of the products installed in this chapter, a separate ActiveMovie setup disk was provided. ActiveMovie is also available as a free download from the Microsoft Web site.*

Setting Up The StarCast MultiCaster

Starlight requires users to meet minimum hardware and software specifications before running the MultiCaster. Minimum hardware requirements are:

- A Pentium 133 or higher, with at least 16 MB RAM.

- An Ethernet (or Fast Ethernet) network card compliant with NDIS 3.0.

- An MPC II-compliant audio card (such as the Creative Labs SoundBlaster 16).

- An MPEG video capture card (either the FutureTel PrimeView II or the Optibase MPEG Lab Suite) or the Intel Smart Video Recorder Pro (ISVRP).

Minimum software requirements to run MultiCaster are:

- Microsoft Windows 95.

- ActiveMovie 1.0 or higher.

- If you're using the ISVRP, you'll need to have the Indeo codec version 3.22.01.20. You should be able to get this easily at the Intel Web site at **www.intel.com**.

In this example, we'll install the StarCast MultiCaster on a Pentium 133 with 32 MB of RAM running Windows 95. This is the basic machine that Starlight recommends for the MultiCaster (as opposed to the Viewer). Here are the steps you should follow:

1. Put Disk 1 of the StarCast MultiCaster in a floppy drive (Drive A assumed).

2. Navigate to Drive A with the Desktop Explorer, and double click on the Setup program. Figure 14.2 shows the initial Installer screen.

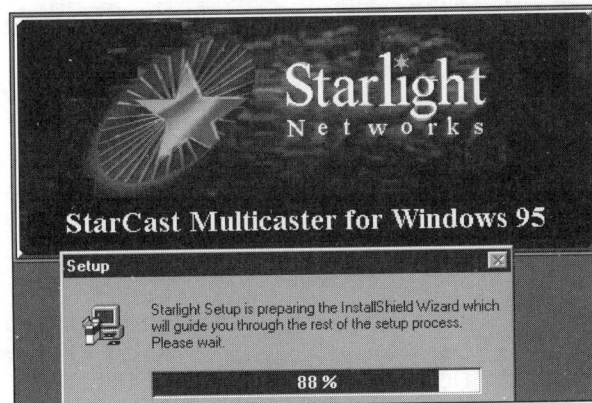

Figure 14.2   Welcome to the StarCast MultiCaster Installer.

3. Click your way to the standard InstallShield panel where you can select the target directory. C:\Program Files\Starcast is a good choice. Then click on Next.

4. Unless you have a reason not to, accept the Starlight Program Folder, then click on Next.

5. InstallShield will show you all its progress indicators as it copies files to your system. After a brief wait, you'll be prompted for Disk 2 of the MultiCaster setup kit.

6. When Disk 2 has off-loaded its cargo, you may or may not see the panel shown in Figure 14.3. If you do, accept the default value by clicking on the Next button.

7. In the dialog box shown next (see Figure 14.4), check the radio button that corresponds to the type of video capture card on your MultiCaster machine. If you don't have a FutureTel or Optibase board (or have no video capture card at all), check the Video For Windows radio button. The machine used in this example has a FutureTel board, as we'll see later in this chapter.

8. Now, it's time to change the Windows 95 Network configuration, as shown in Figure 14.5. If you're familiar with using the Network applet in the Windows 95 Control Panel, this is very straightforward. Click on the Finish button to complete the StarCast MultiCaster installation, and enter the Network applet. Make sure

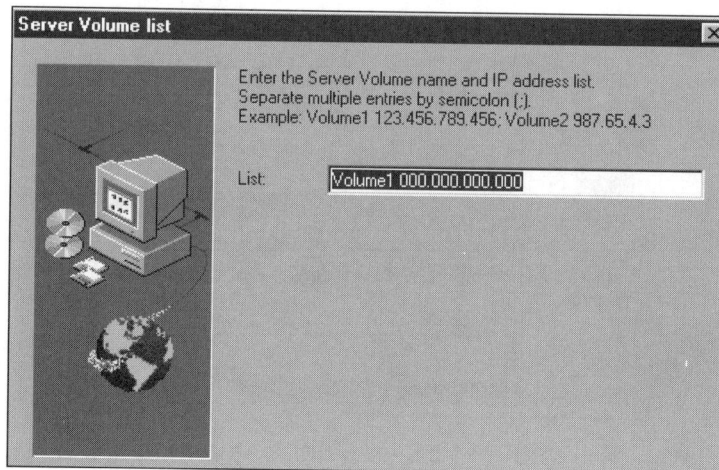

Figure 14.3 It's safe to ignore this for now.

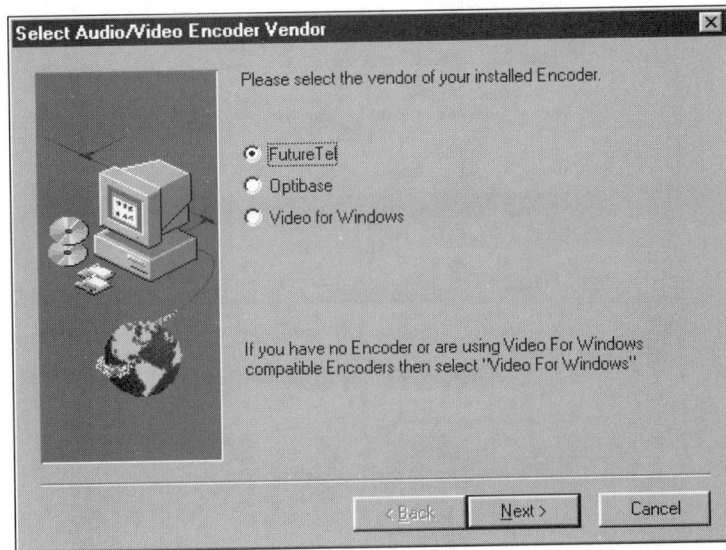

Figure 14.4 Selecting the video capture card.

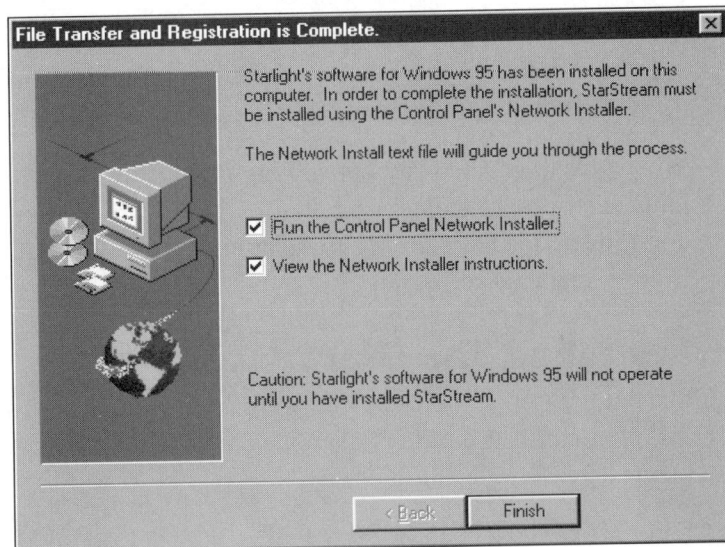

Figure 14.5 Preparing to change the Windows 95 Network configuration.

to check both checkboxes so that the instructions appear along with the network configuration dialog boxes.

9. For the sake of brevity, we'll skip the network configuration details because they are well documented in the text file that comes with the Windows 95 Network configuration file (see Figure 14.6).

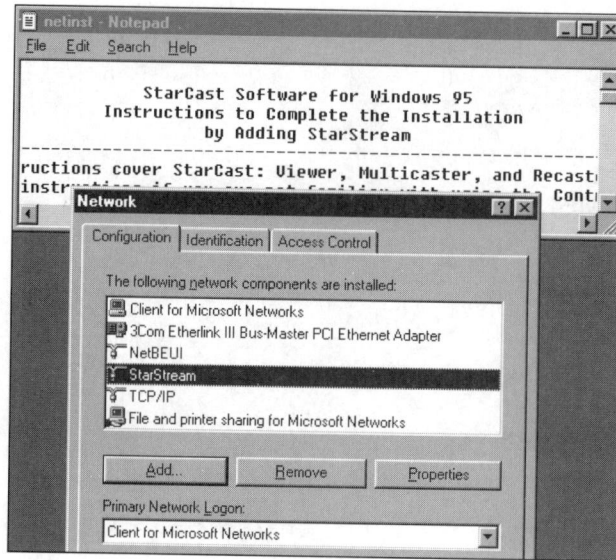

Figure 14.6 Adding the Starlight network driver for the StarCast Viewer.

10. When the network configuration is complete, Windows 95 will probably ask you if you want to reboot your system. Go ahead and do this, even if you're not asked.

When your machine is rebooted, you might want to verify that everything is still functioning normally (no reason why it shouldn't be) but don't fire up the StarCast MultiCaster just yet. Let's install the StarCast Viewer application first.

Installing The StarCast Viewer

Starlight requires minimum hardware and software specifications before you can use the StarCast Viewer. Minimum hardware requirements are:

- For MPEG-1, a Pentium 90 or higher, with at least 16 MB RAM. For Indeo, at least a 486/66 with 16 MB RAM.

- An Ethernet (or Fast Ethernet) network card compliant with NDIS 3.0.

- An MPC II-compliant audio card (such as the Creative Labs SoundBlaster 16).

Minimum software requirements to run the StarCast Viewer are:

- Microsoft Windows 95.

- ActiveMovie 1.0 or higher.

- Indeo version 3.22.01.20. You should be able to get this easily at the Intel Web site at **www.intel.com**.

Assuming you're at a different machine than the one on which you installed the MultiCaster, we'll now run the Viewer Setup program. For the record, our Viewer PC is a Pentium 90 with 16 MB of RAM running Windows 95. This is the basic machine that Starlight recommends for the Viewer (as opposed to the MultiCaster). Here is the recipe:

1. Put Disk 1 of the StarCast Viewer in a floppy drive (Drive A assumed).

2. Navigate to Drive A with the Desktop Explorer, and double click on the Setup program. Figure 14.7 shows the initial Installer screen.

3. Click your way to the standard InstallShield panel where you can select the target directory. C:\Program Files\Starcast is, again, a good choice. Then click on Next.

4. Unless you have a reason not to, accept the Starlight Program Folder, then click on Next.

5. InstallShield will show you all its progress indicators as it copies files to your system. After a brief wait, you'll be prompted for Disk 2 of the Viewer Setup Kit.

Figure 14.7 Welcome to the StarCast Viewer Installer.

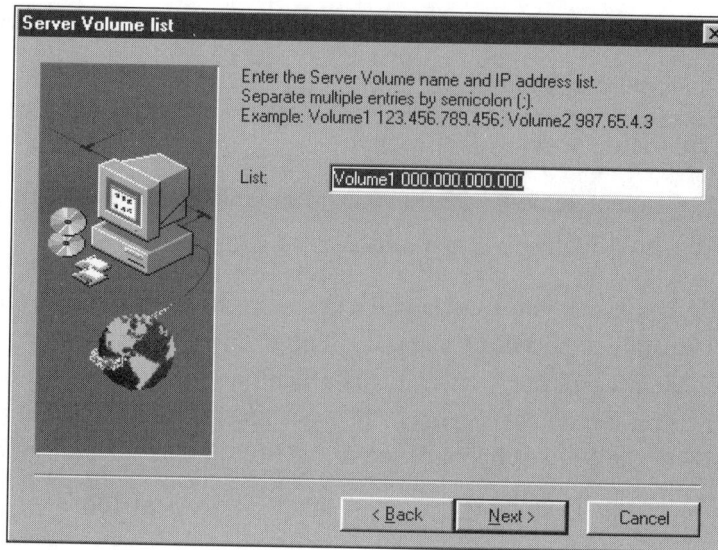

Figure 14.8
It's safe to ignore this for now.

6. When Disk 2 has off-loaded its cargo, you may or may not see the panel shown in Figure 14.8. If you do, accept the default value by clicking on the Next button.

7. Once again, it's time to change the Windows 95 Network configuration (shown in Figure 14.9). If you're the least bit familiar with

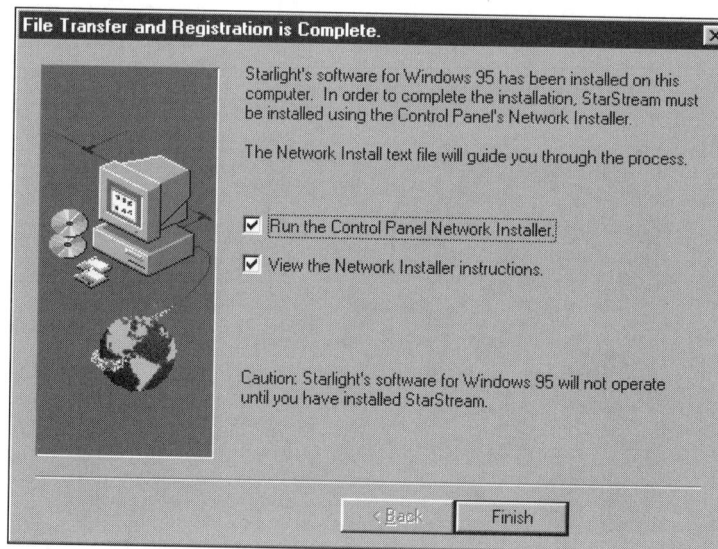

Figure 14.9 Preparing to change the Windows 95 Network configuration.

using the Network applet in the Windows 95 Control Panel, this is very straightforward. Click on the Finish button to complete the StarCast Viewer installation, and enter the Network applet. Make sure to check both checkboxes so that the instructions appear along with the network configuration dialogs.

8. As we did in the MultiCaster Setup (for the sake of brevity), we'll skip the network configuration details because they are well documented in the text file comes with the Windows 95 Network configuration File (see Figure 14.10).

9. When the network configuration is complete, Windows 95 will probably ask you if you want to reboot your system. Go ahead and do this, even if you're not asked.

When your machine is rebooted, you might want to verify that everything is still functioning normally. Once again, there is no reason it shouldn't be.

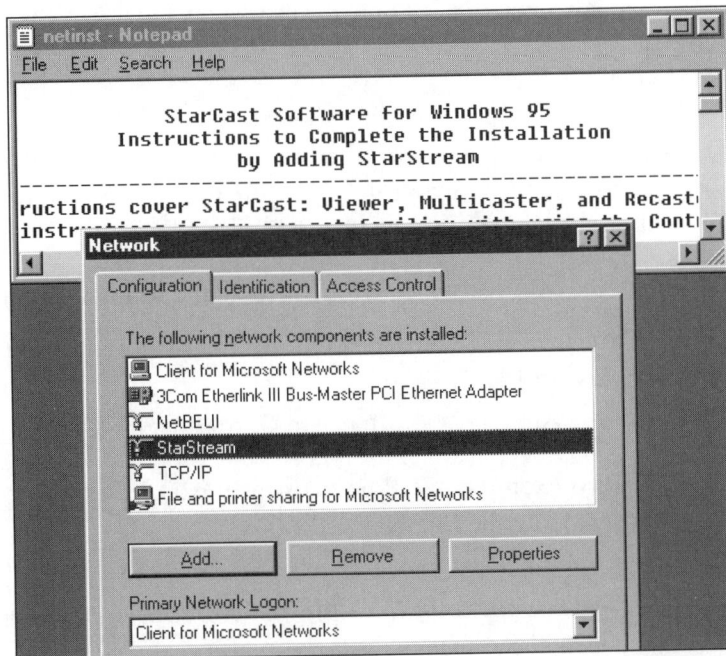

Figure 14.10 Adding the Starlight Network drivers for the StarCast Multicaster.

Stored Media Multicasting With StarCast

With the StarCast MultiCaster and Viewer installed successfully, we're now ready to make some noise. The current version of StarCast can currently handle both MPEG and AVI movies, either live using a video camera and capture card or stored (on CD-ROM, a hard drive, or other storage medium). We'll begin with a demonstration of a stored media multicast.

Running The MultiCaster With Stored Media

Like the Precept IP/TV Server, the StarCast MultiCaster application does not run as an NT Service *per se* (when running on an NT machine). In other words, you launch it and shut it down like any other standard executable. You may remember that Microsoft's NetShow is an official NT Service and is controlled from the Services applet in the Control Panel.

So, let's get to it. Assuming your StarCast MultiCaster machine was rebooted following the installation and a shortcut is now on your desktop, go ahead and double click on the shortcut icon. The main MultiCaster interface is shown in Figure 14.11.

To put the MultiCaster to work, execute the following steps:

1. From the File Menu, select the Multicast stored file item, as shown in Figure 14.12.

2. A File Open dialog will appear, as shown in Figure 14.13.

3. In this example, we'll be multicasting an MPEG file, which we'll select from the File Name list box.

Note! *If you want the file to play continuously, make sure to check the Loop checkbox.*

4. The Channel Selection dialog appears next, as shown in Figure 14.14.

5. We'll choose Channel 1 for this demonstration. Now, click on the Multicast button.

Figure 14.11 The main MultiCaster interface.

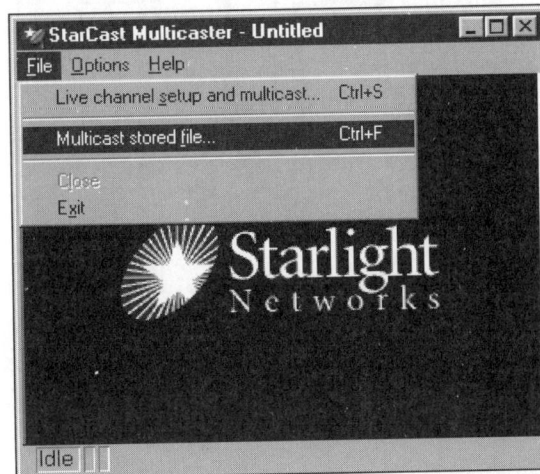

Figure 14.12 Launching a stored file multicast.

Note! *It's a good idea to be as consistent as possible with your channel selection. For instance, multicasting your MPEG movies on one channel and your AVI clips on another helps keep the MultiCaster running smoothly, according to Starlight.*

6. A dialog asking for a channel name now appears. We'll use MPEG, as shown in Figure 14.15. Click on OK to continue.

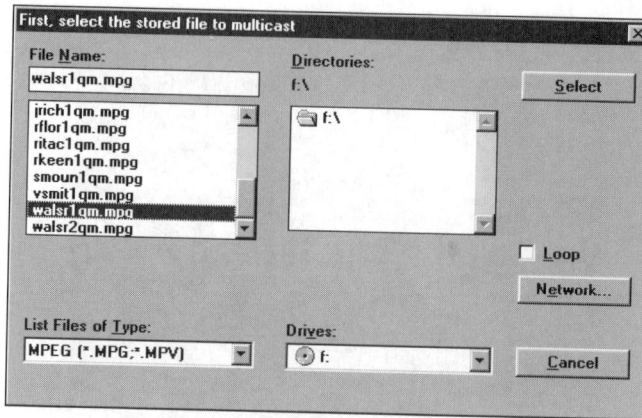

Figure 14.13 Selecting a file to multicast.

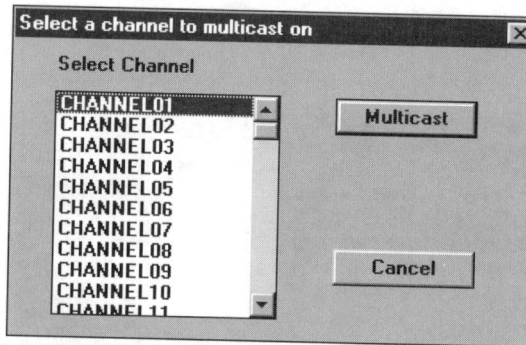

Figure 14.14 Selecting a channel to multicast on.

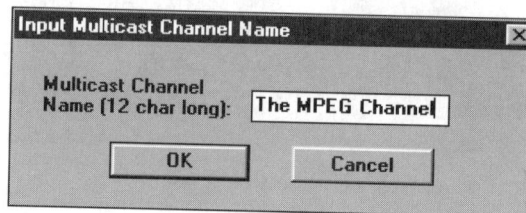

Figure 14.15 The Input Multicast Channel Name dialog.

7. The MultiCaster now goes to work (see Figure 14.16). No video is displayed in the user interface, although some menu items are active, as shown.

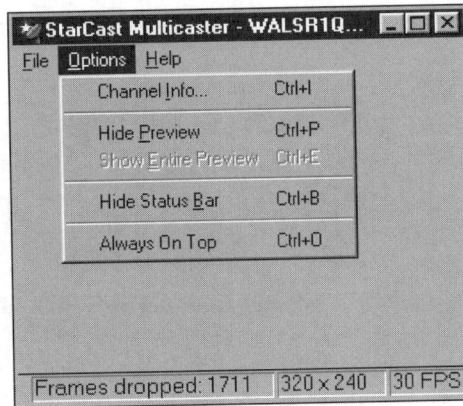

Figure 14.16 The MultiCaster in action.

> *Because multicasting is quite labor-intensive for the CPU, any user input (like clicking on menu items and performing subsequent actions) will adversely affect the MultiCaster's performance.*

Now, let's go to our StarCast Viewer machine.

Running The StarCast Viewer

Now, let's fire up the Viewer on our other machine (on the local LAN). Performing the following actions should tune in the stored MPEG movie we just started streaming from the MultiCaster:

1. Assuming this machine was rebooted following the StarCast Viewer installation and a shortcut now appears on the desktop, go ahead and double click on the shortcut icon. The window shown in Figure 14.17 should quickly appear.

2. Click on the down arrow of the combo box at the bottom right of the Viewer UI. You should see the drop-down list of available channels, as shown in Figure 14.18. Click on the one that says *CH01:MPEG*.

3. After a moment, the clip being streamed by the MultiCaster on the other machine should start to play in the main StarCast Viewer window, as shown in Figure 14.19.

This is the basic multicasting experience using the StarCast MultiCaster and Viewer. StarCast's overall range of capabilities is much greater, as

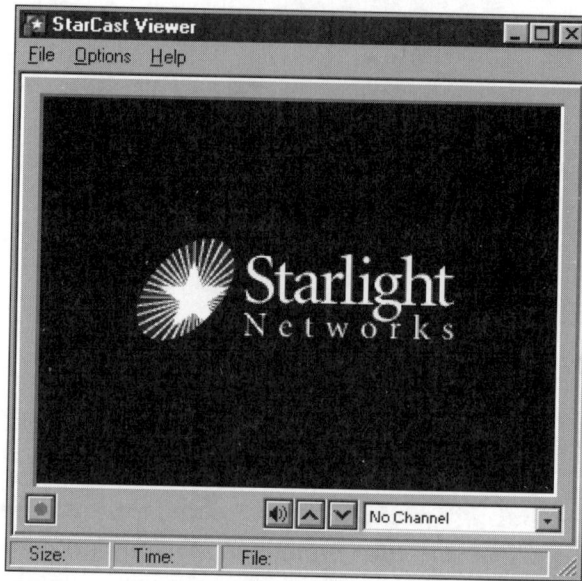

Figure 14.17   The main StarCast Viewer UI.

Figure 14.18   Scanning for channels.

you'll discover by visiting Starlight's Web site and reading the product documentation. A detailed feature outline is provided at the end of this chapter. For now, let's continue the demonstration with another one of StarCast's fortes—live multicasting.

Figure 14.19 Receiving a StarCast multicast of stored media.

Live Multicasting With StarCast

As noted in the StarCast Setup section, the MultiCaster basically supports three types of video capture cards: FutureTel, Optibase, and Video for Windows compatible—such as the Intel Smart Video Recorder Pro (ISVRP). The following section covers operations on a machine using the FutureTel PrimeView II MPEG card.

> **Note!** *Live multicasting is also supported by Precept's IP/TV, as demonstrated in Chapter 8.*

Running The MultiCaster With Live Video

The procedure here is quite similar to multicasting stored video. To begin, double click on the shortcut icon for the MultiCaster or fire it up from the Start|Programs menu. The main UI appears as shown in Figure 14.20.

> **Note!** *A video camera, cabled correctly to a video capture card in the multicasting machine, is assumed in this example.*

Figure 14.20 The main MultiCaster interface.

Now, execute the following steps:

1. From the File Menu, select the Live channel setup and multicast item, as shown in Figure 14.21.

2. The Channel Selection dialog will appear, as shown in Figure 14.22.

3. If you need to change the configuration of your video capture card, click on the Options button. Figure 14.23 shows the configuration panel for the FutureTel card used in this example.

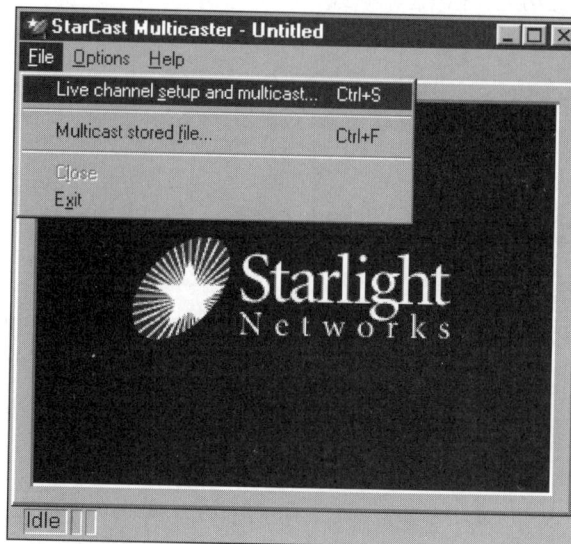

Figure 14.21 Launching a stored file multicast.

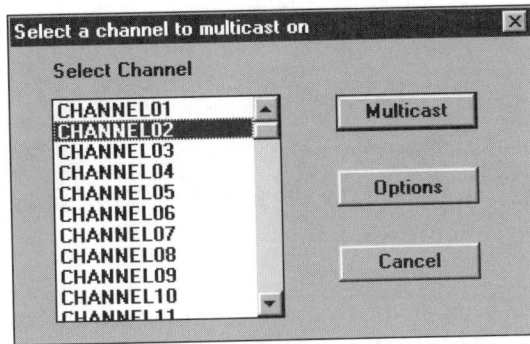

Figure 14.22   Selecting a channel for the live multicast.

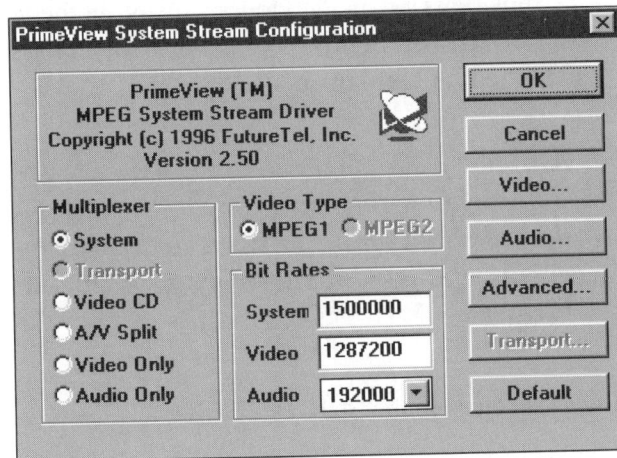

Figure 14.23   Configuring the FutureTel PrimeView II.

4. After selecting the channel on which you wish to multicast (Channel 2 in this case), click on the Multicast button. The dialog in Figure 14.24 appears next. Fill in a name for the channel (*LIVE* is used here), and click on OK.

5. Make sure your camera is recording, then click on OK.

As noted earlier, it's good form to keep your channel selections sorted out. Multicasting MPEG on one channel and, say, AVI clips on another helps keep the MultiCaster running smoothly.

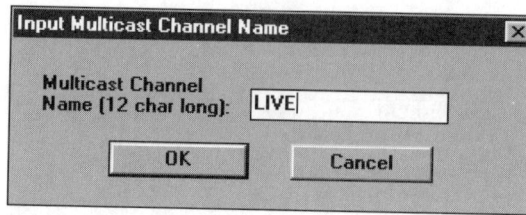

Figure 14.24   Name that channel.

6. Once again, the MultiCaster goes to work (see Figure 14.25) with no video displayed in the user interface (although certain menu items are active). If you want to preview your live multicast, click on Show Preview in the Options menu. In the version of the software tested here, only Indeo video—when using the ISVRP—is supported for Preview mode.

> **Note!** *Again, it is worth noting that, because multicasting is quite labor-intensive for the CPU, any user input (like clicking on menu items and performing subsequent actions) will adversely affect the MultiCaster's performance.*

Now, let's return to the StarCast Viewer.

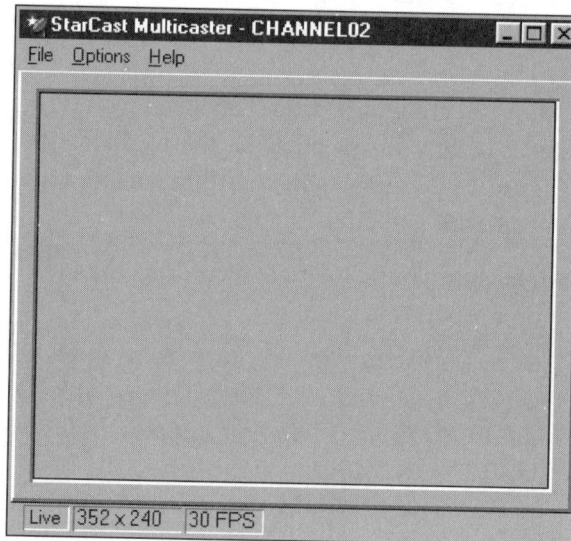

Figure 14.25   Multicasting live video.

Receiving A Live Stream With The StarCast Viewer

Invoke the Viewer on your other machine. As in the stored video example, performing the steps that follow should tune in the video we're now streaming live from the MultiCaster:

1. Double click on the shortcut icon or do a Start|Programs on the StarCast Viewer. The window shown in Figure 14.26 should appear.

2. Click on the down arrow of the combo box at the bottom right of the Viewer UI. You should see the drop-down list of available channels, as shown in Figure 14.27. Click on the one that says *CH02:LIVE*.

3. After a moment, the live clip being streamed by the MultiCaster on the other machine should start to play in the main StarCast Viewer window, as shown in Figure 14.28.

This is the basic experience of running the StarCast MultiCaster and Viewer with live video (in this case, MPEG). Again, StarCast's complete range of features is much more robust. Also, note that the production skills necessary for properly preparing a theatre for live video capture of any type are formidable and not covered here.

Figure 14.26 The main StarCast Viewer UI.

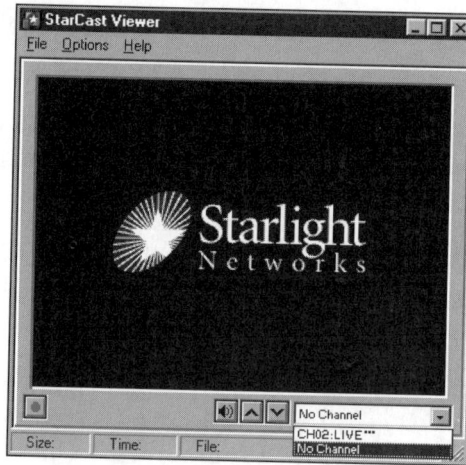

Figure 14.27 Scanning for channels.

Figure 14.28 Receiving a live StarCast multicast.

About The Recaster

The third major component of the StarCast product suite is called the *Recaster*. Unfortunately, the software was not available for demonstration purposes in this chapter, but it should be shipping with the MultiCaster and Viewer components by the time this book is published.

Simply stated, the StarCast Recaster provides an interface for taking digital media from a satellite communications system and multicasting that content on a corporate intranet. Starlight has been working with

Hughes Network Systems to integrate DirectPC technology (**www.direcpc.com**) with StarCast technology to bypass traditional land lines.

How does the Recaster work? The material that follows is taken from Starlight's marketing literature as of February 1997. Figure 14.29 shows a basic schematic of the Recaster topology.

Recaster Functionality

StarCast Recaster Integrates Seamlessly With Hughes Networks Systems (HNS) DirecPC

- Multicasts a digital channel received from HNS DirecPC satellite service.

- Stores selected digital feeds from HNS DirecPC satellite service locally or to StarWorks or StarWare media server for on-demand playback.

- Runs on the same PC as the DirecPC application and hardware.

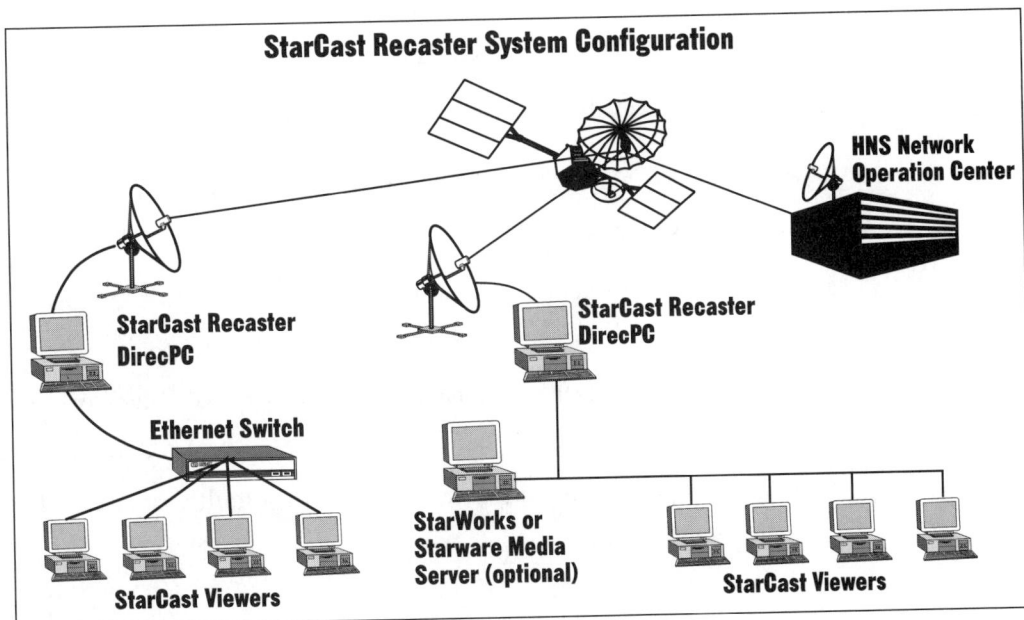

Figure 14.29 The network served by the Recaster.

- Supports distribution of multiple channels from a single satellite antenna with multiple DirecPC stations.

- Leverages satellite delivery investment by providing information access to an unlimited number of PC clients.

MANAGES STREAMING MEDIA TO PEACEFULLY COEXIST ON ENTERPRISE NETWORKS

- Uses IP Multicast to send a single stream across the network to an unlimited number of PC clients running StarCast Viewer.

- Uses StarStream traffic-shaping, buffer management, and efficient error recovery mechanisms to condition streaming traffic without disrupting mission-critical data traffic.

WORKS IN INDUSTRY-STANDARD COMPUTING ENVIRONMENTS

- Supports standard IP routers and networks, and works with Ethernet and Fast Ethernet.

- Supports Windows NT and Windows 95 PC clients.

- Supports MPEC1 and Indeo compression formats.

- Complies with OLE 2 specification for rapid application development.

WORKS WITH STARCAST VIEWER FOR DESKTOP ACCESS TO MULTICAST STREAM

- Allows users to select available multicast audio/video channels on the network.

- Supports recording of multicast stream locally or to a StarWorks or StarWare media server.

- Provides capability to schedule recording of a multicast stream for unattended operation.

INCLUDES STARMONITOR APPLICATION FOR EASY NETWORK MANAGEMENT

- Monitors multicast streams on network and provides information on usage and performance.

- Allows network administrators to monitor and analyze multicast traffic and to select compression type and data rate for a multicast channel.

Recaster Hardware And Software Requirements

StarLight recommends minimum hardware and software specifications for the Recaster. The recommended minimum hardware requirements are:

- A Pentium 133 or higher, with at least 16 MB RAM.

- An Ethernet (or Fast Ethernet) network card compliant with NDIS 3.0.

- An MPC II-compliant audio card (such as the Creative Labs SoundBlaster 16).

- DirecPC hardware.

The recommended minimum software requirements for using the Recaster are:

- Microsoft Windows 95.

- ActiveMovie 1.0 or higher.

- Turbo Internet version 1.3 (for the DirecPC hardware).

Summary

It is unclear as of this writing how the StarCast product suite will be positioned vis-a-vis the global Internet (Precept's IP/TV, for instance, is designed as a viable MBone solution). However, the components demonstrated earlier perform very well on both large and small enterprise networks. If the StarCast Recaster lives up to its marketing campaign, Starlight will be well-positioned in the global multicast sweepstakes.

What follows is Starlight's published spec sheet for the MultiCaster component, as promised earlier. Figure 14.30 shows a basic schematic of the MultiCaster topology.

StarCast MultiCaster Features

STARCAST MULTICASTER OFFERS FLEXIBILITY FOR CONTENT SOURCE

- Digitizes analog source from video camera, cable tuner, VCR, etc., and multicasts encoded stream on the network.

- Multicasts digitized files stored on StarWorks or StarWare media servers or on local disk drives.

- Supports broad range of MPEG1 encoders.

MANAGES STREAMING MEDIA TO PEACEFULLY COEXIST ON ENTERPRISE NETWORKS

- Uses IP Multicast to send a single stream across the network to an unlimited number of PC clients running StarCast Viewer.

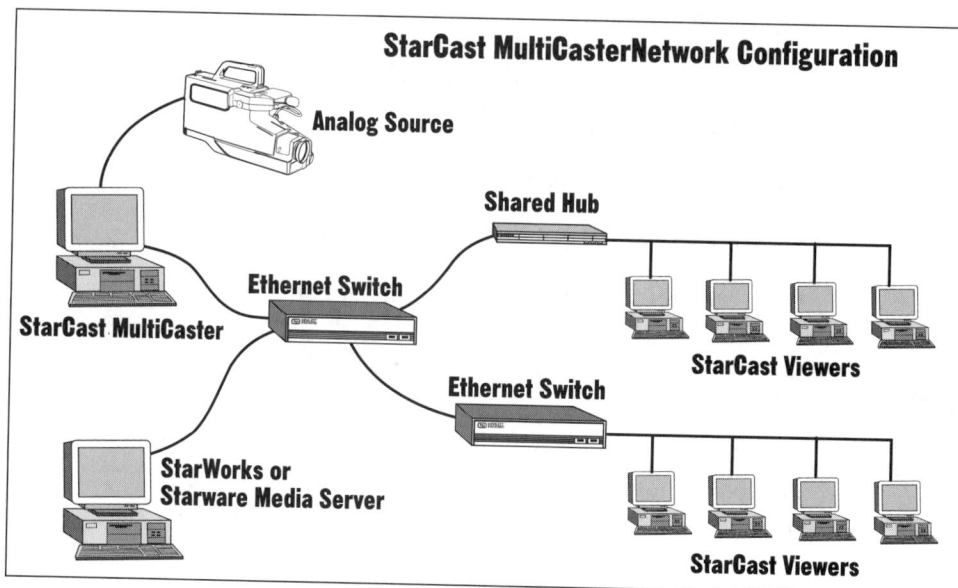

Figure 14.30 The network served by the MultiCaster.

- Uses StarStream traffic-shaping, buffer management, and error recovery mechanisms to condition streaming traffic without disrupting mission-critical data traffic.

WORKS IN INDUSTRY-STANDARD COMPUTING ENVIRONMENTS

- Supports standard IP routers and networks, and works with Ethernet and Fast Ethernet.

- Supports Windows NT and Windows 95 PC clients.

- Supports MPFG1 and Indeo compression formats.

- Supports ActiveMovie interface on Windows NT and Windows 95.

- Complies with OLE 2 specification for rapid application development.

WORKS WITH STARCAST VIEWER FOR DESKTOP ACCESS TO MULTICAST STREAM

- Allows users to select available multicast audio/video channels on the network.

- Supports recording of multicast stream locally or to a StarWorks or StarWare media server.

- Provides capability to schedule recording of a multicast stream for unattended operation.

INCLUDES STARMONITOR APPLICATION FOR EASY NETWORK MANAGEMENT

- Monitors multicast streams on network and provides information on usage and performance.

- Allows network administrators to monitor and analyze multicast traffic and to select compression type and data rate for a multicast channel.

Chapter 15

- **Understanding the current state of the MBone**

- **Implementing MBone tunnels**

- **Finding an MBone/Multicast ISP**

Chapter 15

Accessing The MBone

The goal of this chapter is to put MBone access in perspective for Wintel and Mac Web developers. The issues are generalized, based on the relative lack of direct MBone connectivity for these platforms, but we will go into detail where necessary to make certain points.

As noted in other chapters, the MBone is a stable but maturing part of the global Internet. It is, above all, a multicast environment. In practical terms, it can be thought of as a digital communications space bounded by routers enabled with specific multicast protocols. The better you crystallize this basic image in your mind's eye, the better you'll be able to place other MBone topics in a reasonable context.

Perhaps the most confusing part of conceptualizing the MBone results from trying to visualize its scope. Back in Chapter 4, we suggested a model consisting of multicast islands in a unicast ocean. If you view these islands as finite networks using multicast protocols, separated from each other by a connected sea of network routers employing unicast protocols, the overall image will get a little sharper (see Figure 15.1).

Unicast Infrastructure

| Multicast Island Subnet | Multicast Island Subnet | Multicast Island Subnet | Multicast Island Subnet | Multicast Island Subnet |

——— = Tunnels

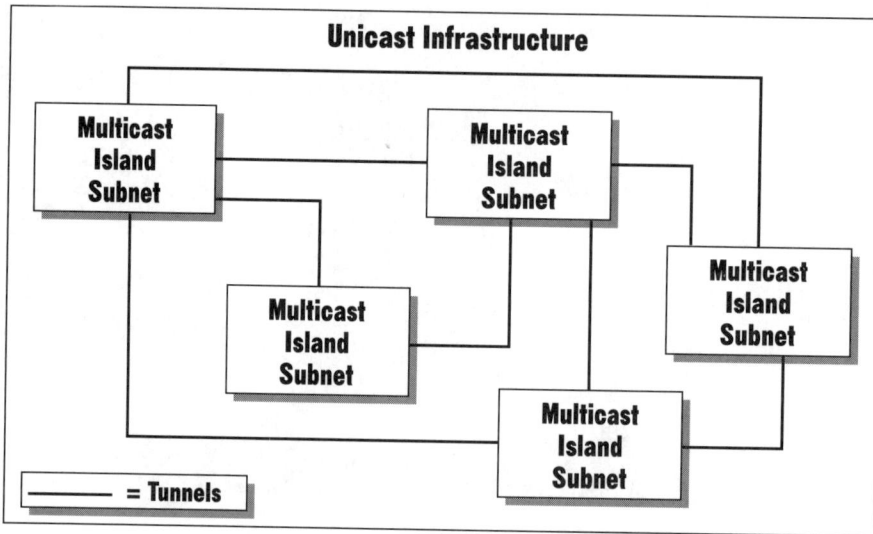

Figure 15.1 Separated MBone subnets.

Now, go a step further and picture the MBone as a collection of physical multicast networks, currently without mass-market ways to connect to each other. Finally, understand that MBone island networks actually do interconnect through a process known as tunneling, which encapsulates multicast IP packets in unicast wrappers (to safely travel the unicast ocean).

If you can keep all these conceptual layers in mind at once, you'll have a good working model for making sense out of the rest of this chapter. Don't let the Unix wireheads muddy the big picture for you. This is essentially what it all boils down to.

So, what's the problem? Why isn't the MBone being colonized with the same Darwinian fervor as the rest of the Internet? A big part of the answer is that market pressures aren't strong enough yet, although they may increase sharply in 1997 and beyond as the general confusion surrounding the MBone clears up.

Other answers have to do with just that: the general confusion (as well as the reluctance of many ISPs to offer MBone service). The rest of this chapter, therefore, attempts to put the technical aspects of the MBone in clear perspective for Web developers and general users.

The Current State Of The MBone

When you get right down to it, what really happens on the MBone is very straightforward, at least from a user perspective. In fact, much of the high-tech glamour associated with the MBone wears off quickly once you get familiar with the standard applications and start worrying about multicasting good content.

If you're excited by surfing the far corners of the Web—and consuming various types of low-bandwidth media *on demand*—you may ultimately prefer free-form Web browsing to viewing scheduled MBone events and joining MBone video conferences.

Actually, none of this should be too surprising, judging by the types of content now playing on the MBone: NASA footage, university research projects, technical conferences, and so forth, although the Summit of Hope Webcast, documented in Chapter 17 and the legendary Rolling Stones MBone feed from the Dallas Cotton Bowl in 1994 (see Figure 15.2) were interesting exceptions.

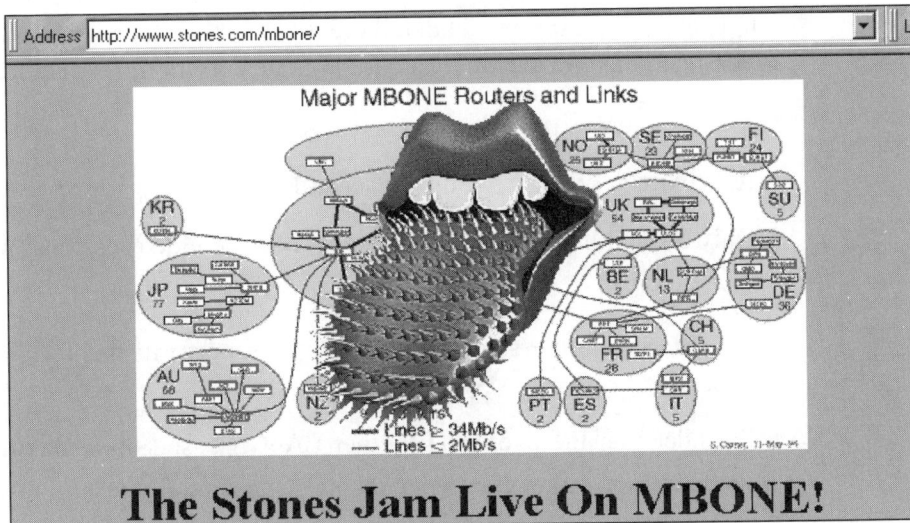

Figure 15.2 The Rolling Stones meet the MBone.

For the record, nobody's suggesting that the MBone is based on dull or trivial technology. As network software (and hardware) development goes, it is one of the most challenging fields around. But the payoff—in terms of a visible return on investment—is deceptively simple. Not everyone understands the possibilities of high-quality, networked digital video compared to standard broadcast television.

Size Of The MBone

It's estimated that around 2,000 MBone subnets worldwide comprised the aggregate MBone at the beginning of 1997. Generally speaking, this is slightly larger than the perceived global Internet circa 1990. Because of the explosive growth of the Internet in the last seven years, however, the MBone is *still* a small fraction of the whole.

As we keep stressing, one of the keys to this imbalance is router technology and deployment. As soon as IP multicast capability is standard in new, inexpensive routers and modems—and ISPs tool up for providing inexpensive MBone access—the MBone should quickly propagate itself across the global Internet.

Bandwidth Limits

Many people seem to perceive the MBone as the mother of all digital communications pipes, perhaps suggested by the long form of the word *MBone* (i.e., *Multicast Backbone*). But even with multicast technology employed, most experts feel that there is a quickly attained upper limit to MBone video traffic, at least based on the current infrastructure.

In practical terms, this limit can be expressed as:

- Approximately 500 kilobits per second, or

- Only a small handful of simultaneous MBone video sessions (more if audio only)

To put these numbers in perspective, let's perform the following exercise:

- Consider that the average Ethernet LAN is based on a maximum bandwidth of 10 megabits per second (substantially less in normal day-to-day use). In very general terms, let's say that this is equivalent to 10 times the recognized MBone bandwidth.

- Reflect on the fact that, if you play an MPEG movie with a data rate of 1.5 megabits per second (approximately 180 kilobytes per second—a common CD-ROM data rate) over an Ethernet LAN using an app like IP/TV, you may see good performance at 320×240 pixels, but you will likely strain overall network efficiency.

Does this mean that the MBone needs an order of magnitude more bandwidth than today's average LAN to deliver a high-quality MPEG movie? In some ways, yes. That's why compressors like H.261 are so popular for MBone video (see Figure 15.3). Of course, other factors intrude here as well, but we're in the right ballpark.

And don't forget that we're still talking about fairly rich bandwidth when it comes to the MBone versus ISDN (128 Kbps) and lower connections, but it always helps to do reality checks like the one demonstrated here when you're extolling the virtues of any new technology.

So, does all this raise issues as to who gets to use the MBone, and when? It certainly does. Fortunately, the number of conflicts to date has been minimal, although they have indeed occurred among the academic and research communities who now form the main user base for the MBone. Whether potential multicasters can regulate themselves going forward remains an important question in the MBone world.

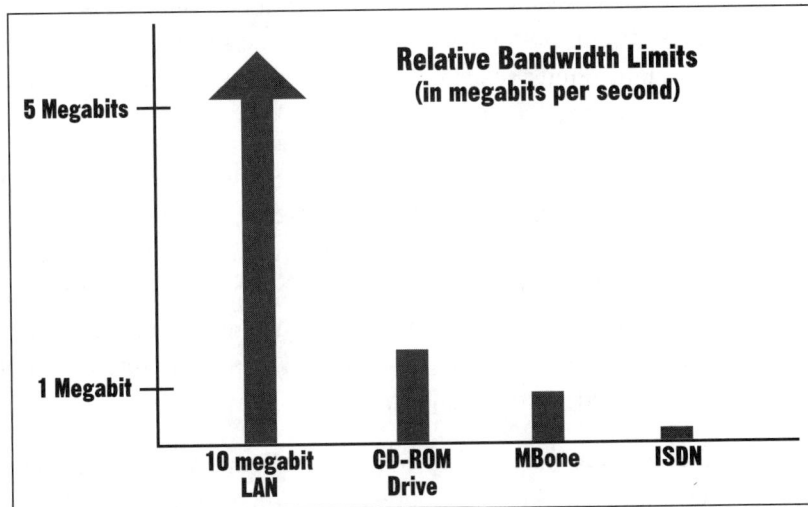

Figure 15.3 Putting MBone bandwidth in context.

MBone Topology

Let's return to the model of MBone islands in the unicast Net for a moment. If this model (complete with tunnels) has significant meaning, what does it suggest about the global topology of the MBone? In other words, to what network connectivity patterns do these strung-together islands generally conform?

Experts say that, within continental boundaries, MBone topology generally combines so-called star and mesh formations. Top-level multicast networks (including the actual backbone) will connect via a mesh of tunnels, many of them redundant for data integrity purposes. Further down the food chain (in regional networks), the star topology will dominate, as non-mesh links are extended to smaller networks.

MBone links among different continents are implemented mostly as tunnels. In the U.S., such tunnels normally terminate on the local networks at the California and Maryland Federal Internet Exchanges (FIXes). As you might expect, smooth operations at these FIXes is crucial to smooth operations for the entire global Internet.

MBone Decorum

Strangely enough, there is not yet an official etiquette for resolving conflicts over use of the MBone. This is because Western-style commerce has not yet established much of a beachhead. As of this writing, the unofficial policy seems based on the expectation that, going forward, interested parties will willingly cooperate for the mutual benefit of all concerned. Right.

The communication mechanism generally used for MBone event scheduling is the mailing list **rem-conf@es.net**. A party wishing to conduct MBone event X can announce it on this list, then wait for other producers to register objections—assuming everybody is monitoring the list. Following this formality, event X is then advertised using the MBone application SD (described later in this chapter), making it convenient for interested viewers to participate at show time.

Other agencies attempting to manage MBone scheduling issues include Web sites such as the one represented by the page **www.cilea.it/MBone/browse.htm** (see Figure 15.4). To reserve transmission time on the MBone, many cooperative parties use the input form **www.cilea.it/MBone/book.htm** (see Figure 15.5).

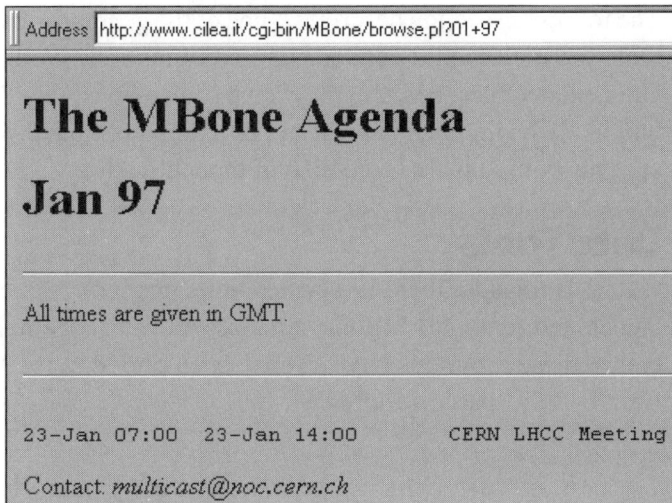

Figure 15.4 An MBone schedule browser.

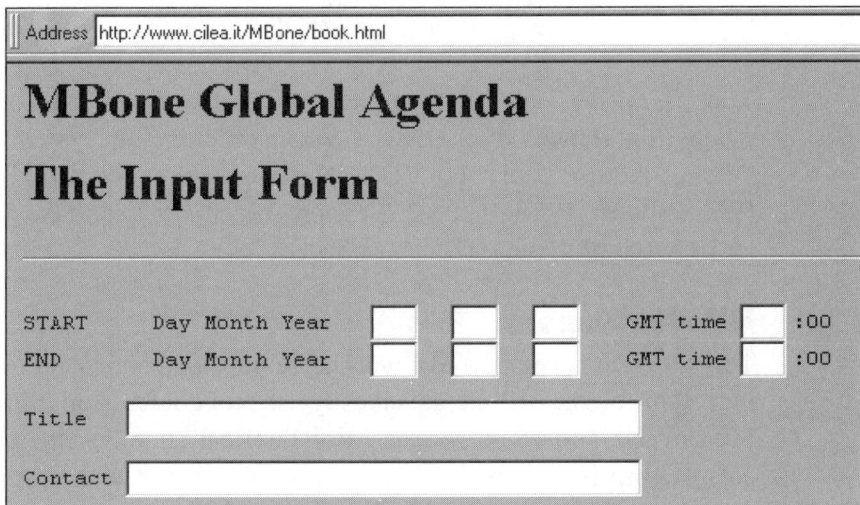

Figure 15.5 An MBone booking agency.

Desktop MBone Applications

As in most areas of desktop multimedia, specific applications define and characterize the underlying technology. This is especially true for the MBone environment (and for multicasting in general), which currently needs as many interesting programs as possible to spur its growth and acceptance.

The following section describes some of the generally available MBone tools for multimedia delivery and consumption. We'll start with the Unix executables, because they have been extensively field tested and will likely be imitated in form and function if ported to Wintel and Mac systems (which is true for some of them already).

Unix Tools

On the Unix side, there is a basic complement of applications used to launch and tune into MBone sessions. As you'll see in a minute, several of these programs have already been ported to the Windows platform by third-party developers.

Note! All of these Unix programs are readily available for downloading from the Internet. Doing Yahoo or Alta Vista searches on their names will provide a variety of download sites.

The essential Unix MBone tools are NV (NetVideo), VIC (VideoConference), IVS (INRIA Videoconferencing System), VAT (Visual Audio Tool), NEVOT (Network Voice Terminal), WB (WhiteBoard), IMM, and SD (Session Directory). Let's take a quick look at each of these.

NV (NETVIDEO)

This program is considered a workhorse for video and audio delivery in realtime on the MBone. It is mostly used for conferencing (like CU-SeeMe) and is based on version 1 of RTP (Real Time Transport Protocol). Key to NV's popularity is a codec that has it both ways: high frame rates and low data rates. See Figure 15.6, which shows a screen shot of the Windows version of NV.

Capture of video images for transmitting with NV is done with a standard frame grabber card, drivers for which come packaged with the main program. NV can also play CU-SeeMe streams compressed with the CUSM codec. Like many applications in the Unix world, operating NV requires supplying raw data like IP addresses and port numbers (as opposed to more user-friendly aliases).

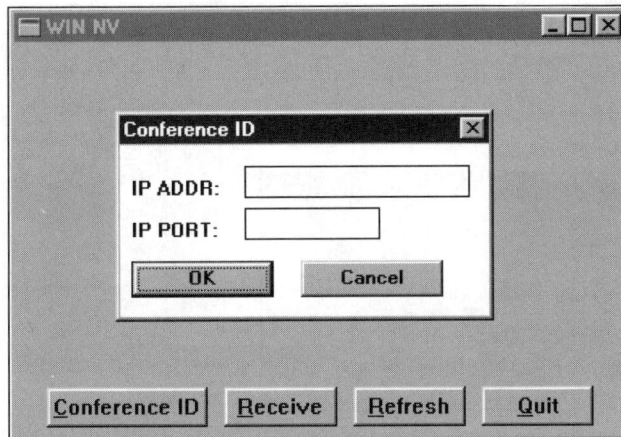

Figure 15.6 The WINNV user interface.

VIC (VIDEOCONFERENCE)

Based on RTP version 2, VIC was designed to be used across a wide range of bandwidth environments. Like NV, it is essentially an MBone conferencing program, but it can also be used in unicast mode for point-to-point sessions. For the record, VIC is backward compatible to RTP version 1.

One of VIC's more interesting features is voice-activated switching to the active speaker video window. Also included are a high-quality H.261 encoder and a robust automatic rate control monitor to inhibit overly rich video streams with high TTL values.

IVS (INRIA VIDEOCONFERENCING SYSTEM)

Developed in France, IVS is the conferencing tool of choice for many European MBone users. It is also used extensively by MICE (Multimedia Integrated Conferencing for Europe) participants and by members of other research institutes.

IVS includes an H.261 video codec, as well as ADPCM and PCM audio compressors, all implemented in software only. The H.261 codec encapsulates UPD/IP datagrams in RTP version 1 streams. An interesting error-control technology is also implemented in IVS.

VAT (VISUAL AUDIO TOOL)

VAT is an application that lets two or more users (each running VAT) conduct an audio-only conference on the MBone. Developed at Lawrence Berkeley Labs at UC Berkeley, VAT is also supported on

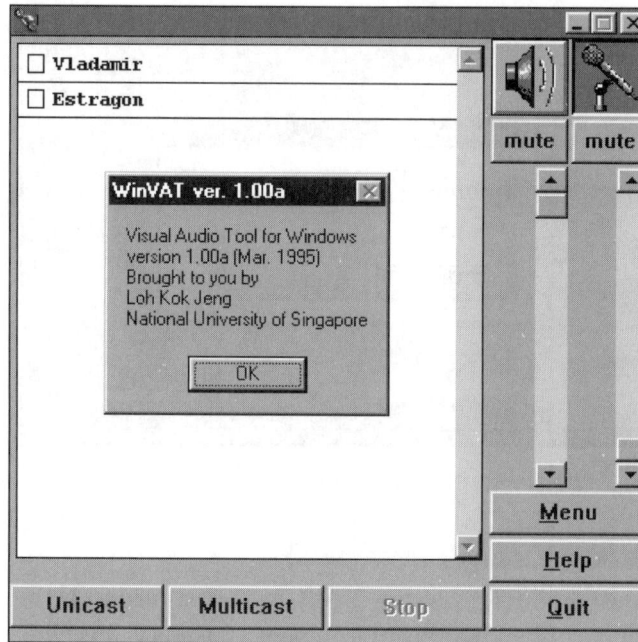

Figure 15.7 The WINVAT user interface.

Intel (as opposed to Wintel) boxes running Linux and FreeBSD. Figure 15.7 displays a Windows version of VAT.

VAT's user interface displays the names of all the participants in a given conference and highlights the name of the current speaker. Audio standards supported by VAT include GSM, PCM, LPC4, and IDVI. Rudimentary encryption is also supported.

NEVOT (NETWORK VOICE TERMINAL)

Like VAT, NEVOT is a dedicated audio conferencing solution for the MBone. In fact, you can configure NEVOT to be compatible with VAT so that both tools can be used in the same MBone audio conference. Unfortunately, while NEVOT's user interface may be a bit more robust, it still generally lives in VAT's shadow.

WB (WHITEBOARD)

WB is a different kind of MBone application than the video and audio tools described earlier, although it does facilitate communication among multiple users. Rather than stream video and audio data, WB allows for document sharing—in much the same way Microsoft NetMeeting supports document sharing on the Wintel platform.

In effect, when a user loads and shares a given document (such as a plain ASCII text file or a graphic expressed in Adobe PostScript), copies of that document are automatically transmitted to the other data conference participants so that they can contribute their own input. Several control modes are available to prevent anarchy during WB sessions.

IMM

This MBone program distinguishes itself in several ways. First, it does not send or receive audio. Second, it operates in very low bandwidth ranges. Finally, it uses a client/server model for image transmission. This approach can be useful for visual data that doesn't need frequent updating (such as weather maps).

SD (SESSION DIRECTORY)

This is probably the primary tool used by producers for scheduling MBone events and by users for tuning them in. As noted in other chapters, Precept's IP/TV solution has a similar *TV Guide*-like feature. SD was originally developed for internal use by MBone researchers but has since become a staple for both multicast publishers and consumers.

As shown in Figure 15.8, SD is one of the MBone applications recently ported to Windows by third parties. A multicaster wishing to create a new entry for an MBone session simply fills in the pertinent data in a dialog invoked by the New button. When a consumer wants to join an ongoing MBone session, he can run SD on his computer and navigate to the session via SD's interface.

Current Windows MBone Tools

As noted earlier, several of the popular Unix MBone applications have already begun porting to Windows. Good examples are referenced at the Web address **http://octavia.anu.edu.au/~markus/webmail/ MBONE/0152.html**, which will point you to an FTP site for downloading the programs, if you wish.

The following are screen shots of several of these programs, along with brief descriptions by the authors, quoted from the previously noted Web page. If you haven't seen the user interfaces of the Unix counterparts or are just interested in seeing the Windows MBone tools that are on the way, you might want to give these images a quick look.

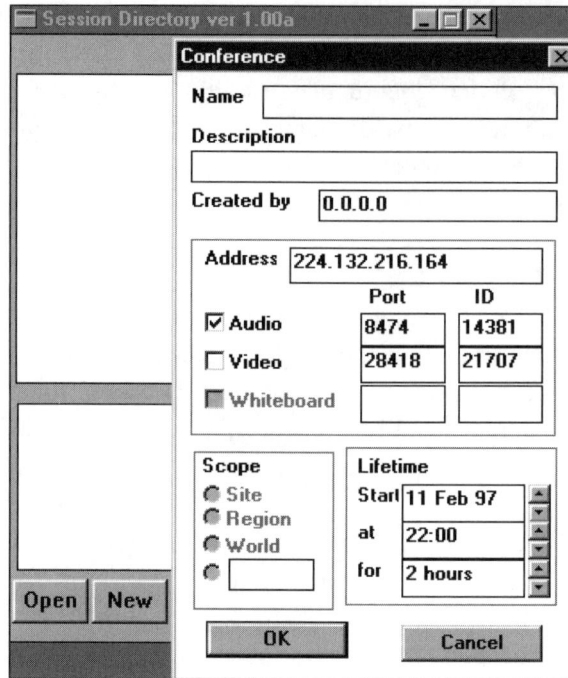

Figure 15.8 The WINSD user interface.

> **Note!** *And don't forget to search Yahoo and Alta Vista frequently with the criteria windows + mbone if you want to keep tabs on even newer applications.*

WINNV

"To run this program [see Figure 15.6], you need a video frame grabber card (e.g., Videoblaster). At present, it can only receive a [multicast] conference. The future version of WINNV will have both sending and receiving capabilities."

WINVAT

"A sound card is needed to run this program [see Figure 15.7]. When it is run as a standalone program, the user can choose to operate in unicast or multicast mode."

WINSD

"This program looks very similar to [Unix] SD [see Figure 15.8]. So if you have experience with using [Unix] SD, you should not have any problem using this program."

For the record, the authors of these three programs also provide the following information in an accompanying readme file:

"The programs should be installed in the same directory. You might need MMSYSTEM.DLL from Microsoft to run WINVAT. These programs were developed on Windows 3.11 using PC/TCP Onnet from FTP Software. They are solely written in C and the networking API used is Winsock 1.1.

We are not sure whether the programs will work on other TCP/IP stacks because we haven't carried out the test yet. The programs are still under development, so they are VERY buggy. Should you encounter any problems or have any suggestions, please contact **eng10213@leonis.nus.sg** or **engp4057@leonis.nus.sg**."

IP/TV

Although Precept Software's IP/TV Server and IP/TV Viewer are positioned primarily as enterprise-class solutions, they are reportedly designed to function normally over the MBone, as well. Because IP/TV is completely standards-based, you should expect this proposition to pan out in actual practice.

Precept's IP/TV Viewer is shown in Figure 15.9. See Chapter 6 for instructions on how to install and run both the Viewer and the Server

Figure 15.9   The Precept IP/TV Viewer.

components. Other examples of how Precept's software is used for multicasting are scattered throughout this book.

StarCast

StarCast is the name of a brand new (as this chapter is written) multicasting solution from Starlight Networks. While Chapter 14 is devoted to covering the operation of StarCast software in detail, it is worth mentioning the product here to round out the list of currently available Windows MBone tools.

Like IP/TV, StarCast is allegedly designed to multicast as well on the MBone as on LANs and WANs. Rigorous field testing will, of course, prove or disprove this allegation in due course. The user interface for the StarCast Viewer is shown in Figure 15.10.

Current Macintosh MBone Tools

As noted in previous chapters, the key to Mac multicasting—and to Mac MBone connectivity—is QuickTime Conferencing technology. While some actual programs have surfaced, like the Apple MBone TV program demonstrated in Chapter 13 (see Figure 15.11), third party development of Mac MBone applications has been dragging. For completeness, however, it is worth mentioning the following tools.

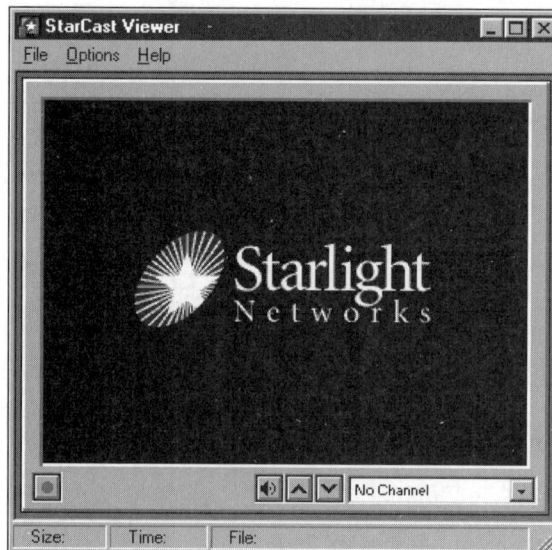

Figure 15.10 The StarCast Viewer.

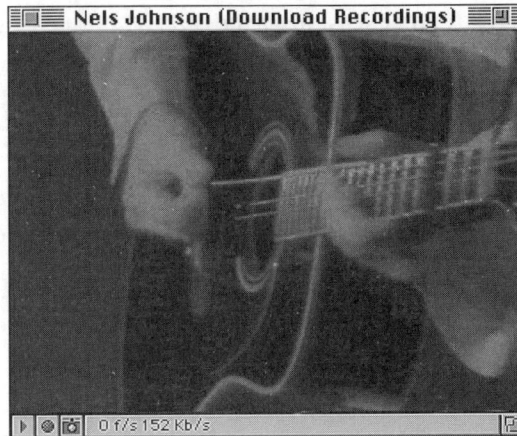

Figure 15.11 The QTC MBone TV interface.

MAVEN

Maven is an audio-only tool for Internet communication on the Mac. Although it does not work on the MBone natively, it is compatible with the Unix VAT (Visual Audio Tool) application. Maven is worth mentioning here because of its multicasting capabilities, although they are more proprietary than standards based (i.e., using IP-Multicast protocol).

CU-SEEME

Although it takes a fair amount of trouble to configure, the Mac version of CU-SeeMe can be made to tune in certain types of MBone events. What it comes down to is proper encoding of both the video and audio streams on the MBone session side. While the overall benefit to the user is small, it does cast the technology in an interesting perspective for developers.

MBone Events And Event Guides

Like public access television, there is always something at least mildly interesting happening on the MBone. Certain programs are perennial, while others tend to come and go. One thing you can always be sure of, the audience is growing. Fortunately, thanks to multicast technology, the performance level is not diminishing as the viewer population increases.

One of the regular sessions is the IETF (Internet Engineering Task Force) meeting. At these events, developers, researchers, and people in related industries exchange ideas regarding new technology, debate proposed resolutions, and generally further the state of the MBone.

IETF sessions are held a few times each year. Video tools are used as often as possible, along with the WB (WhiteBoard) application. If you want to keep informed about the technical side of the evolution of the MBone, these sessions may be the best source of such information.

Other types of events are also ongoing. Examples include symposiums from the MICE project (Multimedia Integrated Conferencing for Europe), the JASON project (which conducts expeditions to exotic locations with scientific/educational themes), and, of course, coverage of NASA missions.

Not to mention musical performances. In June of 1993, a group of musicians named Severe Tire Damage delivered what was probably the first live MBone concert (see Figure 15.12). As mentioned earlier, the Rolling Stones did an MBone feed from a show at the Dallas Cotton Bowl. Other genres of concerts, such as New Age and classical shows, have also been multicast on the MBone.

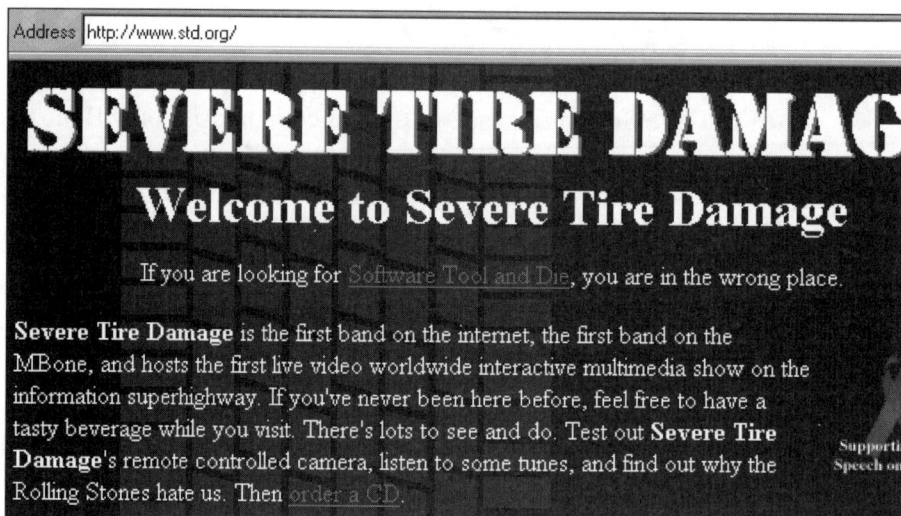

Figure 15.12 The Severe Tire Damage home page.

MBone Event Guides

If you're looking for ways to find out what kind of programming is available on the MBone, you can point your browser at the following Web pages:

- **http://cosmos.kaist.ac.kr/mcast/sched.html** (see Figure 15.13).

- **http://ns.uoregon.edu/~kemp/hotlist/NET-MBONE.html** (see Figure 15.14).

- **http://www.telstra.com.au/rodney/papers/mm_inet/mbonedo.html** (see Figure 15.15).

MBone Tunneling

MBone tunneling has been mentioned and briefly discussed at many points in this book. As explained in several of those places, there is nothing terribly exotic about tunneling, despite the science fiction quality the name implies. What really happens is much more down-to-earth.

The mechanical process involved is actually *encapsulation*—wrapping multicast IP packets in unicast IP packets as they travel from one multicast network to another over unicast highways. The rest of this section covers the technical details of MBone tunneling.

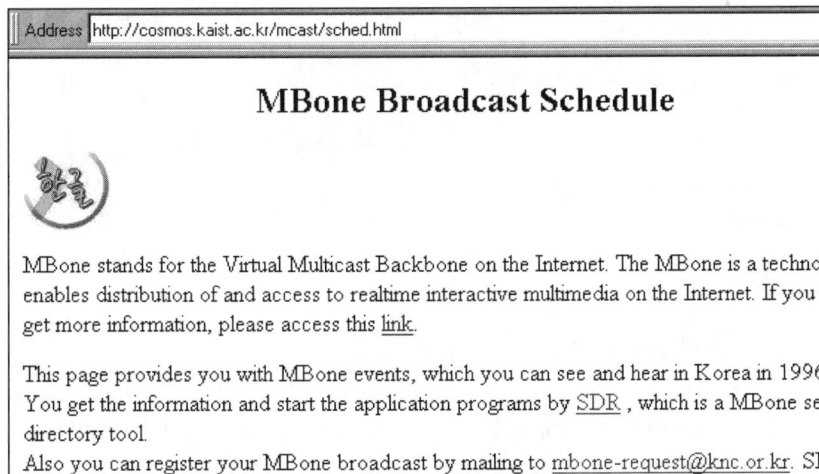

Figure 15.13   A sample MBone event schedule.

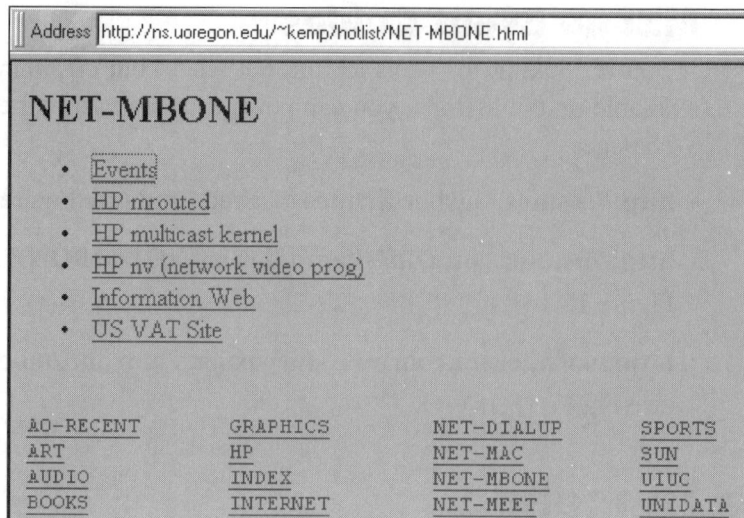

Figure 15.14 A different kind of MBone event schedule.

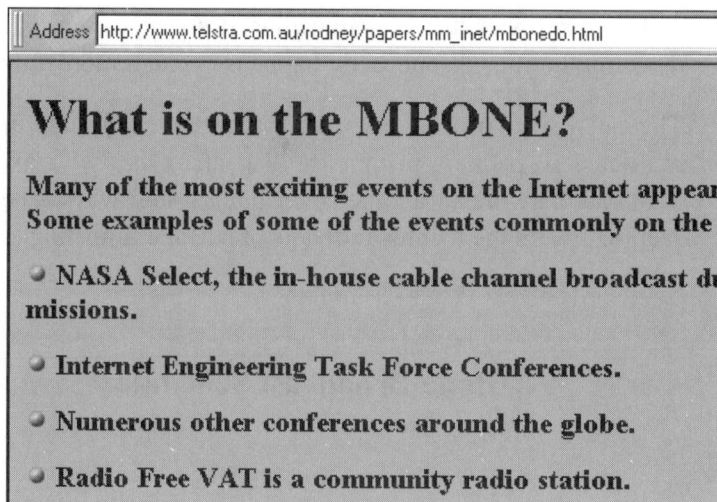

Figure 15.15 Standard MBone events.

Tunneling Overview

It is fair to say that the MBone (as we know it today) would not exist if it weren't for tunneling. Let's use a telephone system analogy. Think of tunnels as the long distance carriers of multicast data between local systems. Each component is dependent on the other, and together, they provide a complete solution for users.

According to published documents, the first multicast tunnel was created at Stanford University in 1988 as an experiment. Apparently, it was successful enough to be embraced wholeheartedly by both the research and commercial communities. Figure 15.16 shows a crude, somewhat dated map of the global MBone tunnel network at high level (as well as an FTP address for procuring better maps).

Most experts believe that, as the installed base of multicast-enabled routers expands, the symbiotic relationship will wane, and tunnels will become less important in the overall connectivity scheme. Of course, it is hard to predict when this transformation will be complete.

Tunnel Truncation And Pruning

When the MBone was first being built, a mechanism known as a *truncated tunnel* was often employed. In this scenario, all multicast routers within a certain number of hops from the sender (as expressed by the TTL value on the sender's IP packets) received the sender's packets.

Nowadays, the preferred process is known as *pruning*. In a pruned tunnel, multicast packets are not forwarded unless the recipient has specifically requested packets being routed to a given multicast group address. Such requests are made using IGMP messages (see Chapter 4). Also, the recipient must reside within the TTL range of the forwarded packets.

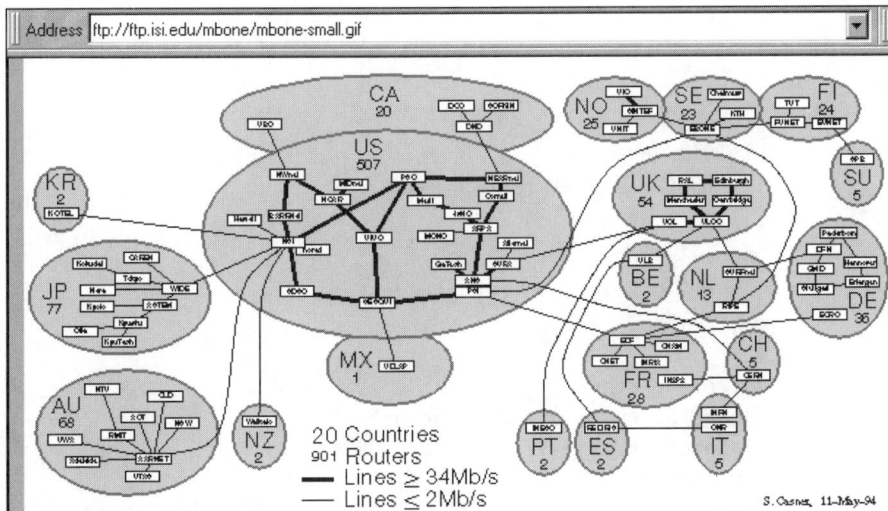

Figure 15.16 A crude map of the MBone.

Pruned tunnels are clearly much more efficient, because they keep out unwanted multicast traffic. In fact, if no node on a subnet attached to a pruned tunnel has registered interest in traffic headed for a given group IP address, no multicast traffic will flow through the tunnel to that subnet. Figure 15.17 shows an interesting graphical representation of global tunnel links (along with a URL for more of the same).

Implementing A Tunnel

In Cisco routers, tunnels are implemented with config files (recall Chapters 11 and 12). Because most other router manufacturers are still refining their tunneling strategies, you should check with them prior to purchase if you are planning on building tunnels for your own systems. Listing 15.1 shows a Cisco config file with a tunnel implemented. Tunnel-specific entries are expressed in boldface.

LISTING 15.1   A CONFIG FILE WITH A TUNNEL.

```
Current configuration:
!
version 11.0
service udp-small-servers
service tcp-small-servers
!
hostname XXX-xxx
!
enable secret level 7 5 $1$EVOH$YDbZYGXpCXDpQ1jle9CyFO
!
ip multicast-routing
!
interface Tunnel0
 ip unnumbered Ethernet0
 ip pim dense-mode
 ip multicast ttl-threshold 127
 ip sd listen
 tunnel source xxx.yyy.zzz.1
 tunnel destination aaa.bbb.ccc.34
 tunnel mode dvmrp
!
interface Ethernet0
 description To Office Ethernet
 ip address xxx.yyy.zzz.1 255.255.255.0
 ip pim dense-mode
!
```

```
interface Serial0
 no ip address
 ip pim dense-mode
 encapsulation frame-relay IETF
 bandwidth 1536
 frame-relay lmi-type ansi
!
interface Serial0.1 point-to-point
 ip unnumbered Ethernet0
 bandwidth 1536
 frame-relay interface-dlci 500 IETF
!
interface Serial1
 no ip address
 shutdown
!
interface BRI0
 no ip address
 shutdown
!
interface Async1
 no ip address
!
ip domain-name XXXXX.NET
ip name-server xxx.xxx.xxx.xxx
ip route 0.0.0.0 0.0.0.0 Serial0.1
```

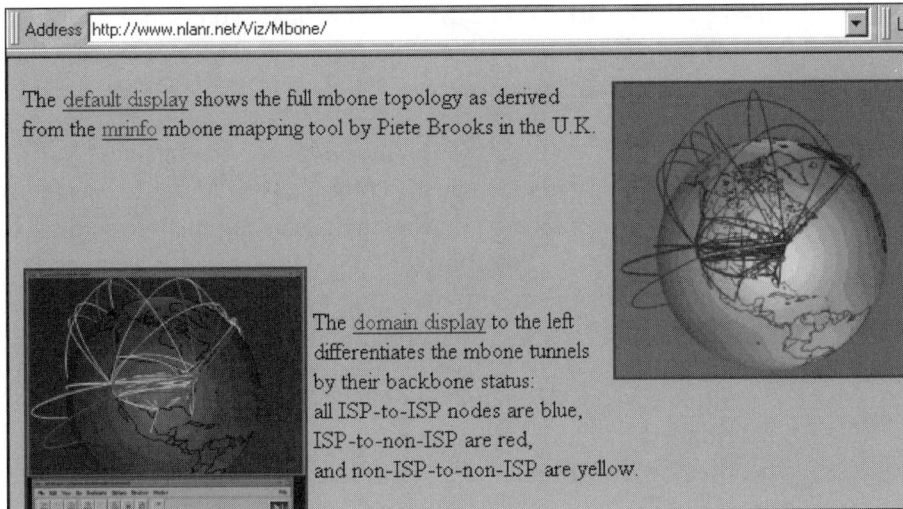

Address http://www.nlanr.net/Viz/Mbone/

The default display shows the full mbone topology as derived from the mrinfo mbone mapping tool by Piete Brooks in the U.K.

The domain display to the left differentiates the mbone tunnels by their backbone status: all ISP-to-ISP nodes are blue, ISP-to-non-ISP are red, and non-ISP-to-non-ISP are yellow.

Figure 15.17   Global tunnels.

Finding An MBone/Multicast ISP

By the time this book is published, you should not be met with a blank stare or a suspicious glance if you ask your current ISP if they can deliver MBone access, complete with tunneling capabilities. This was certainly not the case as recently as a year ago.

Because all Internet service for users and relatively small Web sites comes from ISPs, those ISPs may fairly be considered lynch pins to multicast ubiquity. And because most independent ISPs (unlike ATT, MCI, PacBell, and so on) operate on razor-thin margins, they are necessarily resistant to major hardware upgrades.

So, where does this leave the emerging multicast consumer community? In the slipstream of the free market economy, of course. Actually, it's not that bad. Because of the strong interest in multicasting from the corporate sector, hardware manufacturers will have solid markets in which to sell their gear, which should provide a trickle-down effect for the multicast community at large.

The Role Of The Multicast ISP

In an ideal world, an ISP will offer MBone service to customers as a value-added service on top of plain vanilla Web access. As a functioning node in the MBone, the ISP will have at least one serious multicasting router for connecting to tunnels to other major MBone nodes, and also to the ISP's multicast customers.

Currently, ISPs getting into the multicast service business will likely buy standalone, dedicated gear to provide their MBone service. Down the road, we can expect more sophisticated equipment from the likes of Cisco, Ascend, and Proteon that combines everything in one box, as well as upgrades from the operating system players (like Microsoft, Sun, and Apple) that make overall administration chores easier.

Traditionally, an MBone node (end nodes excluded) has several tunnels implemented. Each tunnel transmits a redundant copy of each packet handled by an MBone node. For this reason, prospective MBone ISPs are well-advised to use so-called *multi-homed hosts* (workstations with multiple network interfaces).

Any ISP planning to offer MBone service to the general public should also be willing to devote time and personnel resources for administration and problem solving in their allotment of the overall MBone space. If this sounds too PC, it's not. The MBone is a highly volatile environment, still in the early stages of development.

For instance, any MBone node has the potential to blast out multicast packets to every other MBone node—in other words, to the whole network. If this potential is misused or managed carelessly, the MBone can get overloaded without anyone half trying. Fortunately, much of the next generation of routing hardware will include scaling capabilities to keep this potential under better control.

Finding A Multicast ISP

Armed with the this chapter's information, you should be able to discuss with your current or potential ISP the realities of getting MBone Internet service. The following list (also available in much greater detail at the Web site **www.mbone.com/mbone/contacts.html**) provides some email addresses to start with if your existing provider can't help you.

- MCInet: **mbone@mci.net**

- Sprintlink: **mbone@sprint.net**

- AlterNet: **ops@uunet.uu.net**

- PSI: **fedor@nisc.psi.net**

- ESnet: **routing@es.net**

- NSI: **mbone-nsi@nsipo.nasa.gov**

Summary

The goal of this chapter is to peel off some of the mystery and misunderstanding about the shape and scope of the MBone. What the MBone is *not* is a limitless bandwidth frontier ripe for exploitation. In reality, the MBone is a relatively *thin* pipe (compared to today's LANs and dedicated WANs), especially if you want to transmit multimedia streams.

As for MBone tunneling, rest assured that it's not a Guild Navigator activity. Rather, it is a form of encapsulation that permits data from one multicast subnet to reach another multicast subnet over today's unicast infrastructure. Even though it sounds like retrofitting, it is the glue that currently holds the MBone together.

But don't swing all the way back to unicast Web surfing. As we've stressed, the MBone is a fascinating communications network that is crucial for the advancement of scientific research and even global politics (see Chapter 17 for coverage of the Summit of Hope MBone Webcast).

Chapter 16

- Using ActiveX Controls and scripting languages

- Working with Netscape plug-ins

- Converting multicasts to unicasts

Chapter 16

Viewing Multicasts On Custom Web Pages

Because of the current state of the multicasting environment, this book is primarily concerned with multicast *applications*—standalone Windows and Macintosh programs that run on the average desktop system. However, technologies like ActiveX, JavaScript, and VBScript now give Web developers ways to customize their HTML pages to include multicast media presentations using a relatively high level of coding.

This chapter covers the tools and techniques that let you create Web pages containing multicast video and audio streams, assuming that you use the custom controls and embeddable objects provided by companies that make the underlying multicast streaming technology. If you wish to write your own controls (ActiveX for instance), you'll need to do so in a language such as C++, although Microsoft Visual Basic v5.0 now has a good facility for doing this. We can expect more sophisticated user interfaces to proliferate as these components mature. When this book was written, only a handful of software companies had released Web-page controls to let developers break away from existing standalone applications.

Working With ActiveX Controls And Scripts

In Microsoft Webland, ActiveX reigns supreme as the framework in which to develop controls that come to life in pages viewed using the Microsoft Internet Explorer. While most multicast software companies are reportedly working on ActiveX Controls, Precept Software has already completed one that will ship with its IP/TV v1.5 solution (in beta, as of this writing). The demonstrations in this section are based on the IP/TV product. But first, to give this section the proper context, a brief review of ActiveX itself.

Note! *Don't forget that Microsoft Internet Explorer also runs on the Mac, along with a lot of ActiveX technology.*

ActiveX Overview

To summarize its description in Chapter 1, ActiveX is built on Microsoft's highly mature OLE code base, which allows for data documents (including media files) to be edited, presented, and otherwise exploited with their native player applications. What ActiveX achieves is bringing all that operability to a desktop computer connected to the Internet (or an intranet).

In other words, if a document such as a video clip is played by a user, it shouldn't matter whether the clip is streaming from a remote Web location or a local CD-ROM drive. As noted, the best way to keep up-to-date on ActiveX is to visit the Microsoft site regularly, where there is already plenty of discussion concerning ActiveX's role in multicasting, video conferencing, and so-called ActiveX conferencing.

The ActiveMovie Connection

The software layer that actually plays a video stream associated with an ActiveX Control is ActiveMovie, Microsoft's successor to Video for Windows (VfW). Previously known as Quartz, ActiveMovie 1.0 (the current release) was designed from the ground up to handle professional quality digital video—and to compete directly with Apple's QuickTime.

ActiveMovie 2.0, due to be released sometime in 1997, is supposed to bring Microsoft's streaming video solution to new performance plateaus. In practical terms, what version 1.0 can do right now is play MPEG streams in software-only mode (something VfW was unable to handle). In any event, it is mainly the combination of ActiveX and ActiveMovie that controls the display of multicast video streams on your Web pages. Figure 16.1 shows a page from the Microsoft Interactive Media center, the current home of ActiveMovie.

VBScript And JavaScript

To complete this picture, we need to include the two principal scripting languages now in general use among Web developers: VBScript and JavaScript. VBScript leverages off of Microsoft's powerful Visual Basic technology. JavaScript brings the power (but not the speed) of Sun's Java to the party.

Both are so-called *interpreters*, which explains their slower execution speed (not necessarily a problem, depending on the application). In essence, a script is processed by a Web browser with the help of an add-in program, which does the actual interpreting of the script. Such add-ins are what make browsers capable of handling VB and Java scripts.

Figure 16.1 Where to learn more about ActiveMovie.

A useful way to view a VB or Java script is to think of it as a program embedded in a Web page. As such, it may contain commands that control the behavior of ActiveX objects also embedded in the page. Generally speaking, these commands get executed when the page is loaded by a browser.

Java was there first, but Microsoft seems intent on making VBScript the alpha geek, at least for pages browsed with its Internet Explorer. We'll look at examples of both types of scripts in this chapter. Figure 16.2 shows the current home page for VBScript.

Note! *Microsoft's version of JavaScript is JScript, which works with the Internet Explorer just like VBScript.*

Precept Software's ActiveX Control

When you install IP/TV v1.5, Precept's ActiveX Control is added to your Windows operating environment along with several other files (not to mention the IP/TV application itself). From that point on, it is up to you—the Web page developer—to make the best use of these powerful components.

Let's get right to an example. Figure 16.3 shows the standard IP/TV Viewer with a multicast movie in progress. Figure 16.4 shows a Web page with the Precept ActiveX Control implemented. As you can see, there is a substantial difference in the overall effect.

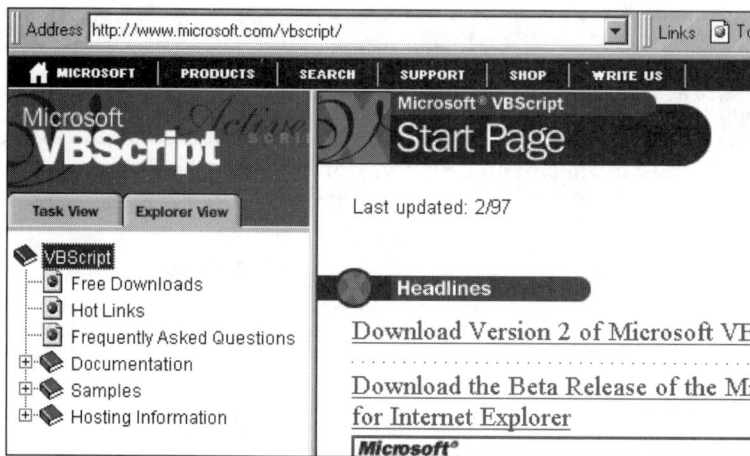

Figure 16.2 The current VBScript home page.

Figure 16.3 The standard IP/TV Viewer.

Figure 16.4 A simple ActiveX implementation.

The Web page shown in Figure 16.4 is obviously composed of several frames. Listing 16.1 shows a generic implementation of the Precept ActiveX Control that could handle the video window in the right-hand frame. The code in this listing would normally be contained in the body of an HTML document.

LISTING 16.1   IMPLEMENTING THE PRECEPT ACTIVEX CONTROL.

```
<OBJECT
 ID="MovieChannel"
 CLASSID="CLSID:05589FA1-C356-11CE-BF01-00AA0055595A"
 STYLE="WIDTH:200pt;HEIGHT:55pt;">
    <PARAM NAME="_ExtentX" VALUE="7038">
    <PARAM NAME="_ExtentY" VALUE="1931">
    <PARAM NAME="ShowPositionControls" VALUE="-1">
    <PARAM NAME="MovieWindowWidth" VALUE="352">
    <PARAM NAME="MovieWindowHeight" VALUE="288">
    <PARAM NAME="AutoStart" VALUE="-1">
    <PARAM NAME="DisplayForeColor" VALUE="65280">
    <PARAM NAME="ShowControls" VALUE="false">
</OBJECT>
```

Web developers experienced with ActiveX will understand the purpose of the components comprising this control. If you are new to ActiveX programming, here's a quick breakdown:

• **<OBJECT> ID**—Precept's name for the control, in this case *"MovieChannel"*.

• **<OBJECT> CLASSID**—As in all ActiveX Controls, this is an identification number generated at the time the control is created, guaranteed to be unique in the known universe (to the extent that's possible).

• **<OBJECT> STYLE**—General specifications describing the control's appearance, such as width and height.

The **<PARAM>** tags are used to set the attributes for the ActiveX Control at runtime. Together, they comprise what amounts to a partial API for programming the control when the page is loaded. The rest of the control's API can be addressed using a VB or Java script, as you'll see in a moment.

If we just dropped this control into a Web page all by itself, the page would look like Figure 16.5 when loaded in Internet Explorer. As you can see, what you get is just the standard ActiveMovie controller. Note that this figure shows the control with the PARAMs ShowControls and ShowPositionControls turned on.

Figure 16.5 The simple Precept ActiveX Control viewed in Internet Explorer.

A MORE COMPLEX EXAMPLE

If you wanted to create a Web page more like the one shown in Figure 16.4, you would have to do a bit more scripting, especially to switch among the various channels and programs being multicast by a Precept IP/TV Server running the Program Guide (discussed in detail in Chapter 11).

Listing 16.2 shows the flavor of the code necessary to create a professional-looking presentation. The code also suggests the robust quality of the Precept ActiveX Control. As you can see, JavaScript is the scripting language used for this example.

Note! *Remember that this example is based on beta-level software and is used here for demonstration purposes only.*

LISTING 16.2 PARTIAL CODE FOR TUNING IN AN IP/TV MULTICAST.

```
<!-- Copyright (c) 1997 Precept Software, Inc. All rights
  reserved. -->
<HTML>
<HEAD>
<TITLE>IP/TV Viewer: iptv Controls, Precept Software, Inc.</
  TITLE>

<SCRIPT LANGUAGE="JavaScript">
<!--
var SdpFileName
var SdpSave
var playing
```

```
function MyInit()
{
    SdpFileName = ""
    SdpSave = ""
    playing = false

    ComboBoxMovieSize.AddItem("Original movie size")
    ComboBoxMovieSize.AddItem("Double original movie")
    ComboBoxMovieSize.AddItem("1/16 of screen size")
    ComboBoxMovieSize.AddItem("1/4 of screen size")
    ComboBoxMovieSize.AddItem("1/2 of screen size")
    ComboBoxMovieSize.AddItem("Full Screen")
    ComboBoxMovieSize.ListIndex = 0

    ComboBoxMovieSize.Enabled = 1

    ScrollBarVolume.Min = -5000
    ScrollBarVolume.Max = 0
    ScrollBarVolume.Value = -2500
}

function MyPlay(button)
{
    if (SdpFileName == "")
    {
        window.alert("You must select a program!")
        return
    }

    if (playing)
    {
        // button.value = "Stop", we were playing a movie
        playing = false
        button.value = "Play"
        if (top.frames[1].bOpenCompleted)
            top.frames[1].MovieChannel.Stop()
    }
    else
    {
        // button.value = "Play"
        playing = true
        button.value = "Stop"
        if (SdpSave == SdpFileName)
        {
            // we did a play+stop, continue playing the same
            movie
            top.frames[1].MovieChannel.Run()
        }
        else
        {
```

```
            // new movie
            SdpSave = SdpFileName
            top.frames[1].MovieChannel.FileName = SdpFileName
        }
    }
}
-->
</SCRIPT>

<SCRIPT LANGUAGE="JavaScript" FOR="ComboBoxMovieSize"
EVENT="Change()">
<!--
if (top.frames[1].bOpenCompleted && playing)
    top.frames[1].MovieChannel.Stop()

top.frames[1].MovieChannel.FullScreenMode = false

if (ComboBoxMovieSize.ListIndex == 5)
    top.frames[1].MovieChannel.FullScreenMode = true
else
    top.frames[1].MovieChannel.MovieWindowSize =
        ComboBoxMovieSize.ListIndex

if (top.frames[1].bOpenCompleted && playing)
    top.frames[1].MovieChannel.Run()
-->
</SCRIPT>

<SCRIPT LANGUAGE="JavaScript" FOR="ScrollBarVolume"
  EVENT="Change()">
<!--
if (top.frames[1].bOpenCompleted)
    top.frames[1].MovieChannel.Volume = ScrollBarVolume.Value
-->
</SCRIPT>

<SCRIPT LANGUAGE="JavaScript" FOR="ScrollBarAudioBalance"
  EVENT="Change()">
<!--
if (top.frames[1].bOpenCompleted)
    top.frames[1].MovieChannel.Balance =
ScrollBarAudioBalance.Value
-->
</SCRIPT>

<SCRIPT LANGUAGE="JavaScript" FOR="ComboBoxChannels"
  EVENT="Change()">
<!--
SdpFileName=top.frames[2].document.programs.getSdpFileName
  (ComboBoxChannels.ListIndex)
```

```
            top.frames[2].document.programs.showPgmbyIndex(ComboBoxChannels.
              ListIndex)

            if (top.frames[1].bOpenCompleted && playing)
            {
                if (SdpFileName != SdpSave)
                {
                    // channel surf
                    top.frames[1].MovieChannel.Stop()
                    SdpSave = SdpFileName
                    top.frames[1].bOpenCompleted = false
                    top.frames[1].MovieChannel.FileName = SdpFileName
                }
            }
            -->
            </SCRIPT>

            </HEAD>

            <BODY BGCOLOR="C0C0C0" ONLOAD="MyInit()">
            <CENTER>
            <TABLE BORDER="0" CELLPADDING="0" CELLSPACING="0" VALIGN="top">
            <TR>
            <TD>
            <CENTER>
            <B>IP/TV Display Controls</B>
            <P>
            <IMG SRC="/iptvgifs/logo.gif">
            <BR>
            <FONT SIZE=-1>
            Programs<BR></FONT>
            <OBJECT ID="ComboBoxChannels"
             CLASSID="CLSID:8BD21D30-EC42-11CE-9E0D-00AA006002F3"
            STYLE="WIDTH:182pt;HEIGHT:6pt;">
                <PARAM NAME="VariousPropertyBits" VALUE="746604569">
                <PARAM NAME="DisplayStyle" VALUE="3">
                <PARAM NAME="Size" VALUE="3600;600">
                <PARAM NAME="ShowDropButtonWhen" VALUE="2">
                <PARAM NAME="Value" VALUE="Select a program!">
                <PARAM NAME="FontHeight" VALUE="72">
                <PARAM NAME="FontCharSet" VALUE="0">
                <PARAM NAME="FontPitchAndFamily" VALUE="2">
                <PARAM NAME="FontWeight" VALUE="0">
            </OBJECT>
            <P>
            <FORM NAME="MyButtons" ACTION=" " METHOD=GET>
            <INPUT TYPE="button" NAME="PlayOrStop" VALUE="Play"
              ONCLICK="MyPlay(this)">
            </FORM>
```

```
<P>
<FONT SIZE=-1>
Video Size<BR></FONT>
<OBJECT ID="ComboBoxMovieSize"
CLASSID="CLSID:8BD21D30-EC42-11CE-9E0D-00AA006002F3"
STYLE="WIDTH:182pt;HEIGHT:6pt;">
    <PARAM NAME="VariousPropertyBits" VALUE="746604569">
    <PARAM NAME="DisplayStyle" VALUE="3">
    <PARAM NAME="Size" VALUE="3600;600">
    <PARAM NAME="ShowDropButtonWhen" VALUE="2">
    <PARAM NAME="Value" VALUE="Original movie size">
    <PARAM NAME="FontHeight" VALUE="72">
    <PARAM NAME="FontCharSet" VALUE="0">
    <PARAM NAME="FontPitchAndFamily" VALUE="2">
    <PARAM NAME="FontWeight" VALUE="0">
</OBJECT>
<P>
<FONT SIZE=-1>
Volume<BR></FONT>
<OBJECT ID="ScrollBarVolume"
 CLASSID="CLSID:DFD181E0-5E2F-11CE-A449-00AA004A803D"
STYLE="WIDTH:182pt;HEIGHT:6pt;">
    <PARAM NAME="Size" VALUE="3400;400">
    <PARAM NAME="Min" VALUE="4294962296">
    <PARAM NAME="Max" VALUE="0">
    <PARAM NAME="Position" VALUE="4294964796">
</OBJECT>
<P>
<FONT SIZE=-1>
Audio Balance<BR></FONT>
<OBJECT ID="ScrollBarAudioBalance"
 CLASSID="CLSID:DFD181E0-5E2F-11CE-A449-00AA004A803D"
STYLE="WIDTH:182pt;HEIGHT:6pt;">
    <PARAM NAME="Size" VALUE="3400;400">
    <PARAM NAME="Min" VALUE="4294957296">
    <PARAM NAME="Max" VALUE="10000">
</OBJECT>
</TD>
</TR>
</TABLE>
</CENTER>
</BODY>
</HTML>
```

A REAL-LIFE APPLICATION

At the end of Chapter 10, a scenario was proposed in which a multicast infomercial of sorts could be conducted with a remote panel of experts and a local audience. If a Web page with multiple ActiveX Controls

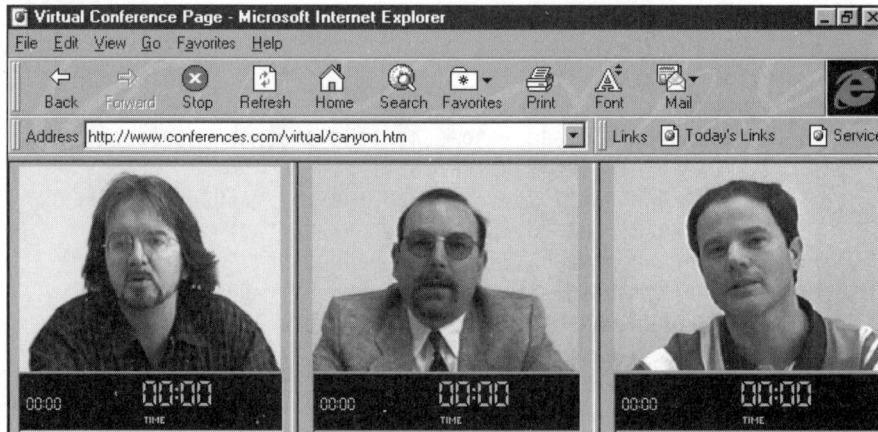

Figure 16.6 Multiple ActiveX movie windows.

(such as Precept's) was developed as the main user interface for such a project, it might look like the one shown in Figure 16.6.

NetShow Live Audio Pages

As already discussed in the sections of this book devoted to Microsoft's NetShow, one of the suggested (by Microsoft) ways to present live audio from a NetShow server is via VBScript/ActiveX-enabled Web pages. When a client browses such pages, VBScript and ActiveX work together to deliver the live audio stream to the client.

Note! *As of this writing, NetShow Live only handles audio—as opposed to NetShow On Demand, which handles both audio and video.*

When you download the installable NetShow Live package, you'll find that it includes some sample HTML documents for you to experiment with. For example, let's take a look at the code shown in Listing 16.3, which is from the Microsoft demo file nlasampl.htm and includes VBScript commands to direct the performance of the ActiveX Controls.

LISTING 16.3   A MICROSOFT NETSHOW LIVE DEMO PAGE.

```
<HTML>
<HEAD>
<TITLE>Audio Control Demo</TITLE>
```

```
</HEAD>
<BODY>
<OBJECT ID="NLAudio" CLASSID="CLSID:56A46023-DB88-11CF-9498-
  00AA00A21BDE" CODEBASE="NLAudio.ocx#Version=-1,-1,-1,-1"
ALIGN="RIGHT" HEIGHT="10" WIDTH="10">
<PARAM NAME="_Version" VALUE="65536">
<PARAM NAME="_ExtentX" VALUE="2646">
<PARAM NAME="_ExtentY" VALUE="1323">
<PARAM NAME="_StockProps" VALUE="0">
</OBJECT>
<H1>Microsoft NetShow Live Audio Control<BR>
Play Multicast Audio</H1>
<FORM>
<INPUT TYPE="BUTTON" NAME="BtnPlay" VALUE="Play">
<INPUT TYPE="BUTTON" NAME="BtnStop" VALUE="Stop">
<INPUT TYPE="BUTTON" NAME="BtnAbout" VALUE="About">
</FORM>
<P>
<B>Note:</B> Make sure the IP address and port matches the
  address and port of the server you want to listen to. This
  sample uses the following parameters:
<UL><LI><B>IP Address:</B> 239.240.100.2</LI></UL>
<UL><LI><B>IP Port:</B> 29102</LI></UL>
<UL><LI><B>Codec:</B> IMA ADPCM, mono, 8 KHz, 4 bits per
sample</LI></UL>
<P>
For more information on how this simple demo works, see the
<A HREF="nlaintro.htm">Audio Control SDK</A>.
<SCRIPT LANGUAGE="VBScript"><!--
Sub BtnAbout_OnClick
    call NLAudio.AboutBox()
End Sub
Sub BtnPlay_OnClick
    call NLAudio.Stop()
    call NLAudio.SetSocket("239.240.100.2", 29102)
    call NLAudio.SetCodec(17,1,8000,4)
    call NLAudio.Play()
End Sub
Sub BtnStop_OnClick
    call NLAudio.Stop()
End Sub
--></SCRIPT>
<H4>Copyright (c) 1996 Microsoft Corp.</H4>
</BODY>
</HTML>
```

Note the **OBJECT** definition and the VBScript section, which refer to the NetShow Live ActiveX Control. Other pages in the NetShow Live sample package illustrate other ways to exploit this object. The page rendered by this particular Microsoft sample code is shown in Figure 16.7.

As you'll see the more you work with ActiveX, one of its key features is its ability to marshal components. For instance, if certain controls referenced in an executing HTML document are not present locally, they can be procured from remote locations—such as other Web sites. Microsoft is strongly focused on this type of design, and the ActiveX development areas deserve close and frequent scrutiny by all types of Web programmers.

Other Web Page/Multicast Techniques

While delivering multicasts to Web pages using custom ActiveX Controls provides developers with the most design flexibility, there are still one or two alternatives to using standalone player applications such as the IP/TV Viewer. The balance of this chapter covers the remaining techniques.

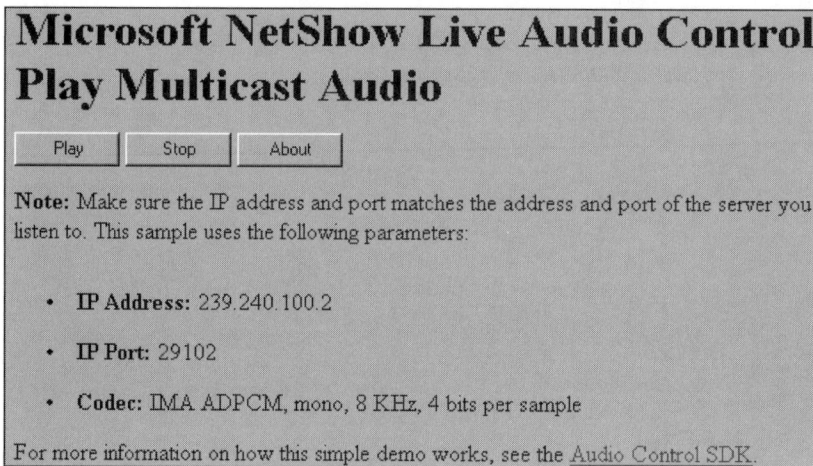

Figure 16.7 A NetShow Live demo page (using VBScript and ActiveX).

Netscape Plug-ins For Multicast Web Pages

Precept Software had a Netscape Navigator plug-in for its IP/TV Viewer in the original version of IP/TV, and the plug-in is still supported in the current release of the Precept product. Like most Netscape plug-ins, Precept's plug-in brings up a player—in this case, the standard IP/TV Viewer. Listing 16.4 shows an HTML document with the IP/TV plug-in implemented.

LISTING 16.4   USING THE IP/TV NETSCAPE PLUG-IN.

```
<HTML>
<HEAD>
<TITLE>IP/TV Plug-in Test</TITLE>
</HEAD>
<BODY>
<CENTER>
<H2>Testing the IP/TV Plug-in </H2>
<HR>
<EMBED SRC="c:\win95\sample.sdp"
WIDTH=360 HEIGHT=300 AUTOSTART=true LOOP=true>
<HR>
</CENTER>
</BODY>
</HTML>
```

As you might remember from the IP/TV test drive in Chapter 6, an SDP file contains information about an available multicast, as opposed to getting that information from a Precept Program Guide running on a remote IP/TV Server. The SDP file referenced in the **EMBED** line in Listing 16.4 could just as easily reside such a remote server as on the local client machine.

Converting Multicasts To Unicasts

Another way to publish a multicast presentation on a Web page is to use a special server-side program to convert, say, an MBone event into a unicast video stream viewable in any browser that visits your Web site. Many so-called Webcasts use this technique, even though it is not true multicasting.

If you view the HTML source behind the pages at **www.netizen.se**, for example, you'll get a feeling for the complexity involved in this sort of approach. Figure 16.8 shows a sample page from that site, which was featured in Chapter 17 (an interview with MBone pioneer Dan Mapes).

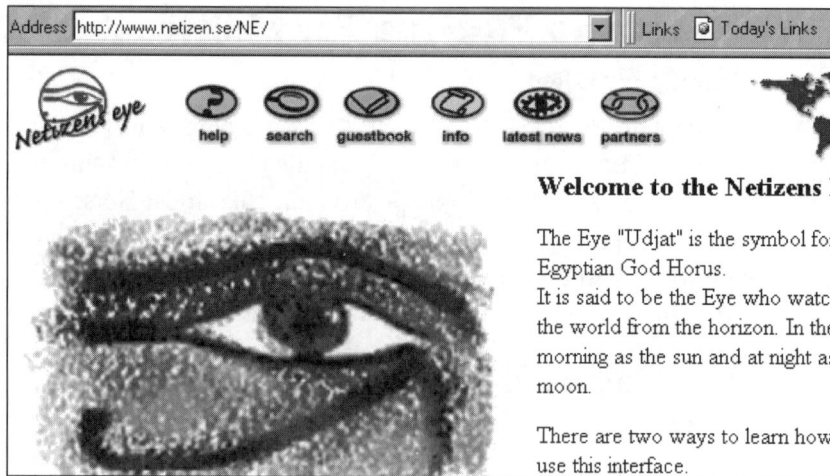

Figure 16.8 A good place to view a Webcast.

Summary

Currently, the most efficient way to consume a multicast on a desktop computer is with an off-the-shelf application like Precept's IP/TV, Starlight's StarCast, or Microsoft's NetShow. This situation is starting to change, however, as these and other software developers create scriptable and embeddable controls and components that let Webmasters add multicast viewing capability to their pages in much the same way as they do the more established types of streaming Web media.

Chief among the scriptable solutions is Microsoft's ActiveX, a powerful and flexible technology that may lock in Microsoft's dominance on the Web when it comes to playing multimedia assets on the local desktop. Look for ActiveX Controls from all the multicast players in the near future.

Chapter
17

- **Producing an MBone Webcast**

- **Bringing the MBone to the PC desktop**

- **Creating a new mode of communication**

Chapter 17

Cruising The MBone

As you've seen, one of the main goals of this book is to demonstrate how you can start multicasting right now, with off-the-rack PC equipment and peripherals. However, as we've also noted, full-on multicasting across the entire global Internet is not yet possible for most people (although this is already starting to change).

The part of the global Internet where multicasting *is* happening right now is called the MBone. Prior chapters defined the MBone as a space limited by routers, switches, and their evolving protocols. Currently, such limitations are surmountable only by people who possess and understand the right equipment and have access to the appropriate communication channels. Traditionally, this happens only within the confines of universities and government research institutions.

One person who thoroughly understands MBone hardware and its underlying communication links is Dan Mapes, a principal in the firm Netizen's Dialog (**www.netizen.se**) and an authority in the field of MBone event production.

Mr. Mapes was instrumental in the successful execution of "The Future of Hope," The First Summit in Cyberspace, a 1996

Webcast involving President Jimmy Carter, President Shimon Peres, President Nelson Mandela, and Mr. Elie Wiesel.

The story is too interesting to describe second-hand, which is why Mr. Mapes has agreed tell it in his own words, punctuated with still frames from video footage shot during the event. The remainder of this chapter consists of Mr. Mapes describing the event and answering some questions about the current state and future of the MBone, based on his day-to-day involvement with it.

Questions are in italics. Answers are in plain text. Also, pictures from the Summit are not necessarily referenced in the text.

The Summit of Hope

Could you set the stage for this story with some background?
Sure. The most wonderful thing about the Internet is its worldwide flow of ideas, which can be put in various forms, from print and pictures to talking-head video all the way up to live feeds of realtime events. In a way, we have a new type of CNN developing here, with people now able to do digital video feeds from all over the planet.

We're now starting to get to the point with this type of technology where nothing can be hidden from view anymore. Also really coming into their own now are VRML worlds, which we'll probably see integrated with streaming video to make a new kind of rich, composite media we've never experienced before.

About Netizen's Dialog

Our company is named Netizen's Dialog. We have a team of people totally dedicated to building the most advanced visual information systems possible. We've also been basing all of our work on multicasting. We already have live multicast camera feeds from different parts of the world, 24 hours a day, 365 days a year.

How are these systems being used?
We're teaching other people how to use multicasting and creating complete systems for them—in a way, we're offering multicasting in a box. You can buy such a system from us right now if you'd like, with training classes and everything you need to get the system online.

Who are your current customers?

Along the way, various companies and musicians have discovered what we're doing, and we've gotten involved in a number of large multicast Webcasts, including working with the United Nations. In December 1995 and January 1996, the UN asked us to host the first summit meeting among world leaders on the Internet. This was the start of the Summit of Hope.

The reason the UN approached us is that the year before we had done a major conference in Tokyo. We opened the conference with an address from the Prime Minister of Sweden, communicating with the other members of the conference in Tokyo over the MBone onto 10×12 foot screens. Technically speaking, the presentation was flawless.

How was this different from traditional technology?

In the past, doing anything like this required direct satellite feeds and was very expensive in terms of transponder time. In contrast, we could conduct a two or three hour MBone presentation at almost no cost, as long as we reserved the MBone time. Because the event in Tokyo was so successful, the UN asked our company to host the Summit of Hope.

The Summit Delegates

The world leaders attending this MBone Summit were Prime Minister Shimon Peres of Israel, President Nelson Mandela of South Africa, President Jimmy Carter of the United States, Elie Wiesel, and various

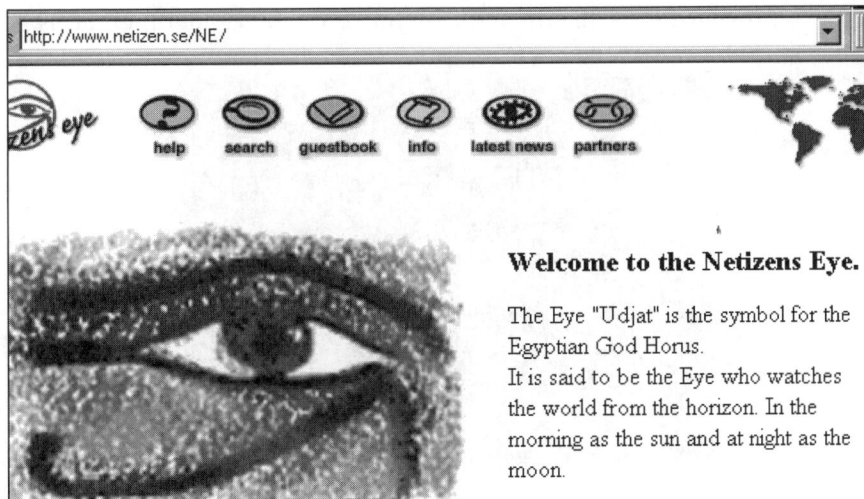

Figure 17.1 The Netizen's Dialog home page.

Nobel laureates and other dignitaries. These leaders were gathered to discuss global security and the potential impact of the Internet and other types of high technology in helping us to have a safer world in the twenty-first century.

Was there a recording made of it?
This project is well documented and can be seen on our Web site at **www.netizen.se**. We feel it was an extraordinary event. We had major world leaders talking *over the Internet*. Thousands of people could dialin and observe the actual Summit as it happened. This had never happened before in history, neither technically nor politically.

In what ways was it unprecedented?
Summit meetings are never televised in their entirety. Interviews with political leaders are generally held after the fact. This was a live, realtime world-class event that anyone with a Web browser could tune into. Back on our servers, we used some of our proprietary software to convert the Summit MBone multicast into a form that people could browse using standard Internet access.

Dealing With The Unexpected

What were some of the unexpected things that happened?
One thing we didn't expect was that we had to fly our own computers into Jerusalem to link up with Prime Minister Shimon Peres. As it turned out, they didn't have compatible systems there, so we had to put our own team on an airplane with SparcStations under their arms.

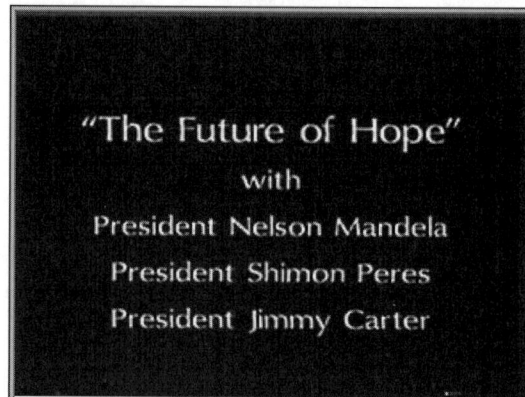

"The Future of Hope"
with
President Nelson Mandela
President Shimon Peres
President Jimmy Carter

Figure 17.2 The Summit leaders.

We had to do this at the last minute, with about three days notice. Fortunately, we had the cooperation of their national security agencies and Israeli Telecom, so we were able to fly in, wire up, and be ready to go on very short notice. Once we got our own gear installed, things were relatively smooth technically.

What about in South Africa?
There the problem was even more difficult, because the phone system is even more primitive. We had to take a satellite truck over to President Nelson Mandela's House to shoot the event, then Microwave the signal over to our team in Johannesburg where we captured it and loaded it onto the Internet for Webcasting out to the rest of the world.

Linking Up
Did you just have to adapt to the situation and hope that it worked?
That's right. But then again, we tend to see everything as just a signal. As long as I'm getting video—whether it's from a camera or from a satellite feed halfway around the world—I'll grab that signal, run it through my computer, convert it, and then send it out multicast on the MBone. I don't really care how I get my raw signal in.

Which you proved by handling all the different conditions at the live sites occupied by the various dignitaries.
All told, this was a very interesting set of links: Jimmy Carter from Atlanta, Georgia; Ted Koeppel and Elie Wisel, the moderators, from Hiroshima, Japan; Shimon Peres from Jerusalem; and Nelson Mandela from South Africa. We controlled the whole event from our headquarters in San Francisco.

How bad were the delays?
They were noticeable, of course, but tolerable. We were working with some very fat pipes once we got the video digitized and onto the Internet, but there are always slight delays.

Was the UN satisfied with the result?
Based on the success of the Summit, we're doing new projects with the United Nations. In fact, we've just signed a contract with them to teach people about the World Heritage sites and the environmental problems Canada is facing in the coming years. We're implementing MBone technology very intensively in cooperation with the UN, and also with other large corporations around the world.

What is it like to work for the UN?

In general, they're ideal to work with because they see the value of this technology for communication, and especially the communication of new ideas—which is what they're in the business of promoting. Of course, there's the expected amount of red tape and politics, but once a radical idea gets rolling, it tends to gather its own momentum.

The Summit of Hope was something special because it completely married form and content—discussing the value of the Internet to international cooperation *on* the Internet itself, with hardly any technical problems.

Breaking The Rules

How jealous were the big networks?

Historically, only AT&T or one of the big networks could have done something like this. Here we are, a little company of about 25 or 30 people, and we're the only ones the UN felt they could trust to do this.

Will the big players now mobilize to start doing what you did?

I don't think so. The Internet is too much of a different world to them. If you compare this whole process to biological evolution, fish are supposed to stay in the ocean while the new species walk on land.

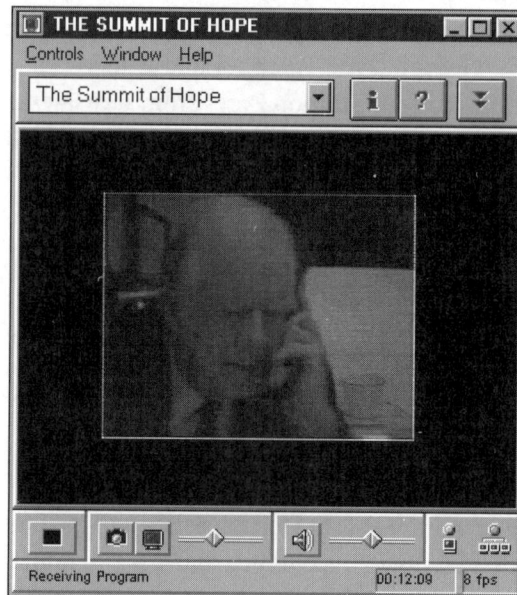

Figure 17.3 President Jimmy Carter as he appeared to the Summit.

In other words, the established broadcasters will continue to broadcast television programming, the big phone companies will continue to provide phone service just like they always have, and we'll see a whole new industry of Internet companies that specialize in areas like ours, which is further proof that you can't be good at everything in this world.

New Communication Modes

Are these new life forms developing new modes of communication?
We believe they are. In a word-based environment, when you're trying to describe something to someone in a remote location, the most cost-effective thing to do is just to write it. A more expensive way is to take a photograph of it and send the photograph. Plus, you have to go out and get the film processed, and so on. Sending realtime video to your recipient has traditionally been even more expensive than that.

And now?
On the Internet, it suddenly becomes very *in*expensive. Computer video cameras can be as cheap as a $100. Suddenly, we have a revolution in the way we can communicate. So, yes, we think new visual languages are evolving, which will link in with new symbol languages.

Think of the complex visual processing centers in our own brains. We've developed very sophisticated pattern recognition systems over thousands of years, all of which can be brought into play in direct visual communication such as what the Internet with multicasting offers.

Better Efficiency

If you're familiar with Von Neuman's Game Theory, it basically says that if you can do something with less energy, you'll migrate toward doing it all the time. Global multicasting makes it possible to communicate with images and sounds that take less effort to understand, which consumes less energy, which makes multicasting inevitable for everyone.

What's the critical mass date?
We think by the year 2000, multicasting will be very common. In fact, don't be surprised if it causes some social revolutions. For example, why should I describe my office and new furniture to you when I can just point a camera at it. In the blink of an eye, you see what would take me several minutes to describe using words.

Plus, there may or may not be a language barrier. If I describe the contents and furnishings of my office in English, but English is not your primary language, you're going to get even less of the information I'm trying to communicate. But if you can look directly at, say, a Bonsai tree, you'll probably know exactly what it is in a flash.

Other MBone Events

Have you been approached by entertainment promoters?

Yes. Actually, we've already done a number of entertainment-based multicasts, involving musical performers and some more experimental Webcasters.

Do you see this expanding rapidly?

To some extent, as big names get involved with experimental events just to have fun and make some noise. But, it's easy to take events like the original Rolling Stones multicast completely out of context.

Do you often hear the word Webcast used in a misleading context?

Not in the environment we work in, but I know what you mean. A lot of the negative perceptions come from the ways inexperienced Webcasters execute their events, not from the nature of the technology itself.

Figure 17.4 The image of Prime Minister Shimon Peres multicast to the Summit.

What kind of equipment does the average Web surfer need to consume these events?

If a person has a Web browser, whether it's a Web TV box or Netscape running on a home computer, that person can now receive a multicast that has been turned into a unicast by a special server. Of course, the higher their line speed the more frames per second of video they'll see. The point is that anyone with a browser can now effectively look through cameras all over the world via these multicasting links.

How crucial is that person's ISP in this process?

That's a good question. When we're Webcasting, we have to have the cooperation of ISPs to go *out* multicast, and we often have to teach ISPs how to implement multicasting. But if you just go to our Web page, you'll get multicast video that has been converted for you to unicast on our server.

Impediments To MBone Deployment

What do you feel are the biggest impediments to the full deployment of MBone technology?

A book called *The Structure of Scientific Revolutions* says that the movement of new ideas is not limited by technology, but by people. So, the real limitation of the growth of the MBone and the Internet in general is waiting for the next generation of kids to grow up.

When those kids do grow up, there will be much more online activity than there is now, because people will understand and accept it. Kids who grew up playing around with this stuff will demand it as adults. It may sound cliché, but that's the way it's going to happen.

What would you say the landscape is like now for trying to do multicasting, MBone and otherwise, with non-Unix equipment like Macs and PCs?

For the last three years, we hosted everything on Sun and SGI workstations, but in the last six months, we've shifted over to Wintel equipment. We are also a beta site for Apple and their MBone-related products. We actually did some early PowerMac Webcasts.

But, like everything else in the industry, this is all moving to the Wintel platform. In general, our company has a strong bias for desktop machines. We use Unix gear when we have to, but we prefer Wintel and Mac.

Platform Specifics

Is the technology equally weighted at this point?

I'd say that as of the Spring of 1997, things are about equal. Up until the end of 1996, I tended to trust the code base on Unix machines more because it was mature and Unix is based on networking.

When we did the Summit of Hope for the UN, we called Intel and spoke to the people who were developing Intel's MBone technology. They said they felt just a little too green at that point to provide any of the hardware and software we said we were interested in.

On the other hand, as soon as the multicasting code's been available for any platform, we've been implementing it. And now, going into the Spring and Summer of 1997, we feel like we're seeing solid implementations on most, if not all, of the major PC and workstation platforms.

Aside from your own, do you think the exciting MBone software is going to come from the major players like Microsoft, Intel, and Apple, or from third-party developers?

I think it will almost always come from third-party developers. Companies like Microsoft, Intel, and Apple pave the way by spending the early R&D money to show that it can be done, but the next steps usually come from committed third-party teams of people who have a vision, and that's all they think about 24 hours a day, 7 days a week.

Like RealAudio?

Yes. That's a good example of really innovative software that was produced by a relatively small brilliant team.

Business Issues

How easy is it going to be launching a business around multicasting and MBone technology?

As opposed to other types of Web-based business, the jury is still out. Because of the current bandwidth problems, multicasting looks good because it solves the problem of things getting a lot worse. Also, it is associated with streaming video, which is a very hot development area.

In the early years of nonnetworked desktop video, video was essentially shoehorned into the PC, especially Wintel boxes. Is video on networks less of a retrofit, or are we still looking at a shotgun wedding?

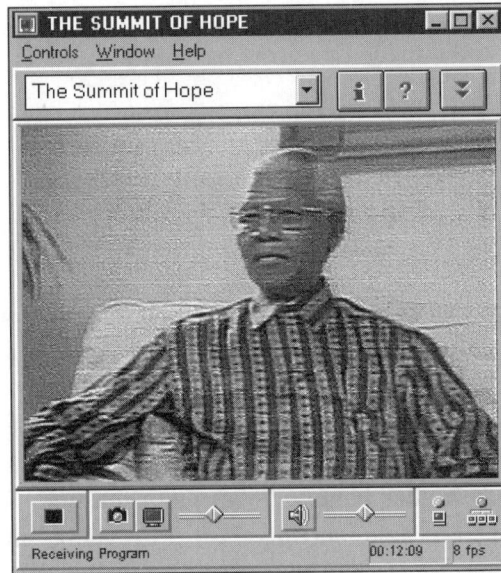

Figure 17.5 President Nelson Mandela at his home in South Africa.

I think there are several answers to that. The first one is that we're standing on the shoulders of the CD-ROM revolution, so we inherit a lot of the work that was done by Macromedia and other companies who implemented CD-ROM multimedia on the desktop.

The Installed Base Is Ready

We now have millions of CD-ROM-enabled computers out there, and those systems are capable of taking media files off the Web and playing them. Also, most of the PCs shipped today are multimedia-ready, without it being a big deal. In fact, if they're *not* multimedia-ready, it's much more noticeable than if they are. So, we've now got a substantial installed base of multimedia machines, PCs and Macs, all generally prepared to play multimedia off the Web.

Secondly, I would say that we're now seeing breakthroughs in ways to get virtual bandwidth, in terms of overall efficiency and better ways of moving media around. When you put these things together, I think we're looking into a very receptive environment for later in 1997.

And beyond that?
To be honest, as a company, we generally view all these powerful rich media technologies as post-2000, in terms of *major* commercial possi-

bilities. Between now and the year 2000, however, there is a lot of money to be made in a growing market.

Are the emerging satellite and cable modem capabilities going to spur this market?
Definitely.

The Role Of Routers

Routers are key to multicasting, at least for now. Do you think modems will be phased out as routers assume a greater importance overall?
It depends if you're looking at this as a producer of multimedia content or as a consumer of that content. Certainly, all serious producers need to have routers, if they don't have them already. Consumers will have access to higher bandwidth through the commercial means we just mentioned—cable modems, DirecPC, ADSL, and so on.

So, there will be a universe of consumers out there with a variety of ways to consume relatively rich media streams. What the producer community needs to understand is what form their media should take if it expects to enjoy the advantages of multicasting.

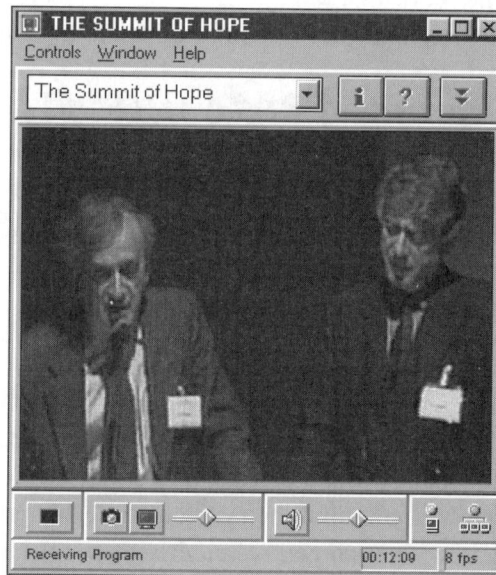

Figure 17.6   The Summit of Hope moderators: Elie Wiesel and Ted Koeppel.

Do you see the MBone as an extension to the Internet at large or as more of an overlay?

The Internet is the large universe of possibilities that we use to communicate with each other digitally. Within that large universe is a subset called the World Wide Web. Also within the framework of the Internet is a protocol capability called the MBone.

That protocol being multicast capability?

Yes. At this point, only a very small number of players are using the MBone as a tool with the larger Internet space by linking it to Web pages. Historically, the MBone was almost a standalone world of its own. But now, our company, and a growing number of other small firms, are integrating the MBone with the World Wide Web.

Integrating The MBone With The Web

So, now we're getting a new growth area in the Web as most people know it, which is growing out of multicasting technology. And it's basically a natural evolution. We're just solving a problem that's inherent in moving ideas around over the Web. Instead of doing straight downloads from a given site, we now have multicasting capabilities as well.

How long will it take until simply browsing the MBone with Microsoft Internet Explorer is possible?

See it for yourself at **www.netizen.se**. At this Web site, which is another project we're doing in cooperation with the United Nations, we have multicasts of live camera feeds from all over the world which you can view with Netscape and Microsoft browsers.

MBone Political Issues

What are the MBone political issues that are surfacing?

We tend to look at the Internet as a hot evolution zone. It's very Darwinian, in that it rewards the efficient and punishes the inefficient in almost realtime. Consequently, it's a great test bed for ideas. This means that if multicasting via the MBone is a better idea, then it will flourish. If someone comes up with an even better approach, we'll go from there. It's really just a question of natural selection applied to technical innovation.

Of course, we feel that multicasting *is* a great idea that *will* flourish over time, especially as people start confronting the realities of moving large volumes of media around networks, and the Internet in particular.

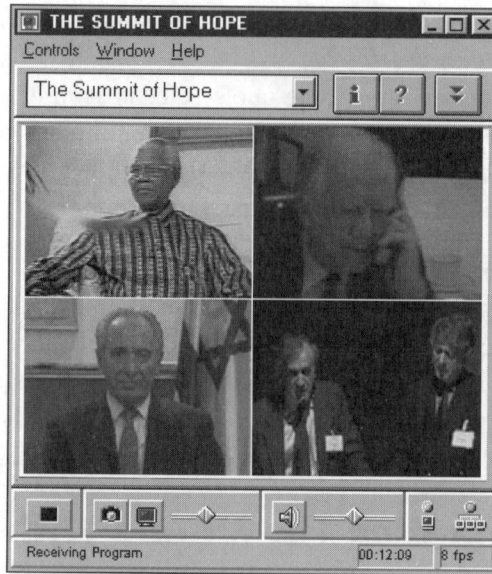

Figure 17.7 What the typical Summit browser saw.

Evolution Rules

The point is, we don't believe that any types of political issues stand a chance in the face of this powerful evolution process. In television, for example, where you've got distribution strategies with large corporations controlling the distribution points, certain political issues do come into play. But I've never seen anything like the Internet when it comes to a pure Darwinian space.

What about political collisions among casual users and the scientific community, which is demanding its right to work without getting distracted and bogged down—as they put it?
Right now, there are two models of commerce on the Web. You've got the flat-fee model and the pay per use model. These two models will probably continue to exist side-by-side. Likewise, we will probably see two distinct Internets, which is already starting to happen.

One for shoppers and one for researchers?
Right. First, we'll have the existing Internet. Then there will be the emerging supercomputer Internet, which is in use by a hundred or so universities right now. This is a secure, high-speed environment for scientists.

And will that space be overrun by carpetbaggers eventually?
Probably not, because it will tend to be fairly exotic to most people.

The Role Of Satellites

How do you see satellite technology evolving for the benefit of the end user?

We work very closely with some of the major satellite companies in both the U.S. and Europe. The great thing is that the new satellites being designed now, to be launched in 1998 and 1999, have massive bandwidth potential. They also have the capability to do things like special targeting of hot spot zones and all kinds of other things.

I think people are going to be quite surprised by the speed at which these DirecPC types of systems are deployed [see Figure 17.8]. Right now, plans are in place to hook up 40 million homes, in the U.S. and Europe, to DirecPC-style systems over the next few years.

What about Teledesic [www.teledesic.com] and the rest of that group of companies?

Those are all interesting, but the existing satellite companies are already providing very useful services—without even adding in technologies used in the Iridium and Teledesic projects. And these existing companies are not slacking. Right now, they're building in high-powered Internet functionality.

The Coming Bandwidth Explosion

So, there's going to be a bandwidth explosion between now and the year 2000?

That's right. But not just because of satellites. The telephone companies and cable outfits are going to play major roles also. When you put all these components together, you're going to see average browsers getting over a million baud asymmetrical.

Just shy of full T1 bandwidth?
Right.

All multicast?
Obviously not all of it, but many of the media-rich portions.

When?
Sooner than most people think.

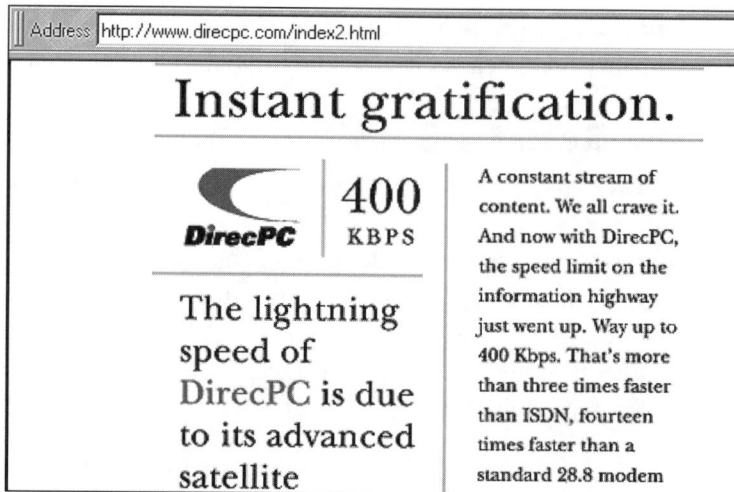

Figure 17.8 The DirecPC home page.

Summary

As you can see, despite its exotic flavor, the MBone is headed for the desktop just like the Internet itself was several years ago. As challenging, public events like the Summit of Hope continue to galvanize interest in the MBone and multicasting in general, this process will presumably accelerate—thanks to the enthusiasm and clear vision of people like Dan Mapes.

Not surprisingly, the best place to keep up-to-date on MBone events is the Web itself. Already, there are several FAQ pages available and a variety of other sites, both academic and commercial, that offer timely technical information and give you an idea where the breakthroughs may happen next.

You can do a Yahoo or an Alta Vista search (on *MBone*) to find these pages quickly. And remember to bookmark **www.netizen.se**.

Chapter **18**

- **Introducing the IP Multicast Summit**

- **Understanding the role of Stardust Technologies**

- **Presenting white papers from the Summit**

Chapter 18

White Papers From The First IP Multicast Summit

At various points in this book, reference is made to the IP Multicast Initiative and to an event called the *IP Multicast Summit*. The first such Summit was held January 16, 1997 in Santa Clara, California, to an overflow audience. Technical presentations on IP Multicast technology were delivered by executives from Precept Software, Cisco Systems, Microsoft, 3Com, Stardust Technologies, and Intel (among others).

The host of this event was The IP Multicast Initiative (IPMI), a diverse group of networking software and hardware vendors, network service and content providers, public institutions, and IT organizations, formed to speed the adoption of native, IETF standards-based IP Multicast.

IPMI provides education and marketing services and a framework for partnerships among the wide range of IPMI members. These services promote the creation, use, and deployment of IP Multicast products and services. You can visit the IPMI Web site at **www.ipmulticast.com** for the most recent information on IPMI activities.

As noted in previous chapters, management of the IP Multicast Initiative is handled by Stardust Technologies, Inc. (**www.stardust.com**). Focused on the promotion of open communication standards, Stardust is best known for its pioneering work with the WinSock group and the Stardust WinSock testing labs.

An independent, neutral third party, Stardust is experienced at technology marketing and has made an immediate and practical impact on the issues that must be addressed for ubiquitous deployment of IP Multicast. Stardust Labs delivers comprehensive development, technological, and marketing services to companies creating software for the Internet.

Among the materials distributed to the IP Multicast Summit attendees were two white papers prepared by Stardust Technologies: *IP Multicast Backgrounder* and *How IP Multicast Works*. Stardust has graciously allowed these two documents to be reprinted in this book, along with a third white paper entitled *Introduction To IP Multicast Routing*. The remainder of this chapter contains the full text of each of these three documents. More white papers are available at **www.ipmulticast.com**.

> **Note!** *No portion of any of these documents may be reprinted without written permission from Stardust Technologies.*

IP Multicast Backgrounder

An IP Multicast Initiative White Paper

How IP Multicast alleviates network congestion and paves the way for next-generation network applications.

Scope Of This Document

This document provides an executive introduction to IP Multicast. It presents the basic concept, highlights its benefits, and provides suggestions for getting started. Whether you are a user of TCP/IP-based technologies or are a vendor interested in implementing or taking advantage of IP Multicast within your product or service, this document will help you.

Introduction To IP Multicast

The Web has proven itself as a communications tool in my organization—what's next?

Most of the widely-used traditional Internet applications, such as Web browsers and email, operate between one sender and one receiver. In many emerging applications, one sender will transmit to a group of receivers simultaneously. These important applications will help increase your organization's ability to communicate and collaborate, leveraging more value from your network investment.

Examples are the transmission of corporate messages to employees, video and audio conferencing for remote meetings and telecommuting, replicating databases and Web site information, live transmission of multimedia training and university courses, communication of stock quotes to brokers, updates on the latest election results, collaborative computing, transmission over networks of live TV or radio news and entertainment programs, and many others.

Yes, I'm hearing requests for some of these capabilities from my users, especially for multimedia. But how can networks handle it?

These new applications are compelling the need for advances in traffic handling to overcome bottlenecks. IP Multicast is an efficient, standards-based solution with broad industry support. IP Multicast is an extension of IP, the internetworking protocol that is used on the Internet.

With IP Multicast, applications send one copy of the information to a group address, reaching all recipients who want to receive it. Without multicasting, the same information must be either carried over the network multiple times, one time for each recipient, or broadcast to everyone on the network, consuming unnecessary bandwidth and processing, and/or limiting the number of participants.

IP Multicasting involves groups of receivers that participate in multicast sessions; only those receivers in a group actually receive the traffic for that group's session. IP Multicast technologies address the needed mechanisms at different levels in the network and internetworking infrastructure to efficiently handle group communications. Under development since the early 1990s by leading researchers and the industry, IP Multicast is an important advance in IP networking.

Comparison Of Point-To-Point Unicast And Multicast Data Flow

As shown [in Figure 18.1], three copies of the same data (D) are sent point-to-point as D1, D2, and D3 to Receivers 1, 2, and 3 in a shared conferencing application. These are "unicast" transmissions, sent point-to-point from one sender to one receiver.

As shown [in Figure 18.2], one copy of the same data (D) is multicast to Receivers 1, 2, and 3 in a shared conferencing application. Note the bandwidth savings locally and across the networks—imagine the bandwidth savings for hundreds of recipients.

IP Multicast Benefits

Multicast sounds like a good technical solution. But what are the business benefits?

There are economic benefits—cost savings in network and server resources—and the value-added of new types of applications enabled by multicasting that are not feasible using unicast transport. If your organization is already taking advantage of cost-effective Internet technologies for internal and external communications, and your users are looking forward to using multicast applications, your network engineers should pursue IP Multicast.

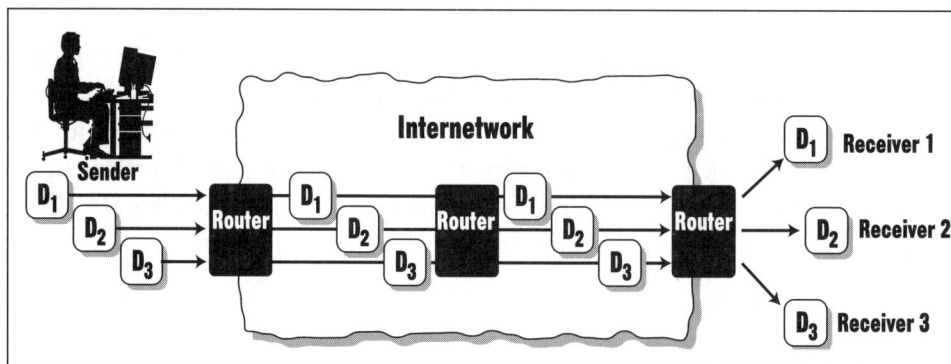

Figure 18.1 Unicast data flow.

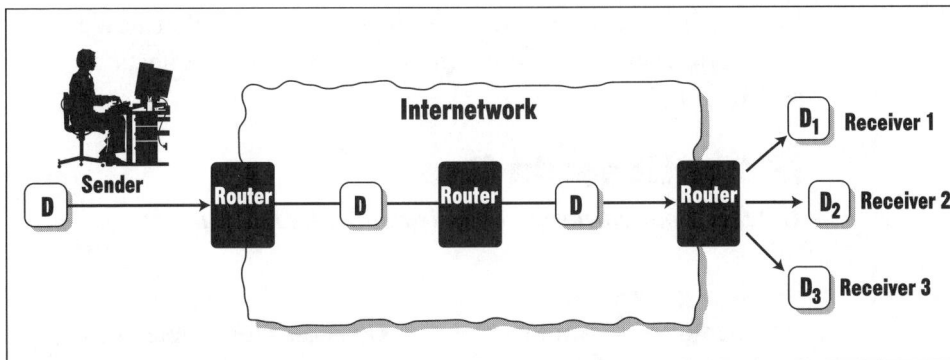

Figure 18.2 Multicast data flow.

One of the most important benefits is that IP Multicast enables a network planner to proactively manage network growth and control costs. IP Multicast is cost-effective compared to other engineering alternatives for increasing LAN and WAN capacities. Upgrading your network infrastructure to support IP Multicast will enable your organization to more quickly take advantage of multicast applications and minimize their impact on your network capacity and response times.

IP Multicast is designed to scale well as the number of participants and collaborations expand, so adding one more user doesn't amount to adding a corresponding amount of bandwidth. Multicasting also results in a greatly reduced load on the sending server, which no longer has to support many sequential or concurrent unicast sessions. This benefit can be just as significant as the bandwidth savings.

Many multicast applications like those described earlier increase productivity—and without IP Multicast they might not even be feasible. IP Multicast can immediately help alleviate network congestion caused by existing applications that are inefficiently transmitting to groups of recipients.

IP Multicast allows corporate users to access content and services not previously available because these application would have consumed too much resources on the network. Furthermore, multicasting enables the simultaneous delivery of information to many receivers. This is a significant benefit for applications involving the delivery of news and financial information such as stock ticker feed applications.

Finally, IP Multicast will work in concert with other new IP protocols and services, such as Quality of Service requests to support realtime multimedia.

IP Multicast In Use

Tell me about corporate experiences with IP Multicast.

Intel

Intel deployed IP Multicast on a 4,000 node Oregon site in early 1996. Intel employees regularly use IP Multicast conferencing software to follow events such as conferences or executive presentations and product launches from their desktops. The deployment was the last phase of a multicast project that started two years ago with the deployment of MAC layer multicast. After the proper planning and testing, IP Multicast was deployed one router at the time over the course of a day.

Toys Я Us

Toys Я Us Inc. uses IP Multicast file transfer software to send software updates to 900 store locations. Before using IP Multicast, the files had to be sent over its VSAT (very small aperture terminal) nationwide network one file at a time. Because this used up so much bandwidth, it had to be performed at night.

During testing, Toys Я Us found that it took 6 hours to transfer a one MB file to 250 clients using the current system, while the same transfer using IP Multicast file transfer took 4 minutes. The IP Multicast-based software is designed to improve product availability in the stores. A Toys Я Us representative believes the system paid for itself immediately.

Microsoft

Microsoft used a phased-deployment approach to multicast-enable its corporate network. Buildings were brought online one by one until it was determined that the test phase was complete. IP Multicast was then fully deployed throughout the campus and to remote locations. Microsoft launched an IP Multicast network service in the fall of 1996 to send information to over 5,000 Puget Sound area seats.

Microsoft employees use IP Multicast software to listen to live executive speeches from industry events and other live broadcasts. Content includes local radio stations, MSNBC, the BBC, and other events. This provides an excellent corporate communications vehicle direct to people at their desktops. Cost savings include reducing employee travel to industry and company events.

What About IP Multicast On The Internet?

The MBone (Multicast Backbone) is a virtual network layered on top of the physical Internet to support routing of IP Multicast packets. It has been in existence for about five years. It originated in an effort to multicast audio and video from the Internet Engineering Task Force (IETF) meetings. Technical meetings and also NASA space shuttle launches, a Rolling Stones concert, and many other live meetings and performances have since been multicast over the MBone.

The MBone is an experimental, cooperative volunteer effort spanning several continents. Research and testing of multicast protocols and services have been conducted extensively on the MBone. The number of participating sites has grown rapidly as a result of interest and utility.

The MBone is an overlay network based on an experimental and volunteer effort. It currently has limited use in commercial environments since it restricts the bandwidth available to IP Multicast and only a small fraction of companies have access to it. However, it has already validated the strengths of IP Multicast.

IP Multicast Applications And Development

Tell me more about uses of IP Multicast.
Demand for multimedia, combining audio, video, and data streams over a network, is rapidly increasing. Users are clamoring for it. Some of the more popular uses of multimedia are realtime interactive applications, such as desktop video and audio conferencing, collaborative engineering, shared white boards, transmission of university lectures to a remote audience, and animated simulations. Even when data compression is used, multimedia applications require lots of bandwidth.

IP Multicast will help in the realization of the full potential of these exciting new applications. For example, consider the transmission of a corporate presentation to workers within a company. Using unicast transmission, it would be possible to support only a small number of recipients, because transmission of multiple copies of the multimedia stream would quickly strain the available network bandwidth. On the other hand, with IP Multicast it would be easy to support thousands of recipients, each sitting at his or her own desk.

Another important type of multimedia application involves the transmission of stored data streams. Examples include updates of kiosks and Web caches, video server to video server updates, corporate announcements to employees, etc. IP Multicast will enable these applications to scale to very large numbers of recipients.

Although multimedia applications are bandwidth intensive, non-multimedia applications that involve the transfer of large databases of information will also benefit immensely from IP Multicast. Examples of realtime applications of this type include stock/commodities quotes and trading information, and shared white boards. Non-realtime applications include multicast file transfer and Web caching.

Are there tools for software developers?
If you are a vendor, or have in-house applications serving some of the functions described earlier, you'll want to consider upgrading them to support IP Multicast. IP Multicast can help you advance to next-generation products. It is also a win for your users because it helps address their concerns about bandwidth-intensive applications.

Most implementations of TCP/IP on major operating system platforms support IP Multicast. Contact your platform and TCP/IP software vendors for more information on their programming interfaces. Some vendors also license high-level development kits and middleware solutions to help developers more quickly implement IP Multicast solutions.

Evaluation And Implementation
What should we do next?
IP Multicast has broad industry backing and is supported by many vendors of network infrastructure elements such as routers, switches, TCP/IP stacks, network interface cards, desktop operating systems, and application software. If you have recent network equipment and software from the leading vendors, you can likely enable or upgrade to IP Multicast at low cost.

Your vendors and network service provider(s) can explain features and help you estimate these upgrade costs. You can also obtain information about the technologies, products, and services from the IP Multicast Initiative described later in this white paper.

A phased approach to evaluating and deploying IP Multicast is recommended. A network analysis will be needed to forecast usage profiles and elucidate categories of benefit and cost. The opportunity cost of being unable to run multicast applications because of network congestion, thereby limiting productivity, should be considered in this analysis.

Plans for WAN deployment should consider several alternatives. For example, satellite data networks can be used for commercial deployment of multicast-based applications over a WAN. In a trial (or in operational use), the entire network need not be simultaneously enabled for IP Multicast. Transitional approaches can be used. One example is tunneling, which enables IP Multicast traffic to traverse non-IP Multicast-enabled network segments. This has already proven useful in the evolution of the MBone.

A testbed evaluation from both the LAN and WAN perspectives is highly recommended, preferably in-house, or at a vendor's facility. Staff training in IP Multicast network administration and diagnosis may be helpful.

When possible, choose IETF standards-based products designed for native IP Multicast. Your network engineers can direct the evaluation and determine which IP Multicast protocols and features should be tested and deployed. Important considerations are supported standards, interoperability with other network infrastructure elements at all sending and receiving nodes and intermediate routers, and performance for typical usage scenarios.

More Information

I'd like our engineers to get started. Where can they get more technical information?

There are many technical aspects of IP Multicast that were not discussed here. The IP Multicast Initiative Web site at **www.ip multicast.com** has a technical resource center that provides more background and in-depth information. The Web site also offers a product and services directory and lists members of the IP Multicast Initiative who can be contacted for information and assistance.

The IP Multicast Initiative provides marketing and educational services to promote the creation, use, and deployment of multicast products and solutions. Supported by a growing number of the most important vendors in the IP Multicast arena, the Initiative and its services are managed and provided by Stardust Technologies, Inc.

For more information about the Initiative, membership, or to see other white papers, contact Stardust Technologies at 408-879-8080, or visit the Initiative Web site at **www.ipmulticast.com**.

How IP Multicast Works

A technical overview of IP Multicast concepts, addressing, group management, and approaches to routing.

Scope Of This Document

This document provides a technical introduction to IP Multicast concepts and technical features. It discusses the requirements for IP Multicast delivery, addressing, and host group management, and approaches to multicast routing. Some familiarity with IP is assumed. If you are an engineer interested in evaluating or implementing IP Multicast, an understanding of the concepts in this document will help you. You may also be interested in other documents in this white paper series, which are available from **www.ipmulticast.com**.

IP Multicast Mechanisms

Many emerging Internet applications are one-to-many or many-to-many, where one or multiple sources are sending to multiple receivers. Examples are the transmission of corporate messages to employees, communication of stock quotes to brokers, video and audio conferencing for remote meetings and telecommuting, and replicating databases and Web site information.

ADVANTAGES OF IP MULTICAST

IP Multicast efficiently supports this type of transmission by enabling sources to send a single copy of a message to multiple recipients who explicitly want to receive the information. This is far more efficient than requiring the source to send an individual copy of a message to each requester (referred to as point-to-point unicast), in which case, the number of receivers is limited by the bandwidth available to the sender.

It is also more efficient than broadcasting one copy of the message to all nodes (broadcast) on the network, since many nodes may not want the message, and because broadcasts are limited to a single subnet.

Multicast is a receiver-based concept: receivers join a particular multicast session group and traffic is delivered to all members of that group by the network infrastructure. The sender does not need to maintain a list of receivers. Only one copy of a multicast message will pass over any link in the network, and copies of the message will be made only where paths diverge at a router. Thus, IP Multicast yields many performance improvements and conserves bandwidth end-to-end.

IP MULTICAST DELIVERY AND GROUPS

IP Multicast is an extension to the standard IP network-level protocol. RFC 1112, *Host Extensions for IP Multicasting*, authored by Steve Deering in 1989, describes IP Multicasting as: "the transmission of an IP datagram to a 'host group', a set of zero or more hosts identified by a single IP destination address. A multicast datagram is delivered to all members of its destination host group with the same 'best-efforts' reliability as regular unicast IP datagrams. The membership of a host group is dynamic; that is, hosts may join and leave groups at any time. There is no restriction on the location or number of members in a host group. A host may be a member of more than one group at a time."

In addition, at the application level, a single group address may have multiple data streams on different port numbers, on different sockets, or in one or more applications. Multiple applications may share a single group address on a host.

AN OVERVIEW OF WHAT'S NEEDED FOR IP MULTICAST

To support native IP Multicast, the sending and receiving nodes and network infrastructure between them must be multicast-enabled, including intermediate routers. Requirements for native IP Multicast at the end node hosts are:

- Support for IP Multicast transmission and reception in the TCP/IP protocol stack.

- Software supporting IGMP (see IGMP section in this white paper) to communicate requests to join a multicast group(s) and receive multicast traffic.

- Network interface cards which efficiently filter for LAN data link layer addresses mapped from network layer IP Multicast addresses.

- IP Multicast application software such as video conferencing.

To run or evaluate IP Multicast on a LAN, only the listed requirements are needed; no routers need be involved for a host's adapter to create or join a multicast group and share multicast data with other hosts on that LAN segment. To expand IP Multicast traffic to a WAN requires:

- All intermediate routers between the sender(s) and receiver(s) must be IP Multicast-capable. Many new routers have support for IP Multicast; older ones may require memory before they can be upgraded.

- Firewalls may need to be reconfigured to permit IP Multicast traffic.

IP Multicast has a broad and growing industry backing, and is supported by many vendors of network infrastructure elements such as routers, switches, TCP/IP stacks, network interface cards, desktop operating systems, and application software. Your vendors can help you select appropriate hardware and software.

The following diagram (Figure 18.3) depicts, at a high level, components that must be multicast-enabled. The direction of traffic shown is for multicast datagrams. Traffic needed to communicate host group membership and routing information is not shown.

IP tunneling is an interim mechanism used to connect islands of multicast routers separated by links that do not support IP Multicast. With this approach, multicast datagrams are encapsulated in a standard point-to-point unicast datagram. Tunneling is used extensively in the MBone. This paper addresses only native IP Multicast. Tunneling is discussed in the IP Multicast Initiative white paper *IP Multicast Routing*.

MULTICAST FILTERING SWITCHES

IP Multicast can be optimized in a LAN by using multicast filtering switches. An IP Multicast-aware switch provides the same benefits as a multicast router, but in the local area. Without one, the multicast traffic is sent to all segments on the local subnet. An IP Multicast aware switch

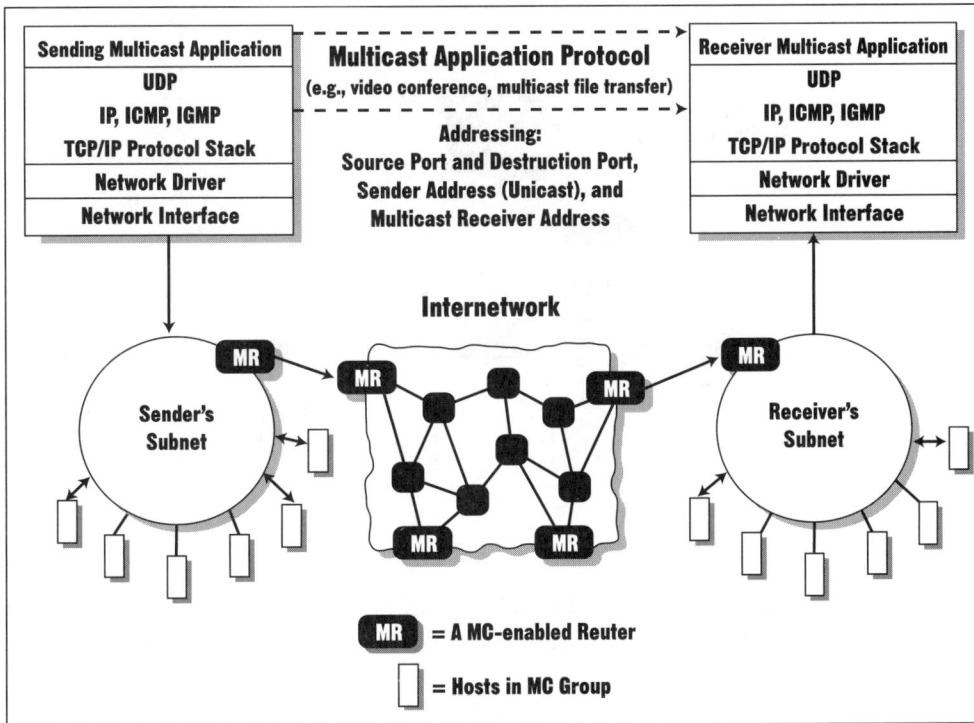

Figure 18.3 Multicast-enabled components.

can automatically set up multicast filters so the multicast traffic is only directed to the participating end nodes [see Figure 18.4].

IP Multicast Addresses And Host Group Management

IP Multicast uses Class D Internet Protocol addresses, those with 1110 as their high-order four bits, to specify multicast host groups. In Internet standard "dotted decimal" notation, host group addresses range from 224.0.0.0 to 239.255.255.255. Two types of group addresses are supported: permanent and temporary.

Examples of permanent addresses, as assigned by the Internet Assigned Numbers Authority (IANA), are 224.0.0.1, the "all-hosts group" used to address all IP Multicast hosts on the directly connected network, and 224.0.0.2, which addresses all routers on a LAN. The range of addresses

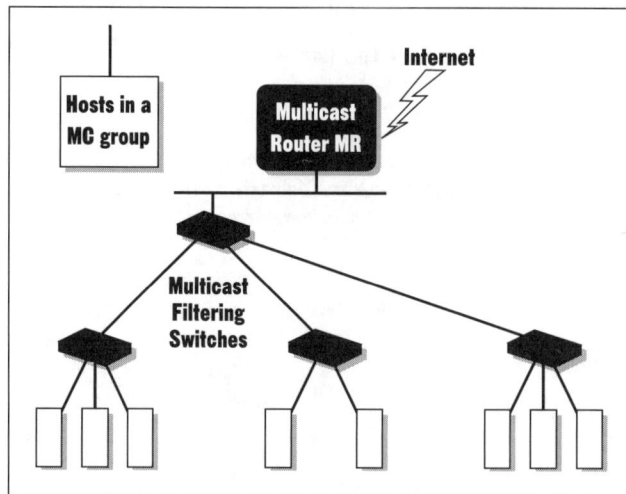

Figure 18.4 Multicast filtering switches.

between 224.0.0.0 and 224.0.0.255 is reserved for routing protocols and other low-level topology discovery or maintenance protocols.

Other addresses and ranges have been reserved for applications, such as 224.0.13.000 to 224.0.13.255 for Net News. These reserved IP Multicast addresses are listed in RFC 1700, *Assigned Numbers*. The Session Announcement Protocol and Session Description Protocol Internet drafts describe how to create and detect MBone session address/port assignments.

To send an IP Multicast datagram, the sender specifies an appropriate destination address, which represents a host group. IP Multicast datagrams are sent using the same "Send IP" operation used for unicast datagrams.

Compared to the sending of IP Multicast datagrams, reception of IP Multicast datagrams is much more complex, particularly over a WAN. To receive datagrams, a user's host application requests membership in the multicast host group associated with a particular multicast (e.g., "I want to view today's live press conference with the President").

This membership request is communicated to the LAN router and, if necessary, on to intermediate routers between the sender and the receiver. As another consequence of its group membership request, the receiving host's network interface card starts filtering for the

LAN-specific hardware (data-link layer) address associated with the new multicast group address.

WAN routers deliver the requested incoming multicast datagrams to the LAN router, which maps the host group address to its associated hardware address and builds the message (for example, an Ethernet frame) using this address. The receiving host's network interface card and network driver, listening for these addresses, pass the multicast messages to the TCP/IP protocol stack, which makes them available as input to the user's application, such as a video viewer.

Whereas an IP unicast address is statically bound to a single local network interface on a single IP network, an IP host group address is dynamically bound to a set of local network interfaces on a set of IP networks. An IP host group address is not bound to a set of IP unicast addresses.

Multicast routers don't need to know the list of member hosts for each group—only the groups for which there is one member on the subnetwork. A multicast router attached to an Ethernet need associate only a single Ethernet multicast address with each host group having a local member.

TIME TO LIVE (TTL)

Each IP Multicast packet uses the time-to-live (TTL) field of the IP header as a scope-limiting parameter. The TTL field controls the number of hops that an IP Multicast packet is allowed to propagate. Each time a router forwards a packet, its TTL is decremented.

A multicast packet whose TTL has expired (is 0) is dropped, without an error notification to the sender. This mechanism prevents messages from needless transmission to regions of the worldwide Internet that lie beyond the subnets containing the multicast group members.

A local network multicast reaches all immediately neighboring members of the destination host group (the IP TTL is 1 by default). If a multicast datagram has a TTL greater than 1, the multicast router(s) attached to the local network take responsibility for internetwork forwarding. The datagram is forwarded to other networks that have members of the destination group.

On those other member networks that are reachable within the IP time-to-live, an attached multicast router completes delivery by transmitting the datagram as a local multicast. TTL thresholds in multicast routers prevent datagrams with less than a certain TTL from traversing certain subnets. This can provide a convenient mechanism for confining multicast traffic to within campus or enterprise networks. Several standard settings for TTL are specified for the MBone: 1 for local net, 15 for site, 63 for region, and 127 for world.

INTERNET GROUP MANAGEMENT PROTOCOL (IGMP)

Multicast packets from remote sources must be relayed by routers, which should only forward them on to the local network if there is a recipient for the multicast host group on the LAN. The Internet Group Management Protocol (IGMP) is used by multicast routers to learn the existence of host group members on their directly attached subnets. It does so by sending IGMP queries and having IP hosts report their host group memberships. The basic version of IGMP dates from 1988 and is now a full Internet standard. It is described in RFC 1112.

IGMP is loosely analogous to ICMP and is implemented over IP. IGMP messages are encapsulated in IP datagrams. IGMP has only two kinds of packets: Host Membership Query and Host Membership Report, with the same simple fixed format containing some control information in the first word of the payload field and a class D address in the second word [see Table 18.1].

Other types are used by extensions to this protocol for use by routing protocols.

To determine if any hosts on a local subnet belong to a multicast group, one multicast router per subnet periodically sends a hardware (data link layer) multicast IGMP Host Membership Query to all IP end nodes on its LAN, asking them to report back on the host groups memberships of their processes.

Table 18.1 IGMP packet layout.

Version(bits 0-3)	Type(bits 4-7)	Code(bits 8-15)	Checksum(bits 16-31)
Multicast Group Address (Class D)			

This query is sent to the all-hosts group (network address 224.0.0.1), and a TTL of 1 is used so that these queries are not propagated outside of the LAN. Each host sends back one IGMP Host Membership Report message per host group, sent to the group address, so all group members see it (thus only one member reports membership). [See Figure 18.5.]

When a process asks its host to join a new multicast host group, the driver creates a hardware multicast address, and an IGMP Host Membership Report with the group address is immediately sent. The host's network interface is expected to map the IP host group addresses to local network addresses as required to update its multicast reception filter. Each host keeps track of its host group memberships, and when the last process on a host leaves a group, that group is no longer reported by the host.

Periodically, the local multicast router sends an IGMP Host Membership Query to the "all-hosts" group, to verify current memberships. If all member hosts reported memberships at the same time, frequent traffic congestion might result. This is avoided by having each host delay their report by a random interval if it has not seen a report for the same group from another host. As a result, only one membership report is sent in response for each active group address, although many hosts may have memberships.

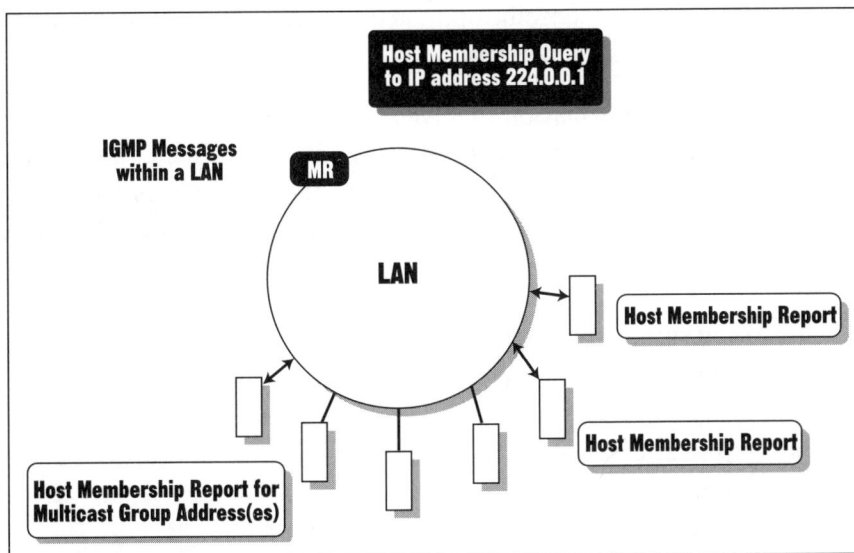

Figure 18.5 IGMP.

IGMP updates are used by multicast routing protocols to communicate host group memberships to neighboring routers, propagating group information through the internetwork. IGMP is used to identify a designated router in the LAN for this purpose.

The bandwidth needed to transmit host group information is usually slight compared to the multicast application traffic, so this propagation method is workable. More sophisticated methods enable routers to determine dynamically how to best forward the multicast application traffic, as discussed in the next section.

Multicast Routing Concepts

The Internet is composed of a myriad of subnetworks connected by routers. When the source of a message is located on one subnet and the destination is located on a different subnet, there must be some way of determining how to get from the source to the destination.

IP ROUTING

This is the function of the IP Protocol. Each host on the Internet has an address that identifies its physical location; part of the address identifies the subnet on which it resides and part identifies the particular host on that subnet. Routers periodically send routing update messages to adjacent routers, conveying the state of the network as perceived by that particular router. This data is recorded in routing tables that are then used to determine optimal transmission paths for forwarding messages across the network.

Unicast transmission involves transmission from a single source to a single destination. Thus, the transmission is directed towards a single physical location that is specified by the host address. The routing procedure, as described earlier, is relatively straightforward because of the binding of a single address to a single host.

MULTICAST ROUTING

Routing multicast traffic is a more complex problem. A multicast address identifies a particular transmission session, rather than a specific physical destination. An individual host is able to join an ongoing multicast session, by using IGMP to communicate this desire to its subnet router.

A naive approach to sending data to multiple receivers would be for the source to maintain a table identifying all the receiving subnets participating in the session and to send a separate copy of the data to each receiving subnet. However, this would be an extremely inefficient use of bandwidth, since many of the data streams would follow the same path throughout much of the network.

New techniques have been developed to address the problem of efficiently routing multicast traffic. Since the number of receivers for a multicast session can potentially be quite large, the source should not need to know all the relevant addresses. Instead the network routers must somehow be able to translate multicast addresses into host addresses.

The basic principal involved in multicast routing is that routers interact with each other to exchange information about neighboring routers. To avoid duplication of effort, a single router is selected (via IGMP) as the Designated Router for each physical network.

SPANNING TREES

For efficient transmission, Designated Routers construct a spanning tree that connects all members of an IP Multicast group. [See Figure 18.6.]

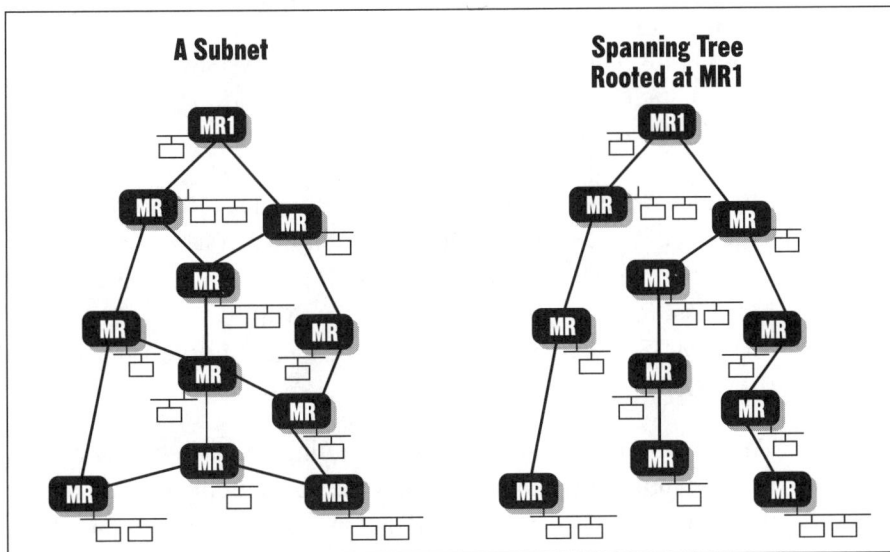

Figure 18.6 Spanning trees.

A spanning tree has just enough connectivity so that there is only one path between every pair of routers, and it is loop-free. If each router knows which of its lines belong to the spanning tree, it can copy an incoming multicast datagram onto all of its outgoing branches, generating only the minimum needed number of copies. Messages are replicated only when the tree branches, thus minimizing the number of copies of the messages that are transmitted through the network.

Since multicast groups are dynamic, with members joining or leaving a group at any time, the spanning tree must be dynamically updated. Branches in which no listeners exist must be discarded (pruned). A router selects a spanning tree based on the network layer source address of a multicast packet and prunes that spanning tree based on the network layer destination address.

The spanning algorithm used and how multicast routers interact depends on the objectives of the routing protocol. Several IP Multicast routing algorithms and protocols have been designed with different objectives and features.

Two Basic Approaches To IP Multicast Routing

IP Multicast routing algorithms and protocols generally follow one of two basic approaches, depending on the distribution of multicast group members throughout the network. The first approach is based on the assumption that the multicast group members are densely distributed throughout the network and bandwidth is plentiful, i.e., almost all hosts on the network belong to the group.

So-called "dense-mode" multicast routing protocols rely on periodic flooding of the network with multicast traffic to set up and maintain the spanning tree. Dense-mode routing protocols include Distance Vector Multicast Routing Protocol (DVMRP), Multicast Open Shortest Path First (MOSPF), and Protocol-Independent Multicast—Dense Mode (PIM-DM).

The second approach to multicast routing is based on the assumption that the multicast group members are sparsely distributed throughout the network, and bandwidth is not necessarily widely available, for example across many regions of the Internet. It is important to note that sparse-mode does not imply that the group has a few members, just that they are widely dispersed.

In this case, flooding would unnecessarily waste network bandwidth and hence could cause serious performance problems. Hence, *'sparse-mode'* multicast routing protocols must rely on more selective techniques to set up and maintain multicast trees. Sparse-mode routing protocols include Core Based Trees (CBT) and Protocol-Independent Multicast—Sparse Mode (PIM-SM).

Other Protocols That Use IP Multicast

There are a number of exciting protocols presently being developed by the Internet community, IETF working groups, and industry vendors to support new applications of IP Multicast. Only a brief introduction is possible here. RTP, the Real-Time Transport Protocol, provides end-to-end network transport functions suitable for applications transmitting realtime data, such as audio, video, or simulation data, over multicast or unicast network services.

RSVP, the ReSerVation Protocol, enhances the current Internet architecture with support requests for a specific quality of service (QoS) from the network for particular data streams or flows. RTSP, the Real-Time Streaming Protocol is an application-level protocol for control over the delivery of data with realtime properties to enable controlled, on-demand delivery of realtime data, such as audio and video. Reliable multicast protocols are being developed to overcome the limitations of unreliable multicast datagram delivery and expand the uses of IP Multicast.

Conclusion

IP Multicast enables many new types of applications and reduces network congestion and server loads. IP Multicast products and services are receiving widespread industry attention because of their potential benefits. Advances are being made in areas such as reliable multicasting, realtime applications support, and network management and diagnosis.

This paper has introduced the technical concepts and mechanisms of IP Multicast. To learn more, the following references are recommended. Many were used in the preparation of this document. The authors are gratefully acknowledged. We also invite you to review the IP Multicast Initiative white paper series at **www.ipmulticast.com**.

More Information

There are many more aspects of IP Multicast that were not discussed here. The IP Multicast Initiative Web site at **www.ipmulticast.com** has a technical resource center that provides more background, in-depth information, including white papers and relevant RFCs. The Web site also offers a product and services directory and lists members of the IP Multicast Initiative who can be contacted for information and assistance.

The IP Multicast Initiative provides marketing and educational services to promote the creation, use, and deployment of multicast products and solutions. Supported by a growing number of the most important vendors in the IP Multicast arena, the Initiative and its services are managed and provided by Stardust Technologies, Inc.

For more information about the Initiative and membership, contact Stardust Technologies at 408-879-8080 or visit the Initiative Web site.

Useful References

The following additional references are recommended:

Books

Routing in the Internet, Christian Huitema, Prentice Hall, 1995

MBone: Interactive Media on the Internet, Vinay Kumar, New Riders, 1996

Gigabit Networking, Craig Partridge, Addison-Wesley, 1994

Interconnections, Radia Perlman, Addison-Wesley, 1992

Windows Sockets Network Programming, Bob Quinn and Dave Shute, Addison-Wesley, 1996

Computer Networks, Andrew Tanenbaum, Prentice Hall, 1996

IETF RFCs

[**http://ds.internic.net/rfc/rfcnnnn.txt**, *nnnn* is the RFC number]

RFC 1112: *Host Extensions for IP Multicasting*

RFC 1700: *Assigned Numbers*

Session Description Protocol: draft-ietf-mmusic-sap-00.txt, .ps

Session Announcement Protocol: draft-ietf-mmusic-sdp-02.txt, .ps

Introduction To IP Multicast Routing

A technical overview of IP Multicast routing protocols and their features.

Scope Of This Document

This document provides a high-level technical overview of IP Multicast routing protocols. If you are an engineer interested in evaluating or implementing IP Multicast for your organization, product, or service, this document will help you understand the distinguishing features of the routing protocols. It assumes you have a conceptual understanding of IP Multicast addressing, group management, and IP routing. If you are unfamiliar with these, we recommend you first read the IP Multicast Initiative white paper *How IP Multicast Works*.

IP Multicast Routing Approaches

IP Multicast traffic for a particular (source, destination group) pair is transmitted from the source to the receivers via a spanning tree that connects all the hosts in the group. Different IP Multicast routing protocols use different techniques to construct these multicast spanning trees; once a tree is constructed, all multicast traffic is distributed over it.

IP Multicast routing protocols generally follow one of two basic approaches, depending on the expected distribution of multicast group members throughout the network. The first approach is based on assumptions that the multicast group members are densely distributed throughout the network (i.e., many of the subnets contain at least one group member) and that bandwidth is plentiful.

So-called "dense-mode" multicast routing protocols rely on a technique called flooding to propagate information to all network routers. Dense-mode routing protocols include Distance Vector Multicast Routing Protocol (DVMRP), Multicast Open Shortest Path First (MOSPF), and Protocol-Independent Multicast—Dense Mode (PIM-DM).

The second approach to multicast routing basically assumes the multicast group members are sparsely distributed throughout the network and bandwidth is not necessarily widely available, for example across many regions of the Internet or if users are connected via ISDN lines. Sparse-mode does not imply that the group has a few members, just that they are widely dispersed.

In this case, flooding would unnecessarily waste network bandwidth and hence could cause serious performance problems. Hence, *sparse-mode* multicast routing protocols must rely on more selective techniques to set up and maintain multicast trees. Sparse-mode routing protocols include Core Based Trees (CBT) and Protocol-Independent Multicast—Sparse Mode (PIM-SM).

This document compares and discusses the features of these routing protocols. Also presented is a transitional strategy, *tunneling*, which can be used to route IP Multicast traffic over portions of an internetwork that do not yet have multicast capabilities. All of the IP Multicast routing algorithms and protocols are rapidly evolving. For the current status of individual protocols, see the references at the end of this document and the latest IETF drafts and RFCs.

Dense-Mode Multicast Routing Protocols

Following is a breakdown of the dense-mode multicast routing protocols.

DISTANCE VECTOR MULTICAST ROUTING PROTOCOL (DVMRP)

The first protocol developed to support multicast routing is called the Distance Vector Multicast Routing Protocol (DVMRP). It is described in RFC 1075 and an Internet Draft update (see references). It has been widely used on the MBone.

DVMRP constructs a different distribution tree for each source and its destination host group. Each distribution tree is a minimum spanning tree from the multicast source at the root of the tree to all the multicast receivers as leaves of the tree. The distribution tree provides a shortest path between the source and each multicast receiver in the group, based on the number of hops in the path, which is the DVMRP metric. A tree is constructed on demand, using a "broadcast and prune" technique, when a source begins to transmit messages to a multicast group.

To simplify the description of DVMRP, we assume that all routers in the network support DVMRP. The approach used by DVMRP is to assume initially that every host on the network is part of the multicast group. The designated router on the source subnet, i.e., the router that has been selected to handle routing for all hosts on its subnet, begins by transmitting a multicast message to all adjacent routers. Each of these routers then selectively forwards the message to downstream routers, until the message is eventually passed to all multicast group members.

The selective forwarding during the formation of the spanning tree works as follows. When a router receives a multicast message, it checks its unicast routing tables to determine the interface that provides the shortest path back to the source. If that was the interface over which the multicast message arrived, then the router enters some state information to identify the multicast group in its internal tables (specifying interfaces over which messages for that group should be forwarded) and forwards the multicast message to all adjacent routers, other than the one that sent the message. Otherwise, the message is simply discarded. This mechanism, called *Reverse Path Forwarding*, ensures that there will be no loops in the tree and that the tree will include shortest paths from the source to all recipients. This is basically the broadcast part of the protocol.

DVMRP actually uses a forwarding process that is even more selective than the process described earlier, by relying on specific information that is provided by the unicast routing protocol. (Note that this implies that DVMRP must contain its own integrated unicast routing protocol.) A DVMRP router, say router MR1, contains information in its unicast routing tables that enables it to determine if an adjacent DVMRP router, say router MR2, will recognize MR1 as being on the shortest path back to the multicast source. This enables MR1 to forward a multicast message to MR2 only if MR2 will be able to use it to further the construction of the multicast tree. This enhancement potentially results in a considerable reduction in the number of flooding messages that are required to construct the distribution tree.

The prune part of the protocol eliminates branches of the tree that don't lead to any multicast group members. The Internet Group Management Protocol (IGMP), running between hosts and their immediately neighboring multicast routers, is used to maintain group-membership data in the routers. When a router determines that no hosts beyond it belong to the multicast group, it sends a prune message to its upstream router. Of course, routers must update (source, destination group) state information in their tables to reflect which branches have been pruned from the tree. This process continues until all superfluous branches are eliminated from the tree, resulting in a minimum spanning tree.

Construction of a DVMRP spanning tree is illustrated [in Figure 18.7]. Once the spanning tree is constructed, it is used to transmit multicast messages from the source to the multicast members. Each router in the path forwards messages over only those interfaces that lead to group members. Since new members may join the group at any time, and since these new members may depend on one of the pruned branches to receive the multicast transmission, DVMRP periodically reinitiates the construction of the spanning tree.

DVMRP works well for a multicast group that is densely represented within a subnet. However, for multicast groups that are sparsely represented over a wide-area network, the periodic broadcast behavior would cause serious performance problems. Another problem with DVMRP is the amount of multicast routing state information that must be stored in the multicast routers. All the multicast routers must contain state information for every (source, group) pair, either information designating the interface to be used for forwarding multicast messages or prune-state information. For these reasons, DVMRP does not scale to support multicast groups that are sparsely distributed over a large network.

Progression of messages is shown by one hop/time unit:

1. In the first hop the message reaches router 1.

2. In the second hop the message reaches routers 2, 3, and 4.

3. In the third hop routers 3 and 4 exchange messages. Each one just drops the message, because it didn't arrive over the interface that gives the shortest path back to the source. (Note that this exchange would not occur under the more selective forwarding process for DVMRP described previously. It was included for illustration only.)

4. In the fourth hop, the message reaches router 7. Router 7 realizes it is a leaf router and there are no group members on its subnet, so it

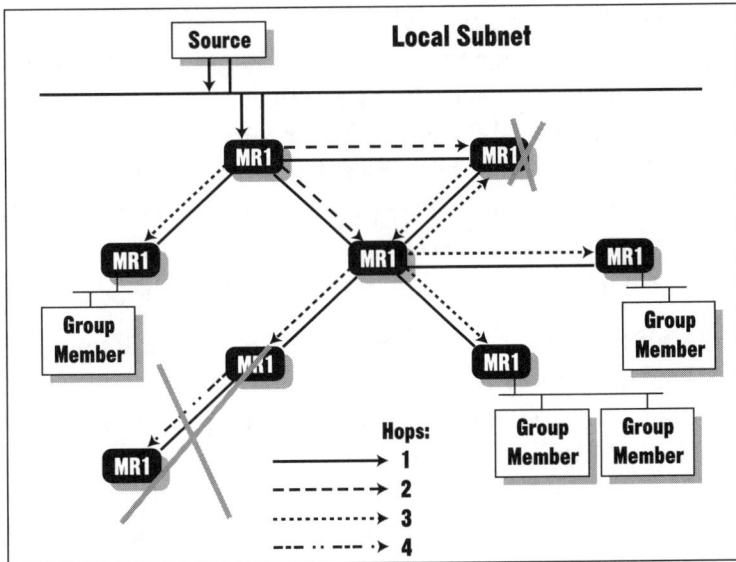

Figure 18.7 Construction of a DVMRP spanning tree.

sends a prune message back to router 6, the upstream router. Router 6, in turn, sends a prune message to router 4. Router 3 also sends a prune message to router 1. The resulting spanning tree is shown [in Figure 18.8].

MULTICAST OPEN SHORTEST PATH FIRST (MOSPF)

Multicast Extensions to OSPF (MOSPF) are defined in RFC-1584. Open Shortest Path First (OSPF), a unicast routing protocol, routes messages

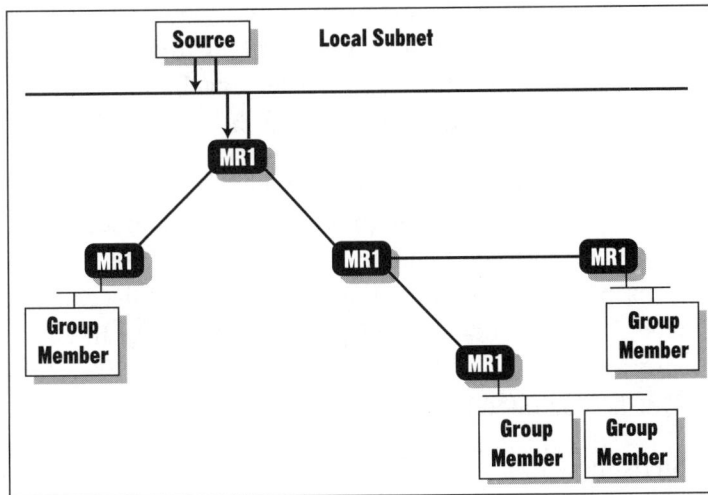

Figure 18.8 The resulting spanning tree.

along least-cost paths, where cost is expressed in terms of a link-state metric. In addition to the number of hops in a path, other network performance parameters that can influence the assignment of cost to a path include load-balancing information (e.g., a link that has very little traffic on it might be assigned a lower cost than a heavily utilized link, in an attempt to balance traffic on the network), an application's desired quality of service (e.g., if an application requires low latency, a path involving a satellite link should be assigned a high cost), etc.

MOSPF is intended for use within a single routing domain, e.g., a network controlled by a single organization. MOSPF is dependent on the use of OSPF as the accompanying unicast routing protocol, just as DVMRP includes its own unicast protocol. In an OSPF/MOSPF network, each router maintains an up-to-date image of the topology of the entire network. This "link-state" information is used to construct multicast distribution trees.

Each MOSPF router periodically collects information about multicast group membership via IGMP. This information, along with the link-state information, is flooded to all other routers in the routing domain. Routers will update their internal link-state information based on information that they receive from adjacent routers. Each router, since it understands the topology of the entire network, can then independently calculate a least-cost spanning tree with the multicast source as the root and the group members as leaves.

This tree is the path that is used to route multicast traffic from the source to each of the group members. Note that all routers will calculate exactly the same tree, since they periodically share link-state information. However, MOSPF does not scale well, due to the periodic flooding of link-state information among the routers.

MOSPF uses the Dijkstra algorithm to compute a shortest-path tree. A separate calculation is required for each (source, destination group) pair. To reduce the number of calculations and to spread the calculations out somewhat, a router only makes this calculation when it receives the first datagram in a stream. Once the tree is calculated, the information is stored for use in routing later datagrams from that stream. This is illustrated [in Figure 18.9].

Steps shown:

1. MR 1 computes tree—knows members of group via IGMP and hence knows path to MR 4 is via MR 2, path to MR 8 is via 5, etc.

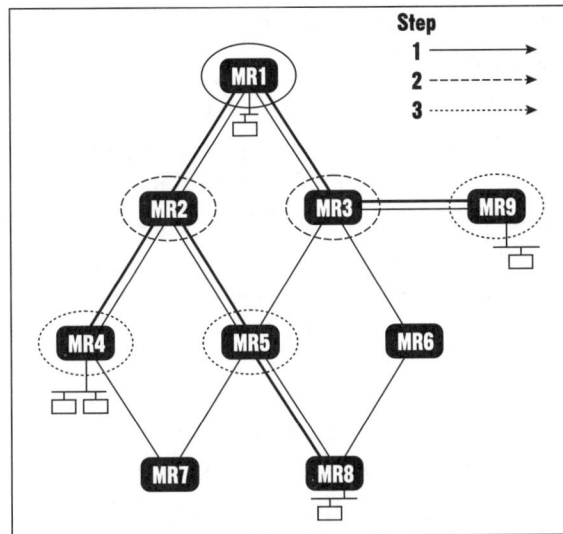

Figure 18.9 MOSPF tree computation.

2. MR 2 computes tree—determines path to MR 4 is direct, path to MR 8 is via MR 5 and MR 3 computes tree—determines path to MR 9 is direct.

3. MR 5 computes tree—determines path to MR 8 is direct.

Note that the multicast transmission triggers this process (i.e., data driven process) and each router, when it receives a message, calculates exactly the same distribution tree as its predecessors and uses it to forward the message.

PROTOCOL INDEPENDENT MULTICAST (PIM)

The Protocol Independent Multicast (PIM) routing protocol is currently under development by an IETF working group. PIM support is currently available in some router products. The objective is to develop a standard multicast routing protocol that can provide scalable inter-domain multicast routing across the Internet, independent of the mechanisms provided by any particular unicast routing protocol.

PIM has two operational modes, one for densely distributed multicast groups and one for sparsely distributed multicast groups. The first mode, called *Protocol-Independent Multicast-Dense Mode*, is described in the following section. The second mode, called *Protocol-Independent Multicast-Sparse Mode*, that is included in the section on sparse-mode routing protocols.

PROTOCOL-INDEPENDENT MULTICAST—DENSE MODE (PIM-DM)

Protocol Independent Multicast-Dense Mode (PIM-DM) is similar to DVMRP. Both protocols employ Reverse Path Multicasting (RPM) to construct source-rooted distribution trees. The major differences between DVMRP and PIM-DM are that PIM is completely independent of the unicast routing protocol that is used on the network, while DVMRP relies on specific mechanisms of the associated unicast routing protocol, and PIM-DM is less complex than DVMRP.

The PIM-DM protocol is data driven, like all dense-mode routing protocols. However, since PIM-DM is independent of the accompanying unicast routing protocol, data packets that arrive at a router over the proper receiving interface (i.e., the interface that provides the shortest path back to the source), are forwarded on all downstream interfaces until unnecessary branches of the tree are explicitly pruned.

Recall that DVMRP can be more selective when it forwards messages during the tree-construction phase by using specific topology information provided by its own unicast routing protocol. The philosophy followed by PIM-DM designers is to opt for protocol simplicity and protocol independence, even though there is likely to be additional overhead due to some packet duplication.

Sparse-Mode Multicast Routing Protocols

The routing protocols in the previous section all rely on the periodic flooding of messages throughout the network. This is an efficient approach within regions where a multicast group is widely represented throughout the network or where there is lots of available bandwidth.

However, consider the problems that could occur if several thousand small conferences were being conducted simultaneously over the Internet; the aggregate traffic from this periodic flooding could potentially saturate wide-area Internet connections. Clearly, if group members are sparsely distributed over a wide area, a different approach is needed so that multicast traffic is restricted to those links which lead to members of the multicast group.

While dense-mode protocols use a data-driven approach to construct multicast distribution trees, sparse-mode protocols use a receiver-initiated process, i.e., a router becomes involved in the construction of a multicast distribution tree only when one of the hosts on its subnet requests membership in a particular multicast group. Two sparse-mode protocols are presented in the following text.

CORE BASED TREES (CBT)

Some multicast applications, such as distributed interactive simulation and distributed video-gaming, have many active senders within a single multicast group. Unlike DVMRP or MOSPF, which construct a shortest-path tree for each (source, group) pair, the CBT protocol constructs a single tree that is shared by all members of the group.

Multicast traffic for the entire group is sent and received over the same tree, regardless of the source. This use of a shared tree can provide significant savings in terms of the amount of multicast state information that is stored in individual routers.

A CBT shared tree has a core router that is used to construct the tree. The process is illustrated [in Figure 18.10]. Routers join the tree by sending a join message to the core. When the core receives a join request, it returns an acknowledgment over the reverse path, thus forming a branch of the tree.

Join messages need not travel all the way to the core before being acknowledged. If a join message hits a router on the tree before it reaches the core, that on-tree router terminates the join and acknowledges it. The router that sent the join is then connected to the shared tree.

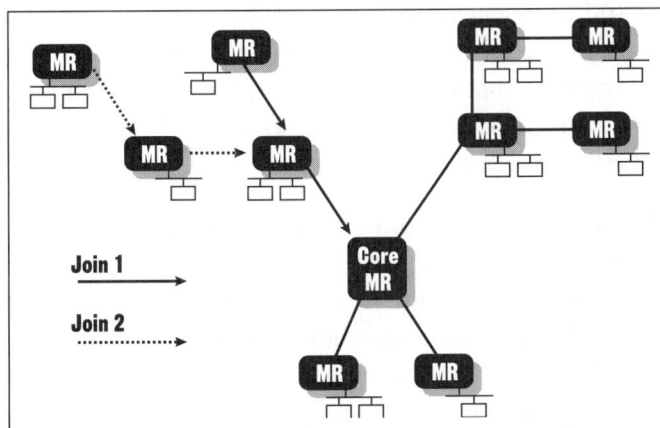

Figure 18.10 A CBT shared tree.

CBT aggregates traffic onto a smaller subset of links that would be used for source-based trees. The resulting concentration of traffic around the core is a potential problem for this approach to multicast routing. Some versions of CBT support the use of multiple cores; load balancing might be achieved by using more than one core.

PROTOCOL-INDEPENDENT MULTICAST—SPARSE MODE (PIM-SM)

Similar to the CBT protocol, PIM-Sparse Mode (PIM-SM) is designed to restrict multicast traffic to only those routers interested in receiving it. PIM-SM constructs a multicast distribution tree around a router called a rendezvous point (RP). This rendezvous point plays the same role as the core in the CBT protocol; receivers "meet" new sources at this rendezvous point. However, PIM-SM is a more flexible protocol than CBT. While CBT with trees are always group-shared trees, with PIM-SM an individual receiver may choose to construct either a group-shared tree or a shortest-path tree.

There are advantages to each type of distribution tree. The shared tree is relatively easy to construct, and it reduces the amount of state information that must be stored in the routers. Accordingly, a shared tree would conserve network resources if the multicast group consisted of a large number of low-data-rate sources.

However, as indicated earlier, shared trees cause a concentration of traffic around the core or the rendezvous point, a phenomenon that can result in performance degradation if there is a large volume of multicast traffic. Another disadvantage of shared trees is that traffic often does not traverse the shortest path from source to destination. If low latency is a critical application requirement, it would be preferable for traffic to be routed along a shortest path. PIM-SM architecture supports both types of distribution trees.

The PIM-SM protocol initially constructs a group-shared tree to support a multicast group. The tree is formed by the senders and receivers both connecting to the rendezvous point, just as a shared tree is constructed around the core with the CBT protocol. After the tree is constructed, a receiver (actually the router closest to this receiver) can opt to change its connection to a particular source to a shortest-path tree.

This is accomplished by having this router send a PIM join message to the source. Once the shortest path from source to receiver is created, the extraneous branches through the RP are pruned. This procedure is illustrated [in Figure 18.11]. Note that different types of trees can be selected for different sources within a single multicast group.

Steps shown:

1. The sender at Source 2 registers at the Rendezvous Point Multicast Router Rpt.

2. A receiver joins at Rpt; there is now a bigger shared tree.

3. The receiver is receiving lots of data from Source 2. The receiver sends an explicit join to Source 2 to construct a shortest path route.

The PIM protocol specifies soft-state mechanisms to periodically refresh system state, adapt to topological changes in the network, and adapt to changes in group membership. While PIM relies on unicast routing tables to adapt to network topology changes, it is independent of the particular unicast routing protocol that is used to construct those tables.

Other features of PIM, such as using multiple rendezvous points to eliminate the problem of having a single failure point, are too numerous to describe in this document. Details of the more subtle aspects of the protocol are presented in the references.

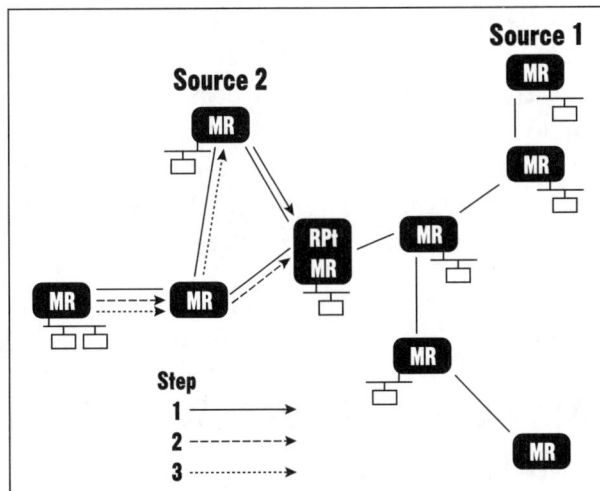

Figure 18.11 PIM-SM join.

Interoperability

It is clearly desirable for different routing protocols to be able to interoperate with one another. Vendors can assist you in assessing your interoperability requirements. There are two broad types of interoperability considerations, 1) interoperability between existing unicast and emerging multicast-capable routers, and 2) interoperability between the various approaches to multicast routing.

As an example of the first type of interoperability, DVMRP, is currently used for multicast routing on the MBone; a mechanism called *tunneling* (discussed in a moment) is used to connect multicast-capable islands within the Internet. In addition, MOSPF was designed on top of OSPF Version 2 so that a multicast routing capability can be introduced into an OSPF Version 2 routing domain.

PIM designers, especially, are addressing the second interoperability issue, both to enable interoperability between PIM-DM and PIM-SM and to enable interoperability between PIM and other multicast routing architectures.

There is a basic incompatibility between the dense-mode protocol approach for constructing distribution trees and the approach used by sparse-mode protocols. Dense-mode protocols are data driven, while sparse-mode protocols rely on explicit join requests.

If a dense-mode group is to interoperate with a sparse-mode group, e.g., to form a group that is sparsely distributed over a wide-area network but that is densely distributed within a single subnet, there must be a mechanism for allowing the dense group to reach out to the sparse group to request to join. The solution proposed by PIM designers is to have "border" routers send explicit joins to the sparse group. Note that the same approach would enable PIM-SM to interoperate with other dense-mode protocols, such as DVMRP.

A formal treatment of interoperability between different multicast routing protocols is presented in a recent Internet Draft (see references).

Tunneling As A Transition Strategy For IP Multicast Routing

Tunneling in the context of multicast refers to the encapsulation of multicast packets in an IP datagram (i.e., unicast packet) to route through parts of an internetwork, such as the Internet, that don't support multicast routing. The most well-known demonstration of multicast tunneling is used in the MBone, with DVMRP. The encapsulation is added on entry to a tunnel and stripped off on exit from a tunnel [see Figure 18.12].

Tunnels are useful as a transition strategy to achieving full native IP Multicast deployment.

Concluding Remarks

IP Multicast enables many new types of applications and reduces network congestion and server loads. This document has described concepts and mechanisms behind several routing protocols used with IP Multicast, and some of their advantages and disadvantages. The selection of routing protocols is an important step in deployment.

Considerations include profiles of expected application usage, scalability, vendor support, performance overhead, dependence on other network protocols, flexibility, interoperability, and router overhead. Evaluating the many new IP Multicast products and services, and tracking the IETF working groups and draft standards will help you assess potential benefits for your organization. Check the IPMI product directory for current product offerings from router vendors.

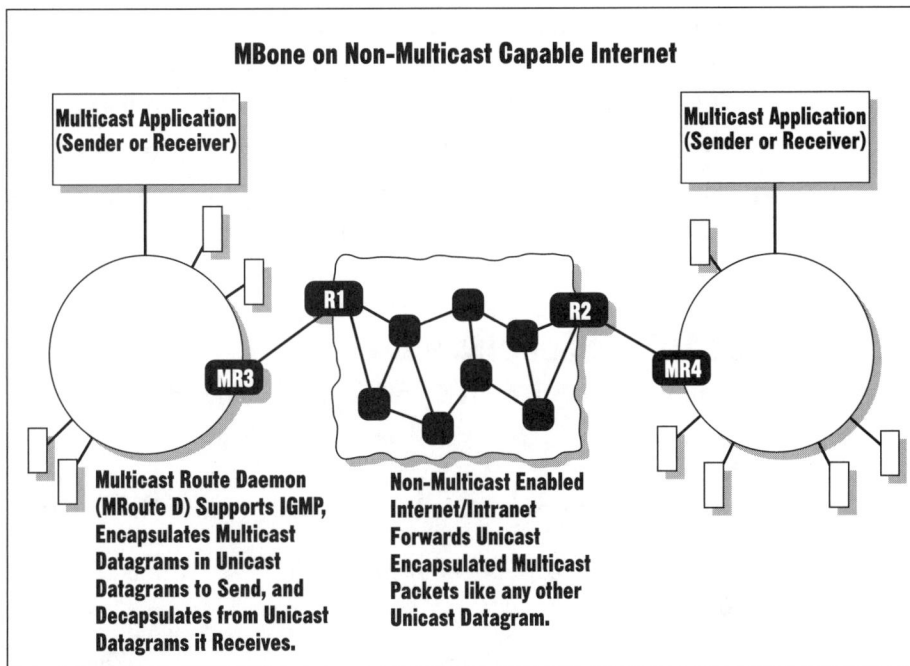

MBone on Non-Multicast Capable Internet

Multicast Application (Sender or Receiver)

Multicast Application (Sender or Receiver)

R1   R2

MR3   MR4

Multicast Route Daemon (MRoute D) Supports IGMP, Encapsulates Multicast Datagrams in Unicast Datagrams to Send, and Decapsulates from Unicast Datagrams it Receives.

Non-Multicast Enabled Internet/Intranet Forwards Unicast Encapsulated Multicast Packets like any other Unicast Datagram.

Figure 18.12 Tunneling.

This white paper has addressed IP Multicast routing as it would be implemented in the Internet or other highly meshed routed networks. Alternative types of network architectures that are used in private networks can also facilitate multicast. These include two-way satellite, where the forward path is inherently broadcast in nature; SMDS (Switched Multimegabit Data Service), which offers multicast as a native service; frame relay networks that are set up as "hub and spoke" configurations with a router overlay; and campus LANs.

The following references are recommended; many were used in the preparation of this document. The authors are gratefully acknowledged.

More Information

There are many other technical aspects of IP Multicast and business benefits that were not discussed here. The IP Multicast Initiative Web site at **www.ipmulticast.com** has a technical resource center that provides more background in-depth information, including white papers and relevant RFCs. The Web site also offers a product and services directory and lists members of the IP Multicast Initiative who can be contacted for information and assistance.

The IP Multicast Initiative provides marketing and educational services to promote the creation, use, and deployment of multicast products and solutions. Supported by a growing number of the most important vendors in the IP Multicast arena, the Initiative and its services are managed and provided by Stardust Technologies, Inc.

For more information about the Initiative and membership, or to see other white papers, contact Stardust Technologies at 408-879-8080, or visit the Initiative Web site.

Useful References

The following additional references are recommended:

Books

Routing in the Internet, Christian Huitema, Prentice Hall, 1995

MBone: Interactive Media on the Internet, Vinay Kumar, New Riders, 1996

Gigabit Networking, Craig Partridge, Addison-Wesley, 1994

Interconnections, Radia Perlman, Addison-Wesley, 1992

Windows Sockets Network Programming, Bob Quinn and Dave Shute, Addison-Wesley, 1996

Computer Networks, Andrew Tanenbaum, Prentice Hall, 1996

PAPERS
"An architecture for Wide-Area Multicast Routing", Deering, et al.

(See **http://netweb.usc.edu/pim**)

IETF RFCs
[**http://ds.internic.net/rfc/rfcnnnn.txt**, *nnnn* is the RFC number]

RFC 1112: *Host Extensions for IP Multicasting*

RFC 1075: *Distance Vector Multicast Routing Protocol*

RFC 1584: *Multicast Extensions to OSPF*

IETF INTERNET DRAFTS
[**ftp://ietf.org/internet-drafts/name-of-file**]

(works in progress)

Introduction to IP Multicast Routing: [draft-ietf-mboned-intro-multicast-00.txt]

Core Based Trees (CBT) Multicast Protocol Specification: [draft-ietf-idmr-cbt-spec-06.txt]

Distance Vector Multicast Routing Protocol (Update to RFC 1075): [draft-ietf-idmr-dvmrp-v3-03.txt, .ps]

Protocol Independent Multicast-Sparse Mode (PIM-SM): Protocol Specification [draft-ietf-idmr-pim-sm-spec-09.txt]

Protocol Independent Multicast-Dense Mode (PIM-DM): Protocol Specification [draft-ietf-idmr-pim-dm-spec-04.txt]

Protocol Independent Multicast-Sparse Mode (PIM-SM): Motivation and Architecture [draft-ietf-idmr-pim-arch-04.txt]

Interoperability Rules for Multicast Routing Protocols: [draft-thaler-interop-00.txt, .ps]

Chapter 19

- **Discerning Precept's role in the industry**

- **Realizing the goals of the IP Multicast Initiative**

- **Understanding the challenges for aspiring multicasters**

Chapter 19

Interview With Judy Estrin, CEO Of Precept Software

At various points in this book, Precept Software is mentioned as a pioneering force in the IP multicast universe. In fact, many of the annotated demonstrations presented in prior chapters show screenshots of Precept's IP/TV software in action. A key factor in Precept's success is their understanding of the role of multicast multimedia—specifically digital video—in the evolving digital future.

Judy Estrin, President and CEO of Precept Software (**www.precept.com**), was gracious enough to be interviewed for this book and to present her vision of the IP multicast landscape—both how it looks now and how it may change in the near future. For the record, Ms. Estrin is the founder of the IP Multicast Initiative (**www.ipmulticast.com**), an organization devoted to the advancement of multicast technology.

General Issues In Multicasting

The first section of this chapter poses general questions about multicasting. Later sections explore more specific areas.

Let's start with some basic questions. What is it like being a leader of the multicast revolution? Is it lonely up there?

When we announced our product early last year, multicasting was already supported by Cisco and a few other hardware vendors. So by the time we started *selling* our product, we assumed people knew a lot more about multicasting than they did. Consequently, the real market took us a little by surprise. It wasn't that the products weren't there, but that the general awareness of multicasting was lacking.

I would say that at this time last year (January 1996), it was real lonely. We kept hearing that the various industry segments were changing and coming together, but still it was a vicious circle.

First, we'd go to the applications guys who'd say multicasting wasn't ubiquitous, so they weren't using it. When we went to PointCast, for example, I asked them how they could architect software that way? Why weren't they using multicast technology for at least some of it? Their answer, of course, was that multicast wasn't ubiquitous yet, the Internet was moving too fast, and they didn't have time to worry about it.

Then we'd go to the ISPs and ask them why they weren't moving forward with multicast faster, and they'd say because the applications weren't there. So, we were clearly in a catch-22 situation, which caused us to start the IP Multicast Initiative.

I had the experience of being in a small company trying to build a market for X-Terminals, and it's very hard for small companies to move markets that require infrastructure changes. So, we launched the [IP Multicast] Initiative by going to a number of vendors and convincing them to join forces with us to make things happen in an organized way.

Now, it's not so lonely because the interest in multicasting has been phenomenal.

About The IP Multicast Initiative

What is the official goal of the Initiative?

Our basic goal is to increase the awareness, and therefore the deployment and use, of multicast products through marketing and education [see Figure 19.1].

The letters IP are significant. Do you differentiate IP multicasting from other types?

Absolutely. The whole idea is that IP multicasting is done at the common IP networking layer. There are some solutions out there that may call themselves multicasting but they do application-level multicasts, or proprietary multicasts, using reflector technology.

The whole purpose of the IP Multicast Initiative is to inform people that the more efficient way to do it, the more standard way to do it, is IP multicasting. If we can get the infrastructure to change—the ISPs and the network hardware vendors—then we won't need application-level or proprietary multicasting anymore.

CU-SeeMe being an example of an application-level product.

Right, and RealAudio, for example.

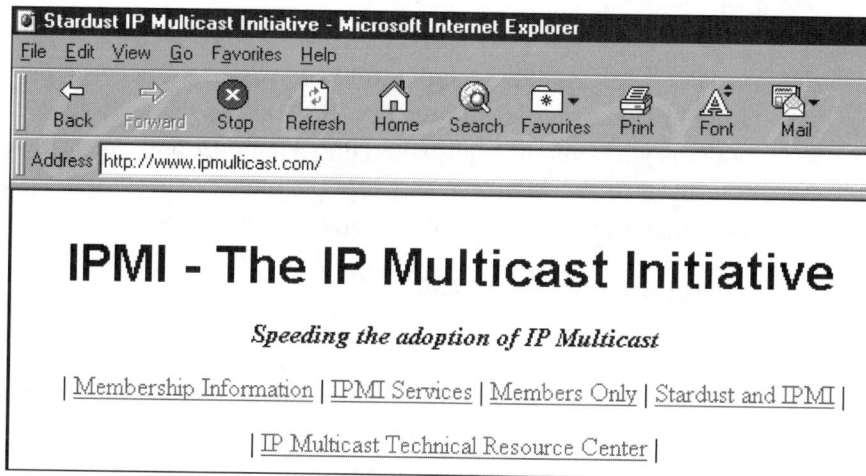

Figure 19.1   The IP Multicast Initiative Web site.

Multimedia Multicasting

What sort of solution does IP multicast provide for networked multimedia bandwidth problems?

I'll go as far as saying I don't believe you can have widespread Internet video, or even enterprise-wide networked video, without IP multicasting. You just can't scale with unicast multimedia, especially video. You can have little clusters of it, but that's all. Using multicast is a necessity for the growth of the Internet (and not just for video) and for integrating video into enterprise networks. I believe that if you keep trying to do all unicast video, it's just not going to happen.

Now that's just part of the answer. You *still* have the issue of video taking a lot of bandwidth. Even if you're multicasting at 56 Kbps, you're still not going to be able to do good quality MPEG video. So there is a combination of issues here, and multicasting is really only part of the solution. We still need higher bandwidth to the home.

From where you sit, how is that scene changing?

Well, for one thing, 56 Kbps modems using Rockwell technology with IP multicast capability are almost here. If you can dial at that speed into a router with, say, Rockwell chips, which the new Ascend routers will have, you will get a different kind of online video experience—especially with codecs such as Vxtreme's which Precept has recently licensed. The difference between 28.8 and 56 Kbps video is very significant.

And don't forget that video doesn't need to be symmetrical, especially video broadcasting [see Figure 19.2]. Because the next generation of modems will support high bandwith to the user and much lower data flow back to the ISP, *and* will support multicasting, there should be some major awareness breakthroughs in 1997.

Will there be 128 Kbps modems?

That's not clear at this point. They always tell us the latest plateau is the top, don't they? And then someone comes up with a clever way to make it go higher. Part of the new increase [to 56 Kbps] is achieved by going to an asymmetrical model. Another factor is making certain assumptions about the quality of the circuit, and so forth.

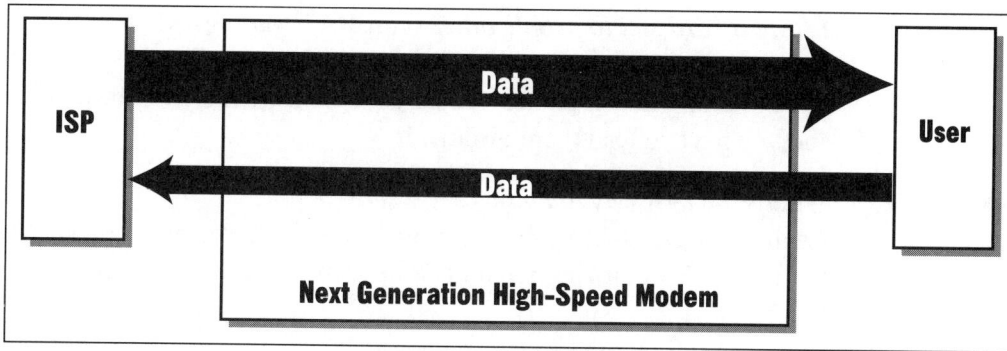

Figure 19.2 Asymmetrical networked data flow.

Speaking of asymmetrical data flow, what about ADSL and cable modems?

Both are technologies which will greatly enhance the ability to make Internet video usable for consumers, but are still only part of the total picture. Someone asked me this morning, "If there's going to be all this bandwidth, do we really need multicasting?" My answer was, "When the freeway system was built, did we ever think we'd need carpool lanes?" We'll find uses for whatever bandwidth is there, no question about it.

So, multicasting is just a good idea anyway.

Yes. And in fact, IP multicast has lots of applications outside of video. Examples are things like multicast file transfers, stock ticker update streams, and so forth. Down the line are Web caching and database replication. In other words, there are lots of applications beyond video that can leverage multicasting.

Internetworked Multicasting

Is internetworked multicasting a good proving ground for doing it on the global Internet?

Again, absolutely. Precept's target is the enterprise. This is partly because that's where our applications will be used, but also because it's where major deployment multicasting will happen first, because the global Internet will take a longer time to be enabled. I believe you will see many private LANs and "private Internets" doing business-to-business multicasting, and that this will happen much faster than multicasting on the Internet at large.

Is that a hard sell to people other than WAN managers?

It depends on the company you're dealing with. Some are very open to it after talking to companies like Cisco; others are more old fashioned, and you have to lead them through it.

What's the best way to do this?

Using analogies to TV broadcasting works well. For many people, it has a very familiar ring if you can describe it in the right terms [see Figure 19.3].

When do the analogies stop working?

One of the biggest problems is that many of the networking guys think that if they turn on multicast, they'll let more video onto their networks, which will then get overloaded. What they don't realize is that, if they *don't* turn on multicasting, video is going to come on anyway in unicast mode, and it's going to be worse.

In other words, they've associated multicasting with video applications in general, and they're nervous about their limited bandwidth. In fact, this is one of the areas in which the IP Multicast Initiative is making progress, which is informing networking professionals about the true nature of multicasting. We do this through white papers, training sessions, special Web sites, etc.

Are there performance problems when crossing multiple subnets in an internetworked environment?

It's really no different than with unicasting. The outstanding problem in multicasting comes when you're working within a very *large* and complex internetwork, like the Internet itself.

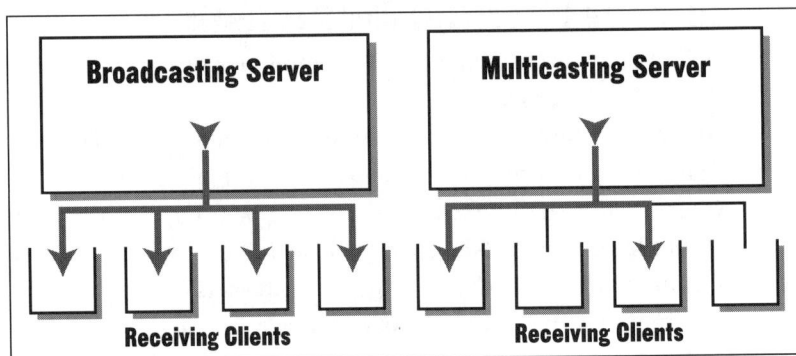

Figure 19.3 Multicasting versus TV-style broadcasting.

Is this due to lack of a hierarchical routing structure?

That's right. It's just one big flat space right now. The amount of information each router needs to keep in that particular environment is immense. If you contrast this to any typical enterprise, with or without WAN connections, it's a completely different story, where things work pretty much as expected and Internet-style problems are not really an issue.

Do you consider the low-end, sub-$1,000 routers from companies like Cisco and Ascend suitable for doing multicasting on a business basis?

It depends on the business, and the amount of traffic, but that's how they're being sold. I'd have to defer answering that until more businesses sign up, at least for that range of equipment. As for the more sophisticated gear from those companies, it's already working fine—as we've seen here in our lab.

The State Of The MBone

Can you sum up the state of the MBone today?

The MBone has changed from being a research tool to a commercially viable pilot. It's not a commercially viable vehicle for mainstream business communications, mainly because it wasn't meant to be and the current infrastructure doesn't support that kind of activity. But it is now a good proof of concept and a great tool with which to continue important research and for viewing conferences and seminars remotely.

Will it continue to change?

I think what will happen over the next few years is that we'll see the MBone slowly merge into the Internet as multicasting on the Internet becomes more common.

Will it be, for lack of a better word, co-opted?

No. I often draw a picture of the Internet in general where it started as ARPAnet, then subsequently broke into three parts: research, consumer, and enterprise. *Enterprise* means intranet, but it also means business-to-business Internet. This enterprise segment must continue to operate and grow or we won't have any new technology [see Figure 19.4].

Where is all the research going on?

In areas like Internet2, DARTnet, and so forth, there is a lot of continuous research. The MBone started out running on DARTnet and then grew beyond it as an overlay of the Internet.

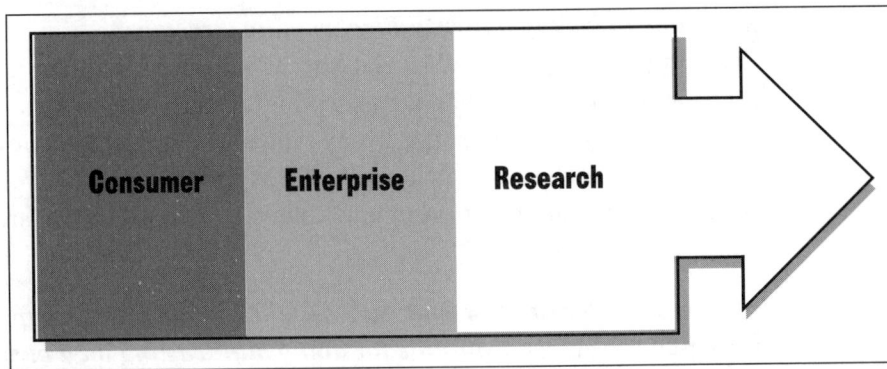

Figure 19.4 Partitioning the Internet.

Getting Into Detail

The following section goes into detail on some of the general subjects already broached.

MBone Tunneling

Let's get into some specific technical areas about the MBone. For instance, many people are confused about the concept of tunneling when they hear about it for the first time. Can you lay this out for us?
First of all, the general concept of tunneling doesn't apply just to multicasting. It can apply to any protocol technology. Let's say you have two sets of network nodes that want to communicate using protocol X (such as multicast). Let's also say that they need to communicate over an infrastructure that doesn't support protocol X but *does* support protocol Y (such as unicast). Tunneling lets you encapsulate your protocol X packets in protocol Y packets to get them across the infrastructure.

So, we're talking about more than just connecting multicast islands on the proverbial unicast ocean.
That's right. You could, for instance, do SNA tunneling using IP protocol. In fact, tunneling will be a very important mechanism in the transition from IP Version 4 to IP Version 6. Again, multicast tunneling is specifically where you have multicast nodes that can communicate with each other over multiple hops in the unicast network environment [see Figure 19.5].

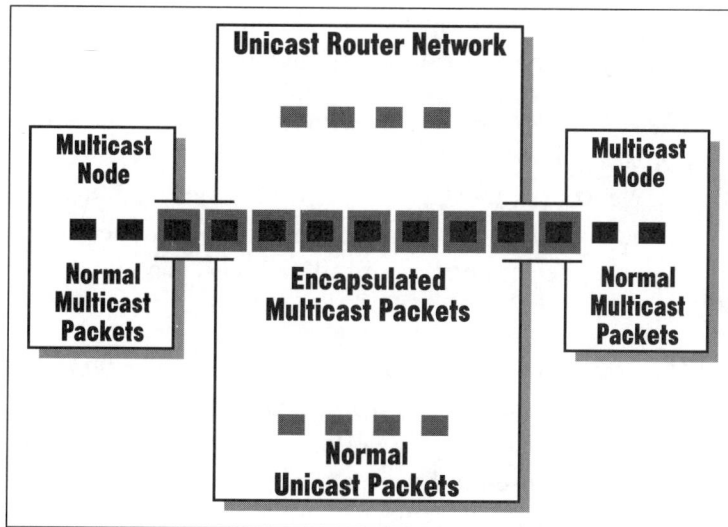

Figure 19.5 How tunneling works.

It sounds exotic, like you're doing some kind of space bending, but you're just putting a temporary wrapper on something to get it through a foreign land, and it still travels just as far.

Yes. Imagine I have a letter to be distributed through internal company mail. I put copies in internal routing envelopes addressed to the individual recipients and then give them to my admin. But one of the recipients is in our UK office so she puts his envelope in a FedEX Pak and FedEX's it to the UK office. The addressee of the FedEX Pak opens it and then delivers the original letter to the recipient.

Does tunneling make the router's job easier?

Not really. It just means that not all the routers along the way need to be multicast enabled. It lessens the number of multicast routers you need, and therefore, defers the problem of scalability.

Are there IETF [Internet Engineering Task Force] standards for tunneling?

I don't think there are standards per se, although I believe there are some IETF drafts which address this subject.

If tunneling solves these kinds of problems, why not exploit it across the board and forget about pushing multicast so hard?

One needs to be careful. Tunneling has its drawbacks, like everything else. For instance, tunneling sometimes causes network traffic to traverse the same link multiple times. It also adds an extra hop, for a technical reason based on encapsulation. So tunneling is good where you specifically need to have it. If you can have native multicast, that's better.

Then if the MBone was ubiquitous right now, we wouldn't need IP tunneling at all.
No, we wouldn't, except for some very special cases not worth going into at this point. The thing to remember is, tunneling is a good place to start if the deployment of full multicast is going to defer your business plans.

How far up in the networking food chain does tunneling need to be supported to make it viable as a multicast substitute?
It's a router issue. Only certain types of multicast routers support tunneling. It used to be a matter of having MROUTE-D, which was software that ran on Unix machines and some other platforms. But now Cisco specifically supports tunneling in their routers.

Does that mean that you can tune in an MBone multicast if you have a Cisco router that supports tunneling attached to, say, your NT machine?
If your ISP supports multicast, yes [see Figure 19.6].

Are you finding many such ISPs?
They're not really advertising it, but many of them can actually do it. There just aren't enough yet to change the overall fabric of the Internet.

Other Specific Issues For Multicasters

Can you advise entrepreneurs to start building business around multicasting technology as it stands now?

Figure 19.6 Tapping into the MBone.

If you mean multicasting video content, you can get into it now, but you might have a relatively long investment period before the payoff. If you have the necessary staying power, you can emerge a leader—just like in any new technology area. Just don't underestimate the fact that a lot of market development is going on and still needs to be done.

What's your opinion about the intersection of multicasting and such technologies as ATM and so-called Gigabit Ethernet.
I think Gigabit Ethernet helps solve current problems, but only in a brute force kind of way, as in the more bandwidth the better. You still need multicasting to route packets efficiently.

And what about ATM?
ATM is good as a fat pipe, but remember that it is a voice/data switching architecture as opposed to an IP-based packet-switching architecture. So, ATM as a data link technology on backbones is fine for enabling high-bandwidth multicasting of video, but I don't believe ATM will come down to the desktop—except in very particular cases.

Would you say that content developers working in the CD-ROM industry and in generic Web media development will have any problems moving into multicast content creation?
I don't think you have to produce special content for multicasting per se. One of the nice things about Precept's products is that you can take content you have on analog tape and just use it—without having to digitize it first.

That's a very powerful concept, isn't it? Just as if it were live—skipping the capture process altogether.
That's right. Except that the presentation obviously can't require interactivity. But any video content you produce for unicasting can easily be multicast. Remember that multicasting is really a deployment vehicle more than anything else.

Multicasting In The Work Place

Many decision makers in large organizations feel that it is hard to justify the cost of networked digital video because they think there's not a lot of corporate video available to begin with. Well, the real problem is that, while there *is* a lot of corporate video in existence, digital video on the desktop has gotten a bad rap in the quality department.

If your digital video isn't as good as your analog assets, then there is no incentive to replace one with the other. But if you can get the quality up to the level of the analog video, then you can transmit the content directly to the recipient at his or her desk without them having to go to a special room to receive the transmission.

And this is true even when the presentation is quarter screen— 320×240?
Yes. If you're sitting in front of a screen with that big of a video window, you can easily watch a training video. And at that size, of course, you have software decoding, which is key when weighing the price/performance factors. If it turns out that you want full screen, 30 frames per second, all you need to do is put in a hardware decoder card, and you've got digital television [see Figure 19.7].

Again, a lot of people have been burned with video—desktop digital video and otherwise. Both enterprise executives and the press like to say: *Look, two years ago you told me digital video was going to happen and it didn't.* I think the main problem has been bad video, which, as you know, is worse than no video.

Finally, this year, the right combination of factors has come together to make it possible from a business perspective—for instance, the Pentium processor, MMX, and desktop performance in general. Also, on the network side, we have the growth in switched LANs and IP networks, and the acceptance of the new standards.

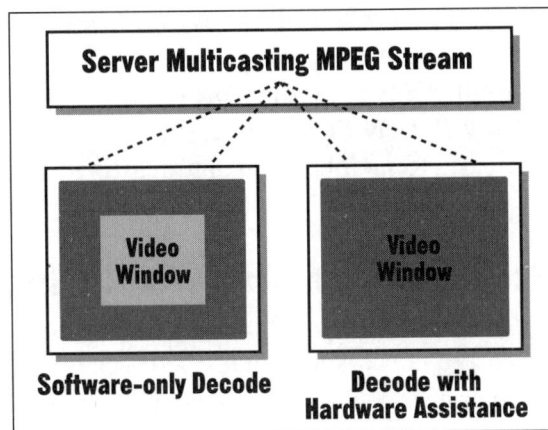

Figure 19.7 Precept's digital TV model for the enterprise.

Like IP multicast itself?

Right, and also protocols such as RTP for transmission of realtime streaming data, such as audio or video, and new compression standards. Now here's where I want to put forth some different thinking about this. When you're talking about digital data, you don't usually talk about the data itself. Instead, you talk about file transfer applications, Web applications, email applications, and so forth.

While video tends to get lumped in with this, people still talk about it as, well, *video*—as opposed to a standard type of digital data—because it's still such a new technology. I don't believe people have thought enough about the different applications of video and the distinct nature of video's various applications.

One of the reasons desktop digital video hasn't been more widespread is that most business people have associated desktop video with conferencing and on-demand streaming. Both of these types of applications are very unicast in nature and use a lot of bandwidth.

Plus, they're more expensive.

Yes. They both have high costs per individual user, mainly due to the cameras and capture cards required by conferencing apps, and because on-demand streaming needs big, powerful servers. As a result, when people say that you don't see video deployed broadly, it's because it's not affordable to deploy these two particular types of applications broadly. Thus, they tend to get deployed in very narrow, targeted ways.

Very true, and I can see where you're headed here.

Push Vs. Pull Models

Good. Well, here it is: Let's add a *third* type of application into this mix, which is *multicast streaming*. One way to think of this is as a push model, as opposed to the pull model used for on-demand video [see Figure 19.8].

Which everyone is talking about these days.

True, but let me also add the idea of *scheduled* video. Here, because you can leverage multicast, you have a very affordable technology that you can deploy across the organization. The thing to remember is not that any one of these types of applications is better or worse, but when you evaluate them on their merits, you'll probably go with the most affordable one in a business environment.

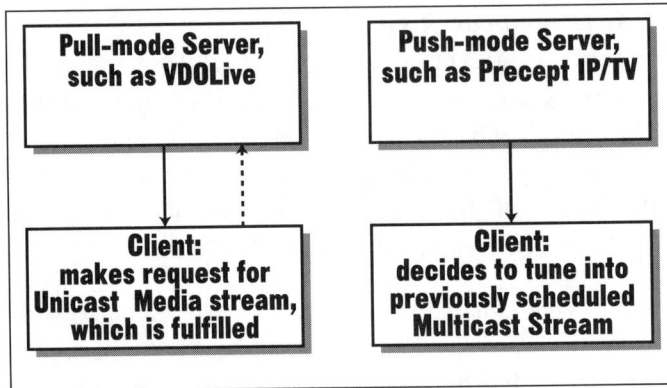

Figure 19.8 Server push versus user pull.

So, if you're stuck in on-demand mode, you might not ever bring video to most of your users.

Exactly. And if you use a prudent *combination* of all three types of video, you'll have even greater success in efficiently deploying video in general [see Figure 19.9].

Now, just to give you an idea of the confusion out there, half of the people I talk to think you can't run video unless you have ATM. The other half think you can do it over 28.8 Kbps.

I sense you're not kidding.

Obviously, the solution is somewhere in between. As everyone is supposed to know by now, video quality is directly proportional to how much bandwidth you have. Because of the traditional focus on conferencing and on-demand, which are unicast, when people tried to scale up, they were forced to go to less and less bandwidth per user…

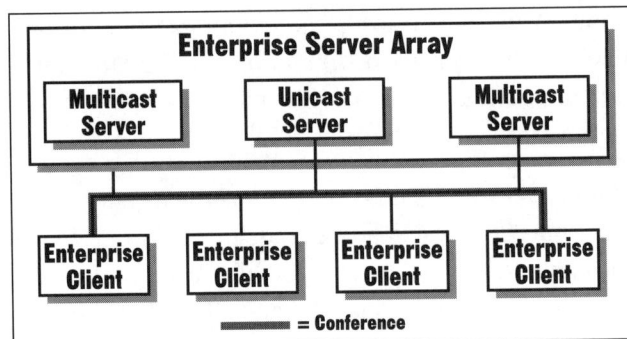

Figure 19.9 Pleasing most of the people most of the time.

..and therefore less and less quality per user...

...which is why conferencing solutions like ProShare ultimately offer only fair quality, or very jerky video performance. With multicast, instead of taking that pipe and dividing it up, you can use the whole thing for the highest quality video possible. Again, multicast saves not just network bandwidth but also server bandwidth. This is an important cost-saving consideration.

I don't think most people fully understand this.

They will, as multicast moves into the mainstream. To make this clear, let's give it some more emphasis here. You need more powerful servers to handle unicast streaming. There are no economies of scale from a cost/benefit perspective. If you have a very large organization with lots of unicast users, and therefore unicast servers, this can be quite expensive when you add it all up.

And how fast is multicast actually moving into the mainstream?

Right now, multicast technology is in almost all the TCP stacks and routers. Unfortunately, not every switch supports it yet. I'm not saying it's everywhere. There are a few places where things are dragging— this is why one of the key functions of the IP Multicast Initiative is education.

Very often the vendors we talk to just need to add little tweaks to their products, as opposed to major overhauls or brand new development and R&D efforts. Plus, we stress the importance of lots of testing. That being said, multicast technology is indeed out there. It's not hard to get or hard to use.

It's in Microsoft's stacks.

Right, and it's in all the major Ethernet controllers.

And how about on the Internet?

Again, it's starting to happen, but it's not completely there yet. There are multicast trials going on with most of the major ISPs. There is now an IETF MBone deployment working group trying to resolve the outstanding technical problems.

Can you say what these are?

The biggest issue is scalability—specifically, scalability for multimedia across the whole Internet.

The same issue faced by the enterprise thinking about implementing on-demand video and conferencing versus scheduled multicasts.
Pretty much. Once again, as your user base for these first two traditional video applications grows, your bandwidth needs will go up dramatically. In video multicasting, the bandwidth requirement is constant.

We should probably add that this is true of scheduled video broadcasting in general, but that video multicasting is even more efficient, as you've demonstrated.
True enough.

As we come to the end here, can you reiterate Precept's role in this arena?
Our focus is enterprise-wide video without compromise. This means a quality level that is acceptable for mission-critical types of applications—not toy video. We have started out with scheduled video, but we plan to offer our own brand of on-demand video and interactive capabilities later this year. Our main goal is to be able to go to the enterprise and solve a whole range of problems revolving around digital video.

Underlying all of this is our common technology: RTP, RSVP, IP multicast, and so forth. We do sell these technology pieces separately. Our newest release also offers optional encryption. On the application side, there is our IP/TV client/server software which includes a Program Guide for managing and scheduling video streams, a Server for capturing and transmitting audio and/or audio/video programming, and a client Viewer for selecting and viewing programs.

Which are all covered in this book. What types of areas are you seeing IP/TV deployed in?
We're seeing four major application areas for IP/TV. First is *employee communications*, which means CEO talks and HR training programs [see Figure 19.10].

Second is *group training*, specifically noninteractive and nonindividual. This is the kind of training normally done in a room where one person speaks and an audience listens. This lends itself very well to scheduled video.

The third category is *distance learning*, which is similar to training but has more of a scholarly feel where, for instance, a university wants to broadcast its courseware to an academic community.

Figure 19.10 Precept's SlideCast feature.

Finally, there is the *TV to the Desktop* category. We could sell into this area from the start, but MPEG makes it a lot more viable.

Is this commercial TV to the Desktop or academic?
It might be commercial, like CNBC, or it might be internal like FedEX TV. But I really want to stress the importance of MPEG for fulfilling our goal to deliver video without compromise. As you know, we have now integrated it with ActiveMovie and the results are very impressive.

This book has a whole chapter on that subject. By the way, do you recommend the ReelMagic card for hardware assisted MPEG?
That's the only ActiveMovie-compatible card we've found to date. Everybody else claims to be working on it. Maybe ActiveMovie is a little more complicated than people think. It's a great architecture, but most developers aren't that far along with it just yet. Obviously this situation will just get better in the future. In the past, each hardware-assist card had a proprietary interface that worked with Video for Windows in its own way. ActiveMovie changes all this.

And now with fast Pentium machines you only need hardware assist if you need to go full screen with MPEG, although this could change in a year or so if current trends continue.

What we're seeing is that most enterprise training only needs high quality quarter-screen presentations, which means no hardware assistance. But you might have, say, a trading floor scenario with a big monitor up in the corner, or a fitness center, where full-screen is required.

Any final comments?
Only that Precept is completely standards-based—unlike some other players—which is crucial for moving this industry forward.

Summary

Clearly, Precept is a company to watch, along with its competitors like Starlight Networks, as the multicasting community expands and gains momentum. Although they have targeted the enterprise, their software also has applications on the global Internet. Again, you can evaluate or purchase IP/TV by going to **www.precept.com**.

And don't forget to monitor the ongoing activities of the IP Multicast Initiative, sponsored by Stardust Technologies (**www.stardust.com**). Information on the latest IP Multicast Summit is available at **www.ipmulticast.com**. Chapter 18 provides a selection of publications from the first IP Multicast Summit.

Chapter 20

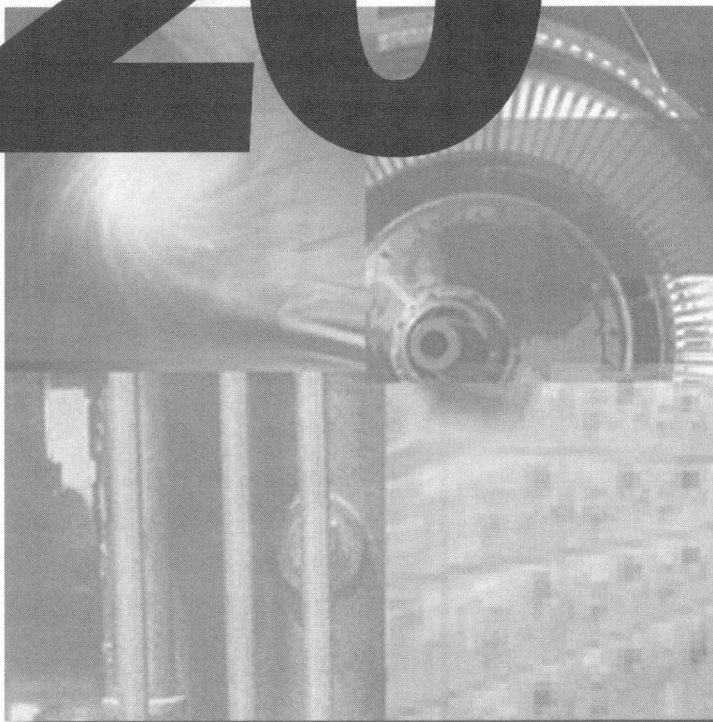

- Mixing video and computer skills

- Producing content for multicasting

- Working with analog media

Chapter 20

Interview With Anne Flatté, Video Producer At S.C.P.D.

In previous chapters, we looked at various aspects of creating media suitable for multicasting, but never from the point of view of a film and video professional who made the transition to CD-ROM-based multimedia and is now developing ways to take digital (and analog) media assets online.

Such a person is Anne Flatté, Producer/Director at the Stanford Center for Professional Development (S.C.P.D.) at Stanford University, located in Palo Alto, California. This institution is the home of the Stanford Instructional Television Network (S.I.T.N.), as shown in Figure 20.1, and the Multimedia Video Production Group.

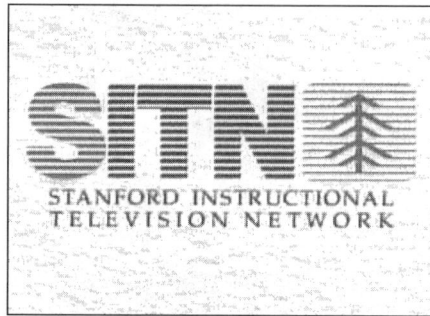

Figure 20.1   The Stanford Instructional Television Network (S.I.T.N.) video logo.

S.I.T.N. is recognized as a leader in the field of distance learning using advanced communications techniques. Ms. Flatté brings an interesting perspective to the digital media production process, as you can see in the interview that follows.

Note!   *Questions are in italics. Answers are in plain text.*

Background Information

Can you begin by telling us about your background?
I went through the graduate program in documentary film and video at Stanford University starting in 1993. The curriculum focused on film and video production and included training on the Avid. While I was there, I started working for the Stanford Instructional Television Network as an Avid editor.

In the second year of the of the program, I started managing various production projects. After I graduated, I was hired as a full-time producer/director. That's what I've been doing ever since.

Acquiring The Necessary Skills

Do you feel your background in traditional video prepared you as much for what you do now as a working knowledge of desktop computers? Do you need both?
I find that both are essential. As it turns out, I was predisposed toward the computer side because of some additional background in desktop publishing. This was mostly on the Mac, and it turned out to be extremely valuable when I began troubleshooting desktop video editing systems.

A computer background does not prepare you for making video content—obviously, I mean *good* video content. But, by the same token, someone who lacks good computer skills and is calling tech support all the time in a deadline situation can be a problem.

Computer Skills Vs. Video Production Skills

So, you look at a person's film and video experience first?

Yes, but the other abilities need to be there also. It would certainly make the difference in deciding between two candidates with equally strong video resumes. I have worked with some highly-skilled computer people who wanted to get into video, but those cases didn't work out so well.

Do you think the skill sets and mentalities are naturally opposed?

I've been in situations where people with both types of backgrounds are working together and there might be a mutual lack of respect for each other's backgrounds. I can sympathize with both sides. I think it would be helpful for both parties to respect the knowledge that each brings to the table.

The Value Of Analog Video Experience

Had you done much analog video editing?

Yes, I have—and I found it somewhat frustrating, to be honest.

Seems like it would give you a valuable perspective, being able to look at projects from all three directions: analog video, digital video, and multimedia.

Since most digital editing interfaces are modeled on techniques developed in analog video and film, I find that my analog experience is very useful when working in a digital environment.

S.C.P.D. Background

Can you give us some background on S.C.P.D.?

I believe it was one of the first institutions of its kind. About 25 years ago S.I.T.N. started producing video courseware for technical professionals interested in graduate and continuing education from Stanford University [see Figure 20.2]. Originally, S.I.T.N. broadcasted classes to participating companies in Silicon Valley. Some time after that, they distributed the material on video cassettes. Later, videoconferencing, satellite transmission and now some Web-based courseware were added.

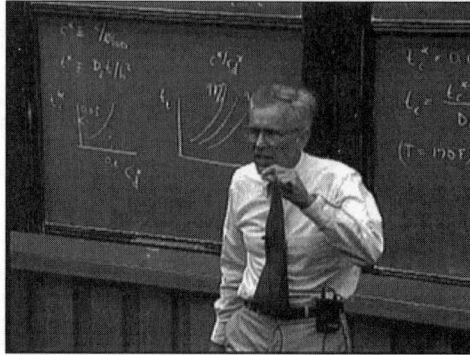

Figure 20.2 An S.I.T.N. course in progress.

Was it driven by professors or by outside producers?
The School of Engineering and a number of computer companies such as Hewlett-Packard pushed the original idea. It was designed as a partnership with industry in which practicing engineers could earn graduate degrees part-time while remaining fully employed, and do most or all of the curriculum without coming to campus.

For the last 10 years, Multimedia/Video Production has provided services to the entire Stanford community, S.I.T.N. as opposed to just the Engineering School, which has led to us being perceived as a multimedia service center for the whole university.

S.I.T.N. Degree Programs

Does Stanford offer degrees in their remote programs?
Yes. many Master's degrees in engineering are offered as well as 23 academic certificates. There is also a full range of continuing education programs for engineers, scientists and technology managers.

If someone were applying for your job, what would be the best degree program that Stanford offers to put on their resume?
The University doesn't offer a multimedia degree at present, but the MA in Documentary Film and Video, which I hold, would be very persuasive. Also, extensive real-world video production experience would also be quite important.

The Value Of Real-world Experience

Do you mean real-world production experience in both traditional video and multimedia?

Right. Actual production experience is at least as valuable as an advanced degree when it comes to finding work, even in university-affiliated situations, such as S.I.T.N. The reason, of course, is that new people get to learn from working editors and producers.

Are there other installations like S.I.T.N. around the country?

There are many distance education providers around the U.S.—with more appearing every day. Most of the business is in the state schools such as Penn State and the California State University System. The largest is the National Technological University, a consortium of 45 universities offering graduate degree programs.

There's a very similar site at MIT, for instance, and also at the University of Arizona and the University of Colorado. I understand more are in development, because we frequently get inquiries about our operation and how we do business. "Distance Learning" is exploding.

Is S.I.T.N. perceived as a viable business, as opposed to being supported by the University?

Yes, the revenue generated is used to support the academic departments who offer distance education courses. But the key is building Stanford/industry relationships and the revenue is an important by-product of this relationship.

How about the competition?

Competition is coming from a number of other universities such as MIT and NTU. The most interesting competition is coming from "Knowledge Product Providers"—private groups such as publishers and computer companies who see distance education as a growth industry, either in partnership with universities or on their own.

Planning A Multimedia Project

Could you now describe a project you would plan and execute knowing it was going to be digitized and presumably multicast?

Sure. Let's start with some general issues, then get into the production details. I should start by saying that if I knew the target audience of the piece was going to be strictly a *multicast* audience, I might consider doing a straight video tape production [see Figure 20.3].

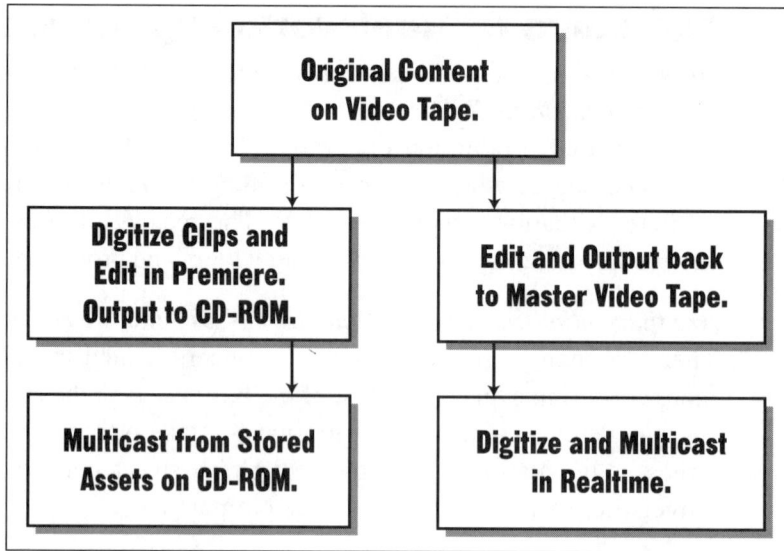

Figure 20.3 Diverging production paths.

For what reason?

As you know, multicasting is being pitched as a distribution mechanism that allows for repurposing existing analog tape assets, so why not just make more, then multicast them out of a VCR—assuming, of course, that the client understands this.

Good point.

Producing Stored Media Assets

Now, assuming that the finished product uses stored video, like desktop video clips in a CD-ROM project—where the media may or may not be multicast—I would approach things in a slightly different manner.

Broadly speaking, the issues fall into two categories: framing and lighting decisions. On the framing side, I would go for tighter shots to begin with and avoid zooming and panning as much as possible.

Based on how desktop video compressors handle such effects?

That's right. Most of the multicasts I've seen of stored media are movies with maximum frame windows of 320×240, compressed with lower data rates than CD-ROM movies with the same dimensions.

As discussed in prior chapters, a popular compressor for multicast streaming video is H.261 using a relatively low data rate such as 400 kilobits per second (50 kilobytes per second). This rate is considered unacceptably low for most CD-ROM products.

And what about lighting issues?

There are some subtleties here that you only learn by doing. Basically, your final digitized video benefits from some brightness and sharpness enhancements if it's going to be presented in a 320×240 or smaller window, but you don't want to over-light your scenes that way. You can add brightness and sharpness later, in Adobe Premiere, say.

Shooting Video As Data Capture

So, you should shoot your scenes with the same lighting as for normal video?

Everyone has their own formula. I let the light sources bring out as much richness and subtlety as possible in the subjects while keeping the contrast levels down. I also pay more attention to overall color schemes, knowing the impact of color in creating mood. A lot of so-called *macro* aesthetics come into play here, given the small windows involved.

Speaking of small windows, what about knowing that, at least in a multicast setting, your audience might have a shorter attention span.

You mean, if they were supposed to be watching a training video on their computer but they moved the quarter screen window to one side and read their email at the same time [see Figure 20.4]?

Exactly.

Outside of making the presentation as dramatic and compelling as possible, I'm not sure how to address that issue. I guess we'll find out what works best the more multicasting we do.

Working With A Crew

What is the size and composition of your crew when shooting for a multimedia project?

Based on my documentary background, I tend to work with small crews anyway. This means a camera person, a sound person, and a gaffer. Maybe a production assistant. I probably wouldn't scale back a lot for

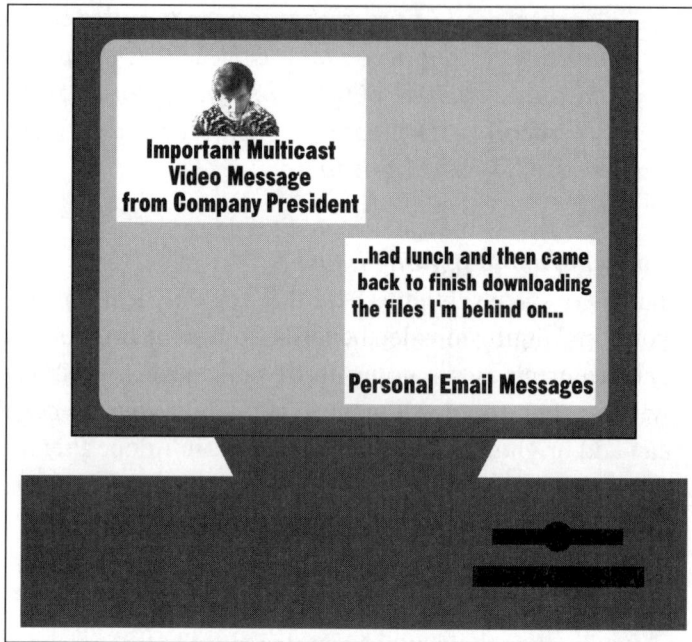

Figure 20.4 Multitasking on company time.

multimedia, but if you don't have to light a big area you don't need as many lighting technicians.

In a way, it just comes down to your budget. If you're making a bid for a client, you should include as much talent as you can so that your work is produced as well as possible.

If the client asks you to scale back, you then have room to negotiate and do so if necessary.

Palette Issues

Do you have any issues about palettes for users that only have 256-color video cards?

When I'm producing for a CD-ROM, I take into account the graphical interface that the video clip will appear in. I try to work with colors that will not conflict with that interface. In CD-ROM production, 256 colors is a requirement that we usually have to address, and there are many tools for converting to 256 colors. With video streaming applications, the situation is the same, but the video window is not as yet surrounded by highly developed graphic elements.

I'd say the same palette strategies will come into play eventually, as applications display more graphical elements along with the video. Besides, all the new PCs being sold have video cards that support more colors. Eventually, I look forward to designing in thousands of colors for both scenarios.

At what point do you stop editing on, say, the Avid and start bringing raw digitized footage into, say, Adobe Premiere for editing?
It depends on the project. Traditionally, we did all our editing on the Avid. Currently, QuickTime export takes too long on the Avid, and is a waste of resources. The goal is to digitize, edit, and output for multimedia using the same application. We're now starting to set up Premiere editing suites so that we can edit and compress on the same machine.

Acquiring High Quality Video Files

What kinds of issues does this raise?
Well, something that I've been thinking about lately is the question of getting the best possible video into a Premiere editing station in the first place.

So that the final compressed assets look as good as possible.
Right. You can read all about detailed post-production techniques to make great Cinepak and Indeo clips, but they don't usually talk about how to get high-quality uncompressed files onto your system [see Figure 20.5].

Don't Blame The Capture Card

Do you mean how to calibrate capture card settings?
Up to a point, but that's just a part of it. Most of the top-quality capture cards out there do an excellent job. If I was trying to build a reputation

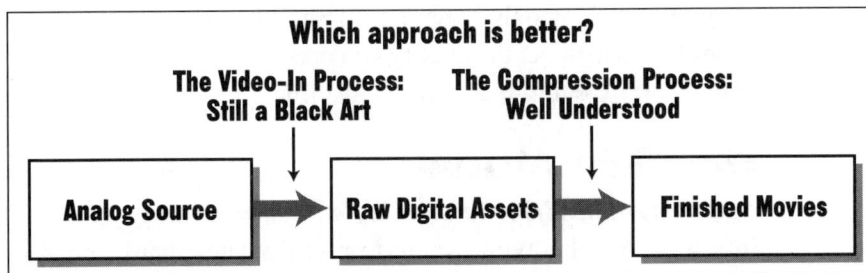

Which approach is better?

The Video-In Process: Still a Black Art

The Compression Process: Well Understood

Analog Source → Raw Digital Assets → Finished Movies

Figure 20.5 Focusing on video input.

for quality, I would want to know that my Premiere system was using the best possible uncompressed clips.

Like knowing you were always working with first generation beta tapes.

Compression is always evolving. But, in the meantime, what I worry about is reducing the number of times the material needs to be processed on its way in and out of the desktop editing station. What I want to do is process it once only on the way in and once only on the way out—for example, to Cinepak for a CD-ROM movie. What I'm really talking about here is a way of looking at this issue philosophically, rather than trying to solve it with specific hardware.

The Philosophical Approach

That can be hard to do, given that multimedia production is so tool-centric.

True. But I don't think I'm alone in thinking this way. It's somewhat abstract in my case because S.C.P.D. provides very good equipment, but for producers with smaller shops, it's probably a much bigger concern. Since multimedia tools are constantly evolving, it's too expensive for many multimedia producers to keep their shops state of the art. If brand new $5,000 cards keep coming out that do better and better raw captures, they're going to get even more depressed if they try to keep everything in-house.

What can they do about it?

If they're willing to go out of house for their initial digitization, they can start feeling good again knowing they've got top-notch raw files on hand. Then, they can do their editing and compressing with confidence.

They'd have to be at the service bureau to oversee the process.

Yes, it's important to supervise the process so that it's done correctly for your needs. It's also important to build a good relationship with a service bureau to get the quality you need. Of course, for some projects your in-house equipment will do just fine.

The Right Attitude

It almost sounds like maintaining a certain attitude.

In a way. And knowing where to rent the latest hardware is crucial.

Also, if you don't have access to service bureaus, or are unwilling to find them and negotiate with them, this idea isn't going to work.

Can you give an example here?
Let's say you have a client who needs MPEG and QuickTime movies. You have a $10,000 Media100 card, but not a $6,000 FutureTel board. If you can use a *third party* outfit to reliably digitize the MPEG files, you can still have a satisfied customer (see Figure 20.6).

All you want to do is get great uncompressed video file onto your system. After that, you can use your own secret formulas to edit and compress in Premiere or whatever tool you like to use. If you use someone else's capture card once in a while, what's the difference? What you're selling is your reputation for the delivery of finished goods—not your production process.

Limiting The Model

This model assumes you have no control over how the source tape was shot and/or edited.
For the sake of argument, that's right. We're also factoring out the nature of the content, because often you have to work with footage not shot specifically for digitization. Boards like the Media100 do fine with pans and zooms using their native hardware-assisted compressors, but Cinepak is the great leveler, at least for CD-ROM movies.

Asset Archives

Let's shift gears and talk about archiving digital assets. Do you think one capture format—like 640×480, 30 fps, CD-quality audio—should be used regardless of what attributes the target assets need?

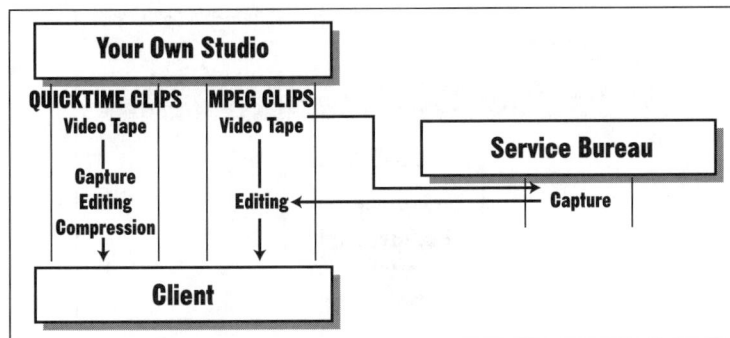

Figure 20.6 Keeping the customer satisfied.

I think it's a very good idea to create a high-quality digital archive file, just like you would create a high-quality digital Betacam master in analog video. Since we currently have to make so many compromises in our finished multimedia video clips, like with compression, frame rates, video window size, palettes, and so on, it's a good idea to archive at 640×480, 30 frames per second to keep your options open for the future when the technology improves.

Capture Card Preferences

Attitude and philosophy aside, what do you think is the best capture card for multimedia?
It's hard to say, because the top two or three are excellent.

So your theory includes boards like the Media100, the Targa 2000, and the Radius Telecast?
Sure, and a few others, including some MPEG cards.

Production Tips

Since we're talking specifically about hardware now, do you have any specific tips for desktop producers obsessed with quality?
Off the top of my head, I would say:

* Always use component video cables, assuming you're capturing from a Betacam deck.

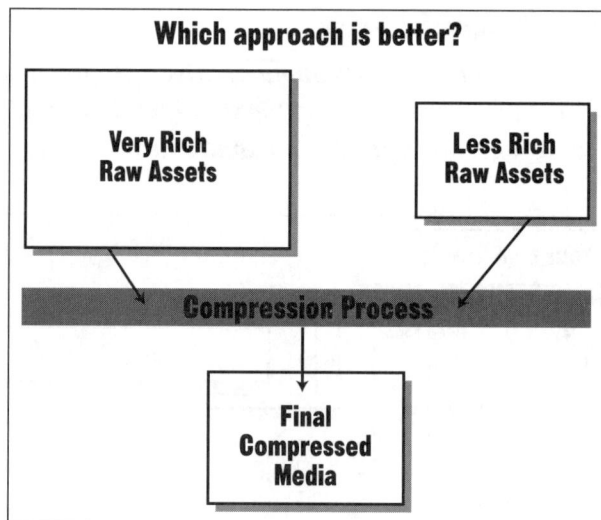

Figure 20.7 An ongoing dilemma.

- Use the fastest SCSI devices possible. Try to get fast-wide drives and controller cards.

- Insist on beta tape, or make sure your client signs off on the consequences. Many multimedia shops are already digitizing from digital betacam.

- Don't be afraid to recapture a clip if you aren't completely happy with it. Play it back to check for defects right after you capture it. If you're doing a batch capture, check the whole batch when its done and redo the ones you're even the least bit worried about.

Cleaning Up Uncompressed Movies

How do you feel about cleaning up your uncompressed movies?
How do you mean, exactly?

This is a technique for having your freshly captured movies safely archived, then performing some cosmetic surgery on them prior to bringing them into a Premiere project. Mainly, it saves you the trouble of doing it later, possibly in the midst of a complex Premiere project on a deadline.
Sounds reasonable so far.

It also helps when another producer inherits them. For example, if the clips are encoded in the JPEG codec native to the capture card, you can convert them to the None format—originally Apple None, but now called None by Premiere for Windows. It takes more hard drive space, but it makes it easier for the person who inherits them. Actually, some people prefer the QuickTime Animation codec, at the 100 percent quality setting, over None.
This sounds similar to the process I use to digitize video into the Avid. I'd be curious to know what techniques you've developed to enhance your video in Premiere.

Sure. The basic cleanup activities are:

- *Scraping off edge noise and possible overscans.*

- *Applying brightness, contrast, and sharpening filters, like you mentioned earlier.*

- *EQ-ing and normalizing the audio track.*

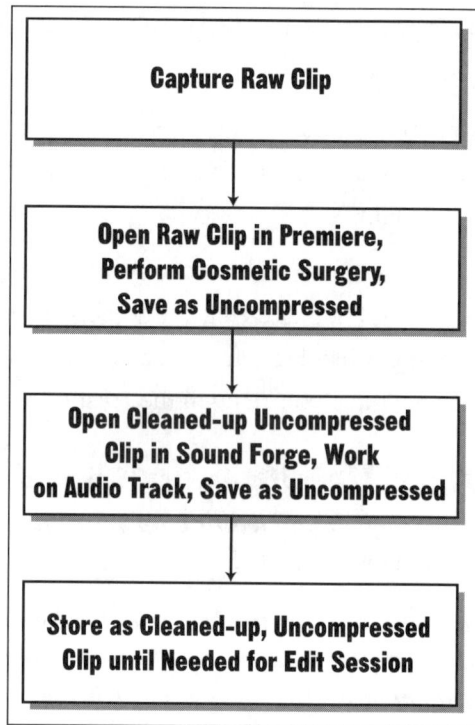

Figure 20.8 Cleaning up your raw captures.

You can do the video portion in Premiere and work on the audio track in Sound Forge for Windows or Sound Edit Pro on the Mac. (See Figure 20.8.)

Of course the problem with all this prep work is that you need lots of scratch hard drive space while you're working.

Unfortunately, that's the drawback. But if you get the basic chores down to a regular exercise, you can save time later in a deadline crunch. Plus, it seems to go along with the spirit of your thoughts about working with the highest quality uncompressed video assets.

Summary

Production facilities like S.C.P.D., with their emphasis on distance learning, are natural proving grounds for multicast technology and presentation aesthetics. As Ms. Flatté has clearly indicated, the sorts of skills required to work at such facilities are within the reach of multimedia professionals seeking new directions.

For further information about S.C.P.D. and S.I.T.N., and the services they offer, you can call (415) 725-8454 or email Ms. Flatté at flatte@leland.stanford.edu. You can also visit their Web site at **http://www-scpd.stanford.edu/scpd/**.

Index

Dense mode multicast routing, 468, 471
   protocols, 472–478
Dense-mode routing protocols
   MOSPF, 475
   PIM, 477
   PIM-DM, 478
Designated router, 467
Device Independent Bitmap (DIB), 26
Digigami
   CineWeb, 15
   MegaPeg, 192
Digital desktop video conferencing, 31–53
Digital Video Producer, 173
Digitizing equipment, 128
   analog media sources, 131
   capture card, 129
   mass storage devices, 130
   platform selection, 128
   role of the CPU, 129
DirecPC, 379, 445
Distance learning, 77, 513
Distance Vector Multicast Routing Protocol.
   See DVMRP.
Document camera, 33
Document sharing, 396
Dotted decimal notation, 461
DPS Perception, 129
Dropping frames, 224
DVMRP, 103, 468, 471, 472
DVP capture program, 173

E

Encapsulation, 403
Equilibrium Technologies
   DeBabelizer, 195
Estrin, Judy, 489 - 506
Ethernet, 266
EtherWAN management, 62
Event guides (MBone), 403
Express Transfer Protocol. *See XTP.*

F

Farralon Computing, 266
Federal Internet Exchanges, 392
File conversions
   between QuickTime and AVI, 352
   converting AVI to QuickTime, 345
   QuickTime to AVI, 342
Filtering, 238
Filtering switches, 460
FireWire, 131
First Summit in Cyberspace, 431
FIXes, 392
FlashStack, 137
FlashWare, 75
Flatté, Ann, 509 - 523
Flooding, 471
Fractional T1 service, 65
Frame rate, 178

Front Page, 244
FTP Software
   PC/TCP Onnet, 399
Future of Hope, 431
FutureTel, 192, 200, 361

G

Gigabit Ethernet, 269, 499
Gold software, 239
Graphics codec, 21
Graphics converters
   DeBabelizer, 195
Group addresses, 461

H

H.261, 171, 172, 331, 395, 515
H.301, 172
Hard disks, 130
Hardware
   digitizing equipment, 128–132
   for multicasting, 60–70
HNS DirecPC satellite, 379
Host group, 459
HOSTS file, 121
HTML
   authoring software, 247
   code for tuning in an IP/TV multicast, 419
   customizing to include multicast media, 413
   for ActiveX control, 417
   implementing the IP/TV plug-in, 427
   NetShow Live demo page, 424
   plug-in for IP/TV Netscape, 427
Hughes Network Systems, 379
Hybrid broadcasting, 42
Hybrid Fiber Coax (HFC), 67
Hyperterminal, 279
   for configuring a router, 282

I

IANA, 461
IETF, 455
IGMP, 103, 459, 464
   packets, 464
   selecting designated routers, 467
IMM, 397
Indeo, 171, 172, 235
   cross-platform issues, 350
   Video Interactive, 25
Inria Videoconferencing System. *See IVS.*
Integrated Services Digital Network
   (ISDN), 64
Intel
   Indeo, 22, 235, 350
   ISVR Pro, 172
   Smart Video Recorded Pro, 361
   Smart Video Recorder Pro, 200
   use of IP Multicast, 454

Reverse Path Multicasting. *See RPM*.
RFC 1112, 459
RIFF, 23
RJ45, 279
Road Pizza, 22
Router protocols, 102–104, 318, 466, 471–485
   dense-mode, 472–478
   interoperability, 482
   PIM-SM, 480
   sparse-mode, 478–482
Router RIP, 318
Routers, 61, 122
   best for multicasting, 255
   config file sample, 308
   config files, 282
   configuring with Telnet, 307
   connecting to an ISP, 282
   designated router, 467
   for ISDN connectivity, 265–268
   future of, 442
   implementing RIP, 292
   join requests, 479
   role in networking, 265
   routing white paper, 471–485
   setting up, 278–293
   setting up client machines, 278–293
   static IP address assignment, 260
   troubleshooting, 318
   unicast-only, 84
   vendors, 266
RPM, 478
RSVP, 101, 469
RTP, 75, 100, 394, 469
RTP/RTCP, 48
RTS Limited, 64
RTSP, 469
Run Length Encoding, 21

S

Samples, 329–336
   H.261 AVI movie, 172–192
   interactive infomercial, 270–273
   live multicasting, 200–207
   the Precept ActiveX Control, 418
   video clip with a 28.8 modem, 256
San Francisco Canyon Company
   TRMOOV, 171
Satellite
   delivery, 68
   downlinking, 258
Scalability, 8
Scripting languages, 415
SCSI, 111, 131, 209
SD, 397
SDP files, 149, 204, 427
Secondary DNS data, 287
Serial communications, 279
Serial port ISDN connection, 264
Server configuration

   adding dialin clients, 290
   computer setup, 292
   configuring the router with
     Hyperterminal, 280
   connecting with an ISP, 282
   enabling multicasting, 289
   for multicasting, 277–300
   implementing router RIP, 292
   router setup, 278–293
   software configuration, 293–299
Servo drives, 216
Session Directory. *See SD*.
Shockwave, 27
Signal to noise ratio, 217
Simple Multicast Routing Protocol (SMRP), 45
Site Mill, 245
SITN, 510
   degree programs, 512
Skills, 511
SMRP, 45
Sonic Foundry, 169
Sound Forge, 169, 189
SoundBlaster 16, 361
SoundEdit16, 195
Spanning trees, 467, 472
   with DVMRP, 473
Sparse-mode, 469, 472
   CBT, 479
   PIM-SM, 480
   routing protocols, 478–482
Spider, 247
SpigotPower, 130
Stanford Center for Professional
   Development, 509
Stanford Instructional Television Network, 509
Star connectivity pattern, 392
StarCast, 359, 400
   as an MBone tool, 400
   features of MultiCaster, 382
   installing, 359–367
   live multicasting, 373–377
   receiving a live stream, 377
   running the viewer, 371
   running with stored media, 368–372
   setting up MultiCaster, 360
   using Recaster, 378
   viewer installation, 364
Stardust Technologies, 57, 450
Starlight Networks, 76, 233, 241
   StarCast, 359
   StarWorks, 76
ST-II, 88, 99
Streaming, 5
   multicast, 501
   video, 7–19
StreamWorks, 11
Studio setup. *See Production Studio Setup*.
Subnets, 90, 255
   configuring a server, 278
   mask, 287
   with MBone, 388

SuiteSpot, 237
Sun Microsystems, 74
    Lyceum, 74
SVR files, 152, 192, 331
Switch boxes, 211
Switches
    filtering, 460
    role in multicast publishing, 127
Synchronization problems, 214

T

T.120 protocol, 47
T1 lines, 65
    multicast enabling, 66
Tape
    heads, 217
    transport, 216
Targa 2000, 129
TBC, 214
TCP/IP, 38–44, 236, 456
    address classes, 92
    assigning numbers, 91
    installing, 85
    video conferencing, 38–44
Technical concepts, 64
Telecommunications Act of 1996, 260
Telnet, 307
Terran Interactive
    Movie Cleaner Pro, 195
Time base correction, 214, 217
Time-to-live field (TTL), 463
Tips
    capturing videos with Premiere, 10
    keeping an eye on the net, 59
Toys R Us, Inc, 454
Transport issues
    using a hard drive, 342
TRMOOV, 171, 196, 352
    restrictions, 353
    target codec, 352
Troubleshooting
    routers, 318
Truncated tunnel, 405
TTL, 104, 463
    settings for the MBone, 464
Tunneling, 119, 460, 472, 483
    defined, 388
    drawbacks, 497
    global, 407
    implementing, 407
    overview, 404
    pruning, 405
    truncation, 405
Tunnels, 496
Turbo Internet, 381
TV RTP Client, 333

U

UDP, 11, 40
Ulead
    Photo Impact, 194
UN MBone implementation, 435
Uncompressed file format, 342
Unicasting, 5, 40. *See also* Video on Demand.
    compared to multicast, 452
    converting from multicasts, 427
Unix
    tools for MBone, 394
UPD/IP datagrams, 395
URLs. *See Web Sites.*
User datagram protocol, 11

V

VAT, 395
VBScript, 415
VCR running with IP/TV, 200
VDOLive, 9
VDOnet
    VDOLive, 9
    VDOPhone, 52
VDOPhone, 52
Versatile Message Transaction Protocol.
    See VMT.
VFW Converter, 343
VIC, 395
VidCap, 193
VidEdit.EXE, 193
Video
    audio features, 218
    camera, 373
    capture meta system, 111
    capture setup recommendations, 210
    capturing, 172
    capturing under Windows, 193
    codec, 22
    conferencing, 31–53
    data types, 19
    decks, 216
    device control, 213
    dropout problems, 215
    equipment issues, 213
    LAN-based, 223–250
    linear, 218
    nonlinear, 218
    production setup recommendations, 208
    signal to noise ratio, 217
    skills needed, 511
    streaming, 5, 200
    tape transport, 216
    transferring film to, 215
Video 1, 25
Video camera with IP/TV server, 206

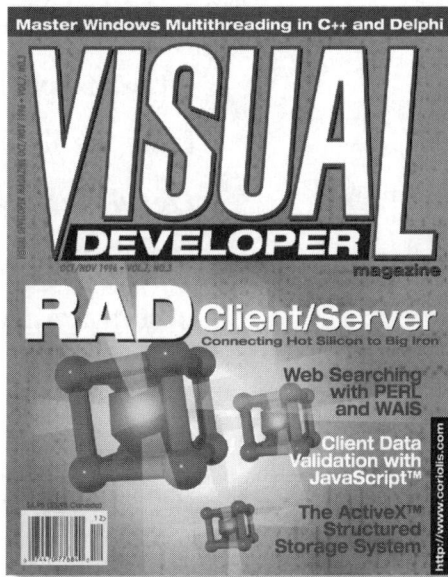